D0433744

ONTARIO SERIES
X

ONTARIO AND THE
FIRST WORLD WAR
1914-1918

ONTARIO
AND THE FIRST
WORLD WAR
1914-1918

A Collection of Documents

Edited with an Introduction by

Barbara M. Wilson

THE CHAMPLAIN SOCIETY
FOR THE GOVERNMENT OF ONTARIO
UNIVERSITY OF TORONTO PRESS
1977

Canadian Cataloguing in Publication Data

Main entry under title:
Ontario and the First World War, 1914–1918
   (Ontario series of the Champlain Society ; 10
   ISSN 0078-5091)

   Bibliography: p.
   Includes index.
   ISBN 0-8020-2255-3

   1. Ontario – History – 1867–1918 – Sources.*
   2. European War, 1914–1918 – Ontario – Sources.
   3. Ontario – Social conditions – Sources.
   I. Wilson, Barbara M., 1931–   II. Series: Champlain Society.
Publications : Ontario series ; 10.
FC3073.057   971.3'03   C77-001161-6
F1058.057

971.3
W746

This book has been published during the
Sesquicentennial year of the University of Toronto

FOREWORD

THE First World War had a profound impact on Ontario. In our social and economic history it marked the watershed between the nineteenth and the twentieth centuries. The stimulus which the war gave to industry greatly accelerated the transformation of a rural, agrarian society into one in which the urban industrial element was becoming ever more predominant. In August 1914, Ontarians, like their fellow Canadians in other provinces, were inclined to regard the war as an adventure that would be over by Christmas, but they were greatly mistaken. The war lasted four long years and touched virtually every Ontario family. It heightened idealism and thereby promoted the success of a movement for prohibition; it radically altered the concept of women's role in society; and it stimulated national pride; but it also stimulated baser emotions and radical prejudices that would be generally regretted once passions cooled. When the armistice finally came on 11 November 1918, probably few people realized how much the events of the past four years had changed them and their society. But the people of the province were intensely aware that they had participated in a national effort of greater magnitude than anything Canada had yet attempted, and as a consequence they shared a strong sense of national consciousness. They looked to the future with greater confidence in themselves, their province, and their nation.

The late Honourable Leslie Frost, with whom the idea of an Ontario Series originated, was most anxious that a volume on the First World War should be prepared for the series. From his own observation, Mr Frost knew the great influence which the war had had on the social and economic history of Ontario. He would have been well pleased indeed with the comprehensive picture Barbara Wilson has given us of the province at war. A member of the staff of the Public Archives of Canada, Miss Wilson brought to the task of editing this volume an outstanding knowledge of documentary sources pertaining to Canadian military and social history during the period. I welcome this opportunity to thank her on behalf of the Government and people of Ontario for such a notable addition to the history of the province.

The Ontario Series is a co-operative enterprise of the Government of Ontario and the Champlain Society, which has been engaged in the production of historical documentary studies for seventy years. The Society selects and guides the editors of each volume while the Government defrays the costs of preparation and publication. The volume editor's objective is to bring together a wide range of significant documents bearing on as many aspects of the subject as possible and to write an introduction that will illuminate the documents and enable the reader to appreciate their full significance. The editor is solely responsible for any opinions expressed.

This volume, the tenth to be published in the series, is the first to deal with a specific subject rather than the historical development of a region or an urban community. In future some volumes will continue to deal with regional themes while others will be devoted to specific subjects and individuals. Two volumes in preparation are concerned with Colonel John Prince and the city of London.

WILLIAM G. DAVIS
Premier of Ontario

Queen's Park,
Toronto
October 4, 1976

PREFACE

THE early months of the First World War were characterized on the home fronts in Great Britain and Europe by excitement, intense patriotism, high morale, and 'business as usual.' These positive attitudes were replaced gradually by weary resignation as tightening state control, shortages, and often disheartening news from the fighting fronts began to affect morale at home. But those on the eventual winning side, particularly the British, never lost their optimism or their determination to see the war brought to a successful conclusion. They were convinced that their armies were fighting to preserve civilization; consequently there must be no relaxation of effort at home or in the fighting zones until the war was won.[1]

Canada was thousands of miles from the front lines, but attitudes and, to a degree, conditions on the home front in Ontario were not unlike those in Great Britain. The enthusiasm and intense patriotism of a large segment of the population showed that Ontario still considered itself to be a very British province, steadfast in its loyalty to the king and to the Motherland.

The enjoyable task of searching for documents reflecting the mood of wartime Ontario was made much easier by the help I received from friends and colleagues at the Public Archives of Canada, National Library, Ontario Archives, Canadian War Museum, the archives of the University of Toronto, Queen's University and the City of Toronto. I am especially grateful to Juliette Bourque, Claude LeMoine, Peter Robertson, Bert Elder, David Russell, Dorothy Kealey, Fred Azar, Scott James, Glenn Wright, and Harold Naugler of those institutions.

The president and Governing Council of the University of Toronto, Marion Beyea of the Anglican Church Archives, A.R.N. Woadden of the Toronto City Archives, the Canadian War Museum, and Ann Henders of the Young Women's Christian Association of Canada have kindly granted me permission to reproduce documents and photographs from their records.

[1]Recent studies of the home fronts in Great Britain and Europe during the First World War include Arthur Marwick, *The Deluge: British Society and the First World War* (London, 1965; pbk. ed., 1967) and John Williams, *The Home Fronts, 1914–1918* (London, 1972).

I have been most fortunate in receiving the advice of many friends and relatives, some of whom have vivid memories of the war years. I cannot thank them enough. Amongst those who have been particularly helpful are John English, William G. Moyer, and W.H. Schmalz, whose knowledge of the complicated Berlin-Kitchener controversy set me straight on a number of the points at issue. Three other friends, R. Craig Brown, H.V. Nelles, and S.F. Wise, read the manuscript and made many helpful suggestions, which were invariably acted upon. Needless to say, the sins of omission and commission which remain are of my own doing.

I would not have had the pleasure of compiling this volume had it not been for the Champlain Society and the Government of Ontario, whose co-operation makes this Ontario Series possible. I am extremely grateful to them and to the editor of the series, Professor William G. Ormsby, for their support and assistance. I am equally indebted to the staff of the University of Toronto Press, especially to Larry MacDonald, who by his excellent suggestions has skilfully smoothed the rough edges of the manuscript.

Finally, my thanks to a very special friend, Charles P. Stacey, who encouraged me to undertake this project in the first place and who kept my spirits from flagging with his enthusiasm and invaluable advice. Without his help and guidance, I am sure that this volume would never have seen the light of day.

BARBARA M. WILSON

CONTENTS

ILLUSTRATIONS

ONTARIO AND THE FIRST WORLD WAR 1914–1918

INTRODUCTION

A. CIVIC HOLIDAY, 1914

THE HOLIDAY WEEKEND began in an atmosphere of tension and suspense.[1] The European crisis had arisen with startling suddenness and, by Friday 31 July, a general war seemed inevitable. It was highly unlikely that Great Britain could remain neutral, and no one challenged the assertion made by Sir Wilfrid Laurier in 1910 that when Britain was at war Canada was at war. The only question to be answered was When will it begin?

Throughout the province the usual holiday entertainments attempted to divert the minds of Ontarians from the anxieties of the day. The summer meeting of the Hamilton Jockey Club was in full swing, as were such other annual events as the Stratford Old Boys' Reunion and the Canadian Henley Regatta near St Catharines. There were lawn bowling tournaments at Amherstburg and Berlin and Old Home celebrations at Brantford, London, and Seaforth. The latter included the Provincial Firemen's Tournament in its festivities. Toronto had its usual full slate of Civic Holiday events: the Maple Leafs baseball team in the International League was playing at home; the Canadian Tennis Championships were about to begin; the Highland Games were being held at Exhibition Park; thirty soccer games were to be played on Monday; and the Newsboys' Union picnic was to take place at Island Park.

Yet in spite of the diversions, the crisis increasingly held the attention of Canadians. Newspapermen speculated on the effect the war might have on Canada, but the loyalty of its people was unquestioned. Sam Hughes, the Minister of Militia and Defence, told the Bracebridge Chamber of Commerce that 'every Canadian would respond to the old flag,'[2] and none doubted he was right.

As the weekend progressed, news reached Ontario of Germany's declaration of war on Russia and the invasion of France. Monday's *Globe* described the impact of the news in Toronto:

There was but one topic of conversation on the lips of all ... A steady stream of people poured from all quarters to centres where news could be

[1] The date of the annual civic holiday was decided by local governments throughout Ontario. Most chose the first Monday in August.
[2] *Globe*, 1 Aug. 1914, p. 6.

learned ... Round the newspaper offices, where bulletins were posted as
news came in, huge crowds gathered ... Such all-absorbing interest and
feverish anxiety to learn the latest developments has seldom marked a
crowd in Toronto's streets ... A continuous and harassing stream of
inquiries kept the telephones in The Globe office buzzing from mid-day
till after midnight ... Requests for confirmation of some of the wildest
rumours came in. The numbers of people asking whether it was true that
the King of England had been assassinated must have reached some
hundreds ... The calls were not confined to the city. Long-distance inquiries from all over Ontario also came in.[3]

Attendance at church services that Sunday was unusually large
for midsummer. The coming war was the popular subject of sermons.
Christian faith and soldiering were to be combined in a crusade
against the evil of the Kaiser and his allies. The Reverend W.A.
Hincks of Trinity Methodist Church in Toronto told his congregation
that 'instead of being appalled and panic-stricken, we Canadians
should thank God that we are allowed to bear our part of the burden
to resist and, God willing, to forever put down this military mad
group of dreamers.'[4]

Militia Headquarters in Ottawa took the first step towards mobilization when it placed all units of the country's small Permanent
Force under orders for active service, thereby causing changes in the
personal plans of many of its officers and men. Preparations for a
large military wedding in the fall were abandoned by a Kingston
family when the prospective groom, an officer in the Royal Canadian
Dragoons, was ordered to join his regiment immediately. The couple
was married quietly during the holiday weekend. In Toronto and
London there were cheers from enthusiastic onlookers and tears
from relatives and friends as companies of the Royal Canadian Regiment, Canada's only regular infantry unit, left to strengthen the
garrison at Halifax.

Although there had been no call for volunteers, the Toronto
headquarters of Military District No. 2[5] was filled with men eager

[3]*Ibid.*, 3 Aug. 1914, p. 6.
[4]*Ibid.*, p. 7.
[5]Since 1868, Canada had been divided into numbered military districts, three of
which were in Ontario. Some of the districts were reorganized as divisional areas
before the war, but neither their boundaries nor their numerical designations had
been altered. Since the divisional areas reverted to 'military district' status in 1916,
they are so referred to throughout this volume. Military District No. 1 covered the
Western Ontario counties of Bruce, Huron, Lambton, Essex, Kent, Elgin, Middlesex,
Oxford, Perth, Wellington, and Waterloo. Headquarters were in London. Military
District No. 2 encompassed the counties of Lincoln, Welland, Haldimand, Norfolk,
Brant, Wentworth, Halton, Peel, York, Ontario, Grey, Dufferin, and Simcoe. It also

to enlist at the first opportunity, and a large group gathered in the armouries at Hamilton. Some of the men were former British soldiers, others were members of the Active Militia, but most were civilians with no previous military experience.

The tension and enthusiasm heightened with the passing of each hour during the weekend. The *Globe* reported that feeling in Toronto on Civic Holiday

reached a pitch of patriotic fervour seldom before approached. As a result of the civic holiday the whole population was freed from their ordinary duties and thousands spent the day in the city streets. Holiday festivities could not draw them apart, for the all-engrossing war-spirit had seized all in its grip.

Toronto's streets witnessed remarkable scenes last night ... The people jammed every available inch of space, vibrating with unrestrained enthusiasm and a display of what might be termed 'Britishism' ... As each bulletin, flashing its pregnant message, was read, the crowds cheered and swayed as if possessed. Hats shot aloft, ten thousand throats boomed out a concentrated roar – a warning to the enemy, an inspiration to every soul in the British Empire, Canadians still belong to the breed ... Up and down several principal thoroughfares a unique procession passed, leaving a storm of awakened feelings in its train. Some hundreds of men, waving the Union Jack and Canada's flag, with drums beating and rousing British airs stirring the atmosphere, marched along, an undeniable testimony of Canada's unswerving loyalty.[6]

On Tuesday 4 August the holiday weekend was over. That evening Canada learned that Great Britain and the Empire were at war. The announcement touched off further celebrations (A 1). The suspense had ended. The tension remained.

---

included the districts of Muskoka, Parry Sound, Algoma, and Nipissing north of the Mattawa and French rivers (including the townships of Ferris and Bonfield). This huge district was administered from Toronto. Military District No. 3 included the western Quebec counties of Wright, Pontiac, and Labelle, as well as the eastern Ontario counties of Glengarry, Stormont, Dundas, Grenville, Leeds, Frontenac, Prescott, Russell, Carleton, Lanark, Renfrew, Lennox, Addington, Hastings, Prince Edward, Northumberland, Peterborough, Haliburton, Durham, and Victoria. It also included the district of Nipissing south of the Mattawa River, except the townships of Ferris and Bonfield. District headquarters were in Kingston. The districts of Thunder Bay and Rainy River were in Military District No. 10, whose headquarters were in Winnipeg.

[6]*Globe*, 4 Aug. 1914, p. 6.

B. THE HOME FRONT

1914

CANADA'S WAR BEGAN with the stationing of units of the Active Militia at public buildings, canals, bridges, and other vulnerable points across the country, thus heightening the tension which had developed over the weekend. People everywhere spoke excitedly of the events of the past few days and speculated about the effects the war might have on them. They worried about possible shortages of food and other commodities and about an increase in the cost of living. They wondered how many men would be needed to fight the war and who among their friends and relations might volunteer for the Canadian force which would soon be formed for service overseas. Everyone considered how they might make their own contribution for king, country, and empire, while eagerly awaiting news of the government's plans for the war effort.

Ontario's urban residents could hardly contain their patriotic enthusiasm; but in rural Ontario the excitement was less visible because farmers were busy harvesting the year's crops. The weather was good, and so was the yield. There would be an increased demand for Canadian produce to offset the decreased production in Europe; James Duff, the provincial Minister of Agriculture, appealed to Ontario farmers to increase their wheat production. They responded by doubling the amount of winter wheat usually sown in the province.

Food was vital, but the primary need was for fighting men. The first to leave for overseas were the British and foreign reservists who were obliged to join the forces of their homelands.[1] Next were the many British ex-servicemen who responded to the appeal of the newly authorized Princess Patricia's Canadian Light Infantry, which promised immediate service with the British Expeditionary Force. Meanwhile men flocked to armouries throughout Ontario, impatient for the government to announce its plans for an overseas force. Some of the men had had previous service, but for most of them military life would be a new experience. Those who passed the rather cursory medical examination were enrolled in the Active Militia and immediately began drilling, to the great delight of spectators who crowded the armouries' galleries. Uniforms and equipment were scarce; the

[1]Reservists were members of the armed forces of their native countries who, after completion of their military service, were liable to be called up in emergencies.

more fortunate among the new recruits traded their civilian clothing for the scarlet tunics, blue trousers, and white helmets of the Active Militia. Khaki was still a rare commodity in Canada.

The anxiously awaited mobilization order was issued on 5 August. Canada's overseas contingent would be composed of volunteers, who would assemble at a hastily prepared camp at Valcartier, Quebec. The Ontario men had a few days in which to settle their personal affairs before leaving for Valcartier. Local councils and organizations quickly arranged for the presentation of gifts of money, fountain pens, sweaters, tobacco, or wristwatches to them. Later, when the soldiers were settled in camp, carloads of fruit and vegetables would be sent as gifts to provincial units from Ontario farmers and municipalities. The pattern of departure was the same throughout Ontario. The volunteers paraded to the railway station, where they listened to farewell speeches by local dignitaries. As their train began to move, a band played patriotic and sentimental songs, the crowd cheering and waving. Everyone hoped that the war would end before the boys completed their training.

There was no difficulty in filling the ranks of the First Canadian Contingent. Indeed, the supply of men far exceeded the demand. The country was full of recent British immigrants, and they formed the majority of the recruits.[2] Although they had chosen to live thousands of miles away, they still regarded Britain as their home. When she was endangered, their first duty was to go to her aid. Native Canadians, on the other hand, had grown up unaware of the dangers and destruction of war. For some the motive was patriotism, for others it was a craving for adventure, but for many it was an economic necessity. A soldier's pay of $1.10 a day was not much, but it was better than none at all in a country hit hard by depression and unemployment. Economic conditions in Ontario during the winter of 1913–14 had been grim, and the prospects for 1914–15 appeared no brighter. The *Labour Gazette* reported that on 31 July in Ottawa alone there were four thousand unemployed, about half of them skilled workmen, and that the city was providing employment for three to four hundred on the city's streets.[3] If there were so many out of work during the summer, what would winter bring?

The outbreak of war caused an immediate worsening of the situation. The Dominion Textile Company mills in Kingston went on half

[2]After the First Contingent arrived in England, the Department of Militia and Defence released enlistment statistics which showed that less than 30 per cent of the recruits had been born in Canada. This prompted newspaper editors and public speakers to urge more native Canadians to enlist for the sake of their country's pride.

[3]*Labour Gazette*, v. 15, Aug. 1914, p. 171.

time because most manufactured cotton was exported to Japan, and that market now appeared cut off. There were rumours that some industries in Preston would close because of the cancellation of orders. Thirty-eight employees of the Noxon Works in Ingersoll were laid off after the cancellation of German orders. A bitter blow was the announcement on 13 August that Massey-Harris would close its plants in Toronto, Brantford, and Woodstock because of the decline of company business in Europe. Critics were quick to observe that industry should be stimulated rather than depressed by the war and that companies like Massey-Harris could adapt easily to the manufacture of vital war supplies and equipment. They concluded that the company had acted in haste. The response to this criticism was published in the *Globe* on 26 August. An official of the company explained that the reason for closing was financial:

Our collection season [in Europe] ... is during the early autumn months, and the war has, therefore, overtaken us at a time when our sales for the year have been largely completed, but no collections made. The result is that we have several millions of dollars completely tied up, probably until the end of the war, with the certainty of substantial ultimate losses. It is obviously impossible for the company to operate its works on the basis of ordinary conditions. Naturally we will desire to run to the full limit of the trade available.

Having in view the best interests of our employees, we have planned that such manufacturing as is possible under the changed conditions will be carried on during the winter months.

In spite of its announcement, Massey-Harris did not close down completely. With reduced staffs in its plants, it produced two thousand wagons for the War Office, and by 1 December all its plants had resumed full operations.

The employment situation improved gradually in Ontario as local industries obtained war orders, but complete recovery seemed far away. By the middle of November, employees of the Dominion Textile Company in Kingston were working overtime to produce sheeting, and the Kingston Hosiery Company was filling extensive orders for hose, underwear, and sweaters for Canada's new soldiers.

The one major industry in Ontario to be stimulated immediately by the outbreak of war was, quite naturally, steel. Munitions were urgently needed. When the Canadian Shell Committee[4] placed its

[4]The Shell Committee was formed in September 1914 by Canada's Minister of Militia and Defence, Sam Hughes, and continued in operation until November 1915, when it was replaced by the Imperial Munitions Board. The Shell Committee acted

first four orders in September, three went to Ontario firms: John Bertram and Sons of Dundas, Goldie and McCulloch of Galt, and the Canada Foundry Company of Toronto. Electric Steel and Metals of Welland began manufacturing fifteen-pounder shells shortly thereafter.

The pulpwood and mining industries of Northern Ontario shared the good fortune of the steel manufacturers. The numerous 'extras' reporting the latest war news resulted in an enormous demand for newsprint. The Abitibi Company of Iroquois Falls was shipping 160 tons of pulp daily by the middle of October and expected that its new paper plant would be in operation within nine months. Mineral prospecting and mining were given new impetus when the Allied nations turned to Canada, and especially to Northern Ontario, for vital metals and ores formerly supplied to them by Germany. The increased interest in Ontario's mining industry was a source of gratification to the Ontario government, which had long encouraged the development of the northern part of the province. But the war emphasized one glaring omission of which the provincial government had long been aware. The Sudbury area had for some years provided an estimated 80 per cent of the world's nickel ore, but most of it was refined in the United States. American neutrality now raised the possibility that some of the refined nickel could find its way into enemy hands. The government renewed its long-standing plea that all Ontario nickel be refined within the province.[5]

Northern settlement was, in the eyes of the provincial government, as important as the mining and pulpwood industries, and it did not want the success achieved so far to be hampered by the war. At the same time, it realized its responsibilities in encouraging recruiting throughout the province. Consequently an order in council was passed protecting the prospecting rights of men enlisting from Cobalt and Haileybury: 'all necessary extensions of time for performance of assessment work will be granted.'[6] The government also

---

as agents for the British War Office, 'arranging for and supervising the letting and the carrying-out of the contracts in such factories as they thought best suited to undertake the work' David Carnegie, *The History of Munitions Supply in Canada, 1914–1918* [London and Toronto, 1925], p. 291). The Imperial Munitions Board, agents for the British Ministry of Munitions, had wide powers and a large staff of experts and, unlike its predecessor, was directly responsible to the British government.

[5]The nickel controversy is explained fully in H.V. Nelles, *The Politics of Development* (Toronto, 1974).

[6]Quoted in J. Castell Hopkins, *The Canadian Annual Review (CAR) for 1914*, p. 459.

announced that soldiers who had purchased or located on Crown land, but who had not yet received patents, were in no danger of losing their land as a result of their enlistment.[7]

The first of the many substantial war contributions by the Ontario Government was a grant of $500,000 to the Imperial War Fund on 20 August 1914. Soon there were grants to relief funds and grants for recruiting, military supplies and equipment, donations of food for refugees and troops, and the gift of a military hospital in England for the treatment of Canadian soldiers.[8]

Although gratified by their government's display of patriotic generosity, Ontarians were impatient to participate in the war effort individually. They did not have long to wait. Money was urgently needed to help alleviate the sufferings of the war's victims. Appeals were launched early in the fall for the Red Cross and for Belgian Relief, and Ontarians exceeded their objectives in both appeals. The most generous support, however, was reserved for the Canadian Patriotic Fund, organized late in August 1914 to raise and distribute money to soldiers' families. Contributions by individuals to these funds was supplemented by the proceeds of patriotic concerts, the earnings of movie houses on advertised days, and contributions by employees of the civil service and business of one day's pay.[9]

Patriotic generosity took other forms in Ontario in the early months of the war. The Walkerville Council devised a plan to place the wives of local soldiers on the town's weekly payroll. Soldiers in Kingston rode free on local streetcars. The Toronto City Council contributed one hundred horses for training purposes, a carload of canned provisions for Belgian refugees, and $105,000 for insurance on the lives of the city's soldiers. Local governments in other parts of Ontario also voted funds for soldiers' insurance policies.[10] Doctors

[7]J. Castell Hopkins, *The Province of Ontario in the War* (Toronto, 1919), p. 36.

[8]A detailed account of the Ontario government's war effort will be found in Hopkins, *The Province of Ontario in the War*.

[9]After the war it was estimated that Ontario, 'with less than one-third of the people of Canada ... had subscribed more than one-half the total amount received from the entire Dominion' (Philip Morris, ed., *The Canadian Patriotic Fund. A Record of its Activities, 1914–1918* [n.d.], p. 141). The first patriotic fund in Canada was raised by Upper Canadians during the War of 1812. Canadians also contributed to a fund organized in Great Britain at the time of the Crimean War and raised money for the benefit of families of men who enlisted in Canada's South African Contingent.

[10]Life insurance policies were considered to be an important inducement to men contemplating enlistment. Besides those provided by municipal governments, there were the policies issued by fraternal organizations to their members as well as those sold by insurance companies. The latter posed a particular problem since they usually contained a 'war clause' which nullified the policy if the holder died as a result of war. The problem was overcome when the life insurance companies instituted an

and druggists offered their services free to soldiers' families. The Christie-Brown Company of Toronto announced it would pay the salaries of all their employees who served at the front; Massey-Harris decided to give fifty dollars to each employee who enlisted and to guarantee that his position in the company would be held open for him until his return. Clearly, the donors had no idea what the next four years would bring.

The most remarkable gesture by Canadian industry was an offer made on 6 August by Frederick Nicholls, president of the Canadian General Electric Company, to provide a 'company' of twenty-five of its Peterborough employees 'for service in any part of the Dominion' at the expense of General Electric.[11] On 31 August, following a meeting between Nicholls and Lt-Col. G. S. Maunsell, director of engineering services for the Department of Militia and Defence, the government accepted the company's offer (B 1). The men enlisted for the duration of the war, were subject to military discipline, but were paid by General Electric. The group, composed of eight engine drivers, four mechanics, eleven electricians, and one telephonist, was commanded by Hazen Ritchie, a militia officer and a company superintendent. Ritchie and eight men were sent to Esquimalt, the others were dispersed to Quebec City and Halifax, where they remained on duty until 1918.[12]

Fear of attacks on Ontario by Germans and Austrians in the United States prompted the formation of quasi-military home guard units and rifle clubs throughout the province in the early weeks of the war. The movement received little encouragement from the

---

additional premium of fifty dollars on policies purchased by soldiers prior to their enlistment.

Neither municipal governments nor fraternal organizations had anticipated the high number of casualties in the Canadian Expeditionary Force. By November 1915 they were finding the financial burden of the soldiers' insurance almost too heavy to bear. Many municipalities were forced to abandon the insurance scheme, and the fraternal organizations announced that they would pay insurance only on those members who had enlisted already.

[11]P.A.C., MG 26 H, Borden Papers, v. 189, file RLB 646, p. 104128.

[12]The arrangement ended in the summer of 1918 at the instigation of the Department of Militia, which considered 'it is now ... advisable and desirable for the Government ... to assume the liability of their military pay and allowances so that their status will be the same as regularly enlisted non-commissioned officers and sappers in the Royal Canadian Engineers.' It was pointed out, at the same time, that the agreement with the company which had been signed by each man at the time of his enlistment 'is not considered as binding upon any man who is liable to service and is required to serve under the Military Service Act' (Deputy Minister to Canadian General Electric, 17 July 1918. P.A.C., RG 24, Department of National Defence, v. 474, file HQ 54-21-4-7).

Department of Militia and Defence, and since arms and ammunition were scarce the men spent more time drilling than shooting. The most active and enthusiastic of the home guard units appeared to be the Toronto Home Guard Sharpshooters' Association, whose officers persuaded Maj.-Gen. Sir William Otter to be their 'colonel-in-chief.' The ageing former chief of the Canadian General Staff was desperately anxious to share in the country's war effort; since this was the first opportunity offered to him he accepted, but with a good deal of doubt about the home guard's effectiveness. He told its members on 7 October,

Your movement is a patriotic one, but whether or not it will meet the exigencies of the occasion is doubtful. Your organization is cumbersome and takes you away from the Government and King. You are not subservient to military responsibility, nor subject to control which would command you to march and fight. I believe that there are too many Associations of this sort being formed that will not live, because they are not being brought under the proper control.[13]

The Toronto Home Guard Sharpshooters' Association, far from being discouraged by Otter's remarks, sought status as a city regiment in the Active Militia late in October, but their request was refused. The Department of Militia was more concerned about meeting Canada's overseas commitments than creating yet another militia regiment in Toronto.[14]

Another quasi-military venture – but one which neither sought nor required material support from the government – was announced by the Ontario Motor League late in October. It proposed to form an aero club to train pilots and mechanics and an automobile corps whose members would be drawn from among the five thousand automobile owners in the province. Since Sam Hughes did not include an air force in his plans, the OML's aero club did not materialize, but a corps of eight hundred cars and drivers in Toronto, under the command of Dr P.E. Doolittle, prepared itself for any emergency. Similar squadrons were planned in Peterborough and Hamilton by automobile clubs affiliated with the OML. On 18 December, the Toronto corps participated in a test mobilization. Within thirty minutes, two thousand troops were collected from

[13]Quoted in *CAR 1914*, pp. 197–8. Sir William's association with the Toronto Home Guard Sharpshooters' Association was short-lived. On 6 November he was appointed Director of Internment Operations in Canada.

[14]Correspondence relating to the THGSA's application for regimental status will be found in P.A.C., RG 24, v. 1239, file HQ 593-1-29.

forty locations in Toronto and driven to Queen's Park by ten squadrons of sixteen to twenty cars each and by twenty-seven street-cars. A parade formed at Queen's Park and marched to High Park, to the great delight of parade-loving Torontonians.[15]

This was not Toronto's first test mobilization. In the middle of November rumours had circulated in the city of an impending raid by Germans from the United States. The tension was not eased by a newspaper story reporting that the number of sentries on the Welland Canal was being doubled. On 16 November, without advance warning, Maj.-Gen. F.L. Lessard, General Officer Commanding Military District No. 2, ordered a test mobilization of the Queen's Own Rifles, the 48th Highlanders, and the 10th Royal Grenadiers of the Active Militia, convincing some Torontonians that the invasion had begun. Although Lessard pronounced himself well pleased with the demonstrated efficiency of the militia, Sam Hughes was furious. Terming the exercise 'ridiculous nonsense,' Hughes told a patriotic meeting in Toronto that Lessard had used 'the worst military tactics possible.'[16] Toronto newspapers, the City Council, and later the Prime Minister, Sir Robert Borden, leaped to Lessard's defence, but on 27 November instructions were issued from Militia Headquarters that, in future, 'to avoid frightening the inhabitants of cities, towns or villages,' no mobilization exercises were to be carried out without advance warning to the public.[17] Lessard was named Inspector General for Eastern Canada shortly thereafter and was replaced in command of the district by Colonel W.A. Logie.

The men of Canada's First Contingent had arrived in England in October. Within days of their arrival, to no one's surprise, there was an announcement that recruiting would begin for a second contingent for overseas service. Again there was a rush to local armouries. There seemed to be an inexhaustible supply of eager young men in Ontario. No time was lost after the announcement in authorizing new units and appointing commanding officers, so that recruiting could get under way as quickly as possible in the geographic area specified for each unit. With winter approaching and Valcartier unsuitable for use in colder weather, it was decided that training would be conducted in the headquarters cities of the military districts in which the units were recruiting. Troops in Military District No. 2 occupied the grounds of the Canadian National Exhibition (which became 'Exhibition Camp'), forcing the cancellation of the

[15]CAR 1914, p. 221 and Globe, 19 Dec. 1914, p. 7.
[16]Ibid., p. 219.
[17]P.A.C., RG 24, v. 4287, file 2D. 34-1-25.

annual motor show and the Ontario Horticultural Exhibition. In London, buildings in Queen's Park were prepared, and Wolseley Barracks were to be used as well. Some of the men in Military District No. 3 were quartered in the Kingston Armouries and in the stables at Artillery Park, but the majority were housed in a cereal mill on Gore Street rented by the Department of Militia.

The recruits undertook their training seriously and with great enthusiasm.[18] They learned to march, dig trenches, master the intricacies of rifle and bayonet drill, and the other arts of modern warfare as well as these could be taught and practised within the confines of the makeshift camps. Morale was high as the troops looked forward to an early departure for Europe and the action for which they were training so diligently. Senior officers, knowing that the Second Contingent could not leave for England until the First Contingent had moved to France, and that this might not happen for some time, were concerned about maintaining the high level of morale. The men were kept busy during their training hours, but it was important that they be kept happy and occupied in the camps when they were off-duty. If there were proper and varied activities available in the camps, Ontario's bars might be less of a temptation to the men. The YMCA and similar organizations responded by organizing boxing and fencing tournaments and by providing movies and reading rooms in each camp. They also organized special entertainments at Christmas and New Year's. Morale remained high, and drunkenness did not become a major problem.

The war was not over by Christmas as many had hoped and, as the year drew to a close, Ontarians remembered the excitement of those early August days. Except for separation from husbands, sons, and friends, their lives had been little altered by the war. The Canadian National Exhibition and the fall fairs had taken place as usual, but with greater crowds than ever. The Ontario Winter Fair in Guelph and the Santa Claus parade in Toronto had lost none of their appeal. To the relief of sports fans, football leagues played their usual schedules in spite of the weakening of many teams by the enlistment of key players. And there was a new and popular form of entertainment in Ontario, the patriotic concert which raised money for war charities and generated enthusiasm for 'the British cause'

[18]So great was the enthusiasm in the quarters of the 18th Infantry Battalion in London that apparently no one seriously questioned an order from Lt-Col. E.S. Wigle, their commanding officer, that they were not to shave their upper lips because, according to Wigle, it was a well-known scientific principle that shaving the upper lip affected the nerves which influence the eyes and could thus impair an infantry-man's shooting accuracy (*Globe*, 18 Nov. 1914, p. 8).

(B 2). Food prices had risen slightly since the war began, but there were no shortages. Christmas was observed in much the same fashion as in previous years. Even the traditional toys were available because Canadian merchants had imported their Christmas stocks from Germany, Austria, and England before war was declared. The only difference seemed to be in the large numbers of men missing from their homes during the Christmas season. They were not forgotten by their families, nor by their home towns (B 3).

1 9 1 5

Europe was far away. Canadian newspapers were filled with reports of battles on the Eastern and Western Fronts, but these were of little more than passing interest to their readers. The First Contingent was still in England, making the best of the miserable living conditions and weather on Salisbury Plain. Sympathies were aroused in Ontarians by reports of the plight of the Belgians and French and by the endless lists of British casualties appearing in Ontario newspapers, but there remained an aura of unreality in a province as yet little touched by the war.

Plans were announced early in January 1915 for raising a Third Canadian Contingent, to be recruited immediately. The year would be dominated by recruiters. In spite of Sam Hughes's optimistic statement in the House of Commons on 25 February, 'I could raise three more contingents in three weeks if necessary,'[19] there were already ominous signs that the recruiting officers would find their task increasingly difficult. The first hint came late in January when it was reported that militia regiments in rural Ontario were having difficulty in recruiting their quotas. The *Globe* asked, 'Is rural Ontario losing its Imperial spirit? Must the stalwarts of the breezy uplands, the vigorous manhood of mountain and plain be branded as laggards in the Empire's shoulder-to-shoulder march to the trenches? Will the rural regiments allow the city regiments to put them to shame? So far they have.'[20] Such criticism infuriated Ontario farmers, who could ill afford to encourage their sons and hired hands to enlist if they were to comply with the government's request that they increase farm production.[21] Peter McArthur took up the cudgels on their behalf in his weekly column in the *Globe* (B 4), observing that 'it

[19]Quoted in *CAR 1915*, p. 188.
[20]*Globe*, 22 Jan. 1915, p. 6.
[21]The federal and provincial departments of agriculture were about to begin a highly publicized 'Patriotism and Production' campaign.

is high time that the Department of Militia and the Department of Agriculture got together and decided on a definite policy. If a man is doing his duty by producing more, he should not be open to criticism if he does not enlist.'

Recruiting in Canada received a tragic impetus from Europe and the high seas in the spring. The First Contingent moved to France in February, and by the end of March the first casualty lists were appearing in Canadian newspapers. The figures were relatively small, and most Canadians rationalized that some casualties had to be expected, expressed sympathy for the next-of-kin, and returned with renewed enthusiasm to the tasks of providing comforts for the soldiers and raising money for the civilian victims of the war. They were totally unprepared for what soon followed.

Late in April, reports were received of a terrible battle at Langemarck, near Ypres, in which the 1st Canadian Division plugged a gap in the line created by hastily retreating French colonial troops. Gradually the complete story unfolded. The Allied line had been broken by the first poison gas attack in the history of warfare. The Canadians, their left flank in the air, stood their ground and 'saved the situation.'[22] The casualty toll among them was staggering; their compatriots at home were stunned. Never before had Canadians faced the results of total war. Heavily attended memorial services were held throughout the country as people tried to grasp the reality of war. It was difficult because they were so removed from the centre of it. But they realized it 'was no longer an adventure. It had become something which affected the lives of everyone, a personal responsibility, particularly of the men of military age ... The war had become a crusade.'[23]

While the people of Ontario still reeled from the shock of Langemarck, a second blow deepened the impact. On 8 May the first reports appeared of the torpedoing of the supposedly unarmed liner *Lusitania*. Of the 1198 victims, over one hundred – all civilians – were from Ontario. Canadians were outraged by the brutality of the Germans. In Ontario, amateur theatricals, golf, bridge, and tennis tournaments were postponed as the province assumed a heavy veil of mourning. The air of undisguised enthusiasm with which Ontarians had greeted the declaration of war and which they maintained as they went about their war work was replaced by

[22]The second battle of Ypres, 22–4 April 1915.
[23]Leslie M. Frost, *Fighting Men* (Toronto, 1967), p. 46. 'Langemarck' was not soon forgotten. Each year, for many years thereafter, special services were held across Canada on the anniversary of the battle. It was also known as the Battle of St Julien.

a grim determination and dedication to do all in their power to help
to defeat the enemy as quickly as possible. And their distaste for
those of German origin in their midst became distrust and anger.[24]

The shock of these events to the people on the home front had one
beneficial effect. For several weeks thereafter enlistment figures
soared as young Canadians joined the crusade. It was not to last,
however. By the beginning of July the recruiters once again faced
the problem of obtaining enough volunteers. The need was even
greater now. Not only were men required for the dozens of new units
recently authorized, but now reinforcements were also needed for
the casualty-riddled units already in France.

Recruiting was a purely military affair at this time. Local militia
units were ordered to provide quotas of men for overseas service,
and when the quota was reached recruiting ended in that particular
locality. Because it was difficult to obtain money for advertising from
the Department of Militia,[25] militia units were forced to rely on
regimental funds for recruiting expenses and most of the available
money had been exhausted in raising quotas for the first two contingents. Local councils in some areas gave grants for recruiting, but
they could not be expected to do so indefinitely. Recruiters relied
heavily on posters, literature, and newspaper advertising to spread
their message; where money was not available for this purpose they
could only hope that a man's pride and his sense of patriotic duty
would be sufficient inducement for him to enlist.

Recruiters faced other obstacles. Uniforms, always considered to
be an army's best advertisement, were scarce in Canada at the time.
Several weeks after enlistment, recruits were still wearing civilian
clothing, but with the addition of a distinguishing armband. It was
difficult for the men to take pride in their armbands, and more difficult to evoke envy and admiration in others. Newspaper editors
compounded the recruiters' problem. Headlines and leading stories
recounted happenings on the Eastern Front, in the Balkans and the

[24]See Section C, 'Loyalty in Question.'

[25]By law, 'all printing, lithographing and engraving must be done by or through
the Department of Printing and Stationery ... All newspaper advertising had to go
through the same channel ... Accounts incurred locally were refused payment.' From
an undated memorandum on recruiting, prepared in the Army Historical Section
and based on Militia Orders 329 of 4 September 1916 and 41 of 22 January 1916
(copy in P.A.C., RG 24, v. 2501, file HQS 1050, v. 9). A parliamentary return prepared in May 1917 showed that the federal government had spent a total of only
$26,571.72 on advertising for recruits to 1 April 1917. Of this amount, $18,566.37
had been spent in Ontario (P.A.C., RG 14 D2, v. 24, Sessional Paper 171 of 1917).
It is probable that a large portion of the total was spent in advertising for the Canadian Defence Force, which was recruiting during the early months of 1917.

Dardanelles. Stories about the Western Front were somewhat confusing and contained little news of the deeds of the Canadian Expeditionary Force. But the most serious obstacle was the attitude of many young men. Clergymen, editors, politicians, and platform speakers tried to explain the causes of the war and why Canadians must participate, but the men remained unmoved and unconvinced. They simply could not understand why they should be expected to leave their families, their jobs, and their pleasures to fight in yet another European war.

Obviously the recruiters needed help, both from government and from the community. The latter was the first to respond. A Speakers' Patriotic League, Central Ontario Branch, had been formed in Toronto in March 1915 to 'educate public opinion ... as to the pressing needs of the Empire for men and money, and as far as possible to co-ordinate and stimulate all the various activities now working to this end.'[26] The League's efforts were confined to raising money for war charities, but on 17 June and again on 30 June Dr A.H. Abbott, the honorary secretary, offered the services of his speakers to Colonel W.A. Logie for recruiting purposes. Logie, realizing that recruiting must somehow be stimulated, welcomed Abbott's offer. He convened a meeting between recruiting officers and a representative of the SPL on 5 July, and their recommendations were soon included in the country's new recruiting policy. They advocated a lowering of physical standards for recruits, an adequate supply of uniforms and recruiting posters, and, with the help of civilians, the organization of rallies and parades.

The government had taken its first step towards helping recruiters in the middle of June when it 'intimated' that central, rather than regimental, recruiting offices would be set up 'at specific points' and that recruiting would be continuous.[27] This was followed by a slight lowering of medical standards, the removal of the troublesome requirement for consent of parents or wives, and the repeal of the regulation which permitted recruits to change their minds on the payment of fifteen dollars. Another measure calculated to stimulate recruiting was a militia order of 12 July 1915 (B 5) which permitted harvesting furloughs to men of the CEF who were in training camps in Canada. Harvest prospects were good, but the chronic shortage of farm help in Ontario cast doubts about whether all the crops so

[26]Brochure of the Speakers' Patriotic League in P.A.C., RG 24, v. 4317, file 2D. 34-1-65.
[27]CAR 1915, p. 190.

desperately needed at home and abroad could be harvested without assistance from the soldiers. Undoubtedly the Department of Militia thought that, if it could be demonstrated that the government recognized the plight of the farmers and was prepared to give them practical assistance, the farmers might then be more inclined to encourage their sons and hired men to enlist.

Although the government was not prepared to provide further assistance in recruiting, it was quite willing to allow civilians to participate; many of them were overjoyed. Here, at last, was the opportunity they had waited for. Now they could play an active role in the raising of Canada's army. Branches of the SPL were soon formed in several areas in Ontario (B 6), and in most of the others there arose recruiting leagues. Among the latter was the Hamilton Recruiting League, formed on 7 July 1915 and so highly organized that little was left to chance.[28] The first task undertaken by its merchants' committee was a campaign to ensure that there was always a sufficient supply of arms and equipment for recruits to keep up with the demand.[29] The public meetings committee, besides arranging rallies, took full credit for persuading the Department of Militia to agree to accept recruits with minor physical defects which could be treated after enlistment by army medical and dental officers. A special committee worked with civic officials in assessing claims and awarding compensation to families who were beneficiaries under the city's insurance programme for local soldiers. The manufacturers' committee induced workmen to enlist and found jobs for returned men. The publicity committee was in charge of honour rolls and certificates, newspaper advertisements, electric signs, shop window displays, pamphlets, cards, streamers, parades, 'and scores of other mediums that could carry a message or stimulate patriotic spirit.'[30] There were, in addition, trades and labour, church, and navy committees of the league, as well as a very active women's auxiliary.

The summer campaign of the recruiters began with enthusiasm and a great deal of optimism. Meetings were held in almost every Ontario centre, each with its quota of politicians, prominent citizens, and returned soldiers as platform guests and speakers. A favourite theme was that enlisting was the definitive proof of manhood. The

[28]A full account of this league's work will be found in J.H. Collinson and Mrs Bertie Smith, *The Recruiting League of Hamilton* (Hamilton, 1918).

[29]'The spectacle of ill-clad, slip-shod recruits marching through the streets was shocking. The military ardour of these patriotic youths deserved and needed all the stimulus and glamour which could be provided' (*ibid.*, p. 5).

[30]*Ibid.*, p. 21.

favourite technique was shaming. At a meeting in St Mary's, Judge John A. Barron proclaimed:

Because others do their duty is no justification for another neglecting his duty; because one brother goes to fight is no reason why another brother should abstain from fighting. The young man had better lose his position and retain his manhood than retain his position and lose his manhood. Better far that the boy should do his bit, with all his might, even should he fail, than remain at home like a bump on a log, which no one can or cares to move.[31]

There was no escaping the message of recruiters who resorted to any form of promotion they could devise. Special recruiting sermons were preached in most Ontario churches,[32] and one, delivered in Ottawa by the Rev. W.T. Herridge before the summer campaign got under way, was published and distributed 'by request of the Honourable the Minister of Militia and Defence' (B 7). In Toronto, the 109th Regiment hired a streetcar which toured the city bearing the regiment's recruiting officers. A sign on the front of the car proclaimed 'To Berlin, via the 109th Regiment,' another on the fender, 'Your King Calls You, How Will You Answer Him?' and one on the side, 'If You Want to Enlist, Jump on This Car.' The number of passengers was not reported.[33] Ontario composers wrote songs which could be sung at recruiting meetings and patriotic concerts as well as by families at home. Many were published by the Thompson Publishing Company of Toronto. Among the first were 'When Jack Comes Back' and 'We're From Canada' (B 8). A few months later 'Johnnie Canuck's the Boy'[34] appeared. By early fall, Thompson's added two more to their list: 'For King and Country' and 'Why Aren't You in Khaki?' The latter, written by Muriel E. Bruce, was advertised as the official song of the Recruiting League.

Recruiting displays were prominent at many fall fairs. The Canadian National Exhibition now had a distinctly patriotic flavour,

[31]Quoted in the *Globe*, 2 August 1915, p. 3. Two months earlier, Judge Barron had told jurors at Stratford that harsh criticism of men who did not enlist was cruel. (London *Free Press*, 9 June 1915, p. 5).

[32]A clergyman's lot was not a happy one in wartime. He urged young men to join the great Christian crusade against the enemy, but all too often he had to comfort their next of kin, explaining that death in battle was the supreme Christian act, both glorious and right.

[33]Kingston *Daily British Whig*, 21 July 1915, p. 1.

[34]Written by Mrs Lorne Mulloy of Kingston and described by the *Daily British Whig* on 17 February as 'a gift to the Kingston Red Cross Society. That means that every copy sold will provide a pair of socks.'

and a recruiting station was set up on the grounds. The feature attractions at the Ex that year included

Grand march of the Allies. The review of the British fleet. Bursting shrapnels and bombs in wonderful fireworks display.
Model military camp, showing every branch of army work on the field of battle.
Grand collection of war trophies taken from the Huns on the battlefield.
Grand array of vaudeville features and the production of the spectacle 'Forcing the Dardanelles,' fireworks and musical ride by the Dragoons in front of the Grand Stand.
A 'Gott Straffe England' brooch and relics of the baby-killing raids on English coast towns.
Blood-stained and torn clothing worn by soldiers in the trenches who have given their lives in the service of their country as well as metal badges and other things which have saved their owners' lives are also to be seen.[35]

It is unlikely that the latter display appealed to many prospective recruits, but at the close of the Exhibition the *Globe* announced in headlines: 'Canadian-born flock to the colors. Exhibition shows help to bring home responsibility.'[36]

The response of Ontario men during the summer was gratifying, but not spectacular. By the end of September, the figures had declined again and further inducements were needed. Sir Sam Hughes announced that during the coming winter Ontario troops would be housed, where possible, in their home localities in local drill halls, unused buildings, and schools. Every village or centre which could raise a minimum of twenty-five recruits could have the men billetted within its boundaries, and preliminary training would be conducted there. In addition, battalions would be limited to men within one county and would be commanded by local citizens, thus encouraging local interest and ensuring an *esprit de corps* in the unit from the beginning. The Department of Militia was hoping, of course, that local units, commanded by local men, would have far more appeal to prospective recruits and their families than units commanded by officers completely unknown to them.

It appeared at first that Sir Sam and his staff had been right and there would be no difficulty in securing enough men for most of the units then recruiting. Enlistment figures during the fall were encouraging; the Sunday recruiting meetings and entertainments were

[35] *Globe*, 28 Aug. 1915, pp. 7, 8.
[36]*Ibid.*, 10 Sept. 1915, p. 12.

popular affairs. But recruiting organizers knew that it could not last unless more aggressive policies were adopted. A conference of civilian recruiting leagues was held in Hamilton on 13 November at which an Ontario Recruiting Association was formed. After hearing reports on local recruiting methods throughout Ontario, the delegates agreed that the most successful campaigns were those in which men received personal appeals. They recommended, therefore, that each organization which had not already done so should conduct a local census of men of military age to enable the recruiters to approach each man directly. Military recruiters were as concerned as their civilian counterparts. After a conference of officers on 2 December, the men living within the limits of Military District No. 2 were given fair warning that the recruiting campaign would be pursued with greater vigour. There would be more extensive canvassing and advertising, a greater number of street corner meetings and parades. All men of the CEF and the Active Militia would be liable for recruiting duty, and the aid of women as recruiters would be sought.[37]

Some officers lost no time in adapting their campaigns to the new mood. Lt-Col. W.B. Kingsmill of the newly authorized 123rd Battalion submitted to District Headquarters on 8 December copies of five handbills he was distributing throughout Toronto as well as the plan for his recruiting campaign (B 9). Most of the handbills employed the shaming technique and one of them was directed to women (B 10). General Logie was not pleased. Kingsmill was told that 'some of the advertising matter is a little too strong ... You should be careful and avoid anything of the "bullying" nature. Be good enough to submit, in future, all printed matter ... for approval before distributing.'[38] In contrast, Lt-Col. Vaux Chadwick planned a quiet campaign to garner recruits for the 124th Battalion, another Toronto unit. Letters were written to churches, lodges, and clubs (B 11) explaining Chadwick's idea of having a battalion of 'Pals,'[39] with a one-dollar bounty to be paid to recruiters for each man brought in.

[37] *CAR 1915*, p. 226.
[38] P.A.C., RG 24, v. 4301, file 2D. 34-1-59.
[39] The 'Pals' idea originated with Lord Derby, who told his audience at a recruiting meeting in Liverpool in 1914 that he would like to form a 'battalion of pals' for Britain's New Army. The response to Derby's speech was immediate. The idea soon spread throughout Britain. In Canada, a circular letter was sent by Militia Headquarters to all districts on 23 November 1914 pointing out the desirability of having units of the Second Contingent 'composed as far as possible of men who are well known to each other, of those coming from the same locality, athletic associations, institutions, etc., in order that chums may be put together in the same unit' (P.A.C., RG 24, v. 6999, file HQ 593-1-40).

The *Canadian Annual Review* for 1916 reported that Chadwick's campaign was so successful that one thousand men were recruited in twelve days.[40] Not many battalions then recruiting in Canada could match that record. Late in December, recruiting officials admitted that the negative method of scolding and shaming had been ineffectual and indeed harmful. Such methods were to be discarded immediately.

In spite of the less than satisfactory methods of attracting recruits, it was reported at the end of 1915 that there had been 15,898 enlistments in Military District No. 1, 44,456 in No. 2, and 21,412 in No. 3.[41] But recruiting in rural Ontario was still a cause for anxiety which was not relieved by announcements in December that the Huron, Lambton, and Peel county councils refused requests for recruiting grants. They felt that governments at a higher level should finance recruiting and that farms had already contributed too many men to the army. Reeve Leckie of Huron County complained: 'They [the recruiters] will go up and down our concessions taking our farm hands who make money for the country and let shiftless young men continue to hang around towns and cities.'[42]

Recruiting was one major concern in 1915; the care of wounded soldiers was another. The injured began to return to Ontario in the early summer, and there were soon complaints from the men about the lack of interest shown in them from the moment of their arrival.[43] Local councils, stung by charges that they were not interested in their wounded heroes, responded quickly by arranging formal welcomes at railway stations and by announcing that veterans would be given preference in civic employment. The Ontario Motor League, ever anxious to serve, asked Torontonians to use their cars to convey men from the station to hospitals or to trains which would take them to their home towns. Car owners responded cheerfully, continued the service throughout the war years, and by so doing earned the gratitude of General Logie (B 12).

The men had far more serious complaints to lodge as well. They felt that governments had failed to make adequate preparations for their treatment and convalescence, education, and training to prepare them for their return to civilian life. They complained of the absence of employment opportunities and of the long delay in re-

[40]*CAR 1916*, p. 307.
[41]*CAR 1915*, p. 524.
[42]Quoted in the London *Free Press*, 10 Dec. 1915, p. 17.
[43]It should be mentioned that many of the trains arrived at their destinations very late at night or early in the morning and that little, if any, advance warning was given to civic officials of the time of their arrival.

ceiving their back pay after being discharged. Many of the complaints were justified. In July, several weeks after the return of the first group of veterans, the federal government established a Military Hospitals Commission, which soon arranged a meeting in Ottawa with representatives of each provincial government. The consensus of the meeting was that there should be a committee in each province to work closely with the MHC; accordingly the Soldiers' Aid Commission of Ontario was created by order in council on 10 November, under the chairmanship of W.D. McPherson. The Soldiers' Aid Comission Act, passed during the 1916 session of the Legislature, enabled it to establish local branches and to make suitable arrangements with educational authorities for the training of the men if they so desired. The chief goals of the commission were to ensure satisfactory employment for all Ontario veterans as well as to assist the dependants of men killed overseas. By mid-1916 forty local branches had been organized and twelve hundred men had obtained jobs through the commission. Classes were conducted in convalescent hospitals in subjects ranging from basketry and wood carving to shorthand and farm-tractor operation, depending on the physical capacity and wish of the patients. Re-training for new occupations was provided when disabilities prevented a return to previous occupations. The training courses averaged six months in length, the men receiving pay and dependants' allowances during this period. On completion of each course a certificate was issued and pay and allowances were provided for an extra month, during which time, it was assumed, suitable employment would be found.[44] The commission proudly issued a pamphlet in 1919 describing the many ways in which it had helped returned men (B 13).

Many men had difficulty adjusting to civilian life and preferred the company of their former comrades, with whom they felt an inexplicable bond. Patriotic Leagues in the larger centres opened Khaki Clubs where they could meet, read, and play cards and billiards. Wherever the men met the conversation usually turned to the subject of jobs. Unemployment had been a serious problem when they left Canada and was still a problem when they returned. An estimated fifteen to twenty thousand residents of Toronto were out of work in January 1915. In Ottawa in April, two thousand men vied for three hundred labouring jobs on a canal-deepening project. As in 1914,

[44]A detailed but rather dry summary of the work of the Soldiers' Aid Commission was prepared in 1918 for the use of J. Castell Hopkins, who had been commissioned by the provincial government to write *The Province of Ontario in the War*. A copy of the summary will be found in the P.A.O., RG 8, Provincial Secretary's Office, I-1-A, box 96.

unskilled workers were forced to consider enlistment as a way out of their economic dilemma. One rural regiment, the 42nd Lanark and Renfrew, took advantage of the unemployment situation to reach their quota for the CEF. The *Globe* reported on 17 February that Lieut. B.M. Morris had persuaded 133 men from rural areas who were unemployed and living in Toronto to return with him to Smiths Falls to enlist. Toronto's Civic Employment Bureau had 133 fewer jobs to find.

The awarding of war contracts led to a gradual revival and expansion of Ontario industry which was evident by the late spring. Soon the provincial economy was booming. Skilled workers were at a premium, and recruiters complained that their task was made more difficult because employers discouraged their skilled workers from enlisting. While recruiters lamented, the government supported the employers. The flow of war supplies must not be impeded by a shortage of skilled labour. Instructions were issued by Militia Headquarters on 16 November that workers whose services could be used by munitions manufacturers were to be encouraged to remain in industry (B 14). Employers were grateful for this evidence of the government's goodwill towards them. Many had permitted and even encouraged their best men to enlist in 1914 when business was slack and were now bitterly regretting their haste.

There appeared to be an endless supply of money in Ontario for war purposes. Campaigns for the British Red Cross and the Patriotic Fund were oversubscribed; much of the money needed for recruiting was obtained through highly successful Khaki Tag Days held throughout the province. Local organizations raised money to purchase ambulances, machine guns, field kitchens, hospital beds, and barber chairs for the troops overseas, but the most substantial contributions were made by the provincial government. By the end of the year the government had contributed some $2 million, including $32,950 for recruiting grants[45] and $120,000 worth of Ontario farm produce to Belgian Relief. The largest gift was $600,000 for the construction and maintenance of a 1000-bed hospital for Canadian soldiers at Orpington in Kent, of which Dr. R.A. Pyne, the provincial Minister of Education, was placed in charge. Half a million dollars was contributed to the 'machine gun movement,' which had begun spontaneously in January 1915 after it was reported that German

[45]*CAR 1915*, p. 519. The provincial government had announced in July that it was setting aside $25,000 to help defray recruiting expenses in the province and Alexander Fraser, the provincial archivist, was chairman of a committee to investigate and recommend how the money should be distributed. The report was submitted on 30 September 1915 and will be found in P.A.O., RG 8, I-1-A, box 80, file on recruiting.

battalions were supplied with ten or twelve machine guns each while British and Canadian units were equipped with only two to four. The public rashly concluded that two to four guns each was all that could be afforded and donations soon began to pour in to Militia Head-quarters in Ottawa. Finally, on 11 November, it was announced that

the Government desires it distinctly understood ... that no subscriptions or contributions for machine guns are required, as all expenditure for that purpose should be defrayed out of the public treasury. The impression seems to have gained ground that an appeal for such contributions to the public was made by some members of the Government. The Prime Minis-ter has made careful enquiry, and cannot ascertain that any such request was ever put forth.[46]

Another favourite war charity opened in February 1915 when Lt-Col. W.S. Hughes, officer commanding the 21st Battalion and a brother of Sir Sam, appealed to Kingstonians for money with which to buy supplies and equipment to 'insure the health and comfort of the NCOs and men.'[47] The battalion soon found itself with an enor-mous amount of money with which to buy field kitchens and other items which, Hughes implied, were not provided by the government. Other battalions soon made similar appeals with gratifying results. Late in August the Department of Militia issued an order forbidding such solicitations. Ontarians had to look elsewhere for ways to spend money to help the troops.

The campaign for prohibition became a major part of the war effort of a growing number of people. Its proponents claimed that the success of the Russian army in the early months of the war could be attributed largely to the banning of vodka sales in that country.[48] Sam Hughes, not a prohibitionist but a strong advocate of modera-tion, used the British army as his model when he addressed the troops in Exhibition Camp in November 1914: 'The one drawback to a soldier – his greatest enemy – is over-indulgence in liquor. The British army has found it impossible to keep up with the pace if drinking is indulged in and today the British army is the most temperate organi-zation in the world. That is one of the reasons for their splendid

[46]*CAR 1915*, pp. 213–14.

[47]*Globe*, 12 Feb. 1915, p. 11.

[48]The Russian example was not used by the prohibitionists after the disastrous campaign on the eastern front in the fall of 1914, but Premier William Hearst resur-rected it in explaining the Ontario Temperance Bill during its second reading in the Legislature in April 1916. See C.P. Stacey, ed., *Historical Documents of Canada*, v. 5, 1914–1945 (Toronto, 1972) pp. 181–2.

fighting against overwhelming odds in Belgium.'[49] Agitation grew to
keep liquor from Ontario's soldiers; Colonel W.A. Logie was amongst
those most concerned. W.J. Hanna, the provincial secretary, announced on 14 January 1915 that licence holders in the province had
been asked to exercise restraint in selling liquor to men in uniform.
He introduced a bill containing more stringent regulations regarding
licensing and hours of sale on 23 March. Logie still was not satisfied.
After obtaining an interview with J.D. Flavelle, chairman of the
Board of License Commissioners, Logie reported to Sir Sam Hughes
on 1 October: 'I have asked the License Commissioners to close all
bars at 7 o'clock p.m. during the continuance of the war and also
asked the Commissioners to forbid the sale of bottles to soldiers or
to any one who might reasonably be suspected of being about to
deliver his purchase to a soldier.'[50] He also prepared an order forbidding liquor in the armouries, messes, and canteens in his command. Sir Sam mildly rebuked Logie for not consulting him before
approaching Flavelle and offered his own views on how 'the liquor
question' should be handled, based upon his past experience (B 15).

Logie's appeal to the License Commissioners was partially successful. New licensing hours were announced on 14 October and imposed, said Premier William Hearst, partly to keep temptation from
the soldiers. Logie was not satisfied. He wrote that same day to the
Commission's secretary that 'the sale of bottles to soldiers is one of
the worst evils which we have to contend with' and asked that it be
forbidden. E. Saunders, solicitor to the Commission, replied that 'the
Board has no power to do this ... but if the Military Authorities were
to place the shops "out of bounds" and the shop licensees disregarded
the order by selling to the troops, then the Board could use its powers
under section 13.'[51] Logie took Saunders's advice and reported to Sir
Sam on 18 October that he intended to issue an order 'putting all
liquor shops out of bounds' to the soldiers in his command.[52] Hughes
approved; the order was issued and a similar one promulgated in
Military District No. 1 on 5 November.[53]

A meeting of temperance workers was held in Toronto on 15
October, the outcome of which was ultimately to be prohibition in

[49]Quoted in the *Globe*, 16 Nov. 1914, p. 3.
[50]P.A.C., RG 24, v. 4318, file 2D. 34-1-81. Logie became a Brigadier General on
1 September 1915, a Major General on 24 May 1916.
[51]*Ibid*. Section 13 of the Liquor Act read: 'The Board may by resolution at any
time cancel or suspend any license issued by the Board for any cause which it may
consider expedient, and subject to such conditions as the Board may see fit to impose.'
[52]*Ibid*.
[53]P.A.C., RG 24, v. 4254, file 1D. 1-7-51.

Ontario. The meeting resolved

that a Committee of one hundred citizens of Ontario be forthwith formed, to be composed as nearly as may be of an equal number of Conservatives and Liberals, and that such committee proceed to organize constituencies and to secure the nomination of candidates for the next election who shall be pledged to the abolition of taverns, shop and club licences and the prohibition of all sales of intoxicating liquors for beverage purposes.[54]

E.P. Clement of Berlin was elected chairman of the Citizens' Committee of One Hundred; the other officers were James Hales of Toronto, F. Kent of Meaford, Newton Wylie, and G.A. Warburton. The Committee, realizing that it must present Premier Hearst with concrete evidence that the majority of Ontario voters favoured prohibition, immediately made arrangements to circulate a petition throughout the province so that each voter might have the opportunity to sign it.[55] No stone was left unturned in the Committee's efforts to make their campaign a success. Newton Wylie, the general secretary, travelled to Ottawa and obtained Sir Sam Hughes's permission to circulate copies of the petition in military camps, provided 'that there is ... no interference with troops inside the limits of military quarters' (B 16). As the Committee worked towards its goal, Premier Hearst told Sir John Willison that the final decision would be made

by the voice and with the desire of the people of the Province expressed with reference to the subject itself, unbiased and uninfluenced by political motives or aspirations ... I may say that the subject is receiving constant and careful thought by me and when I have come to the conclusion what is right to do in the matter I propose to go ahead irrespective of what course the Committee of One Hundred, the liquor trade, or any other interests may say.[56]

But it would be almost impossible to remain uninfluenced by a petition signed by thousands of the province's voters.

It appeared that hardly any facet of Ontario life would remain untouched by the war. Motion pictures were censored. Only faked battle scenes and scenes considered to be pro-German were censored until June 1915 when the ban was extended to include any scenes of

[54]Quoted in Ruth Elizabeth Spence, *Prohibition in Canada. A Memorial to Francis Stephens Spence* (Toronto, 1919) p. 400.
[55]A copy of the petition will be found in P.A.C., RG 24, v. 4318, file 2D. 34-1-81.
[56]P.A.C., MG 30 D 14, Sir John Willison Papers, v. 40, folder 148. Hearst to Willison (Private and Confidential), 9 Dec. 1915.

war, whether real or faked, because of the adverse effect they might have on recruiting. It was, however, permissible to show pictures of 'troops marching, with bands playing and colours flying.'[57] Sports were particularly hard hit by enlistments. Cricket and soccer teams in the province, largely composed of British immigrants, were practically wiped out for the duration of the war, and yachting events on Lake Ontario were cancelled for the summer of 1915 because so many yachtsmen had enlisted. Both the Ontario Rugby Football Union and the Ontario Hockey Association were able to continue operations, however, many teams in the latter being sponsored and manned by battalions and artillery batteries still recruiting in Ontario. Equipment for some of the soldiers' teams was supplied by Sportsmen's Patriotic Leagues, which were organized in Toronto, Hamilton, London, and Ottawa in September.[58]

A year of tragedy and excitement, 1915 had also witnessed a resurgence in the province's economy. Christmas was celebrated in the traditional manner, but without the usual gaiety. In most households there were feelings of apprehension and loneliness for the men overseas; in many there was sorrow as the war took its toll of Canadian lives. European toys for the children were scarce. But some Canadian-made products were available, including jigsaw figures designed by Toronto artists and sold for the benefit of the Patriotic League.[59] They were inadequate substitutes for the children's beloved lead soldiers, but lead was urgently needed for the war effort.

1916

As the year began, the campaign of the Committee of One Hundred was in high gear. Copies of their petition were circulating throughout the province, and a massive advertising campaign had been launched emphasizing the injurious effects of alcohol and suggesting that the estimated $30 million expended annually by Ontarians on liquor might better be spent on the war effort. The Committee was opposed by the Personal Liberty League, which endorsed 'temperance in all things' and opposed prohibition 'or any legislation which

[57]*Globe*, 24 June 1915, p. 7.

[58]The initial purpose of the Sportsmen's Patriotic Leagues was to raise money for sporting equipment for the CEF. They soon undertook to provide entertainment for returned soldiers and their families and continued this work throughout the war. In December 1915, for example, the Toronto League organized three Christmas parties in Massey Hall for the children and wives of Toronto soldiers at which some 18,640 presents were distributed.

[59]See Estelle M. Kerr, 'Those War-Time Jig-Saw Toys,' *Canadian Magazine*, Dec. 1915, pp. 93–9.

encroaches upon or curtails the purely personal liberties of our
people.'[60] But there was little doubt that the prohibitionists would
win. The Personal Liberty League, bringing too little, too late, could
not counter the prohibition-for-patriotism argument of their opponents. The Speech from the Throne gave a clear indication that a prohibition measure would be introduced during the session. On 8
March a massive parade of ten thousand banner-carrying supporters
and many decorated cars moved through Toronto to Queen's Park to
present Premier Hearst with a petition bearing the signatures of
825,572 Ontario voters. A half-mile-long banner carried by the
marchers read:

To-day is the climax of a great campaign. Five months ago the businessmen of Ontario met and resolved that the waste of $100,000 a day on
booze must stop. They declared for prohibition during the war and for all
time. A campaign was launched under the slogan: 'Ontario dry by First
of July.' Billy Sunday came over and fired the opening shots. The liquor
men didn't like him – called him irreverent – but they couldn't answer
his arguments. The people of Ontario threw themselves into the movement with unusual earnestness. Conservatives joined with Liberals,
Catholics with Protestants, Jews with Gentiles, French with English, mod-
erate drinkers with abstainers – men, women and children without division
on this vital question. An army of 35,000 volunteer workers was raised
to circulate a petition to the Government. More than 825,000 by their
signatures have declared for a dry Ontario. The Government is now going
to allow the people to vote the booze business out of Ontario. This is a
call for us to stand together and see the thing through. Let all unite in
making the majority overwhelming and 'Ontario will be dry by the first
of July.'[61]

It was a day of triumph for the Committee of One Hundred, marred
only slightly by a noisy demonstration by protesting soldiers and returned men along the parade's route. The Ontario Temperance Bill
was introduced in the Legislature two weeks later, and, as expected, it
passed unanimously. On 17 September all bars, clubs, and liquor
shops would close for the duration of the war, after which there would
be a referendum to decide whether or not prohibition should be
extended.[62]

The prohibition campaign, although capturing much public attention, in no way affected the war effort in the province. Ontario was a

[60]Advertisement in the Berlin *News Record*, 12 Feb. 1916, p. 6.
[61]*Globe*, 9 March 1916, p. 1.
[62]*Statutes of Ontario*, 6 Geo. v, chap. 50.

hive of recruiting activity in the early months of 1916 as new units were authorized at an astonishing rate. Practically every county and major city in the province had its own infantry battalion. Toronto had several, some of which were designed to appeal to men of particular interests or characteristics. Besides the 124th 'Pals' Battalion, there were the 180th 'Sportsmen's,' the 216th 'Bantams,' and the 201st, which tried to recruit temperance men who had previously served in high school cadet corps.[63] Recruiting organizations faced the increasingly difficult task of filling the ranks, and several turned to census-taking as a means of ensuring that each man received a personal appeal from the recruiters. Hamilton and some other cities successfully used the services of local assessment officials to complete the census. Toronto, on the other hand, could not overcome the antagonism resulting from a decision to employ the police as census-takers. Rural recruiting leagues used voters' lists and asked schoolteachers to supply the names, addresses, and ages of all men residing in the school section. Many local recruiting organizations asked the young men to complete registration cards, providing such information as age, occupation, marital status, religion, and general physical condition and whether or not they were willing and able to enlist.[64] Most leagues sent personal letters of encouragement to prospective recruits (B 17).

Long after the recognition that the personal approach was likely to be the most successful means of acquiring recruits, Sunday meetings remained a major event on the weekly social calendar in many Ontario cities and towns. The movie houses, theatres, and other public buildings in which they were held were usually filled to capacity as Ontarians sought escape from an otherwise dull day. In addition to speeches, audiences could enjoy motion pictures and performances by singers and dancers.The performers were supposed to limit their acts to patriotic themes, but as the crowds at the meetings responded they drifted away from the strictly patriotic. Although the audiences loved it, civic and church officials frowned upon such proceedings. Mayor Thomas L. Church resigned the presidency of the Toronto Citizens' Recruiting League in January in protest against such defamation of the Lord's Day.[65] Clergy and laymen in other parts of the province called for the abolition of the Sunday frivolity (B 18).

[63]The 201st, commanded by Principal E.W. Hagarty of Harbord Collegiate, was singularly unsuccessful in recruiting and was disbanded at Camp Borden in September 1916. Few battalions were disbanded in Canada.

[64]A typical registration card, as well as an outline of organization of the Durham County Recruiting League will be found in P.A.C., RG 24, v. 4431, file 3D. 26-6-1.

[65]He allowed himself to be re-elected within a few days.

Their efforts were successful. Late in March, in response to protests from across Ontario, the provincial censor decreed that no one under the age of sixteen would be permitted to perform on stage at a Sunday recruiting meeting and that all pictures and songs must be of a patriotic or religious nature. The censor also forbade recruiters on stage calling upon men in the audience to come forward. Instead, they were to be asked to consider seriously the question of enlisting; anyone deciding to do so was to sign up at a recruiting office on a weekday. This sound advice should have been adopted months before by the recruiters themselves. Most young men were willing to listen to reasoned appeals for their services, but they objected strongly to any attempts to coerce or to embarass them into enlisting. The *Globe* noted on 24 January that at a recruiting meeting in Toronto 'the greater proportion of the audience was composed of women, men over age and soldiers,' probably because the shaming technique was still practised at some recruiting meetings, months after it was admitted by the majority of recruiters to have been a failure. A case in point was a meeting held in the Star Theatre in Toronto on 2 January on behalf of the 97th Battalion. The *Globe* reported that Lieut. J.B. Price

in an eloquent appeal for recruits, called on all the men in the audience over forty-five years of age, but who would be willing to serve if possible, to stand up. All the ladies were then invited to join the first group. Then followed the men who had not passed the doctors, and then the soldiers. By this time practically all the audience that remained seated was composed of young men of military age. An appeal to those who were willing to serve King and country to stand was answered by a score or more of the latter individuals. Class after class were then allowed to resume their seats till only those who professed to be willing to join the colors remained standing.[66]

The number of recruits obtained by the 97th at this meeting was not reported.

The practice of shaming died hard. At a meeting in Hamilton in May, Sergeant C.W. Niemeyer, a well-known figure on Ontario recruiting platforms, said that single men who were not munitions workers and who refused to enlist were cowards. Twenty-three men volunteered at the conclusion of his speech, but less than half actually reported at the recruiting office across the street. The *Globe* observed that, in future, 'recruiting officers who are trained in the work will be

[66]*Globe*, 3 Jan. 1916, p. 19.

told off to help Sergt Niemeyer, so that volunteers will not have a chance to escape before being taken before a medical examiner.'[67]

Recruiters used any gathering to place their message before the public. They spoke at concerts, church teas, and meetings of any organization to which they were invited. They asked local clergy to preach on the subject (B 19). They also relied heavily on advertising: posters, leaflets (sometimes called dodgers), streamers, blotters, and newspaper and streetcar advertisements were in abundance everywhere, a sloganeer's delight (B 20).

In spite of their efforts, the recruiters knew by the beginning of March that they could not supply volunteers in the numbers required. Aware of the developing crisis, Militia Headquarters asked district officers commanding on 14 March to consult with leaders of civilian recruiting organizations in their districts and to prepare reports, offering 'any suggestions as to any improvements which you consider could be made in recruiting methods suitable to your command.'[68] The reports were both discouraging and alarming. Enthusiasm for recruiting was replaced by calls for national registration and, in some cases, for compulsion. Major George H. Williams, the officer in charge of recruiting in Military District No. 2, advised General Logie to report that

education and inspiration through public meetings and personal appeals [are] still indispensable; but this should now be augmented by universal registration and industrial classification. Such registration, to be acceptable and effective, should be undertaken, or at least authorized by the Dominion Parliament for the whole Dominion. Competent and authorized local authorities could then indicate from among these names the eligible recruits whose enlistment would least disturb necessary industries.[69]

The report of Colonel T.D.R. Hemming, the officer commanding Military District No. 3, went further, pointing out that 'compulsory enlistment, if not entirely necessary at present, will, in a short time be so under present conditions' (B 21).

By this time many prominent people across the country were advocating the enforcement of those clauses of the Militia Act which called for the compulsory enlistment of certain classes of men when

[67]*Ibid.*, 27 May 1916, p. 2.
[68]P.A.C., RG 24, v. 4331, file 3D. 26-6-1.
[69]*Ibid.*, v. 4301, file 2D. 34-1-59. Williams had suggested in February that older men as well as women and youths in such organizations as the Boy Scouts should be mobilized to work on farms and in factories to take the place of men of military age (*Globe*, 11 Feb. 1916, p. 6).

the country was endangered. Others called for a system of compulsion more drastic than that contained in the Militia Act because 'the latter seemed to shelter certain classes of the community, and seemed likely to affect the economic welfare of the country.'[70] The Hamilton Recruiting League prepared a memorial urging the Borden government to conduct a census of men, classifying them according to occupation and conscripting those not engaged in essential war industries. Copies of the memorial and its 'Explanation' (B 22) were sent to every recruiting league across the country; forty-three endorsed it, over half of them in Ontario. A delegation presented the memorial to Sir Robert Borden on 14 April. He told them that the statistics prepared for him showed that enlistments were averaging one thousand per day and that as long as this figure could be maintained there would be no need for conscription.[71] The delegates, knowing the difficulties at the local level, were sure that Sir Robert's statistics did not reflect the present situation. The sharp decline in enlistments during the past month coincided with the publication of huge casualty lists, the result of the bitter fighting at St Eloi and Ypres. They returned to their homes discouraged and frustrated.

The recruiters' task had not been easy. They suffered from a lack of central control which might have co-ordinated their work throughout the country and thus have prevented the all too frequent occurrence of several units recruiting in competition with each other. Such practices led to squabbles among recruiting organizations and resentment by men being tapped on the shoulder by a succession of recruiters. A central organization might have ensured sufficient money and an adequate supply of suitable advertising material for local recruiters. It might also have been able to prevent the use of some of the more questionable techniques which only antagonized potential recruits. Newspaper editors had proven to be both a help and a hindrance to recruiters. They had eagerly published stories, editorials, and advertisements encouraging men to enlist, but they had just as eagerly published veterans' complaints and harrowing tales of trench warfare which possibly tended to discourage recruiting. Even the military had made the work of recruiters more difficult. The Department of Militia encouraged the creation of units which represented geographic areas or special interests in an effort to stimulate recruiting, but such units on arrival in Britain were broken up to provide reinforcements for casualty-riddled battalions already in

[70]Collinson and Smith, *The Recruiting League of Hamilton*, p. 8.
[71]*Ibid*. and *CAR 1916*, pp. 322–3.

France.[72] The appeal of similar units still recruiting in Canada thereby diminished.

These, however, were only contributing factors in the country's recruiting difficulties. The causes lay in the pocket and the conscience. Full employment and high wages at home lessened the possibility that men might enlist for economic reasons.[73] But the most widespread and important cause was the inability of recruiters, clergy, or politicians to alter the conviction of those who felt that the war was a European affair of little concern to Canadians and that too much Canadian blood had already been shed in battle. The printed expression of such sentiments, however, could not be countenanced in wartime. A front-page editorial in the *Sault Express* on 23 June (B 23) so enraged A.C. Boyce, Member of Parliament for West Algoma, that he complained to P.E. Blondin, the Secretary of State, that it was detrimental to recruiting. Blondin's wartime responsibilities included press censorship, and he ordered the seizure of the paper's printing press and plant as well as the seizure and destruction of all copies of the issue of 23 June. This was the first occasion upon which seizure was imposed, but since legal business in the community was dependent upon the publication of notices in the local newspaper the order was modified on 27 June to allow the publisher, C.N. Smith, to produce a fly sheet containing serial legal notices.[74]

All military matters seemed to go badly in Ontario in the summer of 1916. Enlistments slowed to a trickle. Several CEF battalions, all well under strength, moved into the newly constructed Camp Borden at the beginning of July to complete their training while their officers continued to try to swell the ranks. Already annoyed, frustrated, and bored by their long sojourn in Canada, the men gave vent to their feelings in the seemingly endless sun, heat, and sand of Camp Borden. A review was planned for Sir Sam Hughes's first official visit to the camp on 11 July, but the day before, after hours of rehearsing in the

[72]It was not uncommon by 1916 for infantry battalions proceeding overseas to be at least four hundred men below the establishment of a little over one thousand. Many battalions received little training in Canada because all the men became recruiting agents almost immediately after enlisting as the units' officers desperately tried to bring them up to strength (P.A.C., RG 9, Department of Militia and Defence, II B 5, v. 7).

[73]The labour shortage became so acute that on 16 Nov. 1916, Albert H. Abbott, then 'Director for Ontario Department of Labour' of the Imperial Munitions Board, suggested to General Logie that men discharged from CEF battalions 'because they are not first-class in every respect' be encouraged 'to apply at the Government Employment Bureau where they can secure information as to those plants which need men' (P.A.C., RG 24, v. 4376, file 2D. 34-7-61-1).

[74]P.A.C., RG 6, E1, Chief Press Censor, v. 68, file 207–12.

heat of the day, the men demonstrated. The review was held as scheduled, but one man died of heat exhaustion, thirty-five were overcome, and Sir Sam was booed as his train left the camp that evening. The Department of Militia minimized the incident, and the Chief Press Censor asked newspaper editors to restrict their coverage 'as much as possible.'[75] Nevertheless, within a few days it was widely reported that over one thousand men were absent without leave from the camp. Four hundred returned immediately after an announcement that their units would soon embark for overseas.

Harvest leave removed thousands from the training camp. Colonel S.C. Mewburn, Assistant Adjutant General in Military District No. 2, reported that 3549 men were on harvest leave on the weekend of 22 July, 3853 on 29 July, 4369 on 5 August, and 4111 on 12 August. He commented:

I regret to say that this Harvesting Furlough has been very much abused, and while we are very glad to help with the movement of crops, where absolutely necessary, yet, a very large number of men have abused this furlough, and instead of being working have been loafing around towns and villages, and in several cases, I have found it is very easy to get a certificate from an unprincipled farmer, and the men never actually work with the farmer.

This Harvesting Furlough has been a source of great worry and caused a great deal of trouble on account of the seriousness of the whole question as far as the training standpoint of the troops goes.[76]

As recruiters made plans for their fall and winter campaign, the Lord's Day Alliance warned General Logie that they would not tolerate again the defamation of the Sabbath by amusements at Sunday recruiting meetings (B 24); Logie was 'entirely in accord.'[77] Recruiting meetings would never be the same, but they had outlived their usefulness in any event, and recruiters continued their endless search for new and successful methods by which to attract men. Those in Toronto, Hamilton, Ottawa, London, Galt, and Kingston now turned to a technique which, they heard, had been successful in Winnipeg. This was the 'Give Us His Name' scheme in which newspaper readers were invited to complete a coupon indicating the name of a prospective recruit, his occupation, and address. At the bottom of the coupon was a note: 'You may sign this coupon or not, as you

[75]*Ibid.*, v. 25, file 142–8.
[76]P.A.C., RG 24, v. 4372–3, file 2D. 34-7-45. Mewburn to B.J. Roberts, 20 Aug. 1916.
[77]*Ibid.*, v. 4303, file 2D. 34-1-59. Logie to the Rev. W.M. Rochester, 19 Oct. 1916.

wish.' Many readers used the coupon to submit the names of suspected 'slackers,' their enemies, or simply those on whom they wished
to play a practical joke. Less than a week after the coupon first
appeared in Toronto newspapers, the 255th Battalion reported that
one thousand names had been received. But when the *Globe*
published the final results of the campaign in March 1917 it had
obviously been a total failure. Some 11,608 names had been submitted, calls had been made on 5662, of whom 589 had promised to
appear at the Toronto Recruiting Depot. The strength of the 255th
in March was only 321 men.

Recruiting across Canada was at a virtual standstill by the end of
1916. Conscription seemed to be the only solution, but the Borden
Government still hesitated. Almost two hundred thousand Ontario
men had already volunteered for overseas service,[78] a very respect-
able figure for a province whose total population was estimated to be
2,500,000. But the loss of the services of these men on the home
front meant that there was an increasing shortage of men for farming
and war industries. The time had come when governments, federal
and provincial, would have to co-ordinate the war effort to ensure
that adequate manpower was available at home without diminishing
military manpower requirements overseas. The initiative in Ontario
was taken by N.W. Rowell, the Leader of the Opposition, who introduced a resolution in the Legislature on 28 March 1916:

That the most thorough organization possible of our resources should be
secured for the successful prosecution of the War and the maintenance
of our agricultural and industrial production ... and that a Select Committee ... be appointed to inquire into and report as to the further assistance which this Province can render in securing such organization of our
resources, particularly in assisting in the work of recruiting men for the
Canadian Expeditionary Force; ensuring a sufficient supply of labour for
the agricultural interests and the necessary industrial operations of the
Province; and in promoting thrift and economy among the people, thereby
strengthening our financial position during the War and preparing for the
period of reconstruction after the War.[79]

The Select Committee submitted a bill to the Legislature which
received royal assent on 27 April as the Organization of Resources
Act.[80] The Organization of Resources Committee, whose chairman

[78]Enlistments in Ontario, up to 31 October 1917, were 191,632. (quoted in C.P.
Stacey, ed., *Historical Documents of Canada*, v. 5, p. 568.
[79]*Journals of the Legislative Assembly, 1916*, p. 108.
[80]6 Geo. v, chap. 4.

was the Lieutenant Governor, Sir John Hendrie, was composed of members of the Legislature, agricultural experts, businessmen, and other prominent citizens who were eventually organized into finance, labour, agricultural, and housing subcommittees. Local branches were formed throughout the province to assist, but not to supplant, the multitude of organizations already organized and dedicated to the war effort. Premier Hearst asked the local branches

1. To assist in enlisting more men.
2. To aid in keeping production in agricultural, necessary manufacturing and other essential industries as high as possible.
3. To encourage thrift and economy to enable us to finance further war expenditure and to meet the heavy obligations which the war will place upon our people.
4. To aid in absorbing the soldiers into civilian life and in caring for wounded and disabled soldiers.
5. To aid in placing and absorbing the large number of immigrants who may come to Ontario after the war.
6. In short, to assist in securing the organization of the resources of Ontario in the prosecution of the war, and to educate and pave the way for new social, industrial and economic conditions, a high ideal of citizenship and a quickening of national efficiency.[81]

The central committee concentrated on the encouragement of greater food production and thrift. Full-page newspaper advertisements and free circulars were prepared, beginning in April, which urged the necessity of preventing waste and increasing food production and offered practical suggestions on how both objects could be achieved. Little could be done about the effective distribution of manpower among the army, industry, and agriculture without some action in this field by the Borden government. Finally, on 16 August, 'Regulations for Recruiting' were passed by federal order in council. Directors of Recruiting (soon renamed Directors of National Service) were appointed to supervise recruiting in each military district; they were 'to take into consideration the character and importance of the employment in which any persons proposed to be recruited may be engaged.'[82] A series of amending orders in council[83] led to the creation of a National Service Board, which met for the first time in Ottawa on 9 October. It recommended an inventory of the country's manpower, the granting of badges and certificates to men considered

[81]*Public Service Bulletin*, Sept. 1916, p. 22.
[82]P.A.C., RG 2, Privy Council Office, 1, v. 1410, PC 1944 of 16 Aug. 1916.
[83]*Ibid.*, v. 1414, PC 2251 of 20 Sept.; v. 1415, PC 2287 and 2288 of 23 Sept.; v. 1423, PC 2835 of 14 Nov.

to be of greater value to the country in their civilian occupations than in the army, the release of men who in future might enlist but were more urgently required in their civilian occupations, and finally the creation of National Service Boards for women to ensure the most effective deployment of women in the national war effort.

The most important of the recommendations was that which called for a manpower inventory. Most recruiting leagues across the country were sceptical about its effectiveness. The Hamilton Recruiting League, for example, held several debates on the subject and resolved, on 24 October, 'that the Government's scheme relating to Recruiting and National Service is absolutely useless for the purpose it is intended to serve, and that the only just method to adopt is that of Registration and Selection, followed by Compulsion.'[84] In spite of such criticism, plans were made for a National Service Week, to begin on 1 January 1917.

The mounting manpower crisis had little effect on morale on the home front in 1916. Ontario women and schoolchildren devoted countless hours to knitting, sewing, bandage-rolling, and the packing of comfort parcels for the soldiers. There was a steady increase in the number of 'News from Home' budgets (scrapbooks of newspaper clippings) sent weekly by the Toronto branch of the League of Empire to troops in the trenches and in military hospitals. A Soldiers' Letter League kept in personal touch with Canadian soldiers who had no special friends in the country. War production clubs, gardening leagues, farm help committees, savings clubs, potato-growing associations, and preparedness leagues flourished throughout the province, aided by the Organization of Resources Committee. Money continued to pour into the coffers of the Canadian Patriotic Fund, the Red Cross, and similar war charities. On the lighter side, the Thompson Publishing Company offered a new group of patriotic songs: 'Do Your Bit,' 'Red Cross Nell and Khaki Jim,' 'That Old Tipperary Tune,' 'Every Soldier is my Sweetheart,' 'Fly the Flag,' 'Remember Nurse Cavell' and 'Dreaming of Home.'[85] And, as Christmas approached, children were delighted to see toy shops filled with the products of the fledgling Canadian toy industry and with imports from the United States and Japan (B 25).

1 9 1 7

National Service Week began on New Year's Day. Each male between the ages of 16 and 65 was asked, as his patriotic duty, to

[84]Collinson and Smith, *The Recruiting League of Hamilton*, p. 12.
[85]*Globe*, 3 Feb. 1916, p. 2.

complete a questionnaire distributed by the Post Office, indicating his name, age, place of birth, nationality, parentage, marital status, number of his dependants, physical condition, trade or profession, and present occupation. He was then asked: 'Would you be willing to change your present work for other necessary work at the same pay during the war? Are you willing, if your railway fare is paid, to leave where you now live, and go to some other place in Canada to do such work?[86]

The cards made no reference to military service. In spite of an extensive promotional campaign which emphasized that registration was not a first step towards compulsion, Canadians were suspicious, and National Service Week was a failure. Of the 1,549,360 cards returned, some 206,605 were either only partially completed or had been left completely blank.[87] Meanwhile the cries for some form of compulsory service became more numerous and more vociferous. Voluntary enlistments had all but ceased, except for the non-combatant railway and forestry units, but still the Borden government held back. Sir Robert announced on 14 February the formation of a volunteer Canadian Defence Force for home service, which would release for overseas service some fifty thousand men of the CEF serving in Canada. It was a last desperate attempt to keep alive the hope of a purely volunteer army, and it failed. Only 1858 recruits had been obtained by late May when recruiting ceased.

Borden attended sessions of the Imperial War Cabinet in London in the spring of 1917, and it was there that he learned how critical was the manpower shortage in the CEF. Recent losses had been heavy, especially in the capture of Vimy Ridge. He had no alternative. On 18 May, shortly after his return from London, he announced that conscription was now necessary. So ended, to all intents and purposes, Canada's raising of a volunteer force.[88] After the departure of the first two contingents, few units were able to recruit to full strength, but the presence of a Canadian Corps in France, composed entirely of volunteers, was ample evidence that the volunteer system had not been a failure.[89] This was the first time that the country had

[86]London *Free Press*, 30 Dec. 1916, p. 6.

[87]G.W.L. Nicholson, *Canadian Expeditionary Force, 1914–1919* (Ottawa, 1962), p. 220.

[88]Volunteers continued to be accepted, but in the middle of August recruiting for specific units ceased. Henceforth, volunteers would be placed in newly organized depot battalions in each military district, and, after preliminary training, sent overseas in drafts to units already there.

[89]Statistics of voluntary enlistments to 31 October 1917 indicate that there were 191,632 volunteers from Ontario, 48,934 from Quebec, 23,436 from Nova Scotia and Prince Edward Island, 18,022 from New Brunswick, 52,784 from Manitoba,

tried to raise a large military force, and inexperience was bound to result in mistakes. Too much reliance on local initiative, with an almost complete lack of direction from Ottawa, and the authorization of numerous units, instead of the creation of a rational organization to recruit reinforcements for those already overseas, were the principal causes of recruiting difficulties. The result was increasing pressure on, and frustration of, recruiters in all parts of the country in attempting to fill the ranks of local battalions. Furthermore, neither the length of the war nor the enormous wastage rate had been envisaged by anyone when the war began.

Borden's conscription announcement was greeted favourably by the many Ontarians who attended specially organized meetings and rallies. But hundreds of men and women gathered in the Toronto Labour Temple on 29 May to protest, 'believing as we do that militarism is absolutely opposed to any form of democratic government.'[90] J.C. Walters, president of the Trades and Labour Council of Canada, issued a manifesto on 14 June urging the conscription of the wealth of the nation

to take over and operate the mines, railroads, munition works and other establishments necessary to the prosecution of the war ... to eliminate the last vestige of profiteering, thus giving the nation the benefit, instead of the profiteer, of the work done ... I consider it my duty to sound a note of warning to the organized workers not to permit themselves to be shackled with the chains of Conscription. In the event of its being established any effort on the part of the workers to ameliorate conditions can be frustrated by simply calling them to the colours and placing them under military discipline.[91]

Protest meetings organized by socialists in the larger Ontario municipalities usually ended in confusion and disorder after soldiers and veterans in the audience mercilessly heckled the platform speakers.

Borden, realizing that the conscription issue might split the country, concluded that a union government committed to conscription would be in the best interests of both country and party. The Liberal leader, Sir Wilfrid Laurier, refused Borden's invitation to

26,111 from Saskatchewan, 36,279 from Alberta, and 42,608 from British Columbia and the Yukon. (*Debates*, House of Commons, 25 April 1918, quoted in Stacey, *Historical Documents*, v. 5, pp. 568–9.)

[90]Quoted in *CAR 1917*, p. 419.

[91]*Ibid.*, p. 420.

join the proposed government, but left the door open for Borden to approach other Liberals. After months of consultation and negotiation, Borden was able to announce the composition of the Union Government on 12 October. Two weeks later he called a general election, to be held on 17 December. The campaign in Ontario was vigorous, hard fought, and, with one exception, without disturbance. The exception occurred in Kitchener, a city which, since the war began, had been almost torn apart by bitterness and innuendo.[92] At an election rally there on 24 November Borden had been howled down by anti-conscriptionists in the audience. The incident was widely reported, and local tension was inflamed by the city council's refusal to apologize to the Prime Minister. The Unionists won seventy-four of the eighty-two Ontario seats on election day. North Waterloo, the riding in which Kitchener was located, went Liberal.

Parliament had passed the Military Service Act on 24 July and it came into force on 29 August. Local tribunals, each composed of two men, were appointed to hear claims for exemption which were based on grounds specified in Section 11 of the Act (B 26). The local tribunals were almost overwhelmed by the flood of claims submitted before the deadline of 10 November, but each case had been dealt with by 10 December. Proceedings of the hearings were published in local newspapers and for years to come many men bore the stigma acquired from such unwanted publicity. The tribunals were under fire from many sides. They were criticized for showing too much leniency in some of the cases brought before them, and there were suspicions that men received exemptions because of their 'good connections.' Urban residents resented what appeared to be favouritism in handling the claims of farmers' sons; farmers were furious that their sons and farm labourers could be conscripted at a time when, they were told, it was crucial that food production in Canada be increased. Their protests were finally answered by an order in council passed on 3 December, at the height of the election campaign: 'In any case where a person engaged in agriculture has applied for exemption and such exemption has been refused, the Minister of Militia and Defence, if he is of the opinion that the services of such person are essential for promoting agricultural production, may, by order under his hand, discharge such person from Military Service.'[93] Another order in council, passed on the same date, authorized the Minister of Agriculture to appoint representatives to local tribunals 'to guard the national interests in connection

[92]See Section C, 'Loyalty in Question.'
[93]P.A.C., RG 2, 1, v. 1475. PC 3348 of 3 Dec. 1917.

with the production of foodstuffs.'[94] Undoubtedly the passage of
these orders won many rural votes for the Unionists two weeks later.

Groups automatically exempted from conscription included
returned men, Doukhobors, those Mennonites whose ancestors had
immigrated to the west in 1873, and clergy 'including members of
any recognized order of an exclusively religious character, and
ministers of all religious denominations existing in Canada at the
date of the passing of this act.'[95] The exemption of all Mennonites
had been specified in successive Militia Acts until 1904, when a new
Act removed all reference to them, but declared that 'persons who,
from the doctrines of their religion, are averse to bearing arms or
rendering personal military service' might apply for exemption if
they were called up during a time of national emergency. The claim
of Mennonites in Western Canada was reinforced by an order in
council passed at the time of their immigration from Russia to
Manitoba in 1873 which freed them from any obligation to military
service. But Ontario's Mennonites had no such protection, and they
now found themselves liable to military service for the first time.
Their only recourse was to apply for exemption individually as
conscientious objectors; most of the applicants were successful.[96]
Members of the International Bible Students Association[97] also
sought exemption as conscientious objectors. When the possibility
of conscription was first mooted in 1916, members of the association
attempted to make their position clear regarding military service by
submitting printed affidavits (B 27) to the headquarters of the
military district in which they resided. District officers were puzzled,
and, after several made inquiries, Militia Headquarters issued
instructions that the affidavits were to be filed in district headquarters
and that no further action was required. Bible Students were among
the first to file claims for exemption under the MSA. Their claims
were refused by local tribunals, and several then appealed to Mr
Justice Lyman P. Duff, the Central Appeal Judge and final arbiter
in such cases. Duff rejected the first such appeal because, in his
opinion, the International Bible Students Association was not a
religious denomination within the meaning of the Act (B 28).
Members of the Plymouth Brethren fared no better. Duff rejected
the appeal of one member of the sect because the appellant 'did not
dispute that the taking part in combatant military service would not,

[94]*Ibid.*, PC 3349 of 3 Dec. 1917.
[95]Military Service Act (7–8 Geo. v, chap. 19), Schedule of Exceptions.
[96]Mr Kirk Barons, a student at Carleton University, explained the status of Ontario's Mennonites to me; I am most grateful to him.
[97]Later renamed Jehovah's Witnesses.

according to the corporate views of the Plymouth Brethren, be regarded as a disqualification for membership; wickedness alone, he said, would be a ground of exclusion and that would not necessarily be regarded as wickedness in all circumstances.'[98] Conscription appeared to be necessary if the war was to be won, but the bitterness and anguish it engendered would not soon be forgotten.

Thousands of veterans had returned to Canada by the beginning of 1917. They had a strong desire to band together, not only for companionship but also in the hope that, organized, they might wield some influence towards the betterment of the government's rehabilitation policy and job opportunities for themselves. Many felt alienated from the rest of society. They resented the attitude of some civilians who tended to brand them as troublemakers whose demands on government and society were too extravagant. They were also irritated by the criticism of their conduct and dress by officers, few of whom had served overseas. Maj.-Gen. F.L. Lessard made such a complaint on 4 January about men in Toronto (B 29). In response, Maj. R.S. Wilson of the Military Hospitals Commission command in Toronto suggested that the men about whom Lessard complained were probably discharged men no longer within his jurisdiction (B 30 and B 31). There appeared to be all too little compassion for the men or understanding of their plight.

There were several veterans' clubs in existence at the beginning of 1917, most of them local and informally organized. One, however, the Canadian Association of Returned Soldiers, Ottawa District, sought incorporation as a company under the laws of Ontario. The Provincial Secretary's office referred the application to the federal undersecretary of state to see if 'the proposed name and objects (B 32) are objectionable to any Department of the Dominion Government.'[99] The application was passed to Dr Eugène Fiset, deputy minister of the Department of Militia and Defence, who drafted a reply suggesting that the incorporation would be 'inadvisable' (B 33). Before sending it, however, Fiset decided to obtain the opinion of C.J. Doherty, the Minister of Justice. Doherty wisely suggested that the government 'would not be justified in taking steps to interfere with the liberty of returned soldiers to form an association' (B 34).

The veterans soon realized that they could exert little pressure as autonomous local clubs scattered across the country. They must

[98]P.A.C., RG 14, Records of Parliament, D 2, v. 36, Sessional Paper 97 of 1918.
[99]P.A.C., RG 6 A 12, v. 8, file 133. F.V. Johns, acting assistant provincial secretary, to Secretary of State, 9 Jan. 1917.

unite. Representatives of several clubs met in Toronto in March 1917 to make plans for a nationwide association, which came into being at a convention in Winnipeg in April. The new organization, the Great War Veterans' Association of Canada, was the largest and most active and influential of all veterans' organizations in Canada. By the end of 1917 it had some eighty branches and thirty thousand members.

Veterans and their problems were primarily the concern of the federal government, but provincial and municipal authorities were also involved. The Ontario government announced in January 1917 that a soldier settlement would be established in Northern Ontario, near the Kapuskasing River (B 35). The townships of O'Brien, Owens, Williamson, Idington, and Cumming on the National Transcontinental Railway west of Cochrane were set aside for the settlement, and a training school was organized at Monteith. Every possible measure was taken to ensure that the new colony would be a success. Each applicant was physically examined and then appeared before a board composed of representatives of the provincial Department of Lands, Forests and Mines, the Department of Agriculture, the Invalided Soldiers' Commission, the GWVA, the Soldiers' Aid Commission, the Canadian Patriotic Fund, and the Vocational Training School. The first group of successful applicants left Toronto in the middle of June and went directly to the school at Monteith. They were on their land within a few weeks.[100]

Only a small proportion of the veterans were interested in pioneering in Northern Ontario, and even fewer were eligible to participate. The vast majority remained in the cities and towns of Southern Ontario, dissatisfied especially with the lack of job opportunities. In Toronto a municipal commission was planned to consider ways and means of helping returned men, but it had not materialized when trouble erupted in April. Angered by a lack of jobs, groups of returned men demonstrated at Toronto munitions factories against the employment of aliens, whom they wished replaced by British subjects. The demonstration resulted in action by both the Imperial Munitions Board and the Toronto Board of Control. Mark H. Irish, director of the IMB's Labour Department, sent contractors a list of returned soldiers in Ontario who were employable, commenting 'There is no intention on my part to request employment for these

---

[100]J. Castell Hopkins reported that there were eighty-three men in the colony by 5 November 1918, 'with 500 applications on fyle still to be dealt with and 255 called for examination who had failed to report' (*The Province of Ontario in the War*, p. 40).

men but merely a desire to place their names before you for such action as you may feel personally prompted to.'[101] Board of Control arranged a public meeting at Massey Hall on 9 May to hear the men's grievances, but less than one thousand attended. Besides objecting to the employment of enemy aliens in munitions factories, the men criticized the unsympathetic attitude of Patriotic Fund officials and the paucity of their disability pensions. The grievances were embodied in a resolution presented to Board of Control on 17 May (B 36). Having received a sympathetic hearing, the men seemed satisfied, at least for the time being.

Although veterans with no particular trade were in difficulty, there was no shortage of high-paying jobs for machinists, toolmakers, and other skilled workers in Ontario. The economy was booming as plants across the province were deluged with orders from the Imperial Munitions Board. There were some aspects of munitions manufacture which private enterprise was either unable or unwilling to undertake. This resulted in a decision by the IMB late in 1916 to organize national factories, each of which was a separate company whose stock was entirely held by the IMB. Most of the national factories were in Ontario. Toronto had three: an aircraft factory, British Acetones Ltd, and British Forgings Ltd. Energite Explosives Company, owned by O'Brien Munitions Ltd and manufacturers of nitrocellulose powder in Renfrew since 1915, was leased to the IMB early in 1917 and became British Explosives Ltd. Another national factory, the British Cordite Company, was begun at Nobel late in 1916 and was in production by the middle of 1917. The largest explosives plant owned by the IMB and 'one of the largest of its kind in existence' was the British Chemical Company at Trenton which was also in operation by mid-1917.[102]

Munitions work was dangerous, and the pay was good, but in 1917 money was no guarantee of comfort. As the war entered a critical stage both at home and overseas, 'thrift' became a key word. The effects of the long and costly war were reflected in commodity shortages as well as in an ever-increasing cost of living. Ontario, as well as the rest of Canada, faced a severe coal shortage for a few days in February. Much of the coal produced in Canada and the United States was earmarked for the use of essential war industries; there was also a shortage of rolling stock to move it, and unusually cold weather in the eastern part of the continent increased demands for fuel. Passenger rail services were curtailed; schools, universities,

[101]P.A.C., MG 30 B 4, Flavelle Papers, v. 38, Irish to contractors, 25 April 1917.
[102]David Carnegie, *The History of Munitions Supply in Canada, 1914–1918* (London and Toronto, 1925).

and factories were closed; fence rails, back fences, and sawdust were used as fuel. The crisis eased when new supplies of coal arrived in the province on 18 February, but for a few days the people of Ontario had a first taste of material discomforts which could be wrought by war. The federal government, foreseeing the possibility of a similar crisis during the winter of 1917–18, one that could seriously hamper the industrial war effort, created the office of Dominion Fuel Controller in July (B 37).

The great fear at the beginning of 1917 was that Ontario could not produce enough food to satisfy the needs of the province, let alone contribute to the feeding of the rest of Canada and the world. Late in April the Organization of Resources Committee published *The Crisis*, which appeared as a pamphlet and as a newspaper advertisement. It explained the cause of the worldwide food shortage and threatened famine and exhorted Ontarians to greater food production (B 38). The message was directed towards both farmers and townspeople. The latter responded with great enthusiasm.

Groups of men co-operated in planting fields of potatoes, beans, corn and buckwheat. Rotary Clubs, Boy Scouts, Girl Guides, Women's Institutes, Bible classes, churches, Sunday schools, Patriotic Food Committees, horticultural societies, agricultural societies, town councils, boards of trade, bowling clubs, manufacturers, bank office staffs and almost every sort of organization known were stirred to help increase the world's food supplies.[103]

Farmers heeded the call by increasing their acreages of spring-sown crops, although they were sceptical that enough helpers could be found to bring in the harvest. Boys were released from school in April to work on farms. Provincial civil servants were offered five weeks' holidays if they would spend at least three weeks working on farms.[104] College and schoolgirls, teachers, typists, and milliners all volunteered to work on fruit farms. The Trades and Labour Branch of the provincial Department of Public Works reported that 'city men of all ages, occupations and stages of farm experience responded nobly to the call ... Many of the large stores, manufacturing concerns and warehouses, etc. encouraged their men to go on farms by giving a bonus ... Clergymen, school teachers, lawyers, editors, ignoring their accustomed outing places, spent their holidays on farms.'[105] Provision was again made for soldiers to be granted harvest leave, but after the

[103]*Public Service Bulletin*, Oct. 1917, p. 59.
[104]*Globe*, 25 July 1917, p. 13.
[105]Ontario Sessional Paper number 16 of 1918. Annual report of the Trades and Labour Branch.

experience of previous years the regulations were tightened. Only sons of farmers were eligible; the leave was not to exceed six weeks; the men were liable to be recalled at any time; they received no pay or allowances while on leave; and district officers commanding were cautioned that 'the number on furlough at any time should not exceed 10 per cent of the total number under training.'[106] In spite of the enthusiastic response of Ontarians, the farmers' worst fears were realized. The lack of experienced farm labour meant that much of the increased crop was lost. Undaunted, the Organization of Resources Committee prepared and published in September a circular outlining its 1918 campaign for even greater food production, food conservation, and thrift (B 39).

Once the crops were planted in the spring of 1917, attention turned to the conservation of food. Canning demonstrations were held throughout Ontario under the auspices of Women's Institutes and the Organization of Resources Committee. A province-wide conference on the prevention of food waste was held in Toronto late in July. Canning recipes and 'War Menus' were published in provincial newspapers during September and October during a national campaign to conserve food. Food Service pledge cards were distributed through municipal offices, schools, women's organizations, churches, and local branches of the Organization of Resources Committee. Although it was not stated in the pledge, the principal intention was to encourage savings in the consumption of wheat, beef, bacon, and other less perishable commodities, so that they could be conserved for export. Those signing the pledge received cards to hang in their homes testifying that, 'to win the war,' the householder had 'pledged to carry out conscientiously the advice and directions of the Food Controller.'[107]

In Ontario, as in the rest of Canada, 1917 had been a grim year, and as it dragged to a close there was no improvement. Shortages had by now become a fact of life. There was a serious hydro shortage in October. Street lighting was prohibited between five and eight in the evening, and every second street light in Toronto was turned off. Early in December, Ontario, like the rest of the country, was shocked by news of the Halifax explosion. The provincial government immediately rushed money and supplies to the stricken city. As had become their custom throughout the war years, Ontarians once

[106]P.A.C., RG 24, v. 4372–3, file 2D. 34-7-45.

[107]W.J. Hanna, former minister without portfolio in the Ontario cabinet, was appointed Dominion Food Controller in June 1917. He resigned on 24 January 1918, and the position of Food Controller was abolished. It was replaced by the Canada Food Board, created by order in council on 11 February 1918.

again responded generously to appeals for money, bedding, and clothing for the victims of the disaster. As Christmas approached there were reports that another fuel shortage was imminent. It looked as though the new year would be no improvement on the old.

1918

Early in January Ontario's fuel controller, R.C. Harris, took steps to conserve the province's dwindling supply of fuel by limiting house-holders to a two months' supply and threatening hoarders with prose-cution. Churches were encouraged to hold union services, schools were closed for weeks, and rooms in those which were allowed to remain open were used by several classes on a shift basis. Lighting was restricted in shops, theatres, offices, homes, and streets. The crisis was so serious that early in February the federal government ordered all manufacturing plants in Ontario and Quebec to close between 9 and 11 February, the only exceptions being war plants, newspaper offices, and businesses producing perishable goods. No heat was provided for offices, shops, and warehouses, but doctors', dentists', and government offices were exempt from the ruling. Food shops were limited to heat during the morning hours, and there were 'heatless Mondays' between 18 February and 25 March when all places of amusement were closed. The crisis was relieved only by the coming of spring.[108]

The need for farm labour was even greater in 1918 than in the previous year. The newly organized Canada Food Board and the Organization of Resources Committee announced a campaign in March to recruit schoolboys for service as Soldiers of the Soil. Ontario's quota was fifteen thousand. Enrolment began on 25 March, the beginning of 'a week of dedication and preparation for the solemn duty of greater food production.'[109] Some 16,700 Ontario boys had volunteered within the first two days of the campaign. On 24 April, the local Soldiers of the Soil, farmerettes, five tractors, and three bands paraded through the streets of Toronto.

The news from the Western Front was bad. The Germans launched a massive spring offensive in March which for a time threatened to turn into a rout. The need for Canadian reinforce-ments was more critical than ever. The Borden government

---

[108]Federal regulations for the conservation of fuel were embodied in PC 298 of 5 Feb. 1918 (P.A.C., RG 2, 1, v. 1482).

[109]*Globe*, 22 March 1918, p. 7. Advertisement of the Organization of Resources Committee.

responded by passing orders in council on 20 April cancelling all
exemptions, including those granted to conscientious objectors and
farmers' sons, and making registration compulsory for all unmarried
men of nineteen and those who had reached the age of twenty before
13 October 1917.[110] Farmers were particularly upset by the cancella-
tions and organized protest meetings throughout Ontario. Not only
were they concerned about the loss of their sons' help in food production, they also felt betrayed by the Union Government, which they
had helped to elect. Many were now convinced that the orders in
council passed in December 1917 were nothing more than election
bribes. A large delegation of farmers from Ontario and Quebec met
Sir Robert Borden in Ottawa on 14 May to protest against the can-
cellations and 'the breach of faith' by the Borden government.[111]
Borden's response to their protest was predictable:

If the Channel Ports should be reached through the breaking of our line
it would be, to say the least, problematical whether any of this production
would be made of service to the Allied nations overseas or to our men
who are holding that line. I regard it as the supreme duty of the Government to see to it that these men are sustained by such reinforcements as
will enable them to hold the line. You speak of solemn covenants and
pledges. Do you imagine for one moment we have not a solemn covenant
and a pledge to those men?[112]

The farmers returned to their homes empty-handed. But they had
learned of the necessity for farmers to have a strong organization
through which to plead their cause. As a result, the United Farmers
of Ontario took on a new importance among a growing number of
them.

Food production did not suffer much as a result of conscription.
Most farmers actually called up were treated with leniency. When
they reported for duty, most were granted leave immediately to
return to their agricultural work, but there was no guarantee that
they would be granted such leave. And they were incensed when the
government passed an order in council on 22 June restoring exemptions for conscientious objectors but not altering the status of
farmers.[113]

The first draftees under the Military Service Act had been called
up on 3 January. Since then, there had been hundreds of defaulters.

[110]P.A.C., RG 2, 1, v. 1493, PC 919 and 962 of 20 April 1918.
[111]W.R. Young, 'Conscription, Rural Depopulation, and the Farmers of Ontario,
1917–19,' *Canadian Historical Review*, 53 (1972), p. 311.
[112]Quoted in *CAR 1918*, p. 412.
[113]P.A.C., RG 2, 1, v. 1502, PC 1567 of 22 June 1918.

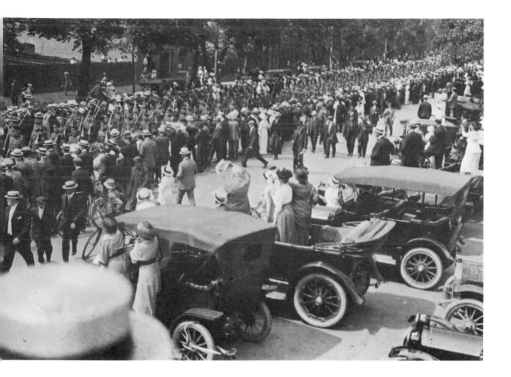

Men of The Queen's Own Rifles
leaving Toronto for Valcartier, August 1914

John Boyd Collection, Public Archives of Canada

'Recruiting Office' in Hamilton, July 1915

John Boyd Collection, PAC

The 35th Battalion's trench exhibit
at the Canadian National Exhibition, September 1915

John Boyd Collection, PAC

Wagon bearing prohibition petition
en route to Queen's Park on 8 March 1916

John Boyd Collection, PAC

Prohibition parade on Yonge Street, Toronto, 8 March 1916,
with its half-mile-long banner. Most of the banner was destroyed
before the marchers reached Queen's Park.

John Boyd Collection, PAC

Recruiting parade for the 198th Battalion
on Albert Street, Toronto, on 8 March 1916,
the same day as the prohibition parade

John Boyd Collection, PAC

Toronto streetcar decorated for recruiting purposes,
3 July 1916

John Boyd Collection, PAC

ROYAL GRENADIERS OVERSEAS BATTALION

123rd. C.E.F.

QUESTIONS TO MEN WHO HAVE NOT ENLISTED.

1. If you are physically fit and between 19 and 40 years of age, are you really satisfied with what you are doing to-day. - - - ?

2. Do you feel happy as you walk along the streets and see **OTHER** men wearing the King's uniform. - - - - ?

3. Do you realize that you have to live with yourself for the rest of your life. - - ? "Gee! and have to look at yourself in the looking glass every time you shave too."

4. If you are lucky enough to have children do you think it is fair to them not to go unless you are going to leave them hungry. ?

5. What would happen to Canada if every man stayed at Home. - - - - ?

Your King and Kitchener and 100,000 more

Canadians at the front are calling you.

---ENLIST WITH---

10th ROYAL GRENADIERS
OVERSEAS BATTALION 123rd. C.E.F.
at the Armouries. - - Toronto.

Leaflet of the 123rd Battalion, of the shaming variety

Military District Records, PAC

'Camp at Sunrise,' by Homer R. Watson

War Collection, No. 8964, Canadian War Museum,
National Museum of Man, National Museums of Canada

Willys-Overland float, with women workers aboard,
prepared for the Women's Day Parade at
the 1918 Canadian National Exhibition

John Boyd Collection, PAC

Armistice celebrants

Celebrations in front of the Toronto City Hall
on the false armistice, 7 November 1918

John Boyd Collection, PAC

The responsibility for their apprehension was assigned to the Dominion Police, who on 31 May were placed under the control of the Department of Militia and Defence and became the Civil Branch of the Canadian Military Police Corps. Theirs was a difficult and thankless job. Detachments frequently 'visited' places of amusement, where young men unable to produce papers identifying their draft status were either arrested immediately, or given a few hours in which to produce them. Many simply disappeared into the hinterland, defying the police to ferret them out (B 40). The most extraordinary 'visit' occurred on 7 June at the Jesuits' St Stanislaus Novitiate in Guelph. It was prompted by complaints from militant Protestants in the Guelph area who were embittered by decisions of the Central Appeal Judge ruling that members of religious orders were exempt from military service, but that theological students were not. The Protestants had chosen the right institution about which to complain because one of the novices was Marcus Doherty, son of the Minister of Justice. No arrests were made, and the raid only deepened the bitterness of the Protestants. Finally, on 7 April 1919, at the instigation of the Rev. Kennedy H. Palmer of the Guelph Ministerial Association, Sir Sam Hughes made specific charges in the House of Commons about the handling of the affair. A commission of investigation was appointed by the government; after hearing evidence presented by twenty-one witnesses, it refuted all the charges[114] (B 41).

A second National Registration was held on 22 June 1918. This time the registration of men and women over the age of sixteen was made compulsory except for cloistered nuns, persons on active service, and inmates of asylums, penitentiaries, and prisons until the time of their discharge. Failure to comply could result in fines, imprisonment, disfranchisement, or loss of elective office or lawful employment. Offenders could also be denied the right to purchase railway and steamboat tickets, and they could not board or lodge in hotels, public houses, inns, taverns, clubs, restaurants, or boarding houses.[115] Each registrant was asked his name, address, age, date and country of birth, marital status, the state of his health, occupation, and whether or not he had agricultural experience or any special training. Women were asked, 'in what capacity do you think you could serve best?' while men were asked to indicate whether 'your

[114]Records of the inquiry will be found in P.A.C., RG 14 D 2, Sessional Paper 101 of 1919 (2nd Session).

[115]P.A.C., RG 2, 1, v. 1493, PC 953 of 22 April 1918. The Canada Registration Board was created by PC 404 of 23 Feb. 1918 (ibid., v. 1485).

circumstances permit you to serve in the present national crisis, by changing your present occupation to some other for which you qualified, if the conditions offered be satisfactory.'[116] After completing the questionnaire each registrant received a certificate which 'must always be carried upon the person.' The compulsory aspect of registration and the stiff penalties for non-compliance ensured that it would be a success.

Meanwhile, westbound military transports on the North Atlantic were filled with wounded Canadian veterans, and early in April some survivors of the First Contingent arrived home on furlough. The idea of such a furlough was suggested first during the summer of 1917, and it received impetus as a result of the work of the Imperial Order Daughters of the Empire, who circulated a petition throughout Canada requesting it. Sir Arthur Currie's views were solicited; he replied on 29 July 1917: 'I would offer no objection to three months' furlough to Canada ... provided their places here [i.e., in France] were immediately taken by a similar number from ENGLAND, and provided further that I had an assurance that the Corps would suffer no permanent disability by reason of leave being granted to these men.'[117] Considering the inadequacy of reinforcements then available in England and the shortage of vessels which could carry the men to Canada, the proposal seemed doomed. No estimate had yet been made of the number of men who might be eligible, but there were suggestions that only native Canadians or only those still serving in the front lines in France be considered. The scheme received impetus on 24 September when the *Canadian Daily Record* reported that Sir Edward Kemp had been sent a petition from the Local Council of Women in London, Ont.:

While appreciating the urgent need of every available man in order to maintain the Expeditionary Force at its proper strength, the opinion is ventured that it is possible, without seriously impairing the efficiency of the Forces, to grant furlough to these few remaining heroes to return for rest and recuperation in Canada. These brave boys are now, unhappily, but a remnant. For the past three years they have been continuously absent from their loved ones, enduring untold hardships without complaint.[118]

With the consent of Sir Robert Borden, Kemp submitted the proposal to Lord Derby, the British Secretary of State for War. Kemp said that the Canadian government felt that,

[116]PC 953 of 22 April 1918.
[117]P.A.C., RG 9, III, v. 90, file 10-12-6X.
[118]*Ibid.*

in order to maintain the morale of the Canadian people, with respect to enlistment, some slight concession is necessary, and after giving the matter most careful consideration, it is thought that the proposal ... will appease public opinion, relieve tension, and will be a proof that the government at least is sympathetic. In view of additional enlistments, particularly under the Military Service Act ... the agitation for leave has become more pronounced.[119]

Derby agreed to the Canadian proposal without hesitation, but, instead of thousands, only 838 men received the furlough. They were greeted with enthusiastic welcomes in their home towns. Kingston, for example, had a 'monster military and civic parade' in their honour, followed by a reception at the City Hall, complete with speeches and 'entertainment extraordinary.'[120] The prospect of returning overseas was not pleasant, and forty-one Toronto men met on 10 April to pass a resolution asking that they be permitted to remain in Canada (B 42). Their timing was bad. The great German spring offensive was still pushing the Allies back, and it was unthinkable that the Canadian government could grant the men's request. Many did not return overseas, however. Of the 838 men granted leave, only 27 per cent had returned to Europe by August and the leave of 12 per cent had not yet expired. Most of the remaining 61 per cent were probably placed on military duty in Canada.[121]

Meanwhile the ranks of the GWVA and other veterans' organizations grew enormously. By the end of the year, it was estimated that the GWVA alone had some fifty thousand members in two hundred branches across the country.[122] Ever mindful of their purpose, they now mounted a vigorous campaign to exclude aliens of enemy origin from jobs which could be filled by veterans. Sir Robert Borden received a petition from the GWVA in March which urged that enemy aliens employed in work of national importance should be placed under surveillance, that they should not be allowed to hold public office, that their newspapers should be suppressed, and that they should not receive more pay than that to which Canadian soldiers were entitled. Borden received the petition with thanks and it was put away.

Alien labour was one of the principal topics at the second annual GWVA convention, held in Toronto between 29 July and 3 August 1918. The work of the delegates was not made easier by riots which broke out on the streets of Toronto while the convention was in

[119]*Ibid.*
[120]*Daily British Whig*, 9 April 1918, p. 6.
[121]P.A.C., RG 9, III, v. 90, file 10-12-6X.
[122]*CAR 1918*, p. 585.

progress. The trouble began on 2 August over the alleged ill-treatment of a returned soldier in a Greek-owned café on College Street. A mob of enraged sympathizers wrecked the café and neighbouring ones as well. The unrest continued sporadically until 7 August, when Mayor Church threatened to read the Riot Act. Delegates to the convention were dismayed and passed a resolution on 3 August condemning 'the grave breach of civil and military discipline taken part in by some returned soldiers ... It is just such actions as these that hamper the work of the GWVA and bring our cause into disgrace ... in the public mind.'[123] An editorial in *The Veteran*, although deploring the Toronto disorders, commented:

Without attempting to justify the conduct of the rioters in Toronto, we would draw the attention of the Canadian people to the fact that many returned men do sincerely feel that the Government and people of Canada have failed to implement the gracious promises of special treatment and consideration made to them ere they sailed overseas. Neglect to control profiteering, to work out a sane land settlement and labour policy, and to regulate the alien problem, have all combined as irritants upon men whose nerves have not been improved by their trials in the trenches.[124]

Lord Reading, British ambassador in Washington, telegraphed the Governor General on 4 August for details of 'anti-Greek riots' which had been reported to him by the president of the Greek community in Toronto. Reading's request was passed to Sir John Hendrie, the Lieutenant Governor, whose subsequent report (B 43) minimized the affair. The Toronto Board of Police Commissioners conducted an inquiry, and its report, made public on 19 October, attributed the difficulty in suppressing the riots to poor relations between military and police, but 'the responsibility for the succeeding too vigorous suppression was not directly placed.'[125]

Most Ontarians were far more concerned about the progress of the war, inflation, and their own standard of living than about minor riots in Toronto. Food prices rose steadily, and by the summer it was evident that there soon would be shortages. 'Honour' rationing of sugar was introduced in August when householders were asked to limit their purchases to 1½ pounds per person per month. A similar request to limit creamery butter purchases to two pounds monthly was made in October. By that time consumers were accustomed to the 'war loaf' of bread which was made with 20 per cent substitutes combined with flour. Fuel shortages were expected; the winter supply

123Quoted in *CAR 1918*, p. 587.
124*The Veteran*, Sept. 1918, p. 13.
125*CAR 1918*, p. 587.

of coal was allotted in some Ontario municipalities as early as August. 'Gas-less Sundays' were introduced in September, drastically cutting the number of Sunday drivers on Ontario roads.

Another grim winter lay ahead, but the news from Europe gave reason for hope that the war might be in its last stages. The Allies had launched a major offensive early in August with the Canadian Corps in the vanguard. Casualties were heavy, but people on the home front were elated by the news of successive victories. Then, early in the fall, Ontario was plunged into a crisis so serious that few had either the time or the inclination to worry about shortages, the cost of living, or Toronto riots. Reports had reached Canada of an epidemic of influenza ravaging Europe. It had reached the eastern United States and Montreal by early September. Many Ontario nurses volunteered to assist medical authorities in Boston and New York. In mid-September men of the Polish army training at Niagara-on-the-Lake were stricken. The epidemic spread rapidly. Within weeks, there were thousands of cases throughout Ontario. Factories, schools, and places of amusement were closed; public meetings and sporting events were cancelled. No Masses were offered in Roman Catholic churches in Ottawa for two Sundays in October because of the severity of the epidemic there. Telephone and streetcar services were limited because so many operators were stricken. Women across the province answered the call for Sisters of Service to help nurse the sick and provide them with hot meals. All too often their services were brief. If the women volunteers did not contract the disease in the course of their work they soon found that they were needed at home to care for members of their own families. Makeshift hospitals were set up in public buildings which could be adapted for the purpose; they were usually staffed by women volunteers under the supervision of a trained nurse. Urgent appeals were made for bedding, for people to care for the children of stricken parents, and for cars to convey the sick to hospitals or to take food and nursing volunteers to the homes of victims who could not be moved. Organizations and individuals across the province responded willingly and in great numbers to the call for assistance (B 44). The epidemic appeared to be on the wane by early November, but the toll was staggering. At one time there had been an estimated ten thousand cases in Ottawa. The death toll throughout Ontario was approximately five thousand by November.

The grim news at home was balanced by rumours early in November that an armistice had been signed. The rumour was false, but spirits were lifted. Ontarians knew that the end of the war was very near.

C. LOYALTY IN QUESTION

A FEW HOURS BEFORE WAR WAS DECLARED Magistrate R.E. Kingsford told lawyers in his Toronto courtroom:

We have among us foreigners, some of whom belong to the countries with which we are at war. Many of these have lived among us for years. They are among our most respected citizens. They can be assured they will receive the full protection of our laws. No molestations or insults will be offered them. They will receive the same consideration and protection as our own fellow-subjects and may rely on our good feeling to see that no harm befalls them. All we expect from them is reciprocal fair treatment. I ask you ... the gentlemen of the Bar ... to use all your influence in the direction of impressing on our own people the necessity for the preservation of law and order, and the protection of the foreigners remaining within our borders.[1]

A few days later the Borden government passed orders in council protecting the rights of enemy aliens 'so long as they quietly pursue their ordinary avocations.'[2] Wild rumours of enemy activities were sweeping across Ontario. There were reports that two spies were arrested after having been flown into Petawawa Camp; that attempts had been made to blow up a Canadian Northern train near Parry Sound and a grain elevator at Windsor; that an airship from a German naval force in James Bay had been sighted some three hundred miles away, over New Liskeard.[3] There were proven incidents as well, and people living along the border were nervous about the possibility of invasion from the United States. Four armed Germans were arrested by Gananoque police after allegedly paddling across

[1]Quoted in the *Globe*, 5 Aug. 1914, p. 7.
[2]P.A.C., RG 2, 1, v. 1312, PC 2086 of 7 Aug. 1914.
[3]Probably the wildest rumour of the war on the home front was of an impending air raid on Ottawa. Sir Robert Borden received a telegram at 10.30 in the evening on 14 February 1915 warning him that three or four aeroplanes had been spotted over Brockville, flying in the direction of Ottawa. Lights throughout the capital were ordered extinguished. The *Globe* reported from Brockville on 15 February that 'the first machine was flying very rapidly and very high. Very little could be seen, but the unmistakable sounds of the whirring motor made the presence of the aircraft known.' Next day it was discovered that the planes had been balloons sent aloft by boys in Morristown, New York, perhaps to commemorate the centenary of peace between Canada and the United States (*Globe*, 15 Feb. 1915, pp. 1, 2; 16 Feb. 1915, p. 1).

the St Lawrence River from Clayton, New York. They enjoyed the dubious honour of being the first internees at Fort Henry,[4] though they were soon joined by many others, picked up at border points and in Toronto and Montreal. The population of the fort rose to eighty by the end of August and continued to grow thereafter until the spring of 1917, when it ceased to be an internment camp and its inmates were transferred to the camp at Kapuskasing.

Aliens of enemy origin were required to register and report regularly, and they could not leave the country without a permit. Those who failed to comply were liable to internment (C 1). Camps were set up in Ontario at Stanley Barracks in Toronto, Kapuskasing, Niagara Falls, and Sault Ste Marie. Although the camps were intended only for those who disobeyed Canadian law, the inmates included aliens whose sole crime was being unemployed. Municipal officials were not above inventing charges simply to remove the aliens from civic welfare rolls. Although the internees had lost their freedom, they could still earn a little money. Arrangements were made with the federal government whereby provincial governments could employ internees in public works at a nominal rate. The Ontario government, for example, used internees in Northern Ontario to construct a new experimental farm near Hearst and to clear land adjacent to Port Arthur and Fort William for eventual settlement.

The attitude of Ontarians towards aliens of enemy origin was, on the whole, one of tolerance during the early months of the war,[5] but this changed in May 1915 after the sinking of the *Lusitania* with the loss of many Ontario lives. Thereafter aliens were detained on the slightest provocation; hostile public opinion forced the closing of two German clubs in Toronto; runners of German extraction were excluded from a ten-mile road race at St Catharines on Victoria Day; Toronto civic employees of German origin were dismissed; Mayor Church ordered the removal of an electric sign advertising German beers made in Berlin, Ontario[6]; and street names with German asso-

[4]On 18 August 1914 the Adjutant General ordered the officer commanding, Military District No. 3, to send an escort to Gananoque to pick up the four men. 'These men will be confined at Fort Henry where a detention camp will be established under a proper military supervision' (P.A.C., RG 9, IIB1, v. 676, Log of Telegrams).

[5]There were, of course, exceptions. The incident involving German professors at the University of Toronto attracted widespread attention (see section F) as did the case of H.J. Glaubitz, a native of Germany and general manager of the Public Utilities Commission in London, who was forced to resign after being accused of assisting a German reservist to leave the country (see *CAR 1914*, p. 286 and *CAR 1915*, p. 363).

[6]Church's order was rescinded a month later on the advice of the city solicitor.

ciations were altered.[7] St Paul's Lutheran Church in London closed 'in the hope ... of putting a stop to allegations that it is a pro-German organization'[8] and its members denied that they had celebrated German victories such as the sinking of the *Lusitania*. F.V. Riethdorf, a German professor at Woodstock College who had relinquished his college duties to devote his time to patriotic and recruiting speeches, often under the auspices of the Speakers' Patriotic League, found himself without a sponsor after Claude Macdonell, Member of Parliament for Toronto South, objected: 'I have nothing against Prof. Riethdorf personally. He is a German, he looks like a German, he speaks with a strong German accent ... It is on these grounds I do not consider him a desirable man to address a British audience.'[9] Riethdorf had served in the German Army prior to coming to Canada, and Macdonell was suspicious of his loyalty:

He may be a spy; I do not know; if he is not, he is a deserter from his own country and no man for us to mix up with. The British cause does not need such advocacy. His German accent is so strong and so objectionable that his English is not understandable. He is the typical German soldier from every point of view and I do not think Anglo-Saxon people have any use for such persons. He is a distinct offence to almost all to whom I spoke and my advice if asked by the league, would be to recall this man.[10]

Attitudes towards Germans worsened during the summer of 1915 with the arrest and conviction of Wilhelm Lefler of Detroit for conspiring with Albert Kaltschmidt to blow up factories and public buildings in Windsor and Walkerville. It now became common to attribute any explosion or fire to the work of enemy saboteurs. Rumours abounded across Canada about enemy spying activities, and aliens of enemy origin found it increasingly difficult to find and keep

[7]Bismarck Avenue in Toronto was renamed Asquith, Albertus was changed to Kitchener, Prust became Maidstone, Hanover became Tracy Place, and Schmidt became Lefroy (London *Free Press*, 11 Aug. 1915, p. 1). There was even a suggestion that Wurtemburg Street in Ottawa, on which Sir Robert Borden lived, be renamed in honour of Nurse Edith Cavell (*ibid.*, 29 Oct. 1915, p. 9).

[8]*Globe*, 4 June 1915, p. 13.

[9]Quoted in the *Globe*, 26 Aug. 1915, p. 4. Riethdorf resigned from Woodstock College in August because of criticism of his German background. He enlisted as a private in the Canadian Army Medical Corps in April 1917, transferred to Intelligence, and was discharged in June 1917. He explained to a *Globe* reporter that he was not allowed to join an overseas draft and claimed he was a virtual prisoner, that 'pro-German politics are at the bottom of it all,' and that those who sought pro-German votes feared he 'might get a foothold' (*Globe*, 29 June 1917, p. 7).

[10]Macdonell to W.R. Cochrane of the Speakers' Patriotic League, quoted in the London *Free Press*, 26 Aug. 1915, p. 10.

jobs. One Hamilton man asked to be interned because he was unable to find a job, owing to his German nationality.

There was, by 1916, a distinct difference in the official attitude regarding Germans and Austrians. 'The Austrian in Canada,' reported the Minister of Justice on 9 August 1916, 'has proved to be a thoroughly inoffensive citizen and we have released large numbers of them.'[11] Germans, on the other hand, were considered to be more sympathetic to their homeland and thus more likely to be troublesome. The general public did not always make this distinction. Ten Austrians were released from the internment camp at Hearst in April 1916 to work in tanneries in Bracebridge where labour was scarce and the wages low. Other employees refused to work with the Austrians and burned the house in which they lived. The Austrians were moved to Acton, but again tannery employees refused to work with them.

Anti-German feeling was continually expressed by public speakers and in newspapers, often in a mocking manner. Few opportunities were lost in making derisive comments about the enemy; even a dachshund at the Canadian National Exhibition dog show was not immune:

It is perhaps not to be wondered at that the German national representative in the dog world, the daschund [sic], is in a minority of one at the show this year. This lone elongated native of sausage-land was discovered in a pitiful state of depression and low morale. While all the other fellows were being patted and petted, this forlorn alien enemy looked around it with a woebegone expression and actually whined and shed tears when a charitable onlooker stroked it. If it had been a real Hun it would have bit the hand that fondled it, but the dogs of Hunland are more humane than some of their masters.[12]

Such anti-German mockery and the far more serious attacks on the loyalty of German-Canadians contributed to an already very tense atmosphere in the southwestern Ontario city of Berlin. That prosperous manufacturing centre had had more than its share of public attention since August 1914 because of its high proportion of citizens of German ancestry, many of whom were the descendants of families which had lived in the area for generations. Within months of the war's outbreak the local Board of Education ended the use of German in the schools, and that language was heard less and less in the streets, shops, and factories of the city. In an attempt to dull further the im-

[11]Quoted in *CAR 1916*, p. 387.
[12]*Globe*, 5 Sept. 1917, p. 8.

pact of suspicions of disloyalty in Berlin, the city council, as early as May 1915, had asked for the appointment of a local Registrar of Enemy Aliens, but the request was refused because, 'upon investigation, the conditions at Berlin did not appear to warrant the maintenance of a registration office.'[13] The decision did nothing to lessen attacks by innuendo or to alleviate the sensitivity of Berliners, many of whom feared that the prosperity of Berlin might suffer as a result. As the months wore on, suspicion and animosity between people of British and German origin in the city heightened.

Aggravating the tense situation was the recruiting campaign of the 118th Battalion, CEF, and its subsequent interference in the troubled municipal affairs of the city. The battalion was authorized in the fall of 1915 and recruited in the electoral riding of North Waterloo, whose total population of 35,000 included many Mennonites who were averse to military service. In spite of vigorous campaigning, the battalion's total strength early in January 1916 was only 26 officers and 288 men. Almost every battalion then recruiting in Canada was experiencing similar difficulties,[14] but recruiters in North Waterloo, stung by insinuations of disloyalty in the riding, were determined to raise the battalion to full strength. As a result, they resorted to some very questionable recruiting techniques, and in doing so aroused a good deal of hostility. The recruiting campaign accelerated in the middle of January. Newspaper advertisements were of the shaming variety. On 17 January, the Berlin City Council passed a resolution deploring the failure of so many men to enlist and appealing to parents, sisters, and sweethearts 'to place no obstacle in the way of loved ones who are anxious to play the MAN in this great world struggle.'[15] That same evening the 118th campaigned in the streets of Berlin, asking men why they had not yet enlisted. The soldiers resorted to press gang tactics a week later, 'hustling in the civilians by force [to the recruiting office] if they did not accompany the soldiers willingly.'[16] Such tactics were bitterly resented, but the officer commanding, Lt-Col. W.M.O. Lochead, said they were used because 'all other methods have failed to produce results.'[17] The actions of the soldiers so aroused the Twin City Trades and Labour Council that they passed

[13]Berlin News Record, 9 Feb. 1916, p. 1.
[14]See section B.
[15]Berlin News Record, 18 Jan. 1916, p. 1.
[16]Ibid., 24 Jan. 1916, p. 1.
[17]Ibid. Lochead had said earlier: 'No young man should resent being asked why he is not wearing the Khaki' (Ibid., 18 Jan. 1916, p. 2). The police did not interfere with the soldiers because, as one of them said, it would have been risking his life to have done so.

a resolution strongly protesting against such tactics, which interfered with the conduct of business, insulted women, and violated 'the individual rights and privileges of private citizens when on the streets ... We request the City Council to take immediate steps to try and end such disgraceful conduct ... that they the City Council stop any further payments from the $4000 fund for recruiting and if the taxpayers are insulted, molested and interfered with in future, that Major-General Sir Sam Hughes be requested to remove this 118th Battalion from Waterloo County.'[18] The loyalty of men who could pass such a resolution was questioned by some Berliners.

Loyalty was the most important quality which a Berliner could possess during the war years and was the favourite topic among speakers in the city. Capt. H.A. Fraser, adjutant of the 118th, told listeners at a recruiting meeting in Berlin on 30 January that 'he believed there was a certain element at work ... that was bending its efforts to retard recruiting instead of doing everything to help it along.'[19] The principal speaker of the day, Lieut. Stanley Nelson Dancey,[20] had far more to say on the subject:

Being a stranger to this city I must tell you that the eyes of Canada are turned upon Berlin today. The whole of Canada is watching to see if Berlin and North Waterloo are going to prove their patriotism in men and not money. Unless your battalion is brought to its full strength, Canada will judge you as being pro-German and not British. There is an element here that is a menace to the city and a disgrace to the country. This element must be weeded out before its rotten influence can do any more harm. Already it has, through the press, made a cowardly, slanderous and seditious attack upon Colonel Lochead ... The offence merits the punishment of the slanderers by internment till after the war ... You have creatures in your midst who say success to the Kaiser, and to Hell with the King; and all I can say is, round up this element into the detention camps, for they are unworthy of British citizenship and should be placed where they belong. Already the showing that the physically fit young men of North Waterloo have made is so rotten that I have heard an outside business man say to a traveller from a Berlin wholesale house, 'I'll not

[18]*Ibid.*, 26 Jan. 1916, p. 1.

[19]*Ibid.*, 31 Jan. 1916, pp. 1, 2.

[20]Dancey was a Canadian journalist who claimed he had seen Belgian victims of German atrocities when he was in Breda, Holland, in the fall of 1914. His novel, *Faith of a Belgian*, published in 1916, was widely read at the time. Dancey became a lieutenant in the 30th Wellington Rifles of the Active Militia in December 1915 and was a popular, but controversial, speaker at recruiting meetings throughout Ontario. He was attached to the 207th Battalion of the CEF in August 1916 with the rank of captain, but was struck off the strength of the CEF on 15 May 1917 (P.A.C., RG 9, IIB4, v. 8), apparently retaining his commission in the militia.

buy another damned article manufactured in that German town. Do you think I'm going to give my money to support a pack of Germans? If I did I'd be as bad as they.'[21]

Not only did Dancey's speech attract few recruits, it did almost irreparable harm to civic pride and solidarity, already seriously endangered.

The Berlin situation took a new turn a few days later when the *News Record* printed a letter from 'A Ratepayer' suggesting that the City Council pass a resolution to change the name of the city.[22] A public meeting was held on 11 February at which a resolution was adopted asking the Council 'to take the necessary steps' to have the name changed (C 2). Many Berliners, including Mayor J. E. Hett, saw no real purpose in changing Berlin's name, but to oppose the change-the-name movement actively in February would have led to more charges of disloyalty and pro-Germanism. There were already enough of those in North Waterloo. A few prominent Berliners, however, did express their opposition, only to be attacked by Captain Dancey at a recruiting meeting on 13 February. Dancey then turned his guns on the Rev. C.R. Tappert, an American citizen and pastor of St Matthew's Lutheran Church, the only local church which continued to use German in its services:

Some of you wonder why Canada mistrusts the loyalty of this place. The reason is simple. You have not done your duty by giving men to the cause ... There are men in this community who cheer German successes when thousands of true British hearts are stilled. They applaud when outrages like the *Lusitania* incident are committed. These men living in Canada are not loyal to the land that feeds them. They are traitors and cowards and should be placed behind the bars ... You have a minister in your midst by the name of Tappert who, according to a Toronto paper, said he did not think they should be called 'Huns' ... This minister's remarks are undoubtedly pro-German and why do you allow him to run free to make them? The time is coming when he will no longer be a 'guest' of Canada's and it cannot come too soon. Let him get back among the Germans of the United States where he belongs.[23]

[21]*News Record*, 31 Jan. 1916, pp. 1, 2.
[22]*Ibid.*, 4 Feb. 1916, p. 2.
[23]*Ibid.*, 14 Feb. 1916, p. 1. Tappert was quoted by the *Toronto Star* on 10 February as saying, 'there is a great deal of bitterness here [i.e. in Berlin] among Germans and those of German descent, arising out of the numerous untrue things that have been said about Germany in the Canadian papers. Everyone knows that 90 per cent of the things said about the Germans are untrue' (quoted in the *CAR 1916*, p. 554).

Anti-German violence erupted in Berlin on 15 February. Men of the machine gun section of the 118th Battalion marched 'in a peaceable manner' to Concordia Hall, the meeting place of the German Concordia Club, from which they removed a bust of Kaiser Wilhelm I.[24] They then paraded it through the streets of Berlin. When other soldiers of the battalion learned that the hall contained German flags and pictures, they and some civilians entered and severely damaged the hall and its contents. The incident was reported in morning newspapers the next day. Before questions could be asked by the Opposition, Sir Sam Hughes read a statement to the House of Commons outlining the causes of the affair as provided by Colonel Lochead and promising that an inquiry would be held (C 3). Subsequent courts of inquiry (C 4, C 5) blamed the unrest on the atmosphere then prevailing in Berlin and found that civilians were equally responsible with the soldiers for the damage which resulted. No charges were laid.

The resolution endorsed at the public meeting on 11 February and signed by 1080 citizens was presented to the city council ten days later. The Concordia Club incident being still fresh in the minds of the councillors, the resolution was received with little opposition. Council voted to submit a petition to the Ontario Legislature for permission to change the city's name and decided that, in the event of the Legislature's agreeing to a change, the council would sponsor a contest for the new name. Some councillors felt that amalgamation with neighbouring Waterloo under the latter's name would be an easier and better way out of the present difficulty and succeeded in passing a resolution to explore the possibility of such an amalgamation.

Soon after the meeting local newspapers were deluged with suggestions of names for the city. One writer asked prophetically, 'Why not name it after some of the Generals? I suggest Roberts or Kitchener.'[25] But not all writers favoured a change. The *News Record* published on 26 February a letter written by W.H. Breithaupt, a prominent citizen of Berlin, who argued that nothing would be gained by changing the name (C 6). He was answered by Alderman

[24]For details of this incident see records of two subsequent courts of inquiry in P.A.C., RG 24, v. 1256, file HQ 593-1-87. The bust had originally been on a pedestal in Victoria Park. Men of the First Contingent had thrown it into a lake in the park; later it was recovered from the lake and placed in Concordia Hall. After its capture by the 118th Battalion the bust was melted down and turned into napkin holders.

[25]*News Record*, 23 Feb. 1916, p. 4. It is interesting to note that the London *Free Press* carried a report on 21 April 1915 that a newspaper in Germany had told its readers that Berlin, Canada, had been renamed Kitchener.

W.G. Cleghorn, who fanned the flames of hatred by attacking not only Breithaupt but also others of German descent who, he claimed, had done little to assist in the war effort (C 7).

On 4 March the men of the 118th Battalion again took the law into their own hands. Their victim was the Reverend C.R. Tappert, who had attracted the attention of Captain Dancey. As a result of the criticism levelled against him, Tappert had resigned his charge and apparently had agreed to leave Berlin by 1 March,[26] but he was still there three days later. That evening some sixty men of the 118th forcibly entered Tappert's house and demanded an explanation for his continued presence in Berlin. When the pastor refused to answer he was, according to a report in the Ottawa *Free Press*, 'given two minutes to put on his hat and coat and to go with the soldiers. When the time was nearly up Tappert made a rush for the telephone and called the police number. He was pulled away from the telephone before he could give the message ... The soldiers began dragging the minister from his house ... Tappert received a blackened eye and a cut on the back of the head, which required two stitches.'[27] After being taken from his house, Tappert was paraded through the streets until he was released by officers of the battalion. The American Consul General in Ottawa protested to Maj.-Gen. W.E. Hodgins about the ill-treatment of Tappert at the hands of the soldiers and demanded that he and his family be assured of adequate protection. Hodgins asked for and received a report of the incident from Colonel Lochead (C 8), who assured the acting Adjutant General that he was 'acting in full sympathy and active support of the civil authorities.' Two men were charged and found guilty in a civil court for their complicity in the incident. Both received only suspended sentences. Tappert and his family left Berlin quietly on 8 March. Relative peace returned for a few weeks.

The Berlin delegation appeared before the Private Bills Committee of the Ontario Legislature on 4 April. After hearing both sides of the argument the committee voted not to report the bill to the Legislature, fearing that there might be racial strife in Berlin if a name change were permitted. Charging that they had not received a fair hearing from the committee, promoters of the name change formed a British League in the city 'to promote British sentiments in

[26]Colonel Lochead told a recruiting meeting on 20 February that Tappert, 'who, to say the least, had been indiscreet in his remarks, was resigning his position and would be leaving town in March.' The announcement was loudly applauded by the audience (*News Record*, 21 Feb. 1916, p. 1).

[27]Ottawa *Free Press*, 6 March 1916. Clipping in P.A.C., RG 24, v. 1256, file HQ 593-1-87.

the community.' The league passed a resolution on 14 April urging
the City Council to protest to Premier Hearst about their ill-treatment
by the Private Bills Committee. Council complied, and the bill was
duly introduced and passed in the Legislature as Section 51 of the
Statute Law Amendment.[28] The amendment permitted the council
to submit to the electors the question. 'Are you in favour of changing
the name of this city?' If a majority favoured such a change, 'the
Lieutenant-Governor in Council on the application of the council
may by proclamation change the name of the city and give it a name
chosen by the council.' Council decided on 24 April that the referendum would be held on 19 May. The campaign began almost immediately. On 5 May, in the midst of the battle, the 118th struck again.
This time the target was the Acadian Club in Waterloo; the raid was
remarkably similar to that on the Concordia Club in Berlin. Again
the primary objective was the removal of a bust of the German
Emperor, and again the raiders returned to the scene of the crime to
demolish the premises. The club's president submitted a claim for
damages to the Department of Militia and Defence. Like that presented by the Concordia Club, it was rejected[29] (C 9).

General Hodgins grew uneasy about the presence of the 118th in
Berlin as voting day approached. He wrote a private and confidential
letter to Colonel Lochead on 15 May suggesting that after the men
had had a reasonable time in which to vote, 'it might be well to take
the battalion for a good long route march and that on their return,
they should be kept in barracks. This will avoid any possible trouble
and give no cause for offence to those who might be looking for
trouble ... If, however, you ... do not agree to this, don't forget that I
have gone surety for the battalion, and for their good behavior while
they remain in Berlin, and you must, on no account, go back on me.'[30]
Lochead assured Hodgins that 'the confidence which you have been
good enough to place in me will not be betrayed.'[31]

The campaign was bitterly fought. Opponents of the change questioned the propriety of holding the referendum in wartime, observing
that federal and provincial general elections had been postponed
because of the war. They charged that the promoters had displayed
a lack of justice and fair play which were 'supposed to be characteristic of every true Briton' and blamed them for the bitterness,

[28]*Ontario Statutes*, 1916. 6 Geo. v, chap 24.
[29]P.A.C., RG 24, v. 1256, file HQ 593-1-87; v. 1158, file HQ 57-4-77. Sir Sam
Hughes had told W.G. Weichel MP that the department would pay for the damages
to the Acadian Club if its president submitted a claim.
[30]P.A.C., RG 24, v. 1256, file HQ 593-1-87.
[31]*Ibid.*

discord, and lawlessness prevalent in Berlin. They argued that the present name was no handicap to local manufacturers, who 'are nearly all busier than they have ever before been in their history.' Changing the name, they contended, was not the patriotic gesture argued by the promoters in that it would not add one recruit to the 118th or one dollar to patriotic causes.[32] The promoters stressed patriotism as the main reason for changing the name and warned that 'if the by-law is defeated ... the whole city ... will undoubtedly be branded as pro-German.' Further, 'the name Berlin is a handicap to us in business competition.'[33]

Some three thousand and fifty-seven citizens voted on 19 May in what the *News Record* described as one of the heaviest votes ever recorded in the city. A majority of only eighty-one favoured a change. Still, the result was enough to touch off wild celebrations in the streets of Berlin that evening:

The streets were thronged with thousands of people some of whom were cheering while others were looking gloomy. To give expression to their feelings of joy, many of the celebrators had provided themselves with fireworks of every known kind, from fancy sky-rockets to squibs. So enthusiastic were some of these firework artists that it was a matter of supreme indifference whether sky-rockets were fired into the air or into the crowds on the sidewalks. The inevitable result was numerous minor injuries to eyes, hands and clothing.[34]

The promoters were jubilant. Alderman J.A. Hallman promptly sent a cable to the King: 'The loyal citizens of Berlin Canada rejoice to inform Your Majesty that they have this day cast off forever the name of the Prussian capital.' It is not known whether the King shared their joy. The Duke of Connaught was asked on 23 May to inform Alderman Hallman 'that this telegram has been received by His Majesty.'[35] To his intense relief, General Hodgins heard from Colonel Lochead that the soldiers' conduct on voting day had been 'most commendable'; they had been involved in only one incident (C 10).

City Council immediately began making plans for choosing a new name. A representative Committee of Ninety-Nine was appointed to

[32]The opponents' views were contained in an advertisement in the *News Record*, 16–18 May 1916, p. 2.

[33]Advertisement in *News Record*, 16 May 1916, p. 3.

[34]*News Record*, 20 May 1916, p. 1.

[35]P.A.C., RG 25, Department of External Affairs, v. 1189, file 4065–16. When the bill for payment of the cable was submitted to the city council, it was refused (*News Record*, 6 June 1916, p. 1).

compile a list of names which could then be voted on by Berliners. The Council had already prepared a list of 113 incredible choices, which the committee reduced to six: Huronto, Bercana, Dunard, Hydro City, Renoma, and Agnoleo.[36] The choice provoked a storm of protest. The committee was dismissed with the thanks of the Council, which now assumed full responsibility for selecting the names to be submitted to the people.[37] They received indirect assistance from the German Navy. Local newspapers carried a report on 6 June that Lord Kitchener, the popular British Secretary of War, had been drowned aboard HMS *Hampshire*, which was sunk west of the Orkney Islands while conveying Kitchener to Russia. His name was quickly inserted in the council's short list.

Voting for the new name was conducted between 25 and 28 June. Only 1,055 votes were cast, and of these 163 were spoiled. Kitchener received 346 votes, Brock 335, Adanac 23, Benton 15, Corona 7, and Keowana 3. The *News Record* commented that 'the outstanding feature ... was the absolute indifference displayed by the ratepayers' and reported that the result was greeted by dead silence.[38] Opponents of the change regarded the result as insignificant because of the small turnout and sought signatures on a petition to be presented to the Lieutenant Governor asking for a postponement 'to give the city time to cool off, so that all may act with good judgment in finally deciding this important matter.'[39] The basis of the petition was a 'Statement in Connection With Change of Name of Berlin' (C 11) in which the history of opposition to the name change was related. Waterloo County Council supported the petitioners' cause on 11 July by passing a resolution which called for postponement of the change until after the next municipal election, so that the new city council might then 'negotiate with the council of the Town of Waterloo with a view of uniting the two municipalities under either the name of Waterloo or some other name suitable as may be agreed upon.'[40] A deputation presented the petition signed by 2,068 residents to Premier Hearst on 13 July, but it was too late. The Statute Law Amendment had been complied with; a vote had been conducted and a new name chosen. Now all that was needed was a provincial order in council to make the new name official. The deputation was bitterly disappointed; on their return from Toronto they formed a Citizens'

[36]A copy of the original list will be found in P.A.C., MG 30 B 28, John A. Lang papers.
[37]*News Record*, 1 June 1916, p. 1.
[38]*Ibid.*, 29 June 1916, p. 1.
[39]*Ibid.*, 5 July 1916.
[40]Quoted in *ibid.*, 11 July 1916, p. 1.

League, 'whose purpose is to promote the best interests of the community.'[41] They produced a remarkable document entitled 'The Other Side, An Appeal for British Fair Play,' apparently written by H.M. Bowman. It was printed in the *News Record* on 22 July and also in pamphlet form, but it received little sympathy from Ontario newspaper editors. The most devastating attack was made by the editor of the Berlin *Daily Telegraph*, a paper which had strongly supported the name-change campaign (C 12). The editor of the Welland *Telegraph* dismissed the article as 'so much piffle' and conjectured that 'whatever else that list of 2068 names [on the petition] may contain or omit, it does not omit one solitary pro-German in the town of Berlin.'[42] The *Globe* merely noted that the author was 'a graduate of a Leipsig [sic] university, Germany.'[43] There was now no doubt that the Citizens' League could gather little support outside their own city.

The Ontario cabinet passed the necessary order in council on 23 August providing for the proclamation of the new name on 1 September. There were spontaneous demonstrations on 23 August, and Mayor Hett addressed the celebrants in the evening. He observed that the change in the city's name

has brought joy to many on one hand, and, on the other, it has given sadness to a very large number of our people ... The victors can well afford to be generous to those of opposite opinions ... especially to the older residents who have lived here so long and have done so much for our city. During the past number of months there have existed quarrels and bad feelings. It is to be hoped that we will be united and live more peacefully.[44]

The Citizens' League had lost the battle, but they were determined to win the war. They launched a campaign on 24 August to rally and strengthen their forces for a victory at the polls in January 1917. Their aims were 'to promote good civic government in Berlin ... to further the best interests of the community' and 'to restore Berlin to the place that the city heretofore occupied in the eyes of Canada.'[45] Meetings to attract new members were held throughout the fall. On 28 October the League announced that Alderman David Gross jr,

[41]*Ibid.*, 21 July 1916, p. 1.
[42]Quoted in the *Daily Telegraph*, 15 Aug. 1916. Clipping in the John A. Lang papers (P.A.C., MG 30 B 28).
[43]*Globe*, 25 July 1916, p. 11.
[44]Quoted in *News Record*, 24 Aug. 1916, p. 1.
[45]*Ibid.*, 25 August 1916, p. 1.

would be the official mayoralty candidate. The British League was not idle. W.E. Gallagher was their candidate, and the ensuing campaign was hard fought. The British League drew first blood when it appealed to the Court of Revision against the inclusion of the names of hundreds of voters who, they claimed, were aliens and thus disfranchised. As a result, 207 applied for naturalization on 12 December. The three judges hearing the cases found that fifteen of the applicants were already British subjects and seventy-five already naturalized.[46] They granted naturalization to twenty-four. The remaining ninety-three applicants were unsuccessful because two of the three judges ruled that those born in enemy countries should not be naturalized during the war.[47] All had lived in Canada at least ten years, some for as long as forty-five, and all had been considered 'residents, taxpayers, jurors and voters' before their status was questioned by the British League.[48]

Although both mayoralty candidates publicly declared that the name-change controversy was not an election issue, the bitterness engendered by it and by the naturalization question could not be ignored by the voters. The situation in Kitchener was tense on voting day. A heavy vote was expected. Eligible voters in the 118th Battalion were brought from their camp in London to cast their ballots. This time, however, military authorities had taken precautions to avoid a major incident. Maj. Baron Osborne, the assistant provost marshal of Military District No. 1, was in Kitchener with some military police, and troops in Galt were ready to move in if trouble developed. Osborne's report (C 13) indicates that the situation was kept well in hand. The election resulted in a smashing victory for the Citizens' League. When the outcome was known, men of the 118th formed a parade, many of them shouting 'Are we downhearted?' When someone attempted to snatch a Union Jack from one of the soldiers a scuffle ensued but was soon broken up. A few days later the 118th was granted embarkation leave. After their departure some of the tension in Kitchener was eased. In his inaugural address the new mayor, David Gross, vowed 'to cultivate genuine good will and unity' and promised 'to try to restore peace and harmony in the community' (C 14), but Kitchener remained a troubled city for months. The 1917 general election campaign in

[46]Canadian-born residents were considered to be British subjects. Those born outside the British Empire who wished to become British subjects had to be naturalized.
[47]News Record, 23 Dec. 1916, p. 1.
[48]Ibid.

North Waterloo, a particularly bitter one, saw the defeat of the Conservative incumbent, W.G. Weichel, by W.D. Euler, a fervent anti-conscriptionist.

A final effort to restore the name Berlin was defeated in 1919. Shortly thereafter, the two sides in the controversy agreed to bury their differences in the hope that the city's good reputation and its prosperity might be fully and quickly restored.

D. WOMEN

HOURS BEFORE WORD of the declaration of war was received in Ottawa the Imperial Order Daughters of the Empire completed plans for the first of many contributions by Canadian women to the war effort. Meeting in Toronto, the national executive adopted a suggestion by Miss Mary Plummer to raise money for a hospital ship. The president, Mrs A.E. Gooderham, immediately telegraphed the offer to Sir Robert Borden, observing that the gift was considered 'most fitting as it is the woman's part to minister to the sick and wounded.'[1] Borden sent his thanks to Mrs Gooderham the next day. The Canadian Women's Hospital Ship Fund was organized; and money raised at concerts, tag days, teas, card parties, lectures, and bazaars poured into the offices of the fund.[2] Soon there were other outlets for patriotic Canadian women. They raised money for the Red Cross, Belgian Relief, and the Patriotic Fund; they made countless pillows, sheets, flannel shirts, socks, cholera belts, wristlets, balaclavas, scarves, and 'housewives'[3] for soldiers and refugees; they provided 'comforts'[4] for Canadian soldiers and visited soldiers' families.

Although most women supported their country's war effort wholeheartedly, some hung back, either because of deep pacifist convictions or from fear of the fate which might befall their husbands and sons. Many refused to give their written consent to enlistment of their men, a condition required by the military authorities before recruits could be accepted.[5] As a result many men declared themselves to be single, or used false names on the attestation papers, thereby depriving their wives and families of the separation allowances and pay allotments to which they would otherwise have been entitled.[6]

[1]P.A.C., MG 26 H, Borden Papers, file RLB 646, pp. 104122–4.

[2]Within two months some $300,000 had been collected, but since the Admiralty did not need another hospital ship at the time the money was used to buy motor ambulances for the War Office and to help pay for the construction of the Canadian Women's Hospital Wing on the Royal Naval Hospital at Hasler, near Portsmouth, England. The wing will soon be demolished, but a commemorative plaque will be mounted in the building planned to replace it.

[3]Mending kits.

[4]'Comforts' included socks, underwear, shirts, small towels, handkerchiefs, bootlaces, books, candles, candies, cocoa, soup tablets, writing paper, toilet paper, pencils, games, playing cards, tobacco, and chewing gum.

[5]P.A.C., RG 9, IIB3, v. 29, Militia Order 372 of 1914.

[6]P.A.C., RG 24, v. 2501, file HQS 1050, v. 9.

So many women refused consent that as early as August 1914 one senior officer was prompted to remark, 'If Canada is to maintain her independence the Canadian soldier must do his duty and his wife should not restrain him from selfish motives.'[7]

Suffragists faced a dilemma, wondering whether or not they should suspend their campaign for the vote until after the war, but most agreed with the substance of a resolution passed at the annual meeting of the Canadian Suffrage Association in Toronto in October 1914: 'That the Canadian Suffrage Association is more than ever convinced ... of the necessity of working for political equality ... so that the constructive attributes of women may be utilized in Government to balance the destructive actions now dominant.'[8] A joint meeting of suffragist societies held in Toronto in November 1915 resulted in the formation of a war auxiliary to support the local recruiting campaign and to provide women to do the work of men who, they thought, would then be free to enlist. Soon women were registering with the auxiliary to relieve male stenographers, secretaries, and streetcar conductors, and some volunteered to drive jitneys.[9] So successful was the Suffragists' War Auxiliary in Toronto that another was formed in Ottawa within a month.[10]

Women throughout Ontario took an increasing interest in military affairs as the war progressed. Some felt it was their duty to accost young men in the streets to inquire why they were not in uniform, while others took to the recruiting platform to shame and to scold. Their enthusiasm and zeal were not always appreciated. Their time and effort, counselled the Kingston *Daily British Whig*, might be better spent in 'missionary operations among their own sex. Very many of them in every community are still without any connection with the Red Cross and other movements which claim their devoted attention.'[11] But such admonitions usually fell on deaf ears. Women recruiters were convinced that they could induce men to enlist where male recruiters had failed; what work could be more patriotic than that?

Not content with either knitting or speaking, some women were determined to play a more active and masculine role in the defence of their country. There were at least two ladies' rifle clubs in the Toronto area by March 1915, and some women in Hamilton planned

[7]Quoted in *CAR 1914*, p. 190.
[8]*Globe*, 31 Oct. 1914, p. 8.
[9]*Ibid.*, 17 Nov. 1915, p. 5; 22 Nov. 1915, p. 5; 3 Dec. 1915, p. 8; 4 Dec. 1915, p. 10.
[10]*Ibid.*, 20 Dec. 1915, p. 11.
[11]*Daily British Whig*, 28 Sept. 1915, p. 4.

a Ladies' Home Guard 'to release for active service many middle-aged men who are now serving in the Home Guard.'[12] The Hamilton ladies' idea did not pass the planning stage, but it was adopted enthusiastically by Miss Jessie McNab of Toronto. Her object was to enlist and train one thousand women in the arts of first aid, home nursing, shooting, and military drill. Within days, about four hundred eager recruits had enlisted. They paid a fee for the privilege of serving in the Women's Home Guard and were soon to be attired in khaki-coloured short skirts, blouses, and Norfolk jackets. Miss McNab persuaded Lt-Col. J. Galloway[13] to supervise the training of the women and she announced that her home, Dundurn Heights, would be the training camp.[14] A largely attended patriotic and recruiting meeting on 26 August was thrown into momentary confusion when the crowded verandah on the McNab residence collapsed. Miss McNab suspected sabotage, but she was fearless: 'Threats won't count here. (Cheers) I got my rifle today and with it came one hundred rounds of ammunition. I'm loaded now. (Renewed cheers) And if the law doesn't round them up, I'll try my hand.'[15] The incident did not deter the recruits. They continued to drill under the watchful eye of Colonel Galloway.

Miss McNab faced a mutiny in the ranks a few days later. The treasurer, Miss Laura E. McCully, resigned after charging that Miss McNab used 'Kaiser-like methods' and had assumed too much power. The supporters of Miss McNab retorted that it was Miss McCully who wished to be Kaiser.[16] Most Toronto newspapers treated the affair as light entertainment, but the *Star* commented soberly: 'The grim business of enlisting to bear a hand in a life and death struggle convulsing Europe and the world ought not to be mimicked by a toy movement.'[17] Mayor T.L. Church of Toronto then intervened, calling for the appointment of an advisory committee of prominent Toronto women in the hope that 'the organization would be completed and all work together in harmony.'[18] Undeterred by the controversy, Miss McNab continued her mission. She announced the formation of a Highland section of her Home Guard, to be composed of women at least five feet five inches in height. 'Miss McNab,' the *Globe* noted, 'has not yet decided to don

[12]*Globe*, 30 July 1915, p. 2.
[13]Galloway also served as secretary of the Toronto Citizens' Recruiting League.
[14]*Globe*, 21 Aug. 1915, p. 9.
[15]*Ibid.*, 27 Aug. 1915, p. 6.
[16]*Ibid.*, 31 Aug. 1915, p. 7.
[17]Quoted in *CAR 1915*, pp. 336–7.
[18]Quoted in the *Globe*, 3 Sept. 1915, p. 8.

the kilts.'[19] Miss McCully, in the meantime, was holding a meeting of dissidents in Kew Beach. But the departure of the McCully faction did not end the troubles of Miss McNab. Elections were held early in December for a Women's Home Guard executive. Colonel Galloway emerged as chairman, with Miss McNab as vice-chairman, and the latter was furious. She claimed that she 'must be head of the association or nothing'[20] and that Galloway could not be chairman because 'the constitution of the original Women's Home Guard sets forth that only women can be members of the organization.'[21] She then refused to transfer to the new executive the money she had collected in fees. The executive sought a court order to gain control of the money. The squabble left the Women's Home Guard in ruins, with most of the disputed money used to pay legal fees. Mrs E.W. Herman tried to revive the movement early in 1916 as the Women's Volunteer Corps,[22] but it disappeared quietly from the battlefield, as did Miss McNab.

There were other and far more rewarding tasks to be undertaken by women by early 1916. Ontario's economy was flourishing, and there was an increasing shortage of labour, especially in the rapidly expanding munitions industry. At the same time recruiting was slow, and it was suspected that many eligible men were using their indispensability to their employers as an excuse for not enlisting. Perhaps inspired by the registration scheme of the Suffragists' War Auxiliary, a meeting held in Toronto on 7 January 1916 made plans to organize a Women's Emergency Corps in Military District No. 2 whose purpose would be 'to aid recruiting through a registration of all women available to take the places and do the work of men eligible for active service.'[23] It was made clear from the outset that the women registered and subsequently employed through the corps would occupy their new positions only so long as the men they replaced were on active service. As hundreds of women registered, members of the Toronto Recruiting League and the Women's Emergency Corps interviewed local manufacturers, merchants, and the Board of Trade to explain the intention of the new organization and of the women who registered with it. Most employers, especially those in industry,

[19]*Globe*, 4 Sept. 1915, p. 20.
[20]*Ibid.*, 4 Dec. 1915, p. 8.
[21]*Ibid.*, 9 Dec. 1915, p. 4.
[22]*Ibid.*, 1 Feb. 1916, p. 8.
[23]*CAR 1916*, p. 423. Many of the delegates from some twenty Ontario centres who attended the meeting in Toronto returned home to organize branches in their own communities. Similar work was undertaken by Women's Recruiting and Patriotic Leagues. See, for example, the Berlin *News Record*, 21 March 1916, p. 1 and Collinson and Smith, *The Recruiting League of Hamilton*.

were reluctant to take part in the scheme. They doubted that women could do the work as well as men and shared with their male employees a suspicion that many women would seek permanent employment when the war was over. The missionary work of the Women's Emergency Corps was slow and frustrating, but they did make progress. The first jobs opened to women were in banks, shipping departments of express offices, and the Red Cross; but manufacturers hung back. There was a critical labour shortage by August, and the campaign of women for an opportunity to share the industrial load could be ignored no longer. Dr A.H. Abbott of the Organization of Resources Committee made a strong plea for the employment of women (D 1), and the Imperial Munitions Board appointed Mark H. Irish, a member of the Ontario Legislature, to oversee 'the work which may be performed by women in munition plants.'[24] In October, for the first time in Canada, women were employed in munitions-making. By the end of the war some 35,000 had been employed in war industries.[25] Irish was assisted by Miss Wiseman, formerly on the staff of the Organization of Resources Committee. She visited munitions plants, advising directors of the work which women were capable of doing and of any special accommodation required by women employed in the plants. The welfare of women in industry was a special concern of both Irish and Miss Wiseman. The need for female labour was vital at this stage of the war, and they could not risk losing it through poor working and living conditions. Furthermore, they wished to avoid the possibility of scandal marring the missionary work in which they were engaged on behalf of women. Consequently the Young Women's Christian Association was asked by the IMB in October 1916 to supervise the housing and feeding of the women munitions workers. The YWCA consented, and by the end of the year operated a canteen in a Toronto munitions plant where six hundred women were employed and a hostel for women workers in St Catharines.[26] Irish was also concerned lest newspaper reports of women being molested going to and from the factories might prejudice their employment (D 2). Colonel E.J. Chambers, the Chief Press Censor, eased his mind by asking newspaper editors to 'exclude from publication reports of any occurrence which might tend to discourage a reasonable extension

[24]P.A.C., MG 30 B4, Sir Joseph Flavelle Papers, v. 38.
[25]David Carnegie, *The History of Munitions Supply in Canada, 1914–1918* (London and Toronto, 1925).
[26]Mary Quayle Innis, *Unfold the Years, A History of the Young Women's Christian Association in Canada* (Toronto, 1949), pp. 79–80.

of the system of using female labour in munitions factories on night shifts.'[27]

The work of operating an employment bureau became too great for the IMB and arrangements were made in November 1916 for this aspect of the board's work to be assumed in Ontario by the provincial Trades and Labour Branch of the Department of Public Works. The ubiquitous Albert H. Abbott, now Ontario Director of the IMB's Department of Labour, wrote Toronto manufacturers of the change and again urged the employment of women (D 3). Local offices of the Trades and Labour Branch were deluged with applications from women anxious to work in munitions factories, but employers were slow to respond to the services provided by the government agency. They were gradually converted, however, as they saw that there was a better chance of finding and retaining efficient employees if applicants were first interviewed by the trained staff of the branch. The branch's annual report for the year 1917 (D 4) recorded the conversion of employers and the success attained in placing women in the labour force, especially in munitions work and in farming. Most females seeking steady employment requested work in the munitions industry. Women had heard of the vast sums of money to be made in munitions work and wanted a share. After overcoming their initial prejudice, manufacturers found to their surprise and delight that women were indeed capable, especially in the intricate task of fuse assembling. Bankers, on the other hand, had reservations about the capabilities of female employees. Ten months after they were first employed as clerks and tellers, bank officials concluded that women were temperamentally unsuited to the banking business. They felt that women could not cope with the noon-hour rush which occurred in most branches, and furthermore that they 'required' the conventional lunch hour.[28]

As more and more women entered the labour force, their sisters continued to pursue vigorously their voluntary patriotic labours. But there were some lapses. The *Globe* noted that 'women who are still working as faithfully along patriotic lines as they did in the first flush of excitement after the war's outbreak, are beginning to feel, with the men who are recruiting, that a wave of lethargy is sweeping the country, and are discussing ways of checking it.'[29] And some knitters came under fire for producing badly made socks: 'The feet

[27]P.A.C., RG 6 E1, Chief Press Censor, v. 40, file 178-B-5.
[28]*Globe*, 31 Oct. 1916, p. 7.
[29]*Ibid.*, 26 May 1916, p. 8.

of the brave men who may be laying their lives down for the safety
of the womenkind they leave behind are worth all the care that can
be taken in sock-making.'[30] But the most serious charge was that
many women still refused to allow their sons and husbands to enlist.
The regulation requiring written consent was abolished in August
1915, but now women were accused of wielding too strong an influence on their loved ones. Recruiting advertisements directed at
women urged them to encourage their male friends and relations to
enlist and to have nothing to do with 'slackers' (B 10, D 5).

While some women held men back, others persisted in shaming
and scolding men not in uniform. A 'young gentleman' advertised
in the Berlin *News Record* on 22 January 1916 for a 'cozy' room
with board. He received an anonymous reply, written in a feminine
hand: 'I think a nice suit of khaki with board and lodging free will
suit you better than a cozy room with board. Now just think it over.'
Enclosed with the note were several white feathers. The man wrote
to the newspapers, explaining that he had tried to enlist on three
occasions, but each time had been declared physically unfit. His
father and two brothers were in uniform, and a third brother had
been killed at Gallipoli. He suggested that his correspondent, in
future, should be more careful in selecting recipients of her feathers.[31]

The contribution of women to Canada's war effort had been so
admired and appreciated that women in the four western provinces
had gained the provincial franchise by the end of 1916. Prospects
for the vote in Ontario, however, remained bleak. Premier Hearst
seemed adamant in his refusal to consider the question of votes for
women. 'Now is not the time to pass an act of this kind, not even in
my opinion the time to debate it' he told the Legislature in 1916.[32]
The Women's Patriotic League of Toronto shared the premier's
view, declaring that 'organized societies of women are spending
money, time and energy on a campaign which tends to divide women
at a time such as the present when the united efforts of the women of
Canada should be put forth in valiant service for the Empire.'[33] The
Speech from the Throne opening the 1917 session of the Legislature
made no reference to woman suffrage; when Newton Rowell moved

[30]*Ibid.*, 12 Feb. 1916, p. 10.
[31]Berlin *News Record*, 1 Feb. 1916, p. 1. Young women in Blyth and Seaforth
used a novel shaming technique: they wore white ribbon badges upon which was
written 'Knit or Fight' (London *Free Press*, 15 May 1916, p. 5; 17 May 1916, p. 5).
[32]Quoted in Catherine Lyle Cleverdon, *The Woman Suffrage Movement in
Canada* (Toronto, 1950), pp. 40–1.
[33]Quoted in *CAR 1916*, p. 426.

an amendment that a suffrage measure be introduced, the amendment was defeated.[34] But several days later Premier Hearst surprised his supporters and opponents alike by introducing a woman suffrage bill. It passed through the Legislature with little opposition.[35] Ontario suffragists were astonished by the ease and rapidity of their victory in the final round. Mrs Willoughby Cummings of Toronto, a leading suffragist and corresponding secretary of the National Council of Women, wrote to a friend in British Columbia on 3 March 1916: 'I am sure you are all as much surprised as we are to find we are to have the franchise!! The situation here was really very funny, for after all these years when neither party would touch the subject, suddenly both parties have been having a regular scramble to see which could bring it in first.'[36]

Having won the battle for provincial enfranchisement, Ontario's suffragists joined their sisters in fighting for the federal franchise. Their provincial victories were due in large part to the role women had played in the war effort; federal victory on the same basis could hardly be denied by the Borden government. The War-time Elections Bill, giving the federal vote to women whose husbands, sons, or brothers had served overseas, was introduced in the House of Commons on 6 September, passed and received royal assent on 20 September 1917.[37] The Liberal Opposition and the suffragists opposed the measure because it did not permit universal female suffrage; but it was better than nothing. The suffragists vowed not to rest until they had won complete victory.

Sir Robert Borden announced at the end of October that a federal general election would be held on 17 December. Women eagerly looked forward to casting their votes, many for the first time in any election. The Women's Christian Temperance Union in Toronto set up 'a perfect representation of an actual polling booth ... and it will be in operation from 1 o'clock until 5 ... All women who are still timid about voting for the first time would do well to visit the booth and find how simple and easy is the process of casting one's ballot.'[38] Many took advantage of the opportunity.

The suffrage campaign captured a great deal of attention during

[34]Rowell had supported the women's cause for some time, but never before in his capacity as provincial Leader of the Opposition. See, for example, *CAR 1916*, p. 499.

[35]*Ontario Statutes*, 7 Geo. v, chap. 5.

[36]P.A.C., MG 28 I 25, National Council of Women, v. 67, file on Women's Suffrage Movement, 1912–19.

[37]*Statutes of Canada*, 7–8 Geo. v, chap. 39.

[38]*Globe*, 14 Dec. 1917, p. 4.

1917, but there was still a war to be won. Thrift, food conservation, and self-denial now became the housewife's best means of helping to win the war. The thrift and conservation campaign, begun in Ontario in April 1917, moved into high gear in Toronto in July at a Women's Convention on Food Conservation held under the auspices of the Organization of Resources Committee and the Toronto Women's War-Time Thrift Committee. Delegates came from all areas of the province to hear talks on food values, substitutes for wheat flour, canning, drying, and preserving. Interspersed among the speeches was a wide-ranging general discussion during which delegates spoke on such varied topics as the waste of grain in producing liquor, the need for conscription, registration of the country's womanpower, and whether or not the manufacture and sale of oleomargarine should be permitted. A women's committee, to be affiliated with the Organization of Resources Committee, was formed at the end of the convention.[39]

Thousands of words poured forth on the subject of food conservation, but few were of practical help to housewives buying groceries and planning weekly menus. An exception was a booklet of suggestions and recipes, sold for the benefit of returned soldiers (D 6). Then, in the fall of 1917, newspapers printed a series of 'War Menus,' issued by the office of the Dominion Food Controller, which included recipes for inexpensive dishes and those using a minimum amount of the commodities to be conserved. The series introduced 'war bread' to Canada (D 7), already standard fare in Britain, and housewives were anxious to try a recipe for 'war cake' which appeared in many newspapers (D 8).

Allied to the thrift and conservation campaign was the much publicized campaign for greater food production. The Organization of Resources Committee encouraged Ontario farmers to produce larger crops in 1917, but there was a chronic shortage of farm labour which could not be entirely overcome even with the help of school-boys. President R.A. Falconer of the University of Toronto suggested to the Trades and Labour Branch that female university students and other women be employed to help with the harvesting of fruit and vegetable crops. Farmers were sounded out. When those in Vittoria, Beamsville, Grimsby, Winona, Oakville, and Bronte reluctantly agreed to hire women, an appeal for workers was issued. Over twelve hundred responded to the call. The YWCA hastily organized camps for the women, borrowing 150 tents from the

---

[39]'Report of the Women's Convention on Food Conservation, Held in Convocation Hall, University of Toronto,' P.A.C. Library Pamphlet Collection, unnumbered.

Department of Militia and renting various types of buildings. The women were hired to be pickers, but many of them handled horses, pitched hay, drove trucks, manned fruit stands, took charge of chicken houses, hoed, planted, cultivated, weeded, and worked in canning factories. On the whole the experiment was successful but there were complaints about the uncertainty of work, ten-hour days, low wages, and inadequate housing accommodation. The YWCA, aware of the shortcomings of the latter, prepared to make improvements for the 1918 season (D 4, D 9), which proved to be altogether more successful than the 1917 experiment. Short courses were arranged to prepare women for general farming; an increased number of farmers requested their services; and the women had better housing, wages, and working conditions.

The scope for the employment of women had widened greatly because of the shortage of manpower (D 10). Although many potential employers remained unconvinced, the Imperial Munitions Board thought so much of women's ability and physical prowess that their employment in explosives plants was seriously considered (D 11 to D 13). Mark Irish, however, felt that they should be so employed 'only as a last resort' (D 14) and there the subject rested. But women had proved that they could succeed in almost every form of employment offered to them. They had also shown their devotion and tenacity in voluntary war work. They had come a long way since the summer of 1914, and the *Globe* wondered whether they would sustain the level of their achievements when the war was over (D 15). But women knew they could not afford to backslide if they wished to continue to command the respect of their countrymen.

E. SCHOOLS

SCHOOLCHILDREN WERE ENJOYING their summer holidays when war broke out, but some began patriotic work long before school reopened. School cadets from Ottawa and Toronto eagerly answered the call to serve as messengers at Valcartier; Girl Guides made bandages; other children's organizations collected money for war charities; and many girls joined their mothers in knitting and sewing garments for soldiers and refugees. Teachers supervised such activities after school opened and also encouraged their pupils to prepare 'News from Home' scrapbooks, or 'budgets,' for soldiers, a project sponsored by the League of Empire. Each budget consisted of six or more pages of newspaper clippings of interest to local soldiers far from home, and the children were instructed to fill in spaces between the clippings with 'jokes, funny stories, etc.'[1]

The war officially entered Ontario classrooms on 19 November 1914 when Dr R.A. Pyne, Minister of Education, announced that the war and its causes would be included in the curriculum 'so far as they can be intelligently taken up in the different grades.'[2] The Department of Education prepared a suggested course outline,[3] supplied each school in the province with copies of *Canada in Flanders*, a historical narrative of the war produced by Lord Beaverbrook, and prescribed the use of a series of pamphlets, issued monthly, entitled *The Children's Story of the War*.

British patriotism and loyalty, always instilled in Ontario pupils, assumed greater importance than ever before, and there was a vigorous campaign to eradicate every vestige of German culture from primary school textbooks. The music reader was a principal source of difficulty. Children in the third book class in Toronto's Carlton Street School refused to sing 'The Moon' because it was simply attributed as 'German.' They were finally persuaded that 'German' was, in fact, the English composer Edward German. There were so many complaints about the music reader that Chief Inspector Robert

[1] Berlin *News Record*, 13 Jan. 1916, p. 3. Budgets were also prepared by the Red Cross, women university students, church youth groups, Boy Scouts, and Girl Guides.
[2] Ontario Sessional Paper No. 17 of 1915. Annual report of the Department of Education.
[3] The course outline was printed in annual reports of the department, published in the Sessional Papers.

Cowley of Toronto issued a circular letter to school principals in February 1916 instructing them to

take the necessary steps to see that there shall not be taken up in any class of your school any selection from the music reader that might suggest offence to the proper patriotic spirit of the pupils. The music reader contains at least some selections that should never be sung in a British school, and whatever may have been the opinion as to their general merit at the time they were introduced, they cannot be regarded as a medium fit to develop the high moral and patriotic ideals of British Citizenship.[4]

A new edition was prepared by the Department of Education before the end of the school year. Austrian and German songs written after 1850 were deleted.

German remained a compulsory matriculation subject for entry into certain university courses. As J.E. Wetherell, high school inspector for the Department of Education, commented in his annual report: 'The study of the German language proceeds as if nothing unusual had happened. As many pupils as ever, of choice, pursue the study of German. The bias that justly prevails against the German rulers and the German people does not appear at all in the attitude of the schools toward the German language.' He also noted that the war had stimulated interest in school cadet corps: 'It is manifest everywhere that the boys for the first time feel that military drill is worth while and that it may have for them and for their country a momentous value.'[5]

Many male teachers and older students enlisted by the end of 1915. The Department of Education received numerous requests to grant certificates to students enlisting before the completion of their courses. Keeping in view 'the necessities of the schools as well as the duty of aiding in enlistment of pupils of suitable age,' the Department issued regulations in January 1916 allowing such students, on returning to Ontario after military service, to attend one session in a high or normal school without charge in order that they might complete requirements for the certificate for which they had been preparing at the time of their enlistment.[6] The regulations were amended again in March 1916 to allow enlisting secondary school students to obtain certificates if their work was satisfactory at Easter; but the regulations did not apply to students studying for university matriculation ex-

[4]Quoted in the *Globe*, 12 Feb. 1916, p. 8.
[5]Ontario Sessional Paper No. 17 of 1916. Annual report of the Department of Education.
[6]Circular No. 11 of the Department of Education, Jan. 1916.

aminations.[7] The need for schoolboys to assist farmers in the spring of 1916 led to yet another change in departmental regulations. Boys volunteering for such work could be promoted without sitting the final examinations provided they were engaged in farming for at least three months.[8]

Meanwhile patriotic work continued unabated in the schools of Ontario, with government departments and agencies using the pupils' enthusiasm to advantage. The provincial Minister of Agriculture reported that Children's Tag Days were a feature of the 1917 rural school fairs organized by his department:

A total of $3233.48 was collected and after deducting expenses ... a motor bus ... was purchased and donated to the Military Hospitals Commission to be used specially to convey wounded soldiers from the hospitals to the Vocational Training Classes at the University ... In addition the sum of $500 has been handed to the Soldiers' Aid Commission to relieve special cases of distress amongst returned soldiers. The balance will be used for other patriotic purposes.[9]

The Organization of Resources Committee encouraged primary school pupils to undertake backyard gardening; where that was not possible, 'arrangements should be made for community plots, either on the school property or vacant land'[10] and teachers were expected to supervise the gardening. The committee urged high school students to volunteer for farm work, and on 21 March 1917 an essay contest was announced, the topic of which was farm employment. Contestants were admonished to 'do your very best to write a good answer, your ideas may be useful to your country, as the Empire is sorely in need of more farm products of all kinds.'[11] Thousands of essays were submitted. The winner was Ruth McKinnon of Chatsworth High School (E 1). She received five dollars as the winner in her school and twenty-five dollars in gold as the over-all Ontario winner. The Organization of Resources Committee was delighted with the success of the contest: 'Thousands of Ontario high school boys and girls were thus brought to a serious consideration of the call to help on the farms. This no doubt was a factor in securing the large number of our youth for food production.'[12] The Trades and Labour

[7]Circular No. 11A of the Department of Education.
[8]Circular No. 7 of the Department of Education.
[9]Ontario Sessional Paper No. 29 of 1918. Annual report of the Department of Agriculture, p. 72.
[10]Circular No. 11 of the Organization of Resources Committee, p. 2.
[11]*Public Service Bulletin*, Nov. 1917, p. 80.
[12]*Ibid.*

Branch of the Department of Public Works was equally pleased with its student farm worker programme in the summer of 1917 (E 2).

The patriotism of Ontario schoolchildren and their enthusiasm for tasks related to the war was due in large measure to the work of their teachers. Dr Pyne paid tribute to the devotion of teachers in 1916:

The place of the teacher as a true servant and minister of the State is well exemplified at a time of this kind. The special duties imposed upon the teacher by the war include the instruction of the pupils in the issues and events of the conflict in which Canada as a self-governing state of the Empire plays so glorious a part. There is evidence that the teaching body has discharged its obligation in this respect with the highest intelligence and fidelity, and that, in addition to the systematic teaching of the war, lessons of permanent value in the upbuilding of character, directly tending to a knowledge of the duty of good citizenship, have been impressed upon the youthful minds.[13]

Fidelity, or loyalty, was an essential quality for teachers in wartime Ontario to possess, and there were apparently only two cases where teachers' loyalty was questioned. Both occurred in Toronto.

Harry Erland Lee, a twenty-five-year-old teacher at the Annette Street School and a self-confessed socialist, was suspended in January 1915 after he was accused 'of uttering pro-German sentiments while discussing the war with his pupils.'[14] His accuser was Dr R.R. Hopkins, a trustee of the Board of Education, who, after receiving an anonymous letter from the parents of two pupils in Lee's class, interviewed Lee and found him 'unfit to discuss the war before loyal British children.'[15] So many shadows were cast across Lee's character and loyalty by the ensuing publicity that in March 1915 he requested and was granted leave of absence in order to enlist. He was killed at Courcelette on 16 September 1916, the first Toronto teacher to die in action. A motion to erect a plaque in his memory was defeated by the Board of Education because a majority felt that there should be one plaque erected at the end of the war to honour the memory of all local teachers who might be killed. It appeared that, if Lee's memory were to be honoured, it would have to be done by the school in which he had taught. The Board of Education relented, however. At a ceremony at the school on 22 June 1917, Sir John Hendrie un-

---

[13]Ontario Sessional Paper No. 17 of 1916. Annual report of the Department of Education, p. 5.

[14]*Globe*, 9 Jan. 1915, p. 6.

[15]*Ibid.* The *Globe* reported on 12 January that the authors of the letter to Hopkins were the parents of two children who were a constant source of annoyance to Lee.

veiled a portrait of Lee procured by the pupils of the school and also a plaque provided by the Board. Miles Vokes, chairman of the Board, described Lee as having been 'a man beloved by his scholars.' General Logie, referring to Lee's political convictions and the 1915 controversy, observed that, no matter what Lee may have said, 'it is what he did that counts.'[16] The Lee case was now closed.

The second case involved Miss Freda Held of the Carlton Street School who, in January 1918, was suspected of disloyalty and suspended. Believing that her usefulness as a teacher had been undermined, she resigned shortly thereafter. Her action sparked demands from her colleagues, parents of her pupils, and the Toronto press that the charges against Miss Held be investigated.[17] Encouraged by this demonstration of support, Miss Held applied to withdraw her resignation, but the Board of Education voted against reopening the case. The Board's action prompted Professor C.B. Sissons of Victoria University to write to the *Globe* outlining the background of the case and condemning the treatment Miss Held had received (E 3). *The Rebel*, a publication of students at the University of Toronto, was equally critical: 'If unconventional opinions are to be out of bounds for Toronto teachers, if such opinions, privately expressed, are to be seized upon by detectives in the guise of inspectors, or if patriotism is to be defined in other terms than the faithful performance of duty, then the children of our city are indeed to be pitied.'[18] The Department of Education declined to interfere in an affair considered to be local in nature. The question of an inquiry was raised at successive Board of Education meetings, but decisions reached at one meeting were negated at the next. Finally, in early May, Miss Held asked that her resignation be accepted to put an end to the controversy (E 4). The case was officially closed, but the air had not been cleared.

The Toronto Board of Education's zeal in inculcating patriotism in the city's schoolchildren could be carried to ridiculous lengths. In July 1918 the Board decided that male pupils 'should salute all returned, wounded and crippled soldiers, whether in uniform or mufti, when meeting them in public places.'[19] The decision prompted

[16]*Ibid.*, 23 June 1917, p. 8.
[17]*Ibid.*, 28 Jan. 1918, p. 6; 30 Jan. 1918, p. 9.
[18]Quoted in *ibid.*, 29 March 1918, p. 9.
[19]*Ibid.*, 5 July 1918, p. 6. The idea of saluting was first suggested by Mayor Thomas Church in a memorandum prepared in 1917 for the special parliamentary committee on the reception, treatment, and re-education of returned men: 'There is a lack of proper respect shown to returned soldiers. The school children should be educated to honour them, applaud them and salute them.' (*Proceedings and Report of a Special Committee of the House of Commons Appointed to Inquire into and Report Upon the Reception, Treatment and Future Disposition of Returned Soldiers of the Canadian Expeditionary Forces* [Ottawa, 1917], p. 798.)

many letters to editors. Bertram M. Tate wrote that it was wrong to 'coddle' returned soldiers: 'Anyone who knows anything at all about character-building knows that development of the ego in an individual tends toward a weakening of that character and sets up a process of unfitting the subject for harmonious association with the rest of the community.'[20] Trustee Ada Courtice presumed that soldiers had had enough saluting and doubted whether the Board's decision 'will create the desired effect on the boy.'[21] The Board quietly dropped the matter before the beginning of the fall term.

The practice of thrift became a tangible aspect of youthful patriotism at the beginning of the 1918–19 school year. Thrift, a dominant need in Canada in 1918, was the subject of a massive advertising campaign and of countless speeches by prominent Canadians. But how better to convey the need than through the country's schoolchildren? A *Canada War Thrift Book* was prepared in August 1918 for distribution to Canadian schoolchildren, but it was not ready for distribution until 1919. It contained a highly coloured and jingoistic account of the war and emphasized the need to conserve food and fuel and to buy Thrift and War Savings Stamps. Books for Ontario children included an account of 'Ontario's Part in the Great War' (E 5) calculated to instil provincial pride in the breasts of its young readers. Due credit was given to Ontario's teachers 'in preparing the youth in mind and in character to meet and sustain the severe test imposed by the war.' Now they must prepare for the period of reconstruction which lay ahead.

[20]*Globe*, 9 July 1918, p. 4.
[21]*Ibid.*, 12 July 1918, p. 5.

F. UNIVERSITIES

F.O. WILLHOFFT, A FORMER GERMAN OFFICER and an American university graduate, had taught in the School of Mining at Queen's University for eight years. After hearing rumours that all Germans in Canada would be interned in the event of war, he left Kingston in mid-summer for Watertown, New York. Rumours swept through Kingston that he was a German spy, but Willhofft denied this in a letter published in the *Daily British Whig* on 17 August 1914. The *Whig* defended Willhofft in an editorial on 21 August, declaring that he had been 'a sufferer from the shafts of venomous tongues.' Willhofft resigned from the School of Mining, and the incident was soon forgotten.

Such was not the case in a dispute which erupted in Toronto, within a month of the Willhofft incident, involving three Germans on the faculty of University College, University of Toronto. The conflict began at Harbord Collegiate on 7 September when Principal E.W. Hagarty condemned Germans and 'Germanism' at a students' assembly.[1] Three students, sons of Professor Paul Wilhelm Mueller, took great exception to the principal's remarks. They asked Hagarty for permission to transfer to another collegiate, but Hagarty refused. Seven colleagues of Professor Mueller submitted a memorial to the Toronto Board of Education protesting against Hagarty's 'outrageous conduct' and asking that appropriate action be taken to prevent similar occurrences in the future.[2] They were accused of interfering in matters outside their sphere. A resolution of the Board of Education on 1 October condemned the professors' criticism of Hagarty, called on the provincial government and the university's Board of Governors to enquire into their conduct 'and to require them to retract publicly the language they have used entirely upon hearsay evidence.'[3]

Mueller lost a good deal of sympathy after Hagarty revealed in a newspaper interview that he was not a naturalized British subject. Mueller explained in a letter to the *Globe* on 25 September[4] that he

[1] *Toronto Daily Star*, 9 Sept. 1914, p. 4.
[2] *Ibid.*, 18 Sept. 1914, p. 4.
[3] University of Toronto Archives, Falconer Papers, Hearst file.
[4] *Globe*, 25 Sept. 1914, p. 7.

had recently applied for naturalization, but irreparable harm had resulted from the Hagarty disclosure. It also led to questions of loyalty regarding other German-born members of the university faculty, principally Dr Immanuel Benzinger, professor of oriental languages, and Bonno Tapper, a lecturer in German. The President of the University of Toronto, R.A. Falconer, refrained from public comment, but, in the face of mounting charges and rumours, he finally issued a statement on 14 November. Falconer said he had conducted a thorough inquiry and had concluded 'that they have done nothing that should arouse any suspicion that they are injurious alien enemies. As members of the staff they are all excellent teachers and perform duties which it would be exceedingly difficult for us to have fulfilled otherwise.'[5] Falconer had worked hard to improve standards at the university and to extend the areas of postgraduate studies by hiring the best men possible. His plans would receive a major setback if he lost the Germans, especially Dr Benzinger. When the university's Board of Governors met again on 3 December, Falconer presented his report on the Germans, which concluded that 'it is only just and right that these gentlemen should be kept in their present positions' (F 1). The Board met again the next day to decide the issue. After several motions and much debate it voted to grant the men leave of absence with pay until 1 July 1915. When the decision was announced the *Globe* commented: 'It is the reflection of the antagonistic feeling of the public against anything emanating from Germany rather than the direct penalty for any wrongdoing on the part of any of the three professors ... In other words, it is one of the injustices of war.'[6] Other reactions were more hostile. One member of the Board, Sir Edmund Osler, felt strongly that the men should have been asked to resign or be dismissed. When he failed to convince a majority of his colleagues, Osler announced his intention to resign from the Board. He contended that 'it is only natural that German professors would have a pro-German influence' on their students, and 'I cannot see why we should be paying Germans salaries here when thousands of the young men of Britain are being killed by the Germans at the front.'[7] Thomas Hook, a member of the Ontario Legislature, told a meeting in North Toronto: 'If we can't get university professors of British blood ... then let us close the universities.'[8]

[5]Falconer Papers, 'Germans' file, Statement to Toronto press, 14 Nov. 1914.
[6]*Globe*, 5 Dec. 1914, p. 1.
[7]*CAR 1914*, pp. 267–8. The *Globe* reported on 11 December that Osler's resignation had not been accepted.
[8]*Globe*, 8 Dec. 1914, p. 15.

The decision to keep the Germans from their classes was a severe blow to Falconer and to the university. Overnight the German department was reduced from three to one. The situation in oriental languages was even more calamitous: there was no one at the university who could continue Dr Benzinger's work. It was virtually impossible to fill three vacancies in the middle of the academic year, and the men faced the equally difficult task of finding employment elsewhere. Tapper resigned on 10 December to resume his post-graduate studies at the University of Chicago, and he left Toronto with a warm letter of commendation from President Falconer.[9] Mueller paid Professor Swedlius of McMaster University[10] to substitute for him at the University of Toronto. Mueller had worked on a part-time basis at McMaster, and because McMaster was not a provincial university and thus not supported by public funds he was able to continue his work there.

Falconer had tried to arrange exchanges for Benzinger and Mueller, but he was unsuccessful. The situation seemed hopeless. At the end of 1914 Professor Benzinger resigned, believing that 'the situation in which the University at present finds itself can only be relieved through my withdrawal.'[11] He left the country in January to stay with friends in Princeton.[12] Mueller had not given up hope of resuming his work at the University of Toronto. He wrote Falconer in May 1915 requesting to be allowed 'to continue my work in the University under conditions that may seem wisest for you and the Board of Governors to determine.'[13] The Board refused his request; Mueller's resignation was accepted on 25 June.[14]

The affairs of the University of Toronto were of more than passing interest to Ontario taxpayers. It was the largest Ontario university; it was also 'the provincial university,' financed in large part by the Ontario government. Its faculty had been subject to criticism in the past for failing to provide leadership in the issues of the day: 'The chiefs of the institution appeared to hold the view that education in the varied arts of peace was its sole mission, moral idealism its inspiration.'[15] The declaration of war brought forth little immediate

[9]Falconer Papers, Tapper file.
[10]McMaster was then in Toronto.
[11]Quoted in the *Globe*, 1 Jan. 1915.
[12]He wrote Falconer in May 1915 that he had accepted the professorship of Old Testament and Religious Studies at Allegheny College (Falconer Papers 'Germans' file).
[13]*Ibid.*, Mueller file, Mueller to Falconer, 25 May 1915.
[14]*Ibid.*
[15]*CAR 1914*, p. 264.

reaction from either President Falconer or the staff, causing the *Globe* to ask:

Have the presidents of Canada's great universities no national message for a great national occasion when the nation is involved with the Empire in a life-and-death war of the world? What about the greatest Canadian University, the Provincial University, with its seat here in Toronto and its lines going out into all the earth? Has war brought it no new occasion? No fresh responsibilities for the Nation, for the Empire, for the World?[16]

President Falconer chose to save his words of inspiration for the beginning of the fall term (F 2). Many male undergraduates had answered the call by then, enlisting in local units where they lived or where they had summer jobs.[17] Military activities soon became an important part of campus life throughout Ontario. A Canadian Officers' Training Corps contingent was formed at the University of Toronto in the middle of October. On the 21st, all lectures were cancelled to allow the students to hear an appeal for recruits by President Falconer. Some 550 students enrolled within twenty-four hours, and by early December eighteen hundred men were drilling two or three afternoons each week. There were, as well, COTC contingents at the University of Ottawa, McMaster, the Ontario Veterinary College, and Queen's, and in spite of a shortage of equipment of all kinds the students undertook their military training with great enthusiasm (F 3).

Military activities at the Ontario Agricultural College were delayed by a dispute. A students' committee reported favourably in the fall of 1914 on the suggestion that military training be introduced at the college. Their report was sent directly to the provincial Minister of Agriculture rather than through the office of the acting college president, Professor C.A. Zavitz. Zavitz subsequently resigned as acting president, believing that 'the cause of agriculture should be followed exclusively' at the college.[18] His resignation was construed as a protest against military training,[19] and there were demands that he resign

[16]*Globe*, 14 Sept. 1914, p. 4.
[17]Queen's had the distinction of being the only Canadian university represented by a unit at Valcartier. A militia unit, the 5th Field Company, Canadian Engineers, mainly composed of Queen's students and commanded by Major Alexander Macphail, professor of civil engineering, was ordered to Valcartier in the middle of August to help prepare the site for occupation by the new troops. Macphail was later given command of the 1st Field Company of the First Contingent, and twenty-four university men from the militia unit accompanied him overseas.
[18]*Globe*, 31 Oct. 1914, p. 14.
[19]Zavitz was a Quaker and a pacifist.

from the chair of field husbandry. The crisis was resolved with the return from abroad of the college president, Dr G.C. Creelman, who soon gained authorization for a COTC contingent, which was formed in January 1915 at the same time as a contingent at the University of Western Ontario.

A steady stream of male students left Ontario during the war years. Some joined the Canadian University Company raised early in 1915 to reinforce the Princess Patricia's Canadian Light Infantry. Others enlisted in hospital units raised by the University of Toronto, Western, and Queen's, or with artillery batteries associated with Toronto, Queen's, and OAC.[20] Each university and college passed special regulations granting credit for the whole year to students who enlisted during the term.[21] By 1917 there were few physically fit male students still on campus other than medical students returned from overseas to complete their studies. Female students followed the example of Canadian women elsewhere. Their spare time was devoted to knitting, sewing, and bandage-making. Many were employed in the summers of 1917 and 1918 on Ontario farms.

In spite of the introduction of war-related activities, there had been little disruption in normal campus life during the 1914–15 session, but by 1915–16 the situation had altered. President Falconer reported at the end of the academic year:

At the opening of this session the full effects of the war began to be felt. A greatly diminished enrolment was the first evidence of what was to follow as the academic year ran its course. From every department came the same story of reduced numbers and of the strain under which the students were doing their work. Athletic activities were confined to inter-faculty ... games and played no large part in the general life ... the usual social interests were lessened or vanished.[22]

It was the same elsewhere. At Queen's, 'the intellectual activities of the students in literary societies and meetings have been continued much as usual; but there has been a great decrease in activities of a

[20]Enlistment in the batteries began with students, their friends and relations, and others associated with the university. Those with no university connection could enlist if the battery was not filled to strength by the first group.

[21]Fourth-year medical students who had enlisted as Medical Corps dressers in 1915 were brought back from overseas in late 1915 and 1916 to complete their medical studies so that they might return to the army as qualified medical practitioners. Summer terms were instituted in 1916, placing Canadian medical schools in full operation the year round.

[22]Ontario Sessional Paper No. 18 of 1917, p. 11. Annual report of the University of Toronto.

purely social and sporting character, most of the time formerly given to these having been taken up by the work of the Officers' Training Corps or other military organizations.'[23]

Teaching staff and facilities were, to a great degree, taken up with war-related activities. These began in October 1914 with a series of nine lectures on the causes of the war, sponsored by the University of Toronto's Extension Office and delivered by members of the teaching staff. The series was so successful in Toronto that it was presented in Collingwood, Orillia, Bradford, Midland, and Parry Sound, the average attendance being eight hundred.[24] Money collected at the lectures was donated either to the Red Cross or to Belgian Relief, the lecturers refusing to accept more than their expenses, which usually amounted to five dollars.[25] The warm reception accorded the academics undoubtedly had a bearing on President Falconer's decision in March 1915 to offer the services of Albert H. Abbott, head of the Extension Office, to the newly formed Speakers' Patriotic League.[26]

Universities made numerous practical contributions to the war effort, mostly in the fields of science and medicine. The University of Toronto was in the vanguard because of its size and extensive facilities. The Pathology Department of Toronto's School of Medicine helped combat the outbreak of cerebrospinal meningitis at Exhibition Camp early in 1915. Connaught Laboratories supplied huge amounts of serums and antitoxins throughout the war. Shells were tested in the Strength of Materials laboratory at Toronto. Metallurgists at Queen's conducted research to discover new alloys, while other scientists at Queen's worked on improving the flares in use on the western front.[27] Professor J.C. McLennan of Toronto became Director of Research for the Admiralty in May 1917; before his appointment he and his associates had conducted research into sources of helium for airships. Not the least of Toronto's contributions was the instruction of Royal Flying Corps cadets by members of the Faculty of Applied Science at a training centre established on the campus.

The war dominated every aspect of university life in Ontario by

[23]Queen's University, *Annual Report, 1915–1916*, p. 10.

[24]'We are almost overwhelmed by requests that come to us from outside and many of our lecturers are out at least once a week' (P.A.C. MG 30 D 14, Sir John Willison Papers, R.A. Falconer to Willison, 13 Nov. 1914).

[25]Falconer Papers, Albert H. Abbott file. Queen's professors also delivered lectures, one having spoken in Trenton in November on 'Great Britain and her Treatment of Smaller Nationalities' (*Daily British Whig*, 14 Nov. 1914, p. 5).

[26]See Section B, 'The Home Front.'

[27]Queen's University, *Annual Report, 1916–1917*, p. 9.

1917. Buildings at Queen's and Toronto were converted into hospitals for sick and wounded soldiers and were staffed by the universities' medical faculties (F 4). The University of Toronto made notable contributions towards the rehabilitation of returned soldiers. Dr E.A. Bott of the Psychology Department opened a clinic to treat soldiers suffering from injuries to the nervous and muscular systems caused by wounds or shock.[28] Members of the staff at Toronto organized, for returned men, classes in tractor operation, motor mechanics, electricity, mining and assaying, plan reading, and estimating and taught future instructors in woodwork, basketry, bookbinding, modelling, and drawing.

The extra work was undertaken by the professors to win a war and to heal its veterans, but it proved to be at least of equal benefit to future Ontario university students. The knowledge and experience gained in wartime led to the opening and expansion of fields of study, especially in the social and physical sciences.

[28]G. Oswald Smith, *University of Toronto Roll of Service 1914–1918* (Toronto, 1921), pp. xx–xxi.

G. ONTARIO'S BLACK VOLUNTEERS

ONTARIO'S BLACK POPULATION had had a long association with the military forces in the province, some having been enrolled in the Kent County Militia as early as 1793. A Coloured Company, commanded first by Captain Robert Runchey and later by James Robertson, was stationed along the Niagara Frontier during the War of 1812 and saw service during the battle at Queenston Heights. Coloured militia units were called out during the 1837 Rebellion, and from 1838 until 1850 the Coloured Corps of the Incorporated Militia were stationed along the border to guard against possible attacks from the United States.[1] They also helped keep the peace among labourers working on the Welland Canal.

It was evident in 1914, however, that Negro volunteers were not welcome in the Canadian Expeditionary Force, and Arthur Alexander of Buxton asked the Department of Militia for an explanation. He was told that 'the selection ... is entirely in the hands of Commanding Officers and their selections or rejections are not interfered with from Headquarters.'[2] Mr Alexander did not pursue the matter, but it was taken up less than a year later by George Morton of Hamilton (G 1) who, in essence, received the same reply.[3] J.R.B. Whitney, publisher of the *Canadian Observer*,[4] offered to raise a unit of 150 coloured soldiers in November 1915; he was told by Sir Sam Hughes 'that these people can form a platoon in any Battalion, now. There is nothing in the world to stop them.'[5] Hughes failed to mention that the platoon would have to be accepted by the commanding officer of an authorized battalion before it could be formed. On the strength of Hughes's letter, Whitney began his recruiting campaign in the pages of the *Canadian Observer* (G 2, G 3). When Whitney asked in January 1916 for a 'coloured chap' in the 80th Battalion to accom-

---

[1]The American government apparently complained about the presence of the Coloured Corps along the border, claiming that it 'held out a bounty for American slaves to desert from their masters' (P.A.C., RG 9, IC1, v. 125, Lt-Col. Ogden Creighton to the Adjutant General, 4 Feb. 1847).

[2]P.A.C., RG 24, v. 1206, file HQ 297-1-21, Colonel C.F. Winter to Alexander, 20 Nov. 1914.

[3]*Ibid.*

[4]'The Official Organ for the Coloured People in Canada.'

[5]P.A.C., RG 24, v. 1206, file HQ 297-1-21, Hughes to Whitney, 3 Dec. 1915.

pany him on a recruiting trip to London, Chatham, and Windsor, officers at headquarters realized for the first time that the proposed platoon was not attached to any unit. After General Logie reported in March that no commanding officer was willing to accept the platoon, he was instructed to tell Whitney that 'permission to recruit ... cannot be granted.'[6] An exasperated Whitney asked for reconsideration of his scheme as well as some explanation he might offer to the men who had already signified their willingness to enlist. The reply to Whitney has not been found, but it may have been based on a letter from General Hodgins to Logie which pointed out that battalions then proceeding overseas were to be broken up and used as reinforcements: 'It is, therefore, obvious that it is necessary in their [the Negroes'] interests as well as in the interests of the Service that they should not be placed in such a position that their services would not be welcomed by any unit, of which they originally or subsequently had to form part.'[7] Whitney wrote Sir Sam Hughes on 18 April asking that his platoon be 'placed with some Battalion, otherwise there will be a great disappointment with the Race and ill feeling towards the Government,'[8] but again he was unsuccessful.

On 13 April 1916 General Willoughby Gwatkin suggested the formation of one or more Negro labour battalions for service overseas. No. 2 Canadian Construction Battalion was authorized on 5 July after the War Office had cabled acceptance of such a unit. Headquarters were in Truro, Nova Scotia, and recruiting was conducted across the country. Only 350 recruits were obtained in Ontario,[9] a figure somewhat below expectations and possibly attributable to the earlier rejection of a black unit. The battalion never reached full strength, and after arriving in England it was reduced to a company. In April 1917 it proceeded to France, where it was attached to Jura Group of the Canadian Forestry Corps.[10]

[6]*Ibid.*, Hodgins to Logie, 13 March 1916.
[7]*Ibid.*, Hodgins to Logie, 31 March 1916.
[8]*Ibid.*
[9]Robin Winks, *The Blacks in Canada. A History* (Montreal, New Haven and London, 1971), p. 318. See also the *Globe*, 12 Sept. 1916, p. 9.
[10]P.A.C., RG 9, IIID1, v. 396, folder 747. War Diary of No. 2 Canadian Construction Company.

H. INDIANS

WITHIN DAYS OF THE DECLARATION of war the Militia Department had established its policy with regard to the enlistment of Indians for overseas service. 'While British troops would be proud to be associated with their Indian fellow subjects, yet Germans might refuse to extend to them the privileges of civilized warfare. Therefore it is considered ... that they had better remain in Canada to share in the protection of the Dominion.'[1] But at least eight Ontario Indians had enlisted by 19 August 1914.[2] They were followed by many more during the next four years (H 1). Duncan Campbell Scott, Deputy Superintendent General of Indian Affairs, estimated in 1918 that 35 per cent of Canada's Indian male population of military age had enlisted voluntarily and that the rate of enlistment among Ontario Indians at least matched the national average.[3]

The manner in which the Indians have responded ... appears more especially commendable when it is remembered that they are wards of the Government and have not, therefore, the responsibility of citizenship, that many of them were obliged to make long and arduous journeys from remote localities in order to offer their services and that their disposition renders them naturally averse to leaving their own country and conditions of life.[4]

Several Canadians offered large sums of money for raising units and supplying equipment in the early months of the war. Among the most persistent was William Hamilton Merritt, an honorary chief of the Six Nations Indians and the driving force of the Canadian Defence League, an organization dedicated to the principles of national preparedness and universal training. Merritt offered to contribute £5,000 for the raising and equipping of two companies of Six Nations Indians. Major the Hon. J.B. Campbell, the Governor General's Assistant Military Secretary, replied on 17 October that 'the Militia Council ... considered that it would be inconvenient to

[1]P.A.C., RG 24, v. 1221, file HQ 593-1-7, telegram from the Adjutant General to Colonel L.W. Shannon, 8 Aug. 1914.
[2]P.A.C., RG 10, v. 3180, Red Series file 452124-1.
[3]J. Castell Hopkins estimated that 31 per cent of the male population of Ontario enlisted voluntarily. (*The Province of Ontario in the War*, p. 24).
[4]Department of Indian Affairs, *Annual Report, 1918*, Ottawa, 1918, p. 14.

include this force in the second contingent.'[5] He failed to mention the official policy that 'they had better remain in Canada.'

Merritt, however, had neglected to consult the Indians before making his offer, and when it was made known to them, the chiefs of the Six Nations found themselves in a difficult position. Regarding themselves as a separate nation, the Six Nations believed that they owed their allegiance directly to the British Crown and not through the Canadian government. Following a lengthy discussion at their council meeting on 3 November, the chiefs decided to postpone any decision, 'as the source of the proposition is not in accordance with the customs of their forefathers and their friend the British Government.'[6] On 26 November they decided not to act on Merritt's offer, 'which they think would affect their status.'[7]

Major Campbell's letter to Merritt had been so tactfully vague that Merritt wondered whether or not a decision had been made. After receiving a copy of the chiefs' resolution he wrote to the Military Secretary late in December outlining the importance of the Indians' role in the history of Canada and requesting that the Governor General 'may appeal to His Majesty ... [to] condescend to ask the Six Nations Council for aid to the Empire.'[8] He made further appeals in January and February 1915 for a reconsideration of his offer (H 2, H 3), but he was told bluntly by Lt-Col. E.A. Stanton, the Military Secretary, that 'under no circumstances is it contemplated to ask the Canadian-Indians to furnish a contingent for war service in Europe.'[9]

So many battalions were recruiting during 1915 that there were numerous complaints of recruiting officers 'raiding' outside the geographical area assigned to them. On 20 November 1915 Lt-Col. E.S. Baxter complained about encroachments in the territory assigned to the 114th Battalion (Brock's Rangers):

As you know, I am depending largely on my four Indian companies[10] with regard to the organization of the ... 114th ... and I am of the opinion that the Brantford, Hamilton and Dundas Battalions, or in fact any other Battalions ought not to be allowed to recruit and take from me men who have justly belonged to my regimental area for so very many years ... I ask this because Hamilton and Brantford units have been recruiting some of my Indians since the beginning of the war.[11]

[5]P.A.C., RG 7 G 21, v. 549, file 14071F.
[6]P.A.C., RG 10, v. 3015, Red Series file 218222-181.
[7]P.A.C., RG 7 G 21, v. 549, file 14071F.
[8]*Ibid.*
[9]*Ibid.*, Stanton to Merritt, 27 Feb. 1915.
[10]In the 37th Haldimand Rifles of the Active Militia.
[11]P.A.C., RG 24, v. 4380, file 2D. 34-7-89.

The Assistant Adjutant General in Toronto reminded Baxter of the correspondence that 'took place at the commencement of the year on the subject of recruiting Indians for overseas service, and at that time Ottawa would not approve of Indians being attested.' Baxter retorted that, through F.R. Lalor MP, he had secured permission to recruit Indians from none other than Sir Sam Hughes, who in 1914 had considered 'they had better remain in Canada.'[12] As a result of Baxter's complaint, and undoubtedly because the need for men was acute, a circular letter from Militia Headquarters on 10 December 1915 announced that, 'owing to the large number of applications for enlistment of Indians,' authority was now granted to do so.[13] Baxter lost no time in addressing a recruiting meeting at Ohsweken at which he obtained thirty-five Indian recruits. In the hope of having at least two full companies of Indians in the 114th, Indians enlisting in other units in Military District No. 2 were encouraged to transfer to the 114th. The scheme was resisted, however, both by officers commanding the other units and by the Indians, many of whom did not wish to be in companies in which the Six Nations Indians would be in the majority (H 4). The scheme was abandoned late in January 1916, but Duncan Campbell Scott, apparently unaware of the change, wrote to General Logie on 31 May 1916 'to tell you how much I am interested in the welfare of the 114th Battalion; I hope to see a solid half of the battalion composed of Indians, and I trust that District No. 2 may be able to produce them. It is in the interest of the Indians, I think, that we should have at least two full Indian companies. Personally and officially I have been doing everything possible to bring this about.'[14] In spite of the best efforts of Scott and the recruiting officers, the 114th, like so many other battalions, never reached full strength and on its arrival in England in November 1916 was broken up.

Throughout the war the council of the Six Nations steadfastly adhered to the principle that any appeal for assistance must come directly from the King. Traditionally, regular chiefs or sachems had nothing to do with the conduct of war; this was the function of war chiefs, who were appointed only when war was declared directly by the Six Nations as a body. Within these limits, the council encouraged the Six Nations' war effort, but felt it could not assist directly in recruiting or in raising money for the Canadian war effort. It voted $1,500 for 'patriotic purposes' on 15 September 1914, but stipulated

[12]*Ibid.*
[13]*Ibid.*, v. 4383, file 2D. 34-7-109.
[14]*Ibid.*, v. 4380, file 2D. 34-7-89.

that the money be spent in England (H 5). At the same time it offered the services of Six Nations' warriors, provided the request for their services came from the King. The council's attitude did not discourage enlistment or patriotic work among women of the Six Nations, who organized a Women's Patriotic League in October 1914. They formed the Brock Rangers Benefit Society in February 1916 to provide comforts for Indians in the 114th Battalion and raised the necessary money by means of garden parties and tag days.[15]

Unlike the Six Nations, Indians on other reserves in Ontario had no difficulty participating in the Canadian war effort. Less than two weeks after the declaration of war the Sucker Creek Band at Little Current on Manitoulin Island voted $500 for 'war purposes,'[16] and other bands quickly followed suit. Feeling that their contribution in men and money justified their receiving increased rights, the Grand Indian Council of Ontario (which did not include the Six Nations) advanced their next regular meeting one year in order to discuss their grievances (H 6). A motion for the exemption of Indians from the operation of the Military Service Act was rejected at the meeting, but one calling for the granting of the franchise was carried with a large majority.[17] Unless they had enlisted, however, Indians remained disfranchised.[18] The status of Indians under the Military Service Act was unclear. Since they did not enjoy the full rights of citizenship it was uncertain whether or not they could be liable for military service. The Military Service Sub-Committee[19] ruled on 23 October 1917 that they were to be treated 'the same as any other citizen of Canada,' but the time for their compliance with the terms of the MSA was extended to 31 January 1918.[20] This decision was reversed by an order in council approved on 17 January which made all Indians exempt from combatant military service.

The war effort of Ontario's Indians was not confined to men, money, and knitting. Colonel Merritt had turned his attention to military aviation by 1916, and as Honorary Secretary of the

[15]Brantford *Expositor*, 3 Jan. 1919.

[16]*Globe*, 29 Aug. 1914, p. 5.

[17]P.A.C., RG 10, v. 2640, Red Series file 129690-3.

[18]The Military Voters' Act (7–8 Geo. v, chap. 34) granted the right to vote to Indians who had enlisted for active service overseas.

[19]This committee represented the Department of Militia in its dealings with the Military Service Branch of the Department of Justice and was formed 'to assist the Minister of Militia in administering the Act from the point where the Minister of Justice ceased to exercise control' (*Report of the Director of the Military Service Branch ... on the Operation of the Military Service Act, 1917* [Ottawa, 1919] p. 32).

[20]P.A.C., RG 24, v. 6566, file HQ 1064-30-34.

Canadian Aviation Fund he again turned to his Indian friends for help. This time he wanted to use Indian land on the Tyendenaga Reserve near Deseronto for a school of aviation. The Indians agreed, although Merritt's plans for the school advanced no further than the planning stage. A few months later, however, arrangements were completed between the Canadian and British governments for the construction of aircraft factories and the establishment of aviation schools in Canada, with the Imperial Munitions Board responsible for the site acquisition and construction of the schools. One of the more desirable locations for a school was at Deseronto. Sir Joseph Flavelle, chairman of the Imperial Munitions Board, wrote Duncan Campbell Scott on 13 March 1917 to ask whether the Indian land might be available.[21] The Indians were consulted and agreed to allow the land to be used for an aviation school, provided 'that the Aviation school be responsible for all damage to property and live stock and the said school to pay a herd-man and said herd-man to be one of the members of the Band and [for] all other work to be done, the members of the Band to have the first preference.'[22] Scott explained the terms of agreement (H 7), which were acceptable to the IMB, and before the end of April five hundred men were employed on the site.[23] The school was in operation in May and was used for elementary flying training until the end of the war, when the land once more became a pasture.[24]

[21]P.A.C., RG 10, v. 7615, file 13034-375.
[22]*Ibid.*, Tyendenaga Band Council meeting, 8 April 1917.
[23]*Globe*, 20 April 1917, p. 12.
[24]During the Second World War the Indians of Tyendenaga again permitted the Air Force to use the land for training purposes.

I. ONTARIO'S FIRST WAR ARTIST

HOMER WATSON, the internationally acclaimed painter of Ontario landscapes, was in his late fifties when war broke out, and like so many Ontarians he was eager to undertake some form of useful patriotic work. Encouraged by Sam Hughes, he hurried to Valcartier in September 1914 to make sketches for three paintings of the First Contingent in training. On his return to his home in Doon, he refused another commission in order to devote himself to the work.[1] The paintings were placed on public view for the first time during the last three days of September 1915, and the fifteen hundred people who saw them in Watson's studio contributed $250 to the Doon Patriotic Society.[2] Five months later they were exhibited in an Ottawa department store.

Watson was under the impression that his work had been commissioned by Hughes on behalf of the Canadian government. On 10 February 1916 he wrote to Sir Robert Borden asking for the payment of $20,000.[3] Borden was flabbergasted and asked Hughes for an explanation, including his reason for not telling Borden and the cabinet of his action. Sir Sam remembered 'encouraging' Watson, but he 'completely forgot' to mention it at meetings of the Privy Council (I 1).

Watson wrote another letter to Borden on 15 March in which he told the Prime Minister that 'people of both parties have said it was a thoughtful and good thing for the govt. to have a record of this kind made of the birth of our army so that the impetuous promptings that guide Sir Sam Hughes in action guided him here aright, as in most of the great things in which he has proved himself of late.'[4] Borden undoubtedly disagreed.

No money was forthcoming as a result of his correspondence with Borden. On 29 May, Watson sent his bill to the Department of Militia and Defence. The next day Sir Sam sent a memorandum to Sir Eugène Fiset, his deputy minister, recommending that Watson

[1]P.A.C., MG 26 H, Borden Papers, v. 214, file RLB 1175, pp. 121207–7A, Watson to Hughes, 22 Feb. [1915].
[2]*Globe*, 1 Oct. 1915, p. 5.
[3]P.A.C., MG 27, IID9, Sir A.E. Kemp Papers, v. 112, file 95, Watson to Borden, 10 Feb. [1916].
[4]*Ibid.*, Watson to Borden, 15 March [1916].

'be advanced three to four thousand dollars' (I 2). Another memorandum was submitted to the Privy Council recommending the payment of Watson's account in full (I 3).

Borden, annoyed by yet another unexpected Hughes transaction, asked Sir Edmund Walker, chairman of the Advisory Arts Council, to inspect the paintings and to 'submit a report of the opinion arrived at.'[5] A week later, and again on 11 July, Watson asked Borden for the payment of his account. Borden replied to Watson on 13 July, hardly disguising his annoyance with Hughes (I 4). Watson was not upset by the tone of Borden's letter. He explained that he would rather receive his money from the Department of Militia than from the Advisory Arts Council because 'my work was on order for the depiction of military scenes which of their nature are of an arbitrary character artistically speaking.'[6]

Borden felt pressed, and with no report from Walker forthcoming he sought the advice of his Minister of Finance, Sir Thomas White. White thought Watson's price 'to be extortionate' and suggested that it should be reviewed by the Advisory Arts Council (I 5). Borden had gained nothing in the exchange. Sir Edmund Walker finally submitted his report on 1 August, suggesting that $10,000 might be a suitable price for the paintings (I 6). Borden, reluctant to write to Watson that the government's offer would be only half Watson's bill, asked the painter if he could come to Ottawa 'at your earliest convenience.'[7] The meeting took place in November, after which Watson reluctantly accepted the offer but asked 'something for my expenses in addition to what is recommended' (I 7). Borden replied that 'we are of course most desirous of meeting your views as far as possible'[8] and left the case with Sir Thomas White for final settlement during Borden's impending absence in England. In passing the Watson file to White, Borden commented: 'he is an artist of eminence but Sir Edmund Walker thinks that his selection for this purpose was unfortunate as the subject was not such as to do him justice. I think we should treat him as fairly as possible because he had every right to suppose that the Minister possessed the requisite authority to engage him.'[9]

[5]Borden Papers, v. 214, file RLB 1175, p. 121224, Borden to Walker, 9 June 1916. The Advisory Arts Council was created to advise the government on the purchase of works of art.

[6]Kemp Papers, v. 112, file 95, Watson to Borden, 17 July 1916.

[7]Borden Papers, v. 214, file RLB 1175, page 121239, Borden to Watson, 14 Oct. 1916.

[8]Ibid., page 121248, Borden to Watson, 1 Dec. 1916.

[9]Ibid., page 121247, Borden to White, 1 Dec. 1916.

The decision to pay Watson had been made. Now White had to find the money as unobtrusively as possible to avoid the likelihood of embarrassing questions being asked in Parliament. He turned to his deputy minister, T.C. Boville, who suggested that it could be found in the funds allotted to the National Gallery (I 8), but Sir Edmund Walker was not receptive to the suggestion (I 9). White again turned to Boville, who on 8 January 1917 was able to report: 'I have discussed the matter with General Fiset and the plan of payment from the War Appropriation on the authority of an Order in Council signed by the Premier is the simplest way of making the payment.'[10] Boville's advice was acted upon, and the necessary order in council was approved on 6 February.[11] Watson eventually received his money. In acknowledging it, he told Borden that 'under the circumstances, I am certain you did the best you could for me, and I am glad the matter is settled.'[12] Borden could hardly disagree.

[10]P.A.C., RG 2, 1, v. 1432 (with PC 320 of 6 Feb. 1917).
[11]*Ibid.*
[12]Borden Papers, v. 214, file RLB 1175, pages 121251–1A, Watson to Borden, 22 May 1917.

J. ARMISTICE

NEWS OF THE ARMISTICE in Europe reached Ontario early in the morning on 11 November 1918, although months passed before people in remote areas heard of it (J 1, J 2). The joy and relief everywhere were unbounded. Civic holidays were proclaimed, parades were organized, and countless Kaisers were burnt in effigy (J 3). Services of thanksgiving were held in most Ontario churches the following Sunday. Preachers exulted in the defeat of autocracy and the triumph of good over evil. Some commented on the growth of democracy and fellowship among the troops in the trenches and referred to the difficult days of reconstruction which lay ahead. A whole generation of young Canadian men had been decimated in the fighting, and the survivors had every right to demand and expect a better life in return for the sacrifices they had made in fighting for their king and country. Referring to the returning men, Professor Robert Law told the congregation of St Andrew's Church in Toronto:

By every obligation and honour we are bound to regard this as a first charge upon the sympathy and resources of the nation ... There are hundreds of thousands who have to turn again to work, and it will require the utmost wisdom and sympathy on the part both of our rulers and our people in order that these may find the opportunity they desire ... Neither men nor women are going to be content in the future with the social conditions of the past. From the battlefield we have learned as perhaps never before the truth of democracy.[1]

Returning soldiers would find astonishing changes had occurred on the home front during the four years and four months of war and that lessons of democracy had been learned at home as well as on the battlefield. Canadians, recognizing their social and moral obligations to those less fortunate than themselves, supported the Patriotic Fund, the Red Cross, and other war relief appeals far beyond the expectations of their organizers. Voluntary war work found people from varying walks of life working together for the first time towards

[1]Quoted in the *Globe*, 18 Nov. 1918, p. 6.

a common goal.[2] Women, generally, gained new respect and status
as citizens by their war work and were well on the way to achieving
universal female suffrage. Trade unions had grown in both membership and strength, partly as a result of the astonishing growth of
industry during the war. It was hoped that industrial production
could be sustained, and thus provide employment for the demobilized
men; but veterans' organizations feared that the best jobs in industry
would be held by slackers and aliens. The armistice did not lessen
the bitterness felt toward those whose patriotism was suspect. Such
wounds took time to heal. And time would tell whether the rate of
social progress in wartime Ontario could be sustained, or even
increased, during the peace.

[2]The spirit of co-operation and the breaking down of social barriers in work for
a common cause was particularly evident during the influenza pandemic of 1918.

ONTARIO AND THE FIRST WORLD WAR 1914–1918

DOCUMENTS

A. CIVIC HOLIDAY, 1914

A 1 ONTARIO'S IMMEDIATE REACTION TO THE NEWS
THAT WAR HAD BEEN DECLARED
[*London* Free Press, *5 August 1914, p. 1*]

All Western Ontario was tremendously stirred by news that Great Britain
had joined the melee of nations in Europe. Developments of the past
week were such as to rouse interest to keenest pitch, and the cities and
larger towns of the province were waiting at the end of the telegraph
wires, as it were, for the worst that might come. Residents of communities
all over The Free Press' district called this office on the long distance
telephone in great numbers.

Demonstrations of the people of Brantford, Preston, Woodstock and
other places were reported in dispatches to The Free Press. At Woodstock
the officers of the 22nd Oxford Rifles had opened a recruiting office, and
the recruiting got a sudden impetus from the news. On the streets of
Woodstock the people sang 'Rule Britannia' and the National Anthem,
and there was enthusiasm exhibited in many other places, but most
striking of all was the way in which the Town of Berlin received the news.
Residents of the city sang 'Rule Britannia' where they were gathered in
theatres. There was a parade of members of the 24th Grey's Horse, and
the people cheered the cavalrymen as they went by. Loyalty to the empire
was shown in unmistakeable fashion by the German-Canadian citizens
of Busy Berlin.

St. Thomas City Council heard the news while in session and arose in
a body to sing 'God Save the King.'

The crowds on London streets cheered when war between Germany
and Great Britain was definitely announced. Suspense and pent-up
excitement, generated by the developments of the day, found expression
in a yell when the bulletins told at last that the empire was at war.

'Three cheers for Kitchener' called someone in the crowd in front of
The Free Press office, and they were given heartily.

'Three cheers for the King' was asked for and given ...

The streets were in a turmoil for hours after the fateful announcement
and the Old Boys' Reunion and all other matters were given a very
secondary place of consideration.

At 10.40 enthusiasts started a procession on Richmond Street, with
four Union Jacks and a trombone player from the Seventh Regiment
Band as a basis, and it soon became a big parade, shouting and singing
down the streets.

At 11 o'clock the crowd on Richmond Street was singing 'Three Cheers
for the Red, White and Blue' and the National Anthem.

B. THE HOME FRONT

B 1 COLONEL CHARLES EUGÈNE FISET, DEPUTY
MINISTER, DEPARTMENT OF MILITIA AND
DEFENCE, TO FREDERICK NICHOLLS
[*P.A.C., RG 24, Department of National Defence, v. 474,
file HQ 54-21-4-7*]

31 August 1914

I have the honour, by direction, to tender you the sincere thanks of the Hon. the Minister, for the very generous offer to loan one officer and twenty-four men from your company, for service with the Royal Canadian Engineers in the Dominion during the period of the war, and to inform you that the same is accepted.

In accordance with the spirit of your telegram of the 29th instant, the distribution will be as follows:

1 Officer and 8 other ranks to Esquimalt
8 ” ” ” Quebec
8 ” ” ” Halifax

The Officers Commanding these stations have been asked to state what trades they consider would be the most suitable and the information will be sent to you immediately it is received.

When the information is sent you concerning the desired trades instructions will also be sent concerning transport etc. and names of the officers to whom these parties are to report on arrival.

The following are the conditions which were agreed to between Lieut.-Colonel G.S. Maunsell, R.C.E., and yourself:

1. The Company to place at the disposal of the Department of Militia & Defence, one officer and twenty-four men to be selected from their employees in the different branches of their electrical works for the period of the war.

2. Captain Hazen Ritchie (Corps Reserve) 10th Brigade C.F.A. in command. Graduate R.M.C. 1889. Seniority 9 June 1900. Captain Ritchie is a Superintendent in the employ of the Canadian General Electric Company.

3. All men will be attested for service during the war and be subject to military discipline for that period.

4. The Government to provide clothing, subsistence, arms and accoutrements and transportation.

5. They will be paid by the Company direct – private rates of pay.

6. They will be subject to the orders of the senior Engineer Officer at the station, for work and discipline.

7. They may be employed either individually or collectively anywhere in Canada. Preferably collectively.

8. Military regulations as regards leave of absence.

9. In case of sickness – military doctor.

B 2 PROGRAMME FOR A PATRIOTIC CONCERT, 1915
[*P.A.C., MG 30, E 5, Ponton Papers*]

A Patriotic Concert

Under the auspices of the Women's Patriotic League

NAYLOR'S THEATRE, DESERONTO
FRIDAY EVENING, MAY 28

Col. Ponton, Belleville, Will Be the Speaker of the Evening

PROGRAMME

Trio,	Miss Campbell, Mr. T. Maxwell, Prof. Eppes
Patriotic Solo,	Mr. H. Aylsworth
Address,	Col. Ponton
Piano Solo,	Mr. Marcel Anderson
Tableau,	Good-Bye, Daddy

INTERMISSION

Maypole Dance,	
Solo,	Miss Kathleen McMurrich
Tableau,	The Summer Girl
Girls' Chorus	(a) Joys of Spring (b) Dixie Kid
Recitation,	Miss Florence Hall
Mandolin Solo,	Mr. W. Woodcock
Solo,	Mr. H. Aylsworth
Tableau,	The Execution of Lady Jane Grey
Piano Solo,	Miss Mary Maloney
Tableau,	The Allies

GOD SAVE THE KING

Curtain Rises at 8:15.   Ladies Will Kindly Remove Their Hats

ADMISSION: ADULTS 25c, CHILDREN 10c

THE DESERONTO NEWS CO., LTD.

B 3   CHRISTMAS GREETINGS TO BRANT COUNTY'S SOLDIERS FROM THE BRANTFORD PATRIOTIC AND WAR RELIEF ASSOCIATION
[*P.A.C., MG 30, B 11, Keen Papers, v. 1*]

Brantford, Canada
Dec. 22, 1914.

Dear Comrade,

The Christmas season is at hand. It will be an unusual Christmas for most of you, far different from what you have ever had in the past, and far different, let us devoutly pray, from what you will ever have again.

A few of your number are already on the "firing line", and you have read this letter as best you can amid the ear-splitting and nerve-racking explosions of "Jack Johnsons" and lesser artillery, or the pit-pat of the rifle. Others of you are in the hospital bearing manfully and patiently, as something to be prized, the wounds received by you in the service of your King and Country. The larger part of your number are being fitted on Salisbury Plain, or elsewhere, to take your places at no distant date on the scene of conflict between the forces of civilization and those of barbarism, for such is what this present war involves.

Since you said "Farewell Brantford! Goodbye Market Square!", the old town has witnessed the departure of soldier boys for the front, until it has become a matter of every day occurrence. In proportion to her population, Brantford has probably sent more volunteers for Kitchener's Armies than any other Canadian city. To every call there has thus far been a noble response, and this we feel confident will be the case until Berlin has been reached by the troops of the Allies, and everywhere the glad message of "Peace on Earth" first heard at Bethlehem nearly 2,000 years ago, is once more sounded; this time, it is to be hoped with the glad assurance that war will be no more.

The ladies of Brantford have sent, or are sending you, Christmas reminders, a little something in the way of comfort or of good cheer. To their contribution, we desire to add these few lines of a home letter, by way of assurance that you are not forgotten in your old home city or county, and to wish you all a "Merry Christmas" and a safe return.

B 4   PETER MCARTHUR'S COLUMN, 'COUNTRY RECRUITS'
[Globe, *30 January 1915, p. 13*]

With all the papers lamenting the fact that the rural districts are not contributing a satisfactory number of recruits to the war, it is perhaps unsafe for me to point out a few facts about rural conditions, for the last time I did so I was accused in a section of the press of preparing a defence for people who lack patriotism. I have surely put myself on record often enough as believing that the war must be supported to the utmost, but I am not going to let that belief make me unjust. I have told you how scarce men of military age are in this district and that if they enlist there can be none of the increased production that is being urged as an expression of patriotism. The Department of Agriculture is proclaiming that the man who produces more foodstuffs is doing a man's work for the Empire, and the few young men who are on the farms are practically all producers. Each one who went to the front would leave a hundred acres untilled.

It is high time that the Department of Militia and the Department of Agriculture got together and decided on a definite policy. If a man is doing his duty by producing more, he should not be open to criticism if he does not enlist. To show you how shorthanded this district is it is only necessary to point out that during the past ten years the population of the county of Middlesex has been so greatly reduced that at the recent redistribution one riding was wiped out. I have not the figures by me, but I understand that the population has fallen off something over ten thousand. This decrease is largely due to the exodus of young men to the west and to the cities. If the country had been at war for the past ten years we could not have lost a greater proportion of our population. If every young man of military age enlisted, the county could hardly make a fair showing and it would fall behind in production. Will those who are condemning the rural districts for not sending more recruits kindly tell what should be done in the case of Middlesex county?

While the above paragraph was in course of preparation I received a letter from a correspondent in Caistorville which reports a similar condition. The writer says

"While reading *The Globe* last evening I noticed a considerable complaint that the country districts are not responding very heartily to the call for volunteers to go to the war. In thinking the matter over I felt that there is a danger of not giving the country due consideration for this seeming shortcoming.

"I do not wish to excuse the country where it is lacking patriotism but I feel that the conditions of farmers are not fully comprehended which I will note briefly:

"(1) The smallness of families in farming districts these days is noticeable. There used to be five and six boys in a family on the farm. Today there are only one or two.

"(2) The spare boy that could be gotten along without has gone to the city or the west, and now not one farm in three has even one boy or man eligible to be a volunteer.

"(3) Help is scarce on the farms and in the farming districts. Most of the farmers are and have been running their farms with as little help as possible, and even when we feel we would like to have someone to help it is almost impossible to get it for there are no spare hands in the community.

"(4) If Canada is to provide bread, beef, horses, etc. for the war, the farmer must have sufficient help to do it.

"(5) The overflow of country population has gone to the cities or west. The congestion in the labour market at the present time is found in the cities, therefore it is not surprising that the majority of volunteers should come from that quarter."

This letter is of interest because it shows that conditions in other parts of the country are the same as I find them here in Middlesex. The farmers cannot both increase production and give volunteers to the army.

There is a thought that suggests itself in connection with this state of affairs. In the present national crisis we have a right to expect every man who is capable of rendering service to do so patriotically. The man who enlists to go to the front is making the supreme sacrifice that it is possible for a man to make. He is offering to give his life for his country. The man who is eligible to give similar service but feels that his call of duty is to stay at home and help his country with increased products should also be prepared to make many and great sacrifices. He is not offering his life, and therefore he should not stint in offering his means. If the young men who avoid military service do so because they think that during war times farming will yield them increased profits they must expect to take their profits with a share of public contempt. Never before has the call for unselfish service been so urgent and so great. Those who elect to serve their country as producers must be prepared to give to their full capacity. Even if they give all, they will not be giving so much as those who are offering their lives. As the war progresses public sentiment will probably be educated to a point where men in all walks of life who try to make profits from the unhappy condition of their country will be scorned for their selfishness. If we cannot serve at the front we must be prepared to serve unselfishly at home. As a matter of fact, I think it would be quite justifiable to ask the young married men of military age who are not enlisting what proportion of their products they will give for patriotic purposes over and beyond what they will have to pay in the form of taxes. When the survivors of those who volunteer for service at the front come back wounded and broken the young men who stay at home cannot feel much self-respect if they have spent the time in accumulating profits. This should show definitely whether their "patriotism of production" is real or only an excuse.

B 5 MILITIA ORDER No. 340, 12 JULY 1915
[*P.A.C., R.G. 9, Department of Militia and Defence, IIB3, v. 40*]

CANADIAN EXPEDITIONARY FORCE. — HARVESTING FURLOUGH
FOR N.C.O.'S AND MEN.

1. Subject to the following conditions, furlough for a period not exceeding one month may be granted to non-commissioned officers and

men of the Canadian Expeditionary Force for the purpose of enabling them to take part in the harvesting work throughout Canada.

2. This privilege is limited to non-commissioned officers and men of good character.

3. It is granted so as to enable them to work as harvesters, and for no other purpose, and it will only be granted on proof that promise of work has actually been obtained.

4. They may be provided with return transportation to and from any locality not exceeding a distance of three hundred miles from the station or camp where they are under training.

5. When they proceed on furlough, they will wear their working suits, leaving their clothing and equipment with their units.

6. Pay and allowances will be withheld during the period of the furlough, but will be paid on the return of the non-commissioned officer or man concerned to the headquarters of his unit, and upon proof being furnished that during furlough such non-commissioned officer or man was bona fide engaged in harvesting work.

7. Each non-commissioned officer and man will, therefore, be warned that when he returns to the headquarters of his unit, he will be required to produce a certificate from the person or persons for whom he has been working, or a certificate signed by himself to the effect that he has been working on his own land, and commanding officers, if not satisfied, with such certificates are required to obtain corroborative evidence.

8. Any non-commissioned officer or man, who misconducts himself during furlough, will be liable to forfeit his pay and allowances for such period as may be determined.

9. Commanding Officers will be held personally responsible that these terms and conditions are strictly carried out, so far as the non-commissioned officers and men of their respective units are concerned.

B 6 REPORT OF THE EXECUTIVE COMMITTEE OF THE SPEAKERS' PATRIOTIC LEAGUE, CENTRAL ONTARIO BRANCH, COVERING OPERATIONS FROM THE DATE OF ORGANIZATION TO MAY 31ST, 1916 [*Public Archives of Canada Library. Pamphlet Collection, No. 4426*]

The Speakers' Patriotic League was organized in March, 1915, and commenced active operations in the following month. In the memorandum then issued, the purposes of the League were set forth substantially as follows: –

To educate public opinion throughout the country as to the pressing needs of the Empire for men and money; to co-ordinate and stimulate all the various activities working to this end, and to augment the various patriotic funds without however establishing any fund of its own. Campaigns were to be carried on as the needs of the military and relief situations dictated, it being understood that whenever the recruiting of men for Overseas service, or the raising of funds for patriotic and relief purposes, appeared to be lagging in any particular district, those enrolled in the Speakers' Patriotic League should be available for promoting the organization of local committees to carry on this work, and to provide speakers to address meetings for the purpose of arousing the general public of such districts, and for securing an adequate response.

The formation of the League was due to two somewhat concurrent movements. Mr. N.F. Davidson, K.C., found, early in 1915, as he spoke in various municipalities of our Military Division, the need of some organization which could supply speakers and organizers to aid both in the stimulation of patriotic endeavor and in the organization of it for definite needs. Recruiting was being done in such a desultory way that it had practically no effect upon the community as a whole, and the needs of the Patriotic Fund were being completely overlooked in a great many places. While the Red Cross Society had organizations of women at work, there was no attempt being made to collect money for the Red Cross at all commensurate with its claims. Early in the year, Mr. Davidson called the attention of the Lieutenant-Governor to these facts and, locally, the organization of this League might be said to be due to Mr. Davidson's efforts.

At the same time, Sir Herbert Ames was working in a more statistical way in Ottawa. He found that those counties which had given fewest men were also weak so far as contributions to the Patriotic Fund were concerned. He evolved the idea of having organizations formed in each Military Division, with a central organization at Ottawa, which would aid recruiting and the Patriotic Fund.

His Honour, the Lieutenant-Governor, called a meeting of a number of gentlemen who had manifested their interest in patriotic work. This meeting was held in Government House on March 2nd, 1915, and the work of the League, as defined above, was agreed upon.

Following this, the organization work was continued at meetings held on March 12th and March 19th, and a public meeting was called on March 25th which endorsed the whole scheme. At this meeting the officers whose names stand at the head of this report were elected.[1]

The purposes above outlined – namely, that the League for Central Ontario, related in exactly the same way to recruiting, the Patriotic Fund and the Red Cross Fund, should serve as the central bureau for supplying speakers and organizers – have been consistently followed throughout the year. Every attempt has been made both to organize those districts which stood in need of organization and to assist bodies of citizens in every

[1]Sir John Hendrie, president; Sir John M. Gibson, Sir Edmund Osler, General W.A. Logie, Colonel S.C. Mewburn, Colonel G.A. Sweny, vice-presidents; Hon. Mr Justice Masten, chairman of the executive committee; G.P. Scholfield, chairman of the finance committee; J.R.L. Starr, chairman of the publicity committee; A.H. Campbell, chairman of the campaign committee; A.H. Abbott, honorary secretary.

patriotic endeavor. No assistance that we could render has been refused where it was physically possible to supply it, even in those cases in which it was evident that even the travelling expenses of speakers would have to be borne by the League. That is, the broadest possible attitude has been maintained to patriotic work of every description, and the letters appended to this report, from Lieutenant-Colonel Williams, Sir Herbert Ames and Mrs. Plumptre, show that our work has been uniformly successful in regard to recruiting and the Patriotic and Red Cross Funds.

Before the work of the League is reported in detail, it might be of service to record that similar Leagues were formed for Eastern Ontario, with headquarters at Kingston, and in Montreal. Some months ago the Montreal League disbanded and was merged with the Citizens' Recruiting Committee. In Eastern Ontario, while branches of the League were formed in many places throughout Military Division No. 3 and considerable help was given to recruiting, no attempt was made to organize for either the Patriotic Fund or Red Cross Society, and in recruiting the policy of organization followed in Central Ontario has not been adopted. So far as we are aware, no other branches of the League were formed, and it was found impossible to organize the central league proposed at Ottawa. The consequence is that the Central Ontario League is the only branch which has developed as was originally proposed. The recognition of these facts may assist those who have not been familiar with the inner working of the League to realize the completely unique character of the work which has been done in Central Ontario. The fact that both in the number of men enlisted and in the contributions to the Patriotic and Red Cross Funds, Central Ontario holds an outstanding position, is in no small degree due to the kind of work which this League has done.

Military Division No. 2, to which we have largely confined our attention, is composed of thirteen counties and four districts. The Eastern boundary of the Division is the Eastern limit of Ontario County, the District of Muskoka, the District of Parry Sound, and the District of Nipissing; the Western boundary is the Western limit of the Counties of Norfolk, Brant, Wentworth, Halton, Peel, Dufferin and Grey, and the District of Algoma. No part of this rather large area has been overlooked, and while we have found it possible to do more work in some parts of the Division than in others, owing to both geographical and local conditions, a complete report of the work accomplished would deal with every County and District mentioned. Further, our activities have by no means been confined to our own Division. We have done work as far East as Peterborough in No. 3 Division and in many places in Military Division No. 1.

At the inception of our work, Mr. (now Captain) C.N. Cochrane, B.A., was engaged as organizing secretary. His work consisted largely in the formation of local committees in those towns and counties where no steps had been taken in the direction of organizing for patriotic work. He remained with the League until the middle of November, when he became

Secretary of the Soldiers' Aid Commission. A great deal of the success of the League is due to the splendid work of Mr. Cochrane, in placing local patriotic organizations in our Division on a thoroughly sound and practical foundation.

When it was found that Mr. W.C. Rean, the organizer for the Canadian Patriotic Fund, could not keep pace with the work of organizing the local campaigns for the raising of money which we had ready for him, the League secured, about the middle of June, the services of Mr. (now Lieutenant) B.J. Roberts, who has rendered conspicuous service in the organization of rural municipalities, and who is still with us, as probably the most expert organizer of recruiting campaigns in the Division.

Even with the addition of Mr. Roberts, the work of organization could not keep pace with the demand, and, as the patriotic committees in many places were willing to combine the Patriotic and Red Cross Funds in their campaigns, the whole matter was presented to the Canadian Red Cross Society, with the result that Mr. A.M. Miller, B.A., was, about the 1st of July, engaged by them as organizer and placed at the disposal of the Speakers' Patriotic League. Mr. Miller's work has continued without interruption to the present time, and we have already planned a full Summer's work for him.

In the early Fall, Mr. Melville H. Staples, B.A., was engaged on the same basis as Mr. Miller by the Red Cross Society, and placed at our disposal. Mr. Staples did splendid work until May 1st, when it was felt that he might be released for other work which demanded his attention.

In the early Fall, also, we were able to secure Mr. J.M. Wyatt, B.A., for the Patriotic Fund, with which he has been working since that time. A full Summer's work in Eastern Ontario is already arranged by the Patriotic Fund Executive Committee for him.

The above will at once make evident how close has been the relation between the work of this League and the National Patriotic Fund and the Canadian Red Cross Society.

From the organization of our League we have been in close touch with the recruiting situation, although during the first few months of our existence it was not possible to render material assistance to recruiting, owing to the special conditions under which the work was then being carried on. However, the first civilian recruiting committee in the Division was formed in Collingwood and a recruiting campaign undertaken about the middle of June. This campaign inaugurated the methods which have since been followed with such splendid success throughout the Division; namely, the preparation of a list of the names of eligible men and the personal canvassing of them. While the campaign was productive of good results in men enlisted, probably the most valuable result was the information which it gave us as to the exact state of mind which existed in the country. The information secured was at once utilized and the first public result of this was the Massey Hall meeting, held under the auspices of General Logie and the commanding officers of the local battalions. The Acting

Secretary of the League, Mr. Cochrane, was the Secretary of the Committee which organized this meeting, and the expenses of the meeting were borne by this League. It is unnecessary to speak of the tremendous and unexpected success which attended the meeting. Not only was Massey Hall filled, but it was reported that at least 10,000 people gathered in front of the City Hall in the overflow meeting. At this meeting the first step was taken in the formation of the Citizens' Recruiting League of Toronto, for which Mr. Cochrane acted as Secretary until the organization was completed.

With the Massey Hall meeting, began the active recruiting work throughout the Division, which has continued with such conspicuous success until the present time. The authorization of the formation of county battalions in the Fall led to general activity throughout the whole Division. We were, consequently, called upon to supply speakers for recruiting meetings, and this led to the engagement of returned soldiers, who were trained to address these meetings.

The appointment of Major (now Lieutenant-Colonel) Williams as Chief Recruiting Officer for the Division was a great step in advance. He at once made use of the local committees which we had formed and to these added others in many places. The really significant element in this was the definite recognition by the military authorities of the part which civilian organizations should take in recruiting.

However, the detailed organization of the Division was not undertaken until the formation, on November 23rd, of the Central Recruiting Committee. Mr. John M. Godfrey, who had been prominent in the organization of the County of Peel, took the leading part in the organization of this Recruiting Committee. On its formation, the Recruiting Committee requested the Speakers' Patriotic League to administer the funds which might be placed at its disposal to aid recruiting, and to undertake all the office and organization work which might be required. The consequence has been that from the 1st of December last the activities of the Speakers' Patriotic League have been very largely devoted to recruiting. All the office expenses in connection with the work of the Central Recruiting Committee have been borne by the Speakers' Patriotic League; consequently, all the money provided through voluntary and county contributions by the Recruiting Committee has been used for recruiting purposes only. (The amount disbursed to date is $10,400.) Colonel Williams' letter is as clear and definite a statement as is needed with regard to the place which the Speakers' Patriotic League has taken in the recruiting activities of this Division.

The thanks of the League are due to the many ladies and gentlemen who have given their services as speakers, at the League's request, without remuneration, and have done such excellent service. Many of the speakers whom we have sent out have placed themselves unreservedly at our disposal. This has been of the greatest possible assistance in the arrangement of meetings.

In addition to the speakers, due acknowledgment should be made to the friends of the League who have contributed so generously toward its support. All the money received came from voluntary contributions, and the work of the League was, naturally, in the last analysis, dependent upon those through whose generosity it was supported.

Mention should also be made of our indebtedness to the authorities of the University of Toronto, who have contributed very largely to the work of the League, both in providing office accommodation without cost and in giving the services of Dr. Abbott, the Honorary Secretary.

The following letters, dealing with the work of the League, have been received by the Secretary:

From Lieutenant-Colonel George H. Williams,
Chief Recruiting Officer, Military District No. 2.

"It affords me very great pleasure to bear testimony to the invaluable services you have personally and also officially, through the Speakers' Patriotic League, rendered us in our recruiting campaign in this district. The unusual success attained here has been in a very large degree the result of your splendid organization and efficient staff. Your experience in securing the splendid results to the Patriotic Fund enabled you to come instantly into touch with the most active persons and societies in this area, so that we were able to secure an organization most efficient and adequate for our recruiting campaign. Your assistants, Captain Cochrane and Lieutenant Roberts, chosen by you, have justified the wisdom of your selection by the hearty co-operation afforded the work. You have been successful in securing financial resources by which a number of capable and successful returned soldiers have been at our disposal continually for recruiting, and in addition a most effective and competent body of volunteer speakers have been available without interruption throughout the entire campaign. Your League has been the only source of poster supply, the selection of which has met with general approval and occasioned universal demand. It is impossible to put too high an estimate on the value of the many forms of splendid service rendered by your office and League, and it is to be hoped that in the work yet to be done to secure the quota of recruits in this district we may be assured of your continued assistance in supply of speakers, stock of posters, etc. The future of our recruiting presents peculiar difficulties in the demand for persistent and experienced modes of appeal. There is no existing organization competent to do the work of your Speakers' Patriotic League, and in thanking you for the most estimable assistance afforded in the past year I would express the hope that you may be able to continue the same until our recruiting is complete."

CANADIAN PATRIOTIC FUND
Ottawa, May 13th, 1916.

From Sir Herbert B. Ames, K.T., M.P.
Honorary Secretary.

"As I understand that in the near future the annual meeting of the

Speakers' Patriotic League for Central Ontario will be called, it may not be out of order to give some expression to our appreciation of the services your League has rendered.

"With the ever increasing enlistment, the demands on the Canadian Patriotic Fund steadily grow from month to month. We are to-day paying out twice as much as we did a year ago and 25 per cent. more than we did four months ago. We expect that sum needed for the month of May will not be far from $700,000. Now, we rely entirely upon voluntary subscriptions that may be sent in to us by governing bodies or by private individuals. The spirit of generosity is widespread among our Canadian people, but if it be not appealed to and organized it may not find full expression. Thanks to the splendid service which your Speakers' Patriotic League has rendered, many communities have given most generously to the Patriotic Fund, and, on behalf of the National Executive, I want to express to your League our highest appreciation and our heartiest thanks. During the past year it has been only necessary for us to indicate that any given community, within the area under your supervision, did not appear to be seized with a sense of the *full* responsibility as to their duty towards our Fund, to have your League stimulate such communities with most gratifying results.

"I trust that your Board may appreciate the splendid personal service which you are rendering and may give you and your associates, for the coming year, such efficient support as may enable a continuance of your excellent work."

THE CANADIAN RED CROSS SOCIETY
Toronto, May 22nd, 1916.
From Mrs. H. P. Plumptre,
Corresponding Secretary.

"As I believe your annual meeting of the Speakers' Patriotic League is to be held shortly, I am writing in the name of the Executive to thank your speakers and yourself personally for the very valuable assistance rendered to the cause of the Canadian Red Cross Society through your organization.

"We feel that the cause of the Red Cross has profited greatly by the addresses given by your speakers, by which the general scope of its operations has been made known in places which would not otherwise have been reached.

"Thanking you for your personal readiness to assist our work at all times."

Since its inception, the League has supplied speakers for and aided in the organization of 980 public meetings, including those held for general patriotic purposes, on behalf of the Canadian Patriotic and Red Cross Funds and for recruiting. A total approximately of $1,500,000 was raised for the two above-mentioned funds as a result of the League's endeavor, assisted by local committees.

The following is a summary of the recruiting work done by the

Speakers' Patriotic League in conjunction with the Central Recruiting Committee:

Speakers supplied for	777 meetings
Posters supplied	69,800
Pamphlets supplied	180,000

This report would be incomplete without reference to the services which have been rendered to the League voluntarily by the Honorary Secretary, Dr. A. H. Abbott, ever since its inception. Throughout the period of its activities he has given to the work the most unremitting and whole-hearted service and it is not saying too much to state that without his assistance the successful results which the League has attained could not have been achieved.

> JOHN S. HENDRIE,
> President.
> C. A. MASTEN,
> Chairman of Executive Committee.

Toronto, Ont., June 20, 1916.

B 7 EXTRACT FROM 'THE CALL OF THE WAR,' A RECRUITING SERMON PREACHED IN ST ANDREW'S CHURCH, OTTAWA, ON 27 JUNE 1915 BY THE REVEREND W.T. HERRIDGE
[*Ottawa* Citizen, *28 June 1915, p. 5*]

The eagerness of many of our youth to take part in this struggle is a credit to Canada. I sympathize with those who, while burning to join their comrades, have not been deemed fit for the strain, and with those of like mind who, for various good reasons, must stay where they are. Yet there are others throughout this big land by whom, whether through dullness or indifference, the call of patriotism has been so far disregarded, and private interest held of greater moment than the public weal.

Now the sooner this easy-going selfish spirit is driven out, the better for us all. Whether we buy a sword or not by selling our garment, it will be a poor boast that we have kept our garment, even if we are able to keep it, when it becomes the badge of degradation. By all means let our young lads play their games and make their bodies strong and clean. But the professional sports, where a few are paid to take exercise, while the rest look on: the race-track courses, the moving picture shows and such like things attract too many of our full-grown men who might well ask themselves just now whether their time could not be spent in a more useful way. Perhaps we might even dispense for a while the elaborate sporting columns in our newspapers. They do not fit in very well with the cable-grams from across the sea. We have serious tasks confronting us as a people; and if we fail to discern their importance, and to try, as best we can, to discharge them, any attempt at lighter fun is nothing but a hideous and disgraceful mockery.

THE HOME FRONT

Under certain circumstances, "safety first" is an excellent motto. It is pure foolishness for any one to run risks which can be of no benefit either to himself or others; and every corporation which looks for public patronage is bound to show proper regard for the welfare of all those who have any dealings with it. But, in great crises "safety first" would be the watchword of a coward. The quality of life on this earth ought to mean more than the mere length of it. Many things come before personal safety; honour comes before it; freedom comes before it; righteousness comes before it. Safety is the last consideration when the dearest treasures of the soul are placed in peril; and, however fierce the attack upon them, no one worthy to be called a man would refuse to guard such an inheritance even unto death.

I have no doubt as to the final issue of this strife. It cannot be that military despotism shall yet prove victorious, and an outrage be fastened upon the conscience of the world. Fervent supplication will rise to God that such a calamity may never be, and hope, the last gift that remains to mortals when others have flown away, will turn from an outlook so gloomy and forlorn. But it will not be enough simply to wish for triumph, or to pray for triumph, we must also work for it. We must refuse the blandishments of ease and sloth, and accept the opportunity for heroic self-sacrifice. We must silence all minor discords amongst us in one united chorus whose inspiring refrain shall ring from shore to shore. We must concentrate our best thought and our noblest effort upon the herculean labour which it is our privilege to share, and must not falter till we have fought out and won the battle for liberty, not our liberty alone, but the liberty of all mankind.

God bless our boys who have gone or who may yet go across the sea. We mourn for those who have fallen, and pray that a Divine comfort may rest upon the homes which they shall see no more. Yet we cannot feel that they have given their lives in vain. Their dauntless courage will never be forgotten, nor their splendid obedience as soldiers of the King. The voice of their blood cries from the ground in piercing tones; and it would be strange indeed if even the most careless and self-centred youth amongst us did not feel in his breast the thrill of a new patriotism, and the irresistible pressure of a new sense of duty waking the manhood in him to serve, to suffer, aye, even to die for God and his native land.

For we need more men in training to take some part in this great war; and if they offer themselves, we must see that no removable hindrances bar the way. We need men who discern the signs of the times, and who will prove all the more efficient, whether in counsel or in fight, because they are men of clean hands and pure hearts. This war is no mere vulgar brawl to be settled in a day. It is a struggle between opposing ideals of life, and a long hard road may yet have to be travelled before the happy end is gained. We are fighting for the rights of others, not less than for our own. We are fighting for those intangible possessions which are the crowning glory of mankind, and the loss of which would cover earth as with a funeral pall, and wrap it in eternal gloom. We are fighting for the overthrow of impious pride and cruel oppression, and for the final triumph of Truth and Righteousness.

I see in imagination a stalwart host of young Canadians marching as to war. The cause they espouse should nerve their arm and ennoble their character. They will be "compassed about with a great cloud of witnesses" who watch their valorous deeds and anticipate their final victory. The heroes of past days will seem to share their high endeavour, and from myriads on earth the voice of suppliant prayer will mingle in its ascent to God with the shouts of conflict and the shock of arms. If, when peace has come again, they return to the land they have left behind, they will be greeted with the welcome which befits those who have done their duty; and if they are called upon to lay the sacrifice of their lives on the altar of freedom, their names will be enrolled in the ranks of the immortals, and their memory cherished by generations yet unborn.

B 8   LYRICS OF 'WE'RE FROM CANADA,' BY MISS
IRENE HUMBLE OF TORONTO AND PUBLISHED
BY THE THOMPSON PUBLISHING COMPANY
[*Reprinted in the* Daily British Whig, *29 January 1915*[2]]

> King and our country,
> We're from Canada,
> We're from Canada,
> A land beyond compare.
> Where the sun shines bright
> And the stars at night
> Look down on our fields so fair.
> On to victory,
> On to victory
> We will help to fight the foe,
> And the maple leaf is our emblem dear,
> As marching on we go.

B 9   LIEUTENANT-COLONEL W.B. KINGSMILL,
OFFICER COMMANDING, 123RD BATTALION TO
COLONEL S.C. MEWBURN, ASSISTANT ADJUTANT
GENERAL, MILITARY DISTRICT NO. 2
[*P.A.C., RG 24, v. 4301, file 2D. 34-1-59*]

Toronto, Ont.
December 8th, 1915.

I have just spoken, by telephone, to Captain Trump, who has asked me to refer to you all hand bills I have had printed for distribution in the

[2]This song was described in the *Daily British Whig* as 'British-Canadian through and through, the sentiment is patriotic and the air catchy.'

City of Toronto in carrying out my recruiting campaign, the programme of which was set forth in my letter of December 2nd.

I have had distributed broadcast throughout the City 70,000 of each of the enclosed handbills. My idea is to have a new handbill for each day of this week until I have exhausted the $1,000.00 which is being given to the 10th Royal Grenadiers for the purpose of recruiting.

My own Regiment, 10th Royal Grenadiers, are themselves furnishing a considerable quota of men for the Overseas Battalion, and those who cannot go are acting as Recruiting Agents in distributing the advertising matter.

Captain Trump seemed to think that the appeal to the women is a little too strong.

Regarding this circular I may say that it already appeared in the Evening Telegram on December 3rd, very much stronger than it is set forth in my circular.

I have still a number of this handbill which have not been distributed and I propose to have them placed in the Churches on Sunday morning next. This may not meet with your approval.

What I am doing at the present time is to use each of the men who are handed over to me from the Recruiting Depot as Recruiting Agents. I place these men under the Recruiting Sergeants, who in consequence have a little squad of men at their disposal to assist them in recruiting, and I believe this to be bearing results and the behaviour of these new men, who have come to me, on the streets has been admirable.

I do not see why this scheme could not be very much enlarged. For instance – There are at the present time stationed in Toronto between 7,000 and 8,000 men, at least, who have enlisted for Overseas service. Why not have a recruiting day and turn this 8,000 men loose as Recruiting Agents?

All that it needs is to put the matter into the hands of some person who has ability to carry on an advertising campaign and it would be worked out methodically and every person in the City could be directly approached. In other words – the same methods for obtaining recruits could be used as the Patriotic Association used for obtaining funds.

Please have the enclosed hand-bills marked approved and returned with the Sergeant who delivers this letter.

B 10   123RD BATTALION RECRUITING LEAFLET
[P.A.C., RG 24, v. 4301, file 2D. 34-1-59]

ROYAL GRENADIERS
Extracts from letter which appeared in the *Evening Telegram*, December 3rd, over the name of G.G. Starr :–

To the Women of Canada
In addressing these few remarks exclusively to the women of the

country, it is to be understood that we have arrived at that period in the struggle where we realize the utter futility of recruiting meetings.

The men who have as yet failed to join the colors will not be influenced by any eloquence from any platform.

The reason? The man we are trying to reach is the man who will never listen and the man who never for a moment considers the remarks as applicable to himself.

And so now we appeal to the women – the women who are the main-spring of all masculine action.

In the First Division of the C.E.F. we swept up the young manhood of the country in the first enthusiasm – we secured the cream of the country in the men who flocked to the colors taking thought of neither yesterday or to-morrow.

At the second call men were stopping to calculate and hesitate. Since then the hesitation has developed into stagnation. Men who see a des-perate winter ahead are joining the colors, and a few others; the remain-der are deadwood.

The reason? Firstly, the man who prefers to allow others to fight for him so that he may pursue a comfortable occupation, preserve his youth, be safe from danger, and explain to his friends that he would gladly join the colors could he obtain a commission – and yet take no steps towards that end.

Second. The man who is influenced by the selfish maternal appeal either from mother or wife.

Third. The man who claims his business would go to pieces without him, but is satisfied to let others throw away life and youth to sustain that business.

Fourth. The others – call them what you may.

And now my Appeal to Women

You entertain these wretched apologies in your homes. You accept their donations, their theatre tickets, their flowers, their cars. You go with them to watch the troops parade.

You foully wrong their manhood by encouraging them to perform their parlor tricks while Europe is burning up.

While Canada is in imminent danger of suffering the same were it not for the millions who are cheerfully enduring the horrors and priva-tions of bloody warfare for the millions who stay at home watching the war pictures and drinking tea.

Bar them out, you women. Refuse their invitations, scorn their at-tentions. For the love of Heaven, if they won't be men, then you be women. Tell them to come in uniform, no matter how soiled or mis-fitting – bar out the able-bodied man who has no obligations, show that you despise him. Tell him to join the colors while he can do so with honor. And the day is not far off when he will have to go. The old mother has issued the last call to her sons.

Make your son, your husband, your lover, your brother, join now while he yet retains the remnants of honor. Compulsory training is in the offing.

Get the apologist, the weakling, the mother's pet, into the service. Weed out all, and we will find out who are the cowards. Analyze your friends – you women – refuse their attentions, and tell them why. Make them wake up.

GOD BLESS HIM. THE KING CALLS!
JOIN ROYAL GRENADIERS OVERSEAS
BATTALION, 123rd C.E.F.

B 11 LETTER FROM LIEUTENANT-COLONEL VAUX CHADWICK TO CHURCHES, LODGES AND CLUBS RELATING TO RECRUITING
[P.A.O., RG 8, 1-1-A, box 80, file on recruiting]

Toronto
23rd December, 1915.

In connection with recruiting of the 124th. Overseas Battalion, C.E.F., an effort is being made to have each platoon if possible, or at least each section, specially recruited by some Church, Society, Club or other Association, so that men who are friends may serve together during their enlistment which of course will make their term of service much more congenial.

My desire is, that the Battalion shall be recruited, not so much by those who individually enlist at random, but by parties or groups of young men, who being friends, or members of Church, Mercantile, or other organizations can chum together. The size of a Platoon is sixty, and that of a Section fifteen men.

I will be very glad if you can get us a group of recruits from your organization and in that event, I personally assure you that they will be kept together in that section or platoon to which they were assigned.

I shall esteem it a favor, if you will let me hear from you at your very earliest convenience, and if you think it well, I will have one of my Officers attend you, and render every assistance in his power, by addressing your men and answering probable questions, or otherwise.

I cannot help feeling that at the present time, the urgent need of the proper kind of recruit is a sufficient reason for an appeal to the patriotism of your organization.

B 12 MAJOR-GENERAL W.A. LOGIE TO DR P.E. DOOLITTLE OF THE ONTARIO MOTOR LEAGUE
[P.A.C., RG 24, v. 4287, file 2D. 34-1-25]

149 College St.,
November 8th, 1918.

I wish to acknowledge in the most public way the very great assistance which the Civilian Moter Cars have been in connection with the return of wounded soldiers from Overseas.

Not only would it have been impossible to meet the wishes of the relations of the men returning, but without the assistance of your committee it would have been very difficult to have forwarded out of town returning soldiers, to their trains in time to catch them, the same night. I well recollect the Ontario Motor League, Toronto Corps, of which you were Chief Commandant, Mr. L.B. Howland Assistant Commandant, and Mr. W.G. Robertson, Secretary, which rendered such valuable assistance in 1914.

You will recollect that your Corps was divided into four districts, with the following officers, #1 District Commandant, A.R. Clarke, Assistant Commandant, G.B. Clarke, #2 District, Commandant, O. Hezzlewood, Assistant Commandant, H.S. McMullen, #3 District, Commandant, F. McGilivray Knowles, Assistant Commandant, Frank Roden, #4 District, Commandant, W.W. Digby, Assistant Commandant, E.W. Goulding. Under these were ten subdivisions, each under a Captain with approximately 16 moter cars in each subdivision. Rendezvous were detailed and co-operation arranged for in case of a sudden mobilization of the Militia.

A test took place on the 16th of November, 1914, and the organization was maintained in case of emergency.

I have no doubt that from the experience you then gained, you have been able with the assistance of your friends, to organize so well the Civil Moter Cars, assisted by your Reception Committee, that no matter at what hour the train came in, or how sudden the call, your Committee, has never failed to be present with sufficient moter cars to accommodate everyone.

Again let me thank you and through you your Committee, for your time and trouble in this very important matter.

B 13   SOLDIERS' AID COMMISSION 'APPRECIATORY'
[P.A.C., RG24, v. 4255, file 1D. 1-7-76]

WHAT IS THE SOLDIERS' AID COMMISSION OF ONTARIO? WHAT ARE ITS
AIMS AND OBJECTS? WHERE ARE THE OFFICES OF THE COMMISSION?
The Answers to these Questions are of Vital Interest to
Returned Soldiers.
THE SOLDIERS' AID COMMISSION is established:
To meet the soldier at the Railway Station.
To remove difficulties with regard to pay accounts.
To help in correspondence on the subject.
To aid in finding employment.
To arrange for Vocational Training.
To assist in reinstating discharged soldiers in civil life.
To support claims for Pension and Insurance.
To take affidavits.

To visit homes and hospitals.

To help and advise wives and families of men overseas.

To help the returned soldier in every way possible.

The services of the Commission are entirely free.

The officials of each and every branch are always glad to welcome returned soldiers at their offices and give them help and advice at any time.

It is the desire of the Commission that every returned soldier is given a square deal, and even more, and to help each returned soldier back to civil life and civil activities.

EXTRACT FROM TORONTO SUNDAY WORLD,
21ST SEPTEMBER, 1919.

As to the comprehensiveness of the work performed by such agencies as the Soldiers' Aid Commission of Ontario, few people have any conception. Only those who have directly benefitted can fully appreciate what these provincial organizations have done for many a man in difficulties, and, indeed, for many a chap who has been "down and out." It may seem incredible that returned soldiers should be permitted to reach the "hard up" stage, but through the offices of such organizations as the Soldiers' Aid Commissions of the various provinces many of these most deserving cases have come to light, cases which, if they had not been adjusted by these public bodies, would have remained as stains of ingratitude upon the page of Canadian history.

In a general way, the objects for which the Soldiers' Aid Commission of Ontario, in common with the other provincial organizations of the kind, was organized are known to the public. The actual results attained are not even known in a general way. One reason for this vague conception of the vast volume of work accomplished by the Commission since its inception in November, 1915, would appear to be simply because the officials have avoided publicity.

Examples of Help.

The vocational training given the returned men by the classes established throughout the province under the direction of the Soldiers' Aid Commission, according to the returns ending May 31 last, shows that 14,837 men had availed themselves of this means of becoming better fitted for civil life. Since June 1 the attendance at these classes has considerably increased, and indications point to at least a doubling of the present number of soldier students by the end of this year.

One group of 573 returned soldiers at the Central Technical School constitutes the largest vocational training class in the British Empire.

A few examples, which follow, have been taken at random from the returns of the classes in various parts of the province. Without publishing the names of the men concerned in each case, which are to be found on the files of the commission, but which are not given out for obvious reasons, it can be seen at a glance the nature of the service that has been done the returned men, and to the country in training them for positions of responsibility and trust.

A private, who, before enlisting, was a barber at odd times, and a farm laborer at other times, suffered a disability on active service. Upon returning home, he was granted a course at London, Ont., and is now employed as an accountant at military headquarters of Military District No. 1, on a salary of $125 per month.

A former farm laborer, partially disabled, is now a telegraph operator at $135 a month, through the Soldiers' Aid Commission.

A non-commissioned officer who had left school when only in the third book at 13 years of age, after twenty months' service overseas was returned to Canada, took a course in the civil service classes, and general education, tried his matriculation and passed with highest marks of all the men who had tried that examination in Ontario. He was then admitted to the Ontario Veterinary College where he is now in his second year, and is making good.

A man who had been a farm laborer and rough carpenter before the war, and who got a bullet in his lungs while in France, took a course in roadmaking including surveying and estimating. He is now with the department of public highways in Ottawa at $1,500 per year and expenses.

A soldier who is a farmer's son, and who left school at 11 years of age, took an electrical course under the Soldiers' Aid Commission, and he is now an electrical engineer at Niagara Falls on a salary of $135 per month.

A few of the other long list of new made men include the following: A farm lad now a telegrapher at $145 a month, a soldier who learned shoemaking and now realizing $9 per day, a soldier who at 51 years of age has become a draftsman at $1,200 per year, a former teamster now a cabinet maker at 55 cents per hour.

Enrolment Summary.

The following is a summary of the enrolments for each year since the beginning of the vocational classes:

In the convalescent classes conducted to keep the men employed as a means of bringing them back to health:

In 1917 3,050 joined; in 1918 5,432 joined; in 1919 to May 31 2,723 joined.

The total in convalescent classes was 11,205.

In the re-educational classes: In 1917 343 joined; in 1918 1,243 and in 1919 2,046 joined up to May 31.

The total in re-educational classes was 3,632.

Thus the total in all vocational classes was 11,205 from the convalescent classes plus 3,632 from the re-educational classes, making 14,837 in all up to May 31st last.

Care of Soldiers' Children.

The Commission conducts a children's hostel at 138 Avenue road,

where the soldier's little ones are cared for when the parents are temporarily unable to look after them, or else suitable homes are found for
homeless soldiers' children. There are 34 children in this institution at
the present time. The Commission will not, however, allow any soldiers'
child to become an object of charity, and it makes an actual charge for
food against the parents.

Claims for Back Pay.

Adjustments with the military authorities are frequently made by the
commission on behalf of returned men with regard to their pay and allowances, such as working pay, pension and separation allowance. Thousands of dollars have been recovered for the men through the good offices
of the Commission in this connection. Some of the individual cases have
resulted in $1,000 being obtained to cover the amounts due through
errors made by the military in settling up the accounts of certain men.

Loans Advanced.

Loans on security, but without interest charges, have been made by
the Commission to 12,487 men of the 118,176 who have returned to
Ontario from overseas to date, or in other words, more than ten per cent.
of the returned men of the province have received substantial financial
aid in this way.

The total amount of money advanced by the Commission to the returned men up to the present is $331,882.12. Six branches of the Com-
mission make these cash advances on imprest accounts from the head
office of the Commission on College street, Toronto. The advances of
these branches have been as follows to date:

Toronto, 8,490 loans, totaling $260,807.61; London, 2,231 loans,
totaling $43,675.17; Hamilton, 1,412 loans, totaling $17,468; Kingston,
207 loans, totaling $4,296.01; Windsor, 145 loans, totaling $5,837; Fort
William, 12 loans, totaling $308.34, making the grand totals of 12,497
loans, amounting to $331,882.12.

These advances of money have helped many a returned man out of
work, enabled some to get started in business, others to get in their winter's supply of coal, etc. The officials of the Commission state that the
loans are invariably paid back within a reasonable time, and that they
have had few cases where any trouble has been experienced in securing
refunds on the advances made.

The large number of crippled men who have obtained work through
the Soldiers' Aid Commission, would, if lined up, produce a long procession of railway crossing signal men, caretakers of large buildings, etc.

A department of the work carried on by the Commission and one about
which nothing is ever heard is that of arranging through Canadian banks
for the exchange of Canadian currency into American money for residents of the United States returning to their former homes after service
in the Canadian expeditionary force. Each of these men carries from
$100 to $1,500 with him. The Soldiers' Aid Commission provides each

of these homeward bound men with sufficient cash in American money to meet incidental expenses en route and the balance of their money on a draft, which they can get cashed at a bank in their home town. Thus the men going to their homes in the United States are assured a safe journey home with their cash.

Another quiet and unnoticed service which the Commission renders is in the matter of adjusting many domestic troubles in the homes of returning men. Indeed, in all respects the Soldiers' Aid Commission is the soldiers' friend, and when other helpers fail and comforts flee this help of the helpless is always ready to serve them.

B 14 CIRCULAR LETTER FROM THE ADJUTANT GENERAL TO DISTRICT OFFICERS COMMANDING THROUGHOUT CANADA
[*P.A.C., RG 24, v. 4376, file 2D. 34-7-61-1*]

Ottawa,
16 November 1915.

Enlistment of Mechanics,
Machinists, etc., CEF

I have the honour, by direction, to enclose herewith the names and addresses of all firms at the present time manufacturing munitions in your Command.

You are requested to keep in touch with these firms with a view to ascertaining whether they are in need of skilled labour in order that all such men offering their services will not be enlisted until it is ascertained whether they can be of use to these manufacturers.

It will be unnecessary to submit the names of these men to Headquarters if you keep in touch with these firms.

B 15 SIR SAM HUGHES TO COLONEL W.A. LOGIE
[*P.A.C., RG 24, v. 4318, file 2D. 34-1-81*]

Ottawa,
October 14th. 1915.

Personal

I am in receipt of your letter of the 1st. instant, stating that you have asked the Licensed Commissioners to close all bars at seven o'clock.

I shall be very much obliged if you will be so good as to submit all such matters as this to me before you issue them as official.

Thus far, I have managed the liquor question fairly well without running foul of the public, and I think you will agree with me that the progress of my plan has been great, so far.

There is just the possibility of riding ahead of public sentiment. Personally, I have never had any trouble with men over the excessive use of liquor. Of course, where we have weak Officers commanding Camps, Corps, or detachments, there is likely to be trouble.

I have thought the matter over, and must protest against the soldier being treated differently, before the law, than the Civilian. We must not forget that in ordinary life the soldiers are citizens and entitled to all the rights of citizenship. What I think would be well, and what I am endeavoring to carry out is that all bars should be closed to everyone, soldier and civilian, at eight o'clock.

I believe, also, that if Officers were jerked up a little forcibly for drinking, there would be less trouble with the men. It is further my belief that, among the men, there might be a system organized whereby they, themselves, would, very quickly, place the boozers where they belong. I well remember when I was a mere boy being in a tent at Camp where a couple of fellows insisted on intruding their booze ideas. I promptly went to the Captain of the company and told him that I would hold him responsible that these men did not annoy the occupants of the tent with their odour, their language and their filthiness. He refused to interfere and I promptly, although a mere boy, reported him to the Colonel, who, also, refused to interfere. I then promptly took the matter up with a Member of Parliament who saw the matter through. Meantime, I tried the plan of having the head of one of these fellows punched, one year. The whole action had a very salutory effect on the question of booze in camp.

There is altogether too much dependence placed upon the law, and not enough on restricting the men. Every man before enlisting should be made to state whether or not he is a boozer, and after he has been found to have falsified his record, he should be photographed and dismissed and the photograph sent around to other Units to prevent him unloading himself on them.

I shall not interfere meantime with your action regarding Armouries. I think it would be better, however, to forbid treating. I, also, think, that closing the bar at seven o'clock will do a lot of harm if it is not to include Civilians as well as the soldiers. It would have been much better to have had the authorities close the liquor places at eight o'clock to everyone.

B 16   MAJOR-GENERAL W. E. HODGINS TO
COLONEL W. A. LOGIE
[P.A.C., RG 24, v. 4318, file 2D. 34-1-81]

Ottawa,
19th January, 1916.

I have the honour, by direction, to state that the representative of the Committee of "100 Business men of Toronto" interested in the question of prohibition for the Province of Ontario, has requested the Minister for permission to visit the various Military quarters throughout the Province, in connection with the signing of a prohibition petition.

The Minister desires that all ranks should be given the privilege of exercising their rights as Citizens as to signing this petition or not, as they may desire but that there is to be no interference with troops inside the limits of military quarters, except with the permission of the Commanding Officer.

B 17   LETTER SENT TO MEN IN BRANT COUNTY
[*P.A.C., RG 24, v. 4376, file 2D. 34-7-61-1*]

Brantford,
20 January 1916

Your name, among others, has been handed in to us as a likely person to enlist.

The 125th Brant Battalion must be completed by February 20th. We would be delighted to secure your enlistment before that time. You are the stamp of man we are after, and we can assure you every man now in the ranks will be glad to welcome you.

This is a purely Brant County Battalion and as such should appeal to all Brant County men. There is sure to be a greater number of your personal friends in this Battalion than in any other. This reason alone should help you to decide.

If you have a good reason why you cannot enlist we would consider it a personal favour if you would sign the enclosed card and return it promptly to us, otherwise if we do not hear from you we will assume you are still undecided.

Your prompt attention to this very important matter which concerns the very existence of our Canadian Home and the British Empire will help us considerably in filling up the ranks of the 125th Brant Battalion and bring honour to the County of Brant.

B 18   WILLIAM SHEARER, SECRETARY, SPEAKERS' PATRIOTIC LEAGUE OF BROCKVILLE TO COLONEL T.D.R. HEMMING
[*P.A.C., RG 24, v. 4431, file 3D. 26-6-1*]

Brockville,
21st March, 1916

I beg to acknowledge receipt of your favor of yesterday inviting any suggestions for improvement of methods in this connection.

As Secretary of the Brockville Branch of the Eastern Ontario Speakers' Patriotic League the onus of supplying speakers at meetings and arranging details of programs has devolved to a great extent on His Honor Judge McDonald, President, and myself. We considered the methods adopted by us the best to meet local conditions here and as the results have proved even more successful than were anticipated, in paving the way for the men on recruiting duty, I shall take this opportunity to give you some detail regarding these meetings that may be of assistance to you elsewhere. No matter what improvements in methods are suggested and acted on with the best of motives, these – as in our own experience – will be adversely criticised by well-meaning but impossible people.

The free use of a Brockville theatre was offered to the 156th Battalion for recruiting purposes, on Sunday afternoons. (On a week-day evening this would cost $60.00) Lt.-Col. Wilkinson referred this offer to the writer. We favored accepting it, but before doing so our President, Judge McDonald, felt it due to the Ministerial Association to consult with them. Within that body there was diversity of opinion, and as an Association they decided to have nothing to do with it. We then decided to proceed, irrespective. Our first Sunday afternoon meeting was held Sunday, 16th January.

The first note of dissent was a letter published in the local papers under the signature of "John Derbyshire" (Baptist). His contention being that Sunday is a day set aside to worship Almighty God; he advocated that we should all truly repent and come to Him for help, reminding us that God was a light to the Israelites – caused the waters to be walled back for them, while closing them over the enemy, etc., etc.

His arguments being incontrovertible, we took no notice of his letter.

The next protest, was dated 14th February, and read as follows:

"At a meeting of the Sunday-School teachers of the Baptist Church, held February 13th, it was resolved that we, as teachers and officers of the First Baptist Church Sunday-School, protest against the holding of recruiting meetings on Sunday afternoons as we believe these meetings on The Lord's Day are contrary to our belief as to the proper observance of the Sabbath."

We took no notice of this protest, considering it a piece of impertinence to have sent this resolution direct to us, instead of through their minister, Rev. H. Edgar Allen. This gentleman explained afterwards to us that he was present when the resolution was passed, but as he did not agree with it they had sent it direct. There is therefore diversity of opinion amongst that persuasion – (recruiting addresses have been delivered in the Baptist Church, Cobourg.)

Protest No. 3 came to us in the shape of a delegation of three ministers from the Ministerial Association. They left with us a resolution, reading as follows, and each enlarged on it orally:

"*WHEREAS* the Brockville Ministerial Association, when approached by the Officers of the 156th Battalion and the Speakers' Enlistment League as to the advisability of arranging Sunday Recruiting Meetings resolved in view of the wide divergence of opinion among the members to express no opinion thereupon, and

"*WHEREAS* the Sunday Recruiting Meetings have now been held for several weeks, and

"*WHEREAS* certain features of the meetings have called forth considerable criticism from a large section of the public of the town and district, and

"*WHEREAS* the Brockville Ministerial Association finds itself unanimously in agreement with certain of these criticisms.

"*THEREFORE* the Association begs to urge upon the Speakers' Enlistment League and the Officers in the 156th Battalion that the following changes in the conduct of the meetings be made, being convinced that such changes would materially increase the value of the meetings themselves: –

"(1) That all children under sixteen be rigidly excluded and that this be done not as heretofore by an ineffective advertisement saying that they were not wanted, but by a guard at the door who shall prevent the entrance of any such to the meeting.

"(2) That the doors be not opened until 4 o'clock at the earliest, and that the meeting be dismissed by 5.15 p.m. at the latest.

"(3) That the Moving Pictures and Songs be either discontinued altogether, or at the least be so advanced in dignity and tone as to be worthy of the high patriotic purpose for which the meeting is called, and that nothing in the nature of mere entertainment be introduced to mar the sacredness of the Lord's Day."

We received the delegation courteously as the three ministers comprising it had had the courage of their convictions and had addressed our Sunday gatherings. All protests apparently originated from the same source, and the Ministerial Association a last channel of communication.

We had invited every clergyman in town to address the meetings. Those who did so were:

Rev. J. Edgar Allen (Baptist) Rev. C.W. Shelley (Presbyterian) Rev. W.S. Jamieson, (Methodist), Rev. F. Dealtry Woodcock, (Anglican) Canon H.H. Bedford-Jones, (Anglican).

The other three of the Ministerial Association who did not address the meetings were:

Rev. S.S. Burns, (Presbyterian), Rev. A.E. Runnells, (Methodist) Rev. L.E. Davis, (Anglican).

And after eight of these meetings had been successfully held to capacity houses of over 1200 people, and when the strength of the 156th Battalion had reached over 800 men they come to us with a resolution suggesting improvements! They say, "Owing to considerable criticism." (Unless from themselves and the other protestors named, we have had nothing but words of commendation from the public and press.) They ask, "That the moving pictures be discontinued altogether." (We pay $8.00 for a special reel for each meeting that will be appropriate for Sunday – of an educative or patriotic character. The ministers could not specifically name any objectionable reel that had been shown; we declined to omit the moving pictures.) They ask, "That songs be either discontinued altogether, or at least be advanced in dignity and tone." (We have had the very best musical talent in Brockville – soloists from church choirs, soldiers in khaki with voices equal to any of them; we asked them to name specifically any selection that had proved objectionable. One minister replied – "Nothing in any of them he could call objectionable – only light and trivial" – naming choruses one Sunday by boy scouts as more suitable to a Sunday-School entertainment than to an audience that should expect music of a higher class. The writer asked if their selections "Men of Harlech," or "The Red, White and Blue," were undignified. The same minister responded that he had only repeated what had been said to him by friends who had been there.) We took no further notice of this protest than the conversation with these delegates.

Now, as to the meetings:

We open the doors at 3 p.m., but as early as 2.30 p.m. people begin to come.

The 156th Battalion Band play until 3.30.

The moving picture is put on, occupying 15 to 20 minutes.

The Chairman opens, calling for a vocal selection.

Shortly after 4 p.m. addresses begin. (This is for the benefit of teachers in Sunday-School work, and members of Bible Classes.)

We endeavor and have succeeded, unless on one occasion, in closing at 5.15 to 5.20 p.m. On the occasion referred to we closed at 5.35 p.m. (This gives ample time for those attending to return home for tea and get to the church evening services.)

(And the people we were most considerate about have proved to be the only objectors – the "unco guid."

Speakers at these Sunday meetings have been such as: Hon. Dr. W.J. Roche, Minister of the Interior; H.H. Stevens, M.P., Vancouver; John Webster, M.P.; A.E. Donovan, M.P.P.; Capt. S.J. Robins, Paymaster 207th Battalion; R.H. Greer, C.C.A., Toronto; and Brockville business men: H.A. Stewart, K.C.; J.A. Hutcheson, K.C.; W.A. Lewis, Solicitor; A.C. Hardy; W.G. McClellan; T.J. Storey, etc.

Officers and men of the 156th Battalion: Lt.-Col. Bedell; Lt.-Col. Wilkinson; Capt. T.A. Kidd; Capt. R.J. Gill; Lieut. Long; Sergt. E.A. Stewart; Pte. N.R. Holmes; Pte. J.L. Kenville; Pte. J.T. McCracken; Bugler, Hector MacLean.

We had also Right Rev. E.J. Bidwell, Bishop-Coadjutor, Kingston.

Each speaker knows that our purpose is to stimulate the patriotic spirit in families and in that way indirectly aid recruiting. We leave the speaker to express himself in his own language. We do not prompt or suggest what a speaker should say.

Regarding the selection of songs, we do not ask the singers to rehearse them to us. Each is asked to select one of a patriotic or sacred nature or if "Mother" is extolled we let the selection pass ...

B 19 LETTER SENT BY MAJOR E.E. SNIDER TO ALL CLERGYMEN IN NORTHUMBERLAND COUNTY
[P.A.C., RG 24, v. 4424, file 3D. 26-5-64-2]

The Armouries,
Cobourg, Ont.
Dec. 30, 1915

In view of the imperative needs of the empire, I venture to ask you to make use of the influence you possess on behalf of the cause for which we are fighting to-day. The clergy of the Methodist Church in this district have been instructed by their chairman to preach recruiting sermons on Sunday, the ninth of January, 1916. May I ask you to seriously consider the advisability of pursuing a like course. The great and crying need at the present time, as Lord Kitchener has said is men, more men, and yet more men. There are probably many young men yet left in your congregation who would respond to a personal appeal from you – whose minds have for some time been considering this great opportunity of taking part in this the greatest struggle that Liberty has ever made in the history of the progress of the world. It is a grand thing to have – the right to be in the work that is convulsing the world this day – and the cause of Christianity, which is bound up in the issue of this war gives you substantial reason for laying before the men of your congregation this great need and to definitely ask for recruits for overseas service.

May I ask you therefore, sir, to preach a sermon on Sunday, the ninth of January, setting forth the needs of the country, and the duty and glorious opportunity now coming to all our men of military age.

B 20 COLUMN ON RECRUITING SLOGANS
[Kingston Daily British Whig, 14 July 1916, p. 9]

The great war is responsible for many illustrations of cleverness and evidence of genius. Especially is this seen in the appeals being made for recruiting and enlistment. Not a few of them are models of terseness and directness, making their appeal instantaneously and in a sentence. Alliteration is a favourite form of expression for these clever phrase-makers.

It has been an interesting pastime to collect a column of samples, which may have a suggestive value in other places.

Toronto affords lots of material in this regard, where recruiting advertising has taken on many forms, not only by posters and streamers, but in newspapers, on streetcars, and by many other means. One reads on a blotter: "Young business men of Toronto, quit your pen and give them the bayonet. We can't win this war with ink. Get your chum and enlist in the company for business men of the 170th Battalion."

The street corner speaker in khaki is, as a rule, buttressed by striking placards borne aloft by sturdy volunteers in the King's uniform. The streetcars carry large cotton streamers their full length, calling upon recruits to "Join the Buffs and Hunt the Huns." Another battalion advertises:

Everybody's War!
Everybody's Battalion!
Everybody's Deal!

It was a satirical artist who wrote the following advertisement in one of the city dailies: "For rifles apply at the Orderly Room. For wool, to the Women's Patriotic League."

When in the County of Simcoe recently, I found that the recruiting appeals were most effective and direct. The newspaper advertisements carried such messages as these:

"The women of Simcoe County must help to win the war."

"Every woman knows in her heart that the place of every real man is at the front."

"Every woman can influence at least one man to do his duty."

The recruiting stations also carried some striking posters such as:

"Canada needs you now."

"Let your service be voluntary."

"Will you don khaki today?"

"All the hopes and expectations in the world will not put one German out of business."

"Young man! Is it worth while getting into the greatest game on earth?"

In another town there was a different set of striking bills and these carried such searching items as:

"Oh, Canada: we stand on guard for thee. How about being a guard?"

"Loyal talk alone won't beat Kaiser, Krupp, or Kultur. Trained men will. Enlist now."

The lettering under the figure of a Canadian soldier read: "Let us be as proud of you as you are of him."

Yet another striking example read: "If you were a German you would be fighting for the Kaiser. What are you doing for the King?"

"Thousands have answered the nation's call. You may be the one to turn the scale at the critical moment. Do you realize this?"

A happy idea was struck in Guelph where, underneath the four faces of the city clock at the head of the Square, the timely words stand out with startling effect:

"It's time to enlist."

while a streetcar carried a banner with the crisp device:

"You said you'd enlist when needed; you're needed now."

B 21   COLONEL T.D.R. HEMMING TO THE
SECRETARY, MILITIA COUNCIL
[*P.A.C., RG 24, v. 4331, file 3D. 26-6-1*]

Kingston,
25th March, 1916

Having reference to H.Q. telegram of the 14th instant, relative to the marginally noted subject, I have the honour to state for the information of the Minister in Militia Council that I have been in communication with all the Secretaries of the Speakers Patriotic League in this Division, and am in receipt of replies from practically all of them.

The suggestions set forth all seem to be confined to one general consensus of opinion and that is that compulsory enlistment, if not entirely necessary at present, will, in a short time, be so under present conditions, and all without exception advocate a system of National Registration.

The general idea is for a compulsory drafting from eligible males so registered, and it is pointed out that thousands of young men, who are possibly unapproachable because of their environment or locality, could if registration obtained, be approached, as such registration would make available complete lists of men who should be canvassed.

Further such registration would act as a definite hint to the shirker, and it is considered would put the Nation in a more dignified and resolute attitude towards the war.

So long as the Government adopt a policy which permits the citizens to consider themselves free to maintain any attitude they choose, so long will such citizens consider that the war does not vitally concern them, and a consequent issue is that recruits are not forthcoming with the spontaneous spirit which should obtain.

Meetings, concerts, band recitals, etcetera, have been widely held and little territory wherein the eligible male is to be found has been missed, but an ignorance of true conditions of affairs makes recruiting in certain sections extremely dull.

I, therefore, have the honour to suggest that a system of National Registration go into effect as soon as possible, to be followed by compulsory drafting from such of these males so registered, who are eligible in their various grades for Overseas Service.

B 22   THE HAMILTON MEMORIAL AND
'EXPLANATION'
[*Printed in* The Recruiting League of Hamilton, *Prepared by
J.H. Collinson and Mrs Bertie Smith. Copy P.A.C. Library*]

THE MEMORIAL.
"To the Right Hon. Sir Robert Laird Borden, *P.C., G.C.M.G., K.C.,*

LL.D., Premier of the Dominion of Canada. The Memorial of the Hamilton Recruiting League Respectfully Sheweth:

"That the Dominion of Canada is engaged in a war involving the very existence of British institutions – a war that calls for the most rigid economy of men and means – a war that can be successfully concluded only by the fullest utilization of all our resources.

"That under the present voluntary system there is great waste of the Nation's resources.

"Therefore your Memorialists pray that a Commission be appointed for the purpose of:

"Taking a census of all men in the Dominion from eighteen years of age and upward, specifying those married and unmarried.

"Classifying the men according to their occupations or their fitness or preference for certain kinds of work.

"Classifying the industries with a view to the restriction or the ultimate elimination of such as are non-essential to the welfare of the country or are not economic factors.

"It being understood that the foregoing is urged with a view to the immediate application of some just and comprehensive system of draft, whereby the men necessary to complete the Canadian Expeditionary Forces may be readily secured.

"And your Memorialists will ever pray.

"Dated this Eleventh day of April, One Thousand Nine Hundred and Sixteen.

"Signed on behalf of the Hamilton Recruiting League.

"ARTHUR F. HATCH, President.
"A. W. KAYE, Secretary."

THE EXPLANATION.

The Hamilton Recruiting League has been a very active agency in the enlistment of soldiers. It may fairly claim a share of the credit that is due to Hamilton for her splendid contribution to the forces of the Empire.

From its intimate knowledge of the workings of the voluntary system, the League has reached the conclusion that for Canada to continue its present methods would be highly detrimental to the welfare of the country.

Canada has without doubt attracted to the colours a very superior class of men, who are actuated by the noblest principles of patriotism and duty.

Very many of these have left positions of great importance, for which competent men cannot be found.

Almost every industry and family is suffering unnecessary loss through the present haphazard method of enlistment.

The first class of men who should be called upon for service is the unmarried fit men who could be released from their occupations without serious loss to anyone.

Probably this class would suffice to complete the forces which Canada is pledged to supply.

The country could thus fulfil its obligations without serious loss of revenue, or serious disturbance of its internal economy.

A system of wise Selection should appeal strongly to every loyal member of the community. It is not contrary to the spirit of true Liberty, for which the Empire is fighting. That liberty for which a man will not fight is not deserving of the name. No man is free from the duty of defending the State.

It is not suggested that the proposed system of Selection should be permanent. Extraordinary need justifies extraordinary measures.

It is hoped that all who are in sympathy with the above Memorial will exert their utmost influence to further its objects.

B 23 EDITORIAL, 'NO MORE CANADIANS FOR
OVERSEAS SERVICE. THIS YOUNG DOMINION
HAS SACRIFICED ENOUGH'
[Sault Express, *23 June 1916. Copy in P.A.C., RG 6, E1, Secretary of State: Chief Press Censor, v. 68, file CPC 207-12*]

The Express in its limited sphere has been advocating peace among the warring nations of Europe, but save in the undercurrent of Canadian sentiment which we know exists in the heart of many of our people there appears to be no desire for a termination of hostilities until the Germanic power in Europe has been utterly destroyed and many of the old world wrongs have been made right. We fear that if Canada is to continue to shed her life blood until that day arrives there will not be many Canadians remaining to celebrate the conquest, and the high purposes for which our forefathers on this continent strove will all have been in vain. And more than that, we have grave fears that if this horrible conflict goes on for another two years we shall not have our United Empire to cheer for. These words are spoken in the fullest consciousness of their meaning. The destruction of the Teutonic race is quite as impossible as the destruction of the Anglo-Saxon race, and the destruction of either would be nothing short of a catastrophe handed down to posterity as an example of our present day higher civilization. What our Empire needs right now and what Canada needs right now is PEACE. But we have drifted away from what we started out to say, which was that this Dominion should not send any more of her sons overseas to engage in this frightful cataclysm. The truth is that there has already been too much Canadian bloodletting and the cost of British connection has been away and beyond what our people counted on. We have less than eight millions of population as against three hundred millions in India. If, as we are told, the shedding of blood overseas is the silicon which binds the steel of Empire, then why does England not draw upon her three hundred millions in India as she has drawn upon her seven millions in Canada?

"The Canadian troops made a most gallant stand;" "the soldiers from

Canada well upheld the traditions of the race;" "thousands of our brave Canadian soldiers fell with honour," "we can never forget the heroism of those grand Canadians." That kind of salve from London does not bind up the hearts of the thousands of Canadian mothers and sisters whose loved ones sleep in a foreign land after dying for a foreign cause.

It is about time for Canadians to wake up and realize that they are living in America and not Europe; that old world empires rise and fall; that we are the last great land to the west on this great planet and that the Lord has so ordained; that our neighbors and we are of the same faith, our language is the same and there is a comity of blood existing between us which makes us brothers in the truest human sense. A century of peace exemplifies the silicon in the steel.

Canada will contribute more to the future greatness of the Anglo-Saxon race by pursuing her own ideals and minding her own business on this side of the Atlantic than by sending "her last son and her last dollar" across the water in a futile effort to adjust the wrongs which most of our ancestors left the old world to escape.

Read what J.L. Garvin, the Editor of the London Observer, has to say and then ask yourself the question, "Has Canada not gone far enough along the line of human sacrifice?" Mr. Garvin says:

"The whole Empire congratulates Canada upon this determined example of how to settle accounts with the Boches. There is, however, another moral. Canadians have been called on for months to take more than their share of this deadly ground, which, so far from possessing a military value, is for us a military disadvantage.

It has been held for reasons of feeling, but these ought not to be weighed anew against the lives of men. The situation is quite different from what exists on the Verdon salient where a German advance has a certain amount of real military value, for ultimate defensive purposes. To be driven out of the Ypres salient is one thing, and a bad thing. To choose whether of our own will we should hold or relinquish positions which on their merits no soldier would occupy is quite another thing. Canadians are winning imperishable fame at a grievous loss and have done more than enough for the sake of honor in front of Ypres."

B 24 THE REVEREND W.M. ROCHESTER, GENERAL SECRETARY OF THE LORD'S DAY ALLIANCE, TO MAJOR-GENERAL W.A. LOGIE
[P.A.C., RG 24, v. 4303, file 2D. 34-1-59]

Toronto,
October 17th, 1916.

The representatives of all the religious denominations, including the Roman Catholic, have been in conference upon the use of the moving-picture theatre for recruiting. It was the unanimous opinion that many features of these meetings, last winter, were most objectionable, and that the results to recruiting did not justify the method.

The officers of the Military representing recruiting with whom we conferred differed from our view as to the success of these meetings and stated that it was their purpose to again hold them. In this matter we defer to the judgment of the Military, having no wish to interfere with any method which, in their view, will accomplish the object. We, however, insisted that certain conditions should, this season, be observed and have so represented to the Premier and Provincial Treasurer:

First. That only applications from the military authorities be entertained by the Provincial Treasurer.

Second. That these permits be strictly limited to recruiting and that applications for the purpose of raising money for philanthropic purposes be not entertained.

In the first case we wish to defeat any sinister purpose of the moving-picture men, or of any other promoters of amusement, to encroach upon our day, and we believe we are justified in insisting upon the second provision because such methods of raising money are unworthy and are not necessary, in view of the generous response made by the public. They afford, too, the opportunity for the self-seeking to promote their own ends. They likewise alienate the constituency that support our philanthropies, and by the opening of our Day of Rest to amusement entail a heritage upon future generations from which they will be unable to free themselves.

Representing, as we believe, the best and most loyal of the people of the land, who have hesitated at no sacrifice at the present time in meeting the demands of the war, we would respectfully solicit your earnest cooperation with us for the recognition of these conditions as specified above.

B 25 'TOYLAND AND HOW IT HAS BEEN AFFECTED
BY THE WAR'
[*Article in the Kingston* Daily British Whig, *16 December 1916, p. 19*]

Toyland is another colony which Germany has lost as a result of the war. It has fallen into the hands of the Allies and of neutral countries which are peopling it with china, wooden and metal dolls and animals of their own creation. The new inhabitants of this land, which is the Mecca of childhood, are, perhaps, not as complex, not as finished and not as attractive as those made in Germany, but they are very pleasing to the young eyes which, after all, are not so critical or so exacting.

The "immigrants" arriving in Toyland come from Canada, the States and Japan. The Jap promises to take the place of the German as a maker of toys. Already he is showing much enterprise and ingenuity along this line ...

In touring through Toyland one rarely sees the beautiful doll, with the real hair and eyelashes, the speaking eyes and the lifelike expression. That, of course, has practically become extinct. The doll aristocrats, with refinement and individuality stamped all over them, are no more. But Toyland is not doll-less by any means. It still has its little china ladies which, while not as handsome as their German sisters of biscuit china, are very pretty in their way, besides being much more serviceable. The German doll was a "Airy Fairy Lillian," dainty and delicate, and could only be played with on state occasions. The doll of today, however, belongs to the rompier class, being more robust if less beautiful, and can, therefore, be a more constant companion of its happy young mother. The china doll comes largely from the United States, although some are made in Canada and in Japan. Character dolls are manufactured in Toronto, and they are very quaint in their different costumes.

Dolls can still be had to suit all pocketbooks although naturally there has been some advance in price. To get anything approaching a German doll, which before the war sold at from 35 cents to 50 cents, one must now pay $1 or more. A rag doll with a celluloid face can be bought for fifteen cents, and when all "fixed up" it's a winsome little lassie. If your hens are laying and you have suddenly become a millionaire and desire to get something out of the ordinary in the doll line, you can procure a character doll for only $4 ...

The Other Toys

Many other things usually associated with Santa's wonderful pack may also be found in the toy stores of Kingston. The mechanical toys, however, are not so numerous or so marvellous in construction as they were in the days when Germany held undisputed possession of Toyland. But there are various other kinds of toys, and for these the prices are practically unchanged from those which prevailed before the war, that grim booster of prices. As yet the majority of toys come from Japan, and are mostly of wood, simple in construction and thoroughly Japanese in design. Japan, however, is beginning to use metal in the making of toys, and is starting to turn out the mechanical variety. The martial idea is carried out in many of the Japanese toys. One Kingston store is showing among the toys from Japan several wooden rifles with fixed bayonets, and no doubt many of Kingston's little soldiers will kill countless numbers of imaginary Huns ...

Toy-making in Canada is still in its infancy, but in time it will undoubtedly become a flourishing industry. Many clever games are being turned out, and some creditable toys, although the mechanical toy has not yet been evolved to any noticeable extent.

Rocking horses, carts, sleighs, and Kiddie Kars are Canadian-made, and as perfect as the German goods ever were. Tiny desks, chairs and tables, dolls' beds are awaiting Santa Claus' purchase. Doll carriages, however, will have to be a special treat for exceptionally good little girls as the cost of their manufacture is still high.

Educate The Boy

For the boys, educational toys are in great demand, and consequently in great abundance. Such a toy as the "Erector" for building purposes, is Canadian made. This toy is to meet the needs of the growing boy ...

It is the electrical toys that are the treasure trove of the mechanical toy industry, for they educate while they amuse. Such toys as the "Erector Electrical Sets" are not merely "wonders" for the boy to gaze at, they bring into play his creative powers, and it is only after he has, by his own hands, created mystery of the great force, electricity ...

In the United States, toy-making has reached greater proficiency, but, the high prices asked, coupled with the customs duties, make it practically impossible for Canadian dealers to handle American toys.

B 26 SECTION 11 OF THE MILITARY SERVICE ACT
[7–8 George V, Chap. 19]

(1) ... An application may be made ... to a local tribunal ... for a certificate of exemption on any of the following grounds:

(a) That it is expedient in the national interest that the man should, instead of being employed in military service, be engaged in other work in which he is habitually engaged;

(b) That it is expedient in the national interest that the man should, instead of being employed in military service, be engaged in other work in which he wishes to be engaged and for which he has special qualifications;

(c) That it is expedient in the national interest that, instead of being employed in military service, he should continue to be educated or trained for any work for which he is then being educated or trained;

(d) That serious hardship would ensue, if the man were placed on active service, owing to his exceptional financial or business obligations or domestic position;

(e) Ill health or infirmity;

(f) That he conscientiously objects to the undertaking of combatant service and is prohibited from so doing by the tenets and articles of faith, in effect on the sixth day of July, 1917, of any organized religious denomination existing and well recognized in Canada at such date, and to which he in good faith belongs.

B 27 AFFIDAVIT SIGNED BY MEMBERS OF THE INTERNATIONAL BIBLE STUDENTS ASSOCIATION
[P.A.C., RG 24, v. 843, file HQ 54-21-10-21]

AFFIDAVIT

Province of Ontario

Dominion of Canada.

I,

being duly sworn, upon my oath state: That I am a male citizen of Canada, and am   years of age; that I reside at   ; that I am averse to bearing arms or rendering personal military service under the conditions as prescribed by "AN ACT RESPECTING THE MILITIA AND DEFENCE OF CANADA," R.S.C. (1906) chapter 41, section 11, and I make this affidavit, as provided by Section 12, subsection 2 of said Act for the purpose of obtaining exemption from liability to service in the Militia, and the facts upon which I rest my claim for such exemption are as follows, to wit:

I am a Christian and the religious doctrines which I believe and hold preclude me from bearing arms or rendering military service; I am a member of the International Bible Students Association, a religious Association organized under the laws of Great Britain, with its chief office at No. 34 Craven Terrace, Paddington, London, England, and also with offices at No. 124 Columbia Heights, Brooklyn, N.Y., U.S.A., and which has classes or congregations throughout the Dominion of Canada; I subscribe to and am in harmony with the religious doctrines taught by said International Bible Students Association, which are, to wit, that all members thereof avow a full consecration of will, heart and life to God's service—as footstep followers of the Lord Jesus Christ and the doctrines and teachings concerning His Kingdom of Peace and good will; I am obligated by my conscience and by engagements with said Bible Students Association to "follow peace with all men," and to do violence or injury to none; that such is in harmony with the teachings of the Master, Christ Jesus, that His followers practice non-resistance; that the requirements of the International Bible Students Association are that its members be obedient to the "powers that be" in so far as their laws and requirements do not conflict with the teachings of Jesus Christ; that the provisions of said THE MILITIA ACT R.S.C. (1906) CHAPTER 41, are in conflict with the teachings of the Lord Jesus Christ, as I understand and believe the same.

Dated at Toronto this 6th day of March 1916
Subscribed and sworn to before me, a
Justice of the Peace within and for
City of Toronto and County of York
this 6 day of March A.D. 1916

Justice of the Peace.

B 28 MR. JUSTICE LYMAN P. DUFF'S DECISION ON
THE STATUS OF THE INTERNATIONAL BIBLE
STUDENTS ASSOCIATION UNDER THE
MILITARY SERVICE ACT
[P.A.C., RG 14, Records of Parliament, D2, v. 36, Sessional
Paper 97 of 1918]

The Central Appeal Judge: The applicant claims exemption as a member of the "International Bible Students Association" on the ground that in the language of Section 11 (1) (f) "he conscientiously objects to the undertaking of combatant service and is prohibited from so doing by the tenets and articles of faith, in effect on the sixth day of July, 1917, of any organized religious denomination existing and well recognized in Canada at such date, and to which he in good faith belongs."

There is an unlimited company known as the "International Bible Students Association" incorporated under the Companies Acts of 1908 and 1913 (United Kingdom) ...

The Company as appears from the evidence, issues publications, in which certain views are advocated touching the interpretation of the Bible, and certain religious beliefs advanced and supported; and of the subscribers to these publications, who accept the doctrine so expounded, there are in various countries, including Canada, groups who meet for the study of the Bible and the discussion of questions of theology and ethics.

These groups are not associated by any bond other than their adherence to, and advocacy of, these views and beliefs, but are among themselves collectively known by the same designation as that given to the Company.

These writings, as far as I have examined them, leave some doubt whether according to the beliefs advocated by the writers of them, a member of the Association might conscientiously under the compulsion of legal necessity, engage in combatant military service. I do not, I must admit, find them entirely self-consistent.

It is not necessary, however, to form any opinion upon the exact nature of the doctrine, as touching the subject of non-resistance and kindred subjects advocated in these writings.

The evidence before me does not justify the conclusion that these groups or associations so-called, either individually or collectively come within the description – "organized religious denomination existing and well recognized in Canada" within the contemplation of the Military Service Act.

First: – There is much room for doubt whether these associations so called have for the primary object a common worship, which is, I think, an essential characteristic of a "religious denomination" within the meaning of Section 11. The evidence is certainly consistent with the view that the primary objects of them in so far as they can be said to have a common object, are those expressed in the passage quoted above from the memorandum of association, which in themselves are certainly not sufficient to constitute even an organized body clearly proved to be pursuing them in common, a "religious denomination."

Second: The Statute plainly implies as a characteristic of religious denominations, falling within its scope, that there should be conditions of membership, compliance or non-compliance with which can be ascertained by reference to some practical criterion, and of such conditions there is, although I pressed for it on hearing, no evidence, and there are no indicia to serve as reliable guides for the Tribunals.

The appeal is dismissed.

B 29 Major-General F.L. Lessard, Inspector General, Eastern Canada, to the Secretary, Militia Council
[*P.A.C., RG 24, v. 4323, file 2D. 34-1-122*]

Toronto, Ont. 4th Jan. 1917.

I have the honour to report that the conduct of the men returned from active service, particularly in this City of Toronto, is not what it ought to be.

1. Men are daily seen in the streets of Toronto, improperly dressed.
2. Others have been seen selling Xmas cards and other things while in uniform.
3. The demeanour of some of these men on the whole is disgraceful and is giving a bad example to young soldiers who think that by imitating them they are doing the right thing.

B 30 Major R.S. Wilson to Colonel S.C. Mewburn
[*P.A.C., RG 24, v. 4323, file 2D. 34-1-122*]

Toronto, Jan. 16th, 1917

When the returned soldiers arrive at Toronto they are taken to The Spadina Military Hospital by a reception committee and several addresses are made to them by high city officials and others, filling their heads with all sorts of nonsense so they are off to a bad start.

When the reception is over they are registered and then given seven days leave to visit their homes. On their return to the hospital they come under my command for training and discipline.

Standing Orders issued by me on taking over the command on November 1st, '16 are read to them on their first parade. I enclose you copy of that portion of these orders which refers to dress and behavior while on the street. These orders are read to the men once a week so they are fully aware of what is expected of them, and if they disobey these orders they know they are subject to discipline. An orderly Sergeant is detailed for duty each day at the main entrance to see that every man going out is properly dressed before leaving.

One particular difficulty is to get them to keep their coats buttoned at the top. I am convinced that the reason for this is that most of the men wear returned soldiers' buttons on the left pocket of their tunics, and leave their great coats open in order that these may be seen.

Men on being discharged are supplied with a clothing allowance of $13 in winter and $8 in summer for the purpose of buying civilian clothes, but at the same time they are also allowed to keep their uniforms. I believe many of these men do not use the money for that purpose and still remain in uniform. These men I have no control over and they should be rounded up by the Provo. Marshal. I am quite convinced that these are the men that have been guilty of selling postcards while in uniform.

Many complaints have reached me as to the discipline of returned soldiers while on the street but no definite case has been laid before me.

To my mind, one of the most effective ways of putting an end to this trouble would be for the officers at Exhibition Camp to co-operate with me by stopping any returned soldier who should pass them on the street improperly dressed or any soldier who does not pay the proper compliment. If I could secure his name, number and regiment, it would be of great assistance to me and also to the Service.

I think, Sir, that this is the only way at the present time that this difficulty can be dealt with.

B 31   EXTRACT FROM STANDING ORDERS, 'D' UNIT, MILITARY HOSPITALS COMMISSION COMMAND
[P.A.C., RG 24, v. 4323, file 2D. 34-1-122]

Dress
N.C.O.s and men must at all times be properly dressed and especially when they are walking out. Their buttons and brass must be clean and particular attention must be paid to keeping their great coats buttoned.

There is no reason why because a man has returned from Overseas he should be slovenly and untidy. The fact is he should set an example to all men preparing to proceed Overseas.
Saluting
Particular pains must be taken to salute in a proper manner all officers when passing them on the street.

B 32   OBJECTS OF THE CANADIAN ASSOCIATION OF RETURNED SOLDIERS, OTTAWA DISTRICT
[P.A.C., RG 24, v. 56, file HQ 649-1-69]

1. To perpetuate the close and kindly ties of mutual service in the Great War, and the recollections and associations of that experience, and to maintain proper standards of dignity and honour amongst all returned soldiers.
2. To preserve the memory and records of those who suffered and died for the nation; to see to the erection of monuments to their valor and the establishment of an Annual Memorial Day.
3. To ensure that provision is made for due care of the sick wounded and needy among those who have served including reasonable pensions, employment for such as are capable, soldiers homes, medical care and proper provision for dependent families of enlisted men.
4. To constantly inculcate loyalty to Canada and the Empire and unstinted service in their interests.

B 33 DR. EUGÈNE FISET, DEPUTY MINISTER OF
MILITIA AND DEFENCE, TO THOMAS MULVEY,
THE UNDERSECRETARY OF STATE
[*P.A.C., RG 24, v. 56, file HQ 649-1-69*]

OTTAWA   22nd January, 1917.

In reply to your communication of the 19th instant, I have the honour
to state that it is considered inadvisable that such proposed incorporation
should be permitted.

In doing so, I may state that there does not appear to be any necessity
for such an Association, as already several authorized bodies are laboring
in the interests of the men who have served in the war, in addition to the
provision which the Dominion Authorities have made for those men and
their dependents. Moreover, the proposed Association seems objectionable, in that it appears to have been set on foot in a spirit of dissatisfac-
tion with what those Authorities and the Provincial Authorities have done
and purpose doing on the subject of disabled soldiers.

The proposed Association is designated "The Canadian Association
of Returned Soldiers, Ottawa District", thus styling itself "Canadian"
while limiting its scope to the Ottawa District. If such an Association is
needed at all, it should not be limited to the Ottawa District, nor yet to
the Province of Ontario, as is proposed. It should be Dominion-wide in
its scope, and, if incorporation is essential to its usefulness, it should be
incorporated under the Dominion law, and not under the law of any one
Province.

Further, it is not desirable that the Act of incorporation, whether Provincial or Dominion, should permit the Association to deal with such objects as "reasonable pensions", "soldiers' homes", etc., which are provided by the Government at the public expense – matters which should
not in any way be interfered with by Associations or officials other than
those appointed and controlled by the Government. Moreover, in the
public interest, and in the interest of discipline, it is desirable that, from
the membership of the Association, if incorporated, there should be excluded all persons who belong to the Overseas Force, or to the Permanent
Militia Staff, or to the Permanent Force, or are otherwise in the employment of the Dominion Government.

In view of the foregoing facts, it is considered advisable that such Association should not be given incorporation, and that, at all events, the incorporation, if granted, should be limited in the way suggested in the
foregoing paragraphs.

B 34 THE HONOURABLE CHARLES J. DOHERTY,
MINISTER OF JUSTICE, TO DR. EUGÈNE FISET
[*P.A.C., RG 24, v. 56, file HQ 649-1-69*]

Ottawa, January 26, 1917.

I have your note of the 25th instant, enclosing a file of your depart-

ment relative to an application which has been made for an incorporation of a Company under the name of "The Canadian Association of
Returned Soldiers, Ottawa District", and asking for my views on the
matter.

In reply I beg to say that it does not seem to me that the Government
would be justified in taking steps to interfere with the liberty of returned
soldiers to form an Association such as that contemplated. The purposes
appear to me to be lawful and the reasons advanced in support of action
restricting the formation of such associations do not seem to me to justify
the conclusions reached.

B 35   MEMORANDUM RE LAND SETTLEMENT AND OPPORTUNITIES FOR RETURNED SOLDIERS IN THE PROVINCE OF ONTARIO
[P.A.O., RG 3, Hearst Papers, Box 7. File entitled "War – Employment and Settlement of Returned Soldiers"]

The Province of Ontario is prepared to extend to all soldiers who have
served in the British forces an opportunity of acquiring homes for themselves upon the land in this Province, under the following terms: –

1. All soldiers who wish to go upon the land, and are desirous of obtaining some practical instruction in farming, and learning something of
the conditions in Northern Ontario, will be sent to an agricultural training depot now being established on the Government Experimental Farm
at Monteith.

2. At this depot they will be provided with comfortable living accommodation and board during their period of instruction.

3. The institution will be under the direction of competent men who
have a practical knowledge of agricultural methods, and particularly the
conditions and needs in Northern Ontario.

4. As soon as a sufficient number of men have accumulated at the
institution, whom the superintendent is satisfied know sufficient of farming requirements to enable them to succeed as settlers, a farm colony will
be established along the line of railway, to which these men will be moved.

5. The colony will be in charge of a competent superintendent, under
whom the men will proceed to do whatever clearing may be necessary,
erect the necessary buildings, and do such other work as may be essential
to the establishment of a central community. The men will be housed and
cared for in the central community, and their labours will be directed to
clearing and preparing for cultivation the lands of the colony.

6. Farms containing not more than 80 acres will be laid out in such
manner as to bring the different farm houses as close together as possible.
The work of the men will be directed to clearing on the front of each
farm an area of 10 acres.

7. As soon as a soldier desires to go upon a farm and work for himself, an 80 acre lot with a 10 acre clearing will be allotted to him. He will
be supplied with the necessary machinery and tools, and such cattle, pigs,

poultry, etc., as competent authority may determine, up to the value of $500.00.

8. The 80 acres, with 10 acres of clearing, will be given the settler free of charge.

9. For each day's work that is done from the time he enters the training school at Monteith until he goes upon his clearing, he will be paid a reasonable wage.

10. An advance up to $500.00 will be made to cover the cost of stock, implements, equipment, and any assistance in building that may be given, for which a lien will be taken against the settler's holding and chattels.

11. The lien will be repayable in 20 years, at 6%, but no payment on account of either principal or interest shall be required until after the expiration of three years.

12. At the expiration of five years from the settler locating upon his land, and upon the due performance of certain conditions in the meantime, he will be entitled to receive a patent from the Crown.

13. The community system will apply with regard to the supplying of horses and other stock and implements.

14. An ample supply of these will be kept at headquarters, for the use of the settlers, upon generous terms.

15. The co-operative method will obtain in the carrying out of the work in connection with the colony.

16. The social side of life at the colony will be provided for, and ample provision will be made to make life enjoyable and comfortable at headquarters. A proper public building, where both religious and secular gatherings may be held, will be provided. A school house and educational facilities will be provided.

17. Buying and selling will be done upon a co-operative basis, and every assistance possible will be rendered to hasten the day when the soldier may be established upon a prosperous and independent footing.

18. Provision will be made at as early a date as possible for married men to have their families with them, and to the fullest extent practical returned soldiers with experience will be employed to direct the affairs of the colony.

19. Soldiers who may desire to go into fruit farming and chicken raising, or other like agricultural pursuits, will be given free instructions at the public institutions of the Province.

Maps and descriptive pamphlets are attached hereto.

Toronto, February 6th, 1917.

B 36 RESOLUTIONS OF THE RETURNED SOLDIERS'
GRIEVANCE COMMITTEE, PRESENTED TO THE
TORONTO BOARD OF CONTROL ON 17 MAY 1917
[Toronto City Archives. Board of Control Papers]

1. Resolved that the Dominion Government stop the importation of alien enemy labour from the United States (also physically fit men) and to

exclude them from munition plants and other places where War contracts are being filled and have the same vacancies filled by Returned Soldiers, A.R. Men,[3] British Subjects and subjects of the Allies, and that a reasonable wage be paid.

Above moved by S.E. Graham – Supported by R.N. MacIntosh.

2. That a Committee be appointed by the City to co-operate with the Returned Soldiers and A.R. Mens' Grievance Committee, to visit and inspect all places where labour is employed to ascertain the number of aliens employed in these places, if any, and a report to be made public and forwarded on to the proper authorities.

Above proposed by [?] Livingston – Mr. J.P. Fanning.

3. That the City Council should open an Employment Bureau as soon as possible for the Returned Soldiers, and that a Returned Soldier be placed in charge of said bureau. This bureau will be headquarters for Returned Soldiers and A.R. Men in Toronto. It's nature will be as follows: –

> "To secure employment and attend to the very many
> complaints received from Returned Soldiers."

With all due respect to the existing organizations, they are in our opinion, inadequate to cope with the situation. The first duty of the City Council should be to look after its own men, irrespective of any other organization. Complaints and grievances of the Returned Soldiers are not being dealt with as they should be and many men are out of employment, and unless the Civic Authorities bestir themselves here in the matter, the Returned Soldier question will be beyond them. This bureau will fill a long felt want and could attend to general matters pertaining to the Returned Soldiers and A.R. Men at a little cost to the City.

Above Proposed by Sergt. Williams – Mr. C.W. Lidbetter.

4. That in Munition Plants and other places where War contracts are being filled the preference be given to women whose earnings are needed for household expenses rather than to those who desire pocket money.

Mr. Prothero – Sergt. McFarland.

5. That the Dominion Government be asked to at once re-organize the Pension Board system of Canada and do away with the present system of Political Patronage in all such cases in all Government Departments, and that Returned Soldiers and A.R. Men be given first consideration.

6. That the Dominion Government be asked to relieve from Office, all Officers, N.C.O.'s and Men, holding positions on the Staff, who are eligible for Overseas Service, who do not intend to go to the Front, and that all such vacancies be filled by Returned Officers, N.C.O.'s and Men, or A.R. Men.

7. That steps be taken by the Government to secure a fair and uniform method of distributing the different monies disbursed by Patriotic Fund Branches throughout Canada. We submit that it is unfair for the Toronto Branch of the Patriotic Fund to cut off allowances from soldiers' wives

[3]AR was the abbreviation for 'Applied and Rejected' volunteers for military service.

who go out to work, after those dependents had been assured previously that such action on their part would be considered commendable, and that they would not be penalized for so doing. This Committee is of the opinion that Soldiers' wives and dependents should be encouraged in trying to help the family fortunes while their men are away fighting and the Government is hereby strongly urged to keep the Officials of the different branches of the Patriotic Fund more in line with public opinion.

8. Resolution re Bailiffs. That it be illegal to put in baillifs for rent, taxes, etc. on wives or dependents of Soldiers Overseas, during the War and the Act re Destraint be so amended and sent to the City and Sir Wm. Hearst.

B 37   Order in Council Creating the Office
of Dominion Fuel Controller
[P.A.C., RG 2, 1, v. 1453. P.C. 1887 of 12 July 1917]

The Committee of the Privy Council have had before them a report, dated 7 July, 1917, from the Minister of Trade and Commerce, recommending that the Orders in Council Nos. 1579, and 1651, dated 11th June, and 15th June, 1917; respectively, be cancelled and the following substituted therefor:

The Minister submits the following observations on the coal situation in Canada:

Last winter very considerable difficulty and hardship were experienced owing to shortage of supplies and congestion of transport, resulting in increased prices to consumers, serious temporary curtailment of production in factories and much discomfort and privation in the homes of the poorer classes in towns and cities. These causes bid fair to continue and with increasing force during the present season and are added to by the scarcity of labour for the mines, the increasing difficulties in transport and the larger demand for coal in both the United States and Canada owing to the ever growing exigencies of the war.

At the present moment the outlook for the coming year gives cause for grave anxiety and calls for prompt and efficient action if subsequent shortage and its consequent privations are to be avoided. The Quebec District, which formerly drew for its needs for railways and factories some 2,000,000 tons of bituminous coal from Nova Scotia mines, cannot estimate on more than 200,000 tons from that source. Nearly all the prospective output of these mines will be required for local needs, bunkering purposes and the use of the Intercolonial Railway. The only source of supply for this deficiency, as also of the needs of Middle Canada, is to be found in the mines of the United States.

Here two difficulties are encountered: – First, the high price and shortage of supply in the United States mines, caused by extraordinary demands, and reduced output owing to scarcity of labour. The entrance of the United States into the war and the vast preparations necessary for the equipment of her sea and land forces and the growing needs of the Allies call for vastly increased output of coal and added restriction of export for other than war purposes. In the second place, transport by land and water is daily becoming more inadequate compared to the increasing volume of freights to be moved, and the freight costs are continually increasing.

In the Western Prairie Provinces the supply has been diminished by strikes in some of the mines, and in respect to those working the output is restricted by the tendency to neglect putting in orders during the summer season and consequent failure to haul coal to consuming centres during the slack and favourable season.

The Minister represents that it seems, therefore, to be necessary that a competent Fuel Controller should be appointed:

1. To examine into the coal situation in Canada;

(a) As to the probable demand for consumption therein for the coming season.

(b) As to the output of Canadian coal that can be relied upon towards meeting those demands and what, if any, measures can be adopted to increase this output.

(c) As to the sources outside of Canada from which the deficiency can be provided and the possibility of obtaining the necessary amount.

(d) As to the possibility of providing sufficient transport for the carriage of both Canadian and foreign coal from the points of production to the distributing points.

(e) As to the possibility of early and continuous co-operation between producers, carriers and consumers, with a view to economising and facilitating the needed supply.

2. That in the course of, and in connection with, such investigation the Fuel Controller be authorized to confer with and co-ordinate the different interests with a view to ensure, so far as possible, a sufficient supply of coal for Canadian requirements during the approaching autumn and winter season and from time to time to report and recommend to the Government ways and means for effecting the same.

3. That the Fuel Controller be authorized to make regulations subject to the approval of the Governor in Council governing the price of coal and the distribution, sale and delivery thereof.

4. That for the purpose of any enquiry or investigation held by him under this Order in Council, the Fuel Controller shall have all the powers of a Commissioner appointed under the provisions of Part 1 of the Inquiries Act, Revised Statutes of Canada, 1906, Chapter 104.

5. The powers and duties hereby conferred and imposed upon the Fuel Controller shall not include or interfere with the powers and duties vested in Mr. W.H. Armstrong, Director of Coal Operations by the Order in Council of the 25th June, 1917.

The Minister, therefore, recommends that Charles A. Magrath be appointed Fuel Controller and be charged with carrying out the purposes outlined in the foregoing memorandum, and that all expenses incurred by him for clerical assistance and travelling expenses in connection therewith constitute a charge upon and be paid from the War Appropriation Funds.

The Committee concur in the foregoing and submit the same for approval.

B 38 CONCLUDING PARAGRAPHS OF 'THE CRISIS,'
PUBLISHED BY THE ORGANIZATION OF
RESOURCES COMMITTEE
[*P.A.C. Library, Pamphlet Collection, Number 4585*]

Why the Call to Canada is So Urgent

If this country does not raise a big crop this year, not only will the people of Canada suffer, but the Motherland and her Allies will suffer, and their military power will be weakened if not paralyzed. Therefore, the right solution of the present war problem comes back to the farm, as to a foundation upon which our whole national and international structure must be built and maintained.

The farmers know that they are the last reserve, and that the soil on which crops are grown is the strategic ground on which wars are decided. To their care is entrusted the base of supplies.

To enable the farm to do the work two factors are essential. The *first* is Time. Whatever we are to do must be done at once. Nature waits for no man. The *second* is Labour. Many farmers cannot plant the acres they would because they cannot get the necessary help. Many are afraid to increase their acreage because they fear they would not be able to cultivate and harvest an unusual crop after they had raised it. If they are to do the work that is essential for them to do, the last man in each city, town and village must be mobilized at once.

Every man not on Active Service can help. In every city, town and village are men who, by their training on the farm, or by their present occupation, can readily adapt themselves to farm work. These can render no greater service to the Empire at the present time than by answering the call of the farm. Capable men and boys willing to learn should not allow their lack of farm experience to stand in the way.

Can the employer render a more signal service in this crisis than by encouraging these men to help the farmer to cultivate every available acre and by making it easy for them to go?

Ontario's farm lands are waiting – the implements are ready – the equipment is complete – the farmer is willing – all he needs is labour.

So short is the world's food supply that without increased production many in Canada must go hungry, and even with enormously increased production we cannot expect cheap food. The world is waiting for our harvest.

If peace should be declared within a year, the food conditions will be no better, for the accumulated hunger of the Central Empires must be met. This will absorb a large part of the world's supply.

We do not know when this war shall cease. It is endless – its lengthening out has paralyzed the thought and conception of all men who thought about it and its possible time of conclusion. Three months – six months, we said; nine months, a year, we said; and yet two years and eight months have passed their long, dreary and sanguinary length, and there is no man who can tell how long this gigantic struggle may yet last.

Lloyd George, in a letter addressed to farmers throughout the Empire, said:

The line which the British Empire holds against the Germans is held by those who WORK ON THE LAND as well as by those who fight on land and sea. If it breaks at any point it breaks everywhere. In the face of the enemy the seamen of our Royal naval and mercantile marine and the soldiers gathered from every part of our Empire hold our line firstly. You workers of land must hold your part of our line as strongly. Every full day's labour you do helps to shorten the struggle and brings us nearer victory. Every idle day, all loitering, lengthens the struggle and makes defeat more possible. Therefore, in the nation's honour, heed! Acquit yourselves like men, and as workers on land, do your duty, with all your strength!

So, for the honour of Canada's soldiers in France – and for the glory of our New-born Nationhood – let it be said of Ontario's citizens that, in the hour of our greatest need, their response was worthy of their sons.

We owe a great debt to those who are fighting for us.

B 39   CIRCULAR NO. 6 OF THE ORGANIZATION OF
RESOURCES COMMITTEE, PUBLISHED IN
SEPTEMBER 1917
[P.A.C. Library. Pamphlet Collection, unnumbered]
THE C.P.S. CALL
CONSERVE! PRODUCE! SAVE!
IS YOUR COMMUNITY ORGANIZED?
TO CONSERVE FOOD AND FUEL
TO PRODUCE FOOD
TO SAVE MONEY
TO DEVELOP ITS RESOURCES

LOCAL COMMITTEES WANTED

The Organization of Resources Committee wishes to have in every Municipality in the Province a representative Branch Committee of public-spirited citizens. It does not aim to set up any new organizations,

however, but to co-operate with those already formed, such as War Production Clubs, Gardening Leagues, Farm Help Committees, Savings
Clubs, Potato-Growing Associations, Preparedness Leagues, War Aux-
iliaries, Patriotic Leagues, Red Cross Societies, Women's Institutes,
Farmers' Clubs, etc.

ORGANIZE AND CO-OPERATE

Let us know what you are doing! Let us help you if we can! Ontario has
still much to do! The war is not yet won; and we must get ready for after-
the-war days!

SUGGESTIONS FOR THE 1918 CAMPAIGN

(1) FOR FOOD CONSERVATION

Understand clearly the necessity. – Remember that Canada is asked to
save food so that Britain and our Allies may not be in want and the successful ending of the war prevented. It is not to cheapen the cost of living
for ourselves primarily – but to win the war for democracy that Canadians are asked to economize particularly in the use of wheat and meats.

Co-operate with local organizations. – Work in conjunction with your
local Women's Institute, your Patriotic League, your Red Cross, your
Church Society, your Resources Committee, or with whatever organization undertakes to canvass your community and secure signatures to the
food-saving pledges asked for by the Dominion Food Controller. Pull
together, co-operate. Do not dissipate your energies by overlapping. Make
your town richer in community good-will from your common efforts in
food economies. It is a long pull and a strong pull and a pull altogether
that is needed.

Arrange for demonstrations on canning and drying. – Arrange with the
Women's Institute Branch of the Department of Agriculture, Parliament
Buildings, Toronto, for a public demonstration. Use local talent in this
work too and distribute the Government bulletins widely. Explain to the
pupils in the schools what is required and show them how to can. Give
prizes at the local Fall Fair or School Fair for canned products. Distribute
buttons or some such recognition to those who have canned, say, 100 jars
of perishable garden products.

Educate the public on food values. – Many people misunderstand the
food problem. They think they are asked to do with less food. This is not
so. They are asked to *substitute* other foods for wheat and meat. Arrange
for talks by experts on Food Values. Distribute the Government bulletins
and those published by the Food Controller dealing with this subject.
Have the matter discussed in the schools amongst the older pupils. This
will help to bring it before people in their homes.

Store garden produce safely. – Co-operation in storing potatoes, carrots, cabbage, turnips, etc., will be necessary in some places to save wastage. Some people have cellars that are too warm; some have cellars that

are not frost-proof, and some have no cellars at all. Here's a chance for team-play. Those who have cellars larger than required for their own needs might help their neighbors. Town or village councils may be able to arrange municipal schemes of storage in some places.

Secure community canning outfits. – Make plans early for the 1918 campaign. It may be economical to arrange for the establishment of a Community Canning Club and to purchase an outfit with supplies of cans early. In some places such work might be done in connection with a cheese factory or wherever live steam is procurable. Surplus goods could likely be profitably sold.

Back up the food controller. – Be loyal to the Dominion Food Controller. Remember that his work is a war necessity. Submit to his directions and accept his suggestions. Remember that his work is very difficult. Do not make it more difficult by your indifference or grumbling.

(2) FOR PROVIDING FUEL

Prepare for next winter. – The United States Fuel Administrator has stated that there will be a coal shortage of 50,000,000 tons this year. This means that Ontario will be dependent on its own supplies of wood to a considerable extent. Municipal Councils, Boards of Trade and Organization of Resources Committees should co-operate in securing supplies of wood to carry them through emergencies. The experiences of this winter warrant the taking of early and effective action. The greatest economy should be urged upon all. In several places steps have been taken to provide wood to householders. The City of Guelph, for example, is selling wood cut from its Waterworks Farm. The Town of Smith's Falls has bought a bush property, and it is expected that the sale of wood will cover all costs, so that the municipality will have the land free. A well-stocked municipal wood-yard will help materially in keeping "the home fires burning" next winter.

(3) FOR FOOD PRODUCTION

IN TOWNS AND VILLAGES

Fairs and displays. – Make a display of garden produce at your local Fall Fair, or at a special Thanksgiving Day Exhibit. Have the boys and girls make a display of their garden products at a School Fair. Invite the public. Make the occasion a patriotic one. Point out, too, the educational values that there are in gardening.

Estimate the 1917 effort. – Take stock of your town's gardening enterprises; count the number of gardens; estimate their total area; determine the quantity of material grown and its value. Especially find out what proportion of the potato supplies of the town have been grown by your own townspeople.

Get ready early. – Manure and cultivate your garden this fall in anticipation of an early start next spring. Put away your garden tools cleaned

and in good repair. If you have saved some good seed of your own growing such as beans, peas, lettuce, corn, potatoes and beets, put it away
carefully in a safe, dry place.

Organize for community efforts. – In a great many places in Ontario
there have been commendable co-operative enterprises carried out this
year. For example, a group of men in Jarvis had a six-acre field of buckwheat adjoining the village; the High School girls at Fergus had potato
and bean plots in a six-acre field prepared by the Town Council; the Boy
Scouts at Harriston grew about two acres of potatoes; the Woodstock
Bowling Club had a twelve-acre potato patch.

Plan for a greater effort in 1918. – Increase the number of your gardens. See that no vacant ground that is fit for cultivation is overlooked.
Plan for a larger production of potatoes and beans. Abundance of potatoes makes for the saving of wheat, and beans make a fair substitute for
meats. Maybe your town could grow all the potatoes it needs, estimating
an acre of potatoes as sufficient for from thirty-five to fifty people. Have
unbroken land ploughed this fall.

Interest the children. – Get the school children interested. Send speakers to the school to give talks on gardening and to explain the part Canadian boys and girls must play in the world's food crisis. Help the teachers
to organize School or Home War Plots. Arrange for assistance in supervising the children's work.

Read gardening bulletins. – Write to the Dominion Department of
Agriculture at Ottawa, and the Ontario Department of Agriculture at
Toronto, and ask to be put on their mailing lists for horticultural publi-
cations.

Talks and lectures. – Arrange for talks by your successful local gar-
deners or lectures by Department of Agriculture experts during the winter months.

Newspaper campaign. – Keep your locality interested by arranging for
the publication of gardening news in your local paper.

Arrange farm-help schemes early. – The experience of 1917 should
be useful in planning for the 1918 crop. With the war continuing another
year and Canada sending more men overseas the farm labor shortage
will remain acute. Towns should organize early to help farmers in seeding, in harvesting, and in fall plowing. Local Committees should co-
operate with Township Councils to secure an exact survey of the man
power on the farms of the neighborhood so that any available help may
be distributed to advantage.

Arrange instruction for high school boys and girls. – In 1917 thousands
of High School boys and girls "did their bit" on Ontario farms and did
it well. There will be need for their help again in 1918. For those especially who are going out for the first time, practical talks by local farmers
and others interested in boys' and girls' activities should be arranged for a
few months before school closes.

IN THE COUNTRY

Arrange early for farm help. – Farmers should apply as early as possible to the nearest Farm Labor Bureau. If there is no such Bureau in a near-by town, application should be sent to the Ontario Labor Bureau at Toronto, giving full particulars with reference to wages, size of farm, location of farm, etc. It is an advantage to register with the Labor Bureau a few months ahead of requirements, even if not quite certain at the time what the actual needs will be.

For short-time help required in haying and harvest, early application should be made also, or arrangements made with resources committees in local centres for volunteer helpers from stores or factories. If groups of neighboring farmers could make their needs known together, it would make it easier to send out help.

Co-operate by purchasing tractors, etc. – The demonstrations given throughout the Province by the Ontario Department of Agriculture this year have aroused a great deal of interest. Tractor plows will undoubtedly come into greater use in Ontario. There is a good field here for co-operative buying and using. Potato planters, sprayers and diggers might be secured on the same plan. In some places townspeople might be willing to co-operate in this for the use of such machinery on their Community Potato Plots. Township Councils might consider, too, the advisability of purchasing such machinery either alone or in conjunction with groups of farmers.

Campaign for increased wheat production. – There is a loud cry in the world for wheat. Ontario is asked to do her "bit" in this need. An extra acre next year by every farmer would mean 150,000 more acres, and this, with a fair yield, perhaps 3,750,000 bushels. Figure up what you did in 1917. Try for a 25% increase in 1918. If your Township had 1,000 acres this year, make it 1,250 acres for 1918. Some districts may be able to do even better. If you cannot get in Fall wheat, try a small crop of Spring wheat.

Get the best possible seed. – Good seed pays. Buy the best you can. Ask your District Representative to help you secure such. Co-operate with your neighbors in purchasing a large supply. Or write early to the Canadian Seed Growers' Association, Ottawa, and ask to be put in touch with some of the best growers.

(4) FOR THE SAVING OF MONEY

Prepare for a Rainy Day. – Opinion differs regarding Canada's prosperity after the war. Some say there will be very hard times. Others think that there will be dull times only for a short time. It is the part of wisdom, however, to prepare for a rainy day. There will be an enormous war debt to pay in any case. Everyone will share in this obligation. People everywhere should be roused to the necessity of saving. The best security against distress in hard times is a bank account.

Encourage the use of Savings Banks. – Local Committees might find out how many savings accounts there are and the approximate totals of savings in the local Post Office and chartered Savings Banks. Then start a local campaign to double these. Get the boys and girls interested. Go to the schools and explain the matter. Show them the wisdom and the patriotism of saving. Enlist the teachers' co-operation. Perhaps they will undertake to organize a branch of the Penny Savings Bank.

Some may prefer to invest their savings regularly in the Dominion Government's Old-Age Annuities. Encourage this too.

Get the young people interested. Have the matter put before them in their church organizations. Secure pledges to save 25¢, 50¢, or $1.00 a week. Perhaps the local Banks will co-operate in collecting weekly deposits. Friendly competitions amongst groups such as boys' and girls' Bible Classes may prove attractive. In the country, enlist the support of the Ontario Junior Farmers' Associations wherever such have been organized. Your Agricultural Representative will help you to get in touch with them.

Make your plans known through the local press, and from time to time announce your progress.

Push the purchase of war certificates. – Co-operate with the Dominion Government in this. Secure an estimate of the amount of Certificates that have been bought locally and figure the average amount this represents for your population. Organize to double this, or treble it, or even to increase it a hundredfold. Arrange friendly competition with your neighboring villages in this National Service.

Canvass your community to secure the names of people who will undertake to purchase Certificates systematically – *e.g.*, a $10 Certificate weekly or monthly. Induce your local Postmaster to arrange for a War-Certificate Purchasing Club. Make it a popular thing. Talk about it. Preach about it.

Arrange with employees in factories and stores to have part of their weekly wages held over and applied on the purchase of War Certificates. Employers will be glad to co-operate in this.

B 40   REPORT BY J.J. GRAHAM, CHIEF INSPECTOR,
CIVIL SECTION, CANADIAN MILITARY POLICE CORPS
TO MAJOR J.H. PORTER, ASSISTANT PROVOST
MARSHAL, MILITARY DISTRICT NO. 3
[*P.A.C., RG 24, v. 4436, file 3D. 26-6-90*]

Ottawa
August 7th, 1918.

For your information I beg to submit the following re work done in the month of July ... I have had a number of men almost continuously in the Gatineau District, which District has been very hard to work on account of the long distances to travel and also of considerable antagonism to the Military Service Act. I have had special instructions to try and clean up this District and am continuing to work there at present. I also made a night raid in company with Major Osborne on the shores and islands in the Ottawa River for some thirty miles or more below this city. I also took a number of men and made a raid out of Renfrew to Mont Laurier and vicinity at night, and investigated the conditions of Pembroke thoroughly, and for the time being I have taken the men I had stationed there away. My men at Mattawa have been fairly successful, and I also have had men in the vicinity of Casselman investigating, which spot I hope to get a number of men from shortly, and have made several trips to the vicinity of Hammond, Thurso, Rockland and Clarence Creek. I had men at Smith's Falls on the 12th of July on account of there being a celebration there and we apprehended some 10 men from whom three were fined in the Police Court and I might add that from explanations made in Smith's Falls on the evening of the 12th have heard of several cases where men are giving themselves up voluntarily. The border towns have been looked after by men situated in Kingston and Morrisburg, Ottawa, Hull and vicinity have been very carefully gone over and from now on I propose keeping most of my staff working in the outlying districts.

B 41   REPORT OF THE COMMISSION OF INQUIRY INTO THE RAID ON THE JESUIT NOVITIATE AT GUELPH
[*Published in* A Double Collapse of Bigotry, *issued by the Catholic Unity League of Canada, London, Ont., (1919). Copy in P.A.C. Library, Pamphlet Collection, unnumbered*]

May it Please Your Excellency:
  We, the undersigned Commissioners, appointed by Royal Commission, to inquire into the facts concerning certain charges made by the Reverend Kennedy H. Palmer, of Guelph, and certain additional matters referred to in an address by the Hon. Sir Sam Hughes, M.P., in so far as such charges involve allegations of impropriety or misconduct on the part of the Minister of Justice, the Department of Justice, the Minister of Militia and Defence, or the Department of Militia and Defence, report that sittings were holden at the City of Ottawa on the 25th day of August, and the 8th, 9th, 10th, 11th and 12th days of September, 1919, where we were attended by Sir Sam Hughes in person, and by counsel for the Reverend Kennedy H. Palmer, and by counsel for the Minister of Justice and the Department of Justice, the Minister of Militia and Defence, and the Department of Militia and Defence, and by counsel for the Society of Jesus and St. Stanislaus' Novitiate, Guelph, whereupon, and upon hearing the evidence adduced, and what was alleged by Sir Sam Hughes, and by counsel aforesaid, and after weighing and considering said matters, beg to submit the following report:

Under the provisions of the Military Service Act, 1917, section 2, subsection (1)

"Every male British subject within one of the classes described in section 3 of this Act ... shall be liable to be called out as hereinafter provided on active service with the Canadian Expeditionary Force for the defence of Canada unless (a) he comes within the exceptions set out in the schedule ..."

The schedule to the Act excepts from its operation, "Clergy including members of any recognized order of an exclusively religious character and ministers of religious denominations existing in Canada at the date of the passing of this Act."

Much that took place giving rise to the matters investigated before us arose from the failure of those concerned to rightly understand the full effect of this statute. It clearly excepts from the operation of the Act not only ministers of religious denominations but also "members of any recognized order of an exclusively religious character" existing in Canada at the date of the passing of the Act.

This provision of the statute was not intended to except from the operation of the Act theological students either Protestant or Catholic. This was so held by the Central Appeal Judge on test cases taken before him. If a theological student was a member of any recognized order of an exclusively religious character he was then excepted from the Act, not by reason of the fact that he was a theological student, but by reason of his membership in the order in question. A number of Catholic theological students were members of religious orders, and so were not liable for service under the Act. Many other Catholic theological students were not members of such orders and were, therefore, liable for service, and did not claim to be excepted from the Act by this provision. This misunderstanding of the situation is manifest, for example, in the letter from the District Military Representative, at London, of 28th November, 1917, in which, in referring to this institution he says: –

"There are thirty-nine students in the Novitiate Jesuit class. The rector claims that these men cannot be classed amongst those required to report for service or claim exemption and has declined to do so.

"There is a very strong feeling in Guelph that these men not being ordained ministers do not come within the clauses of the Act exempting them from service and that they should be required to comply with its provisions."

The same misunderstanding is found in a letter from the military representative to the rector of the Novitiate bearing date November 30, 1917, in which he says: –

"I understand from communications I have had with your rector and with your counsel, Mr. Kerwin, that you are of the opinion that novitiate members are exempt under the wording of the Act, but according to what I am told such wording only applies to the ordained clergy of all denominations and it is not intended to apply to those who are not ordained, but who are serving a term of probation, but are students such as I understand you have in the novitiate."

The position of the members of the Jesuit order residing in the novitiate was placed before the Hon. Mr. Guthrie, who is the member for South Wellington, which includes the city of Guelph, and on October 29, 1917, he telegraphed the Minister of Justice as follows: –

"At Jesuit Novitiate school in Guelph there are some thirty or forty members, of the order, including ordained priests, lay brothers, and novices. My understanding was that all these were excepted under the Military Service Act, and do not require to present themselves for examination or apply for exemption. Military representative here states that instructions have been received from London that all students at college must apply for examination and afterwards claim exemption. Please wire me definitely upon this point and if necessary send definite instructions to London Military Headquarters to cover this case."

In response to this, on the following day the Honourable the Minister of Justice telegraphed the Hon. Mr. Guthrie: –

"Your wire yesterday. Members of recognized religious orders are under section two and the schedule to Military Service Act excluded from its operation; they therefore are not bound to make application for exemption. The fact that such member of a religious order may be also a student does not affect his exclusion from the operation of the Act in his quality of member of the order. Am asking that the military authorities be communicated with."

This opinion of the Minister of Justice was communicated to the solicitor and to the rector of the novitiate, and also to the military representative, and, according to the evidence of the Hon. Mr. Guthrie, which we accept, also to the Reverend Kennedy H. Palmer.

Early in November, immediately after what the rector thought was a final settlement of the controversy, he issued to each member of the order resident in the Novitiate in Guelph a certificate either that the member was "a member of the Roman Catholic clergy of Canada," and "also a fully recognized member of the exclusively religious order known as the Society of Jesus," or that he was "a fully recognized member of the exclusively religious order known as the Society of Jesus and resides at St. Stanislaus' Novitiate, Guelph," and instructed that these certificates be kept in the residence, and that no member of the order should leave the residence without taking his certificate with him. Of the fact that these certificates were issued about this date we entertain no doubt.

Matters remained in this situation until the end of May, 1918. On the 30th May the Provost Marshal wired to the Assistant Provost Marshal at London, Major Hirsch: –

"Please ascertain immediately from the Registrar why students at St. Jerome's College, Kitchener, and the Novitiate at Guelph have not been called. Have there been any communications received by Registrar regarding this matter. If so, send copies. Handle with discretion. Decode at Headquarters."

On the following day 31st May, 1918, the Honourable the Minister of Militia having been informed by the Honourable Mr. Guthrie that it was rumoured that the two men named Newman and Craig were improperly harboured at the Novitiate, made a memorandum of instructions to one of his subordinates, Captain Tyndale, reading as follows: —

"I am informed through a very reliable source that there are several men at the Jesuit College, Guelph, particularly men by the name of Newman and Craig, who are escaping the military service. Steps should be taken to get after these men. There is also another very glaring case, and that is James Alexander, son of A.W. Alexander, Guelph. Can you have these cases followed up? Probably the Provost Marshal would help you. S.C.M."

Captain Tyndale sent this memorandum over to the office of the Provost Marshal marking it "P.M. 'for you please'." This memorandum reached the hands of Captain Burrows, Staff Captain, Canadian Military Police Corps, attached to the Provost Marshal's Office. It was his duty to write a letter of instructions based upon the memorandum, but instead of doing so he forwarded a copy of the memorandum to the Assistant Provost Marshal (Major Hirsch) at London. This was done on the 5th June, 1918, his letter reading as follows: —

Novitiate, Guelph, Ont.
"Herewith copy of a memorandum re marginally noted institution from the Minister of Militia this date. Might every effort be made, therefore, to have this place cleaned out at your earliest convenience."

The original of this letter was lost, and so not produced before us. The stenographer's notes show that the expression used by Captain Burrows was "Cleaned up" and not "cleaned out". From the copy of the letter upon the file it would appear that it was erroneously transcribed, and forwarded using the expression "cleaned out."

The copy of the memorandum sent with this letter consisted of the first paragraph only. This arose from the fact that the case of Alexander had been dealt with. As appears by a contemporaneous letter, Alexander was at Petawawa Camp, and on the strength of the 64th Battery. The instructions issued by Captain Burrows to the Assistant Provost Marshal at London embodied in the last paragraph of his letter was entirely unauthorized by the Minister of Militia or the Provost Marshal.

Major Hirsch had in the meantime replied to the telegram of the 30th May on June 1st stating: —

"The Public Representative is now sending questionaires to these institutions, and I am personally going to visit them and procure nominal rolls of the inmates."

Major Hirsch (who was not at London in October and November,

1917, and apparently did not know of what had then taken place), on receipt of Captain Burrows' letter enclosing the extract from the minister's memorandum on 7th June, issued instructions to Captain Macauley, Deputy Assistant Provost Marshal, as follows: —

"You are hereby instructed to proceed to Guelph and visit Bedford Farm, and make a thorough investigation as to the young men who are alleged to be residing in that place with a view to evading the Military Service Act.

"You will take with you for this purpose Inspector Minard of the C.M.P.C., Civil Branch, and a sufficient number of men to enable you to put a guard over all exits and outline to prevent escape of the inmates before your investigation is complete.

"In case of meeting with any unforeseen difficulties or complications you will immediately get into communication with me. Please exercise the greatest tact and discretion in handling this matter."

It is to be noted that, as a result of Captain Burrows' instructions, and these instructions the desire of the minister, that the cases of Newman and Craig who were supposed to be evading military service should be investigated, is thus, by the action of subordinates, expanded into an investigation of all the young men residing at the Novitiate.

Pursuant to these instructions, Captain Macauley and Inspector Minard with constables, the party numbering eleven in all, went to Guelph and arrived at the Novitiate at 9.30 p.m. (daylight saving time) after most of the inmates had retired for the night. Guards were placed at the doors and constables "outlined," and Captain Macauley and Inspector Minard and some of the police entered the college, and Captain Macauley demanded that all the inmates of the establishment should be at once paraded before him.

By the Order in Council P.C. 1013 it is provided that on or after the 1st June, 1918, any male person who apparently may be, or is reasonably suspected to be, within the classes liable for military service, by whom, or on whose behalf it is claimed that he is exempt from service, shall carry a certificate upon his person or in or upon the building or premises in which he is, showing that he is not liable for service, the certificates required in the case of clergy or members of any recognized religious order being signed by an office holder competent to certify to his membership.

The Order in Council further provides that any person not having a certificate shall "prima facie be presumed to be a person at the time liable for military service and to be a deserter or absentee without leave," and he may be taken into military custody, and held until the fact be established to the satisfaction of a competent authority that he is not liable for military service.

No arrests were made by the military authorities in this district under this Order in Council until after the date in question.

It is now suggested that the raid made by Captain Macauley was justified because of the failure of the inmates of the institution to produce the certificates required by the Privy Council order. There is no suggestion in the report made by Captain Macauley that the occurrences on the night in question were justified by the requirements of P.C. 1013, and we are satisfied that the intention of the visit was not to call for the production of the certificates required by this order, but for the purpose of asserting the liability of the young men at the novitiate who were not clergymen, and who were of military age, to perform service. That this was the real object is evident from the report of Captain Macauley in which he states: –

"I am firmly convinced that the majority of these men are defaulters under the Act, and in support of my belief I submit for your consideration the following information I gleaned from the rector himself."
He then sets out these matters and adds: –

"In view of this information I contend that these people do not come within the meaning of paragraph 6, schedule of exemptions ... Should my interpretation of this paragraph be wrong I beg to draw your attention to the fact that all young men of military age could avail themselves of the opportunities thus presented by institutions of this kind, for the express purpose of evading military service."

Upon the arrival of Captain Macauley at the institute those in authority, including the Reverend Father Bourque, the rector, demanded the production of his written authority to enter the building. Macauley refused to produce his instructions, although he says he had them with him, and although Inspector Minard produced and read in his hearing the terms of P.C. 1013 under which he was only entitled to enter the building "if generally or specially authorized in writing by the officer," etc., etc., and "upon reasonable demand for admission and upon producing his authority in writing aforesaid."

Captain Macauley now seeks to justify his course in this respect by the statement that the demand for the production of his written authority came from the Reverend Father Hingston, and not from Father Bourque, but we find upon the evidence that the demand was made by Father Bourque as well as by Father Hingston who was acting as spokesman for Father Bourque, and in his presence. Father Hingston, who had preceded Father Bourque as rector of the novitiate, had been overseas, and on his return was staying temporarily at the novitiate, had been asked by Father Bourque to deal with these military men owing to his greater familiarity with military matters.

There is some conflict of evidence as to what took place thereafter, but this conflict is mainly as to immaterial matters. Captain Macauley sets forth his version of the affair in his report of June 10th, 1918. Father Bourque wrote to the Minister of Militia and Defence on June 8th, 1918, setting forth the matter from his standpoint, and we think that the facts are stated by him with substantial accuracy. There was, however, no evidence that any of the police were in fact armed, and the statement as to the detailed search said to have been made of the dormitories was based on hearsay, and probably has little foundation. On the other hand, there is absolutely no foundation for the statement made in Captain Macauley's report that there was any attempt on the part of any of the inmates of the building to escape from it.

During the course of the evening Marcus Doherty, son of the Minister of Justice, and two others had been arrested by Captain Macauley for supposed violation of the Military Service Act, and Marcus Doherty telephoned the information to his father at Ottawa. The Minister of Justice, thereupon, remonstrated over the telephone with Captain Macauley regarding his conduct, and pointed out to him the illegality of what he was doing, but he did not attempt otherwise to interfere with him in the discharge of his duties. Later in the night the Minister of Justice found that the Minister of Militia and Defence and his Deputy were both away from Ottawa, and he communicated with the Adjutant General. The Adjutant General then communicated with Major Hirsch at London and the latter thereupon instructed Captain Macauley not to arrest the inmates of the novitiate, but to make a full report.

On the 11th June the Minister of Militia and Defence, on receipt of the letter of complaint from the Reverend Father Bourque, wrote to him expressing regret for the action taken by Captain Macauley, stating that the Adjutant General had taken steps for a most thorough investigation.

"and if the facts are as stated in your letter, which of course, I do not doubt, I can assure you that the error in judgment committed by this officer will be dealt with in a proper way, as I will not tolerate any such action on the part of any military officer as far as the operation of the Military Service Act goes."

An investigation was then held by the Provost Marshal under instructions from the Adjutant General, the Adjutant General pointing out six matters in which it appeared to him that the Assistant Provost Marshal and his officers had been at fault.

1st. – "That the investigation was conducted at an unseemly hour, between 9.30 p.m. and 12.40 a.m., and that a demand was made for all members of the community to be paraded within the space of five minutes.

2nd. – "The threat that if the community was not assembled at once the officer would proceed to search the house for deserters and defaulters.

3rd. – "That the officer concerned did not have and did not produce the written authorization required by the Order in Council in order to forcibly enter and search the premises, and in spite of the fact being brought to his attention, he proceeded in direct violation of the law to carry on his work.

4th. – "That he authorized a force of police to form a cordon about the house, thereby making a demonstration of force which was undesirable and unwarranted.

5th. – "That he placed under arrest three members of the community, who were told at 11 p.m. or later to make ready to leave for the barracks.

They were conducted under escort to the dormitories to make the necessary changes in clothing, although it is stated that none of these young men came under the Military Service Act.

6th. – "That the whole proceedings were conducted in a high-handed manner calculated to create the impression that this religious community was in league with deserters and desirous of evading the law, and that secrecy and force were necessary to deal with the situation without regard to the essential principle of all police work that it should be carried out without friction."

The Provost Marshal went to London and Guelph, and carefully investigated the whole matter, and found both Major Hirsch and Captain Macauley to be at fault, his report as to Major Hirsch being: –

"No such drastic action as that of surrounding this establishment with police should have been adopted. Either yourself, or an officer should have been detailed to visit the rector or priest in charge, and all courtesy should have been observed. After all such means had been tried and failed then a report should have been sent in to the G.O.C. the District, and to me as Provost Marshal, with your suggestions as to further action."

With regard to Captain Macauley he was found by the Provost Marshal to be at fault: –

1st. – In that "he performed this duty in mufti."

2nd. – "Even after he was warned that he was committing an illegal act, in that he had no written authorization from either the G.O.C. or the A.P.M., he still persisted in carrying out his duty."

3rd. – His general behaviour towards the earlier part of the interview showed lack of tact and good judgment."

In view of the excellent reports the Provost Marshal had received as to the previous work of Captain Macauley he recommended the officer be transferred to Winnipeg instead of being dealt with in a more drastic manner, as had been suggested by the Minister of Militia. With reference to the second of the findings as to the conduct of Captain Macauley it is now shown that he had written authorization but refused to produce it when demanded, although he knew that it was his duty to produce it without demand under the Order in Council. In this we think his conduct was most improper and unreasonable. With reference to the performing the duty in mufti he states that he was instructed to go in mufti by Major Hirsch, and Major Hirsch accepts responsibility for issuing those instructions.

Upon the evidence before us we think that the conduct of this raid was open to all the adverse criticisms found in the memorandum of the Adjutant General.

We are further of opinion that the Minister of Militia acted with entire propriety in apologising for the incidents which took place by reason of a series of bungles on the part of subordinate officials.

Dealing now with the specific charges referred to us as set forth in the Order in Council: –

"1st. – The Department of Justice at Ottawa interfered with the Military Board at Guelph in their efforts to obtain information as to the status of the inmates of the Guelph Novitiate."

There is absolutely no foundation for this charge. The Minister of Justice, the responsible legal head of the Dominion Government, was charged under the statute with the duty of seeing that the administration of public affairs was in accordance with the law. It having come to his knowledge that Macauley was acting illegally he adopted the entirely proper course of warning him of the illegality of his conduct, and of communicating with the minister or the acting head of the department having charge of the matter, and advising that instructions be sent to Macauley to desist until full investigation could be made. In no other way is it suggested that the Minister of Justice or Department of Justice interfered.

"2nd. – That in doing so the department extended special privileges to an institution which should have been treated like any other institution."

There is no foundation for this charge. The only institution against which a raid was directed was this particular institution. It is not shown that any privilege was ever extended to it.

"3rd. – That the Honourable C.J. Doherty interfered with Captain Macauley on the night of June 7th while he, Captain Macauley was carrying out the instructions of his superior officers."

This is covered by what has been already said.

"4th. – That the Department of Justice through its Minister, prevented the placing in military service of young men of military age residing in the institution."

There is no foundation for this charge. When applied to by the Honourable Mr. Guthrie, the Minister of Justice gave his opinion as to the true construction of the Military Service Act. Later the opinion of the Department of Justice as to the position of the inmates of this Novitiate under the provisions of the Military Service Act was asked by the Department of Militia and Defence. The question was carefully considered by the Deputy Minister of Justice who gave his opinion to the effect that residents of the institute who were bona fide members of the order were not liable for service. This opinion was concurred in by the Judge Advocate General. It was followed by correspondence with the rector of the Novitiate who was asked to give, and gave very full information concerning the case of each inmate. Each case was thoroughly investigated and it was found that no one claimed as a member of the order was liable for service. It may here be said that there was no foundation whatever for the charge freely made in the letters and documents appearing in the file, that young men were being harboured by this institution so as to enable them to evade military service. At the time of admission of each member to the order his case was carefully investigated by the Rector, and in no case where admission followed was there found to be any improper motive.

It may facilitate the understanding of the situation if it is pointed out that the case of all applicants for admission to the order receives the most careful consideration at the hands of those in authority. A "postulant," if he satisfies those in authority, is admitted as a "novice," and then becomes a member of the order. This novitiate lasts for two years, and if the novice during these two years desires to withdraw from the order he may withdraw, or, if he is found unfit he is rejected. At the end of the two years if he is found fit, and so desires, he takes his vows and becomes either a lay brother or a scholastic. In either case he is then a member of the order for life. If a lay brother, he performs such physical services as he is fit for. If a scholastic, after fifteen years of training he is admitted to the priesthood. None of those received as novices in this institution was at the time of reception liable for military service, and since the Armistice only one novice (a man named Ryan) has left the order, his retirement being on account of his physical condition.

"5th. – That the press censorship instigated by a minister of the Crown intensified the feeling that special protection was being given to the institution at Guelph."

There is no foundation for this charge. The Press Censor and the Minister of Justice desired that the incident should not be given publicity. This was not with any desire of promoting the interests of the Jesuits but entirely by reason of the fear that publication of the full details of the harsh and unjustifiable conduct of the military towards the members of this religious order might arouse in other parts of the Dominion the feeling that members of the Catholic Church were not being treated fairly under the law.

Under the terms of the Order in Council we were instructed to investigate these charges with the view of ascertaining whether any of the acts alleged were wrongfully done or improper in themselves.

In our opinion the Minister of Justice, the Minister of Militia and the Adjutant General, and the Provost Marshal acted with great propriety, and with no other idea than to see that the law was fairly, firmly, and uniformly enforced, and the rights and immunities granted by the Act were duly recognized. There is no foundation for the suggestion of any wrongdoing or impropriety in their conduct.

Turning to the charges made by Sir Sam Hughes: –

"1st. – That the Government improperly failed to make the occupants of the Novitiate register for medical examination or for service under the Military Service Act and the Government also failed to punish those harbouring defaulters in the Novitiate."

This charge is not proved and is unfounded. According to the terms of the Act, and the opinion of the Minister of Justice as expressed to Mr. Guthrie, the members of the order residing in the Novitiate were excepted from the operation of the Act, and were not called upon to register for medical examination, or for service.

There is no foundation whatever for the allegation that the Novitiate was a harbour for defaulters. There was only one man resident in the Novitiate at the time of the raid who was liable for military service, a man named O'Leary. This man was a postulant for admission as a lay brother, and had been rejected; but as he was very insistent, he had been allowed to remain for a short time in the institution. It is said that he had already been overseas, and had been returned as unfit, but this was not proved. After the raid he was examined by the medical board and placed in category "D." He appealed to the Medical Board of Review from this decision and was placed in category "A2." He was then accepted for active service. "2nd. – A member of the Government (Mr. Guthrie) informed a member of the Ministerial Association that 'Doherty says they are all right, and they are to be left alone.' This was improper interference."

According to the evidence of the Hon. Mr. Guthrie, which we accept, after he received the telegram above referred to from the Minister of Justice, in October, 1917, he read this to the Reverend Mr. Palmer. This is the incident referred to and does not constitute any improper interference.

"5th. – The Justice Department improperly communicated with Macauley."

This has already been dealt with.

"7. – After midnight the Militia Department communicated with Macauley and improperly ordered him to retire from the novitiate."

This has already been dealt with.

"8th. – The Justice Department improperly ordered the press censorship."

This has already been dealt with.

"9th. – The Minister of Militia, apologized to the principal of the novitiate, and indirectly censured Macauley when the order should have been to the principal to observe the law."

This has already been dealt with.

"11th. – Godson-Godson visited London and it is claimed improperly and surreptitiously had certain letters removed from the military files there."

Colonel Godson-Godson, the provost marshal, stated that it was his duty, in the course of his investigation, to have taken away from London, on the occasion of his first visit the original documents concerning the matter which he was investigating. By oversight he did not do so, and upon a subsequent visit he took the letters from the file and removed them. In doing so he was within his right, particularly as the production of these documents was called for by the Adjutant General and the Minister. He would have acted more prudently had he communicated the fact that he had removed these documents to Major Hirsch; at any rate he should have left a memorandum, stating the fact of removal, in the files at London. In all Colonel Godson-Godson did he acted in absolute good faith.

"12th. – Macauley was improperly removed to Winnipeg by the Militia Department."

In view of what has been already said, in our opinion Macauley was treated most leniently by those in authority. Even if his own statement as to what he did is accepted, he behaved with the utmost lack of tact and discretion in the discharge of a mission which called for the exercise of these qualities; he was cautioned by the document under which he was acting as to the necessity of exercising tact and discretion upon this occasion.

It is quite obvious to us that underlying the attacks made upon the administration in connection with this matter was the suspicion entertained by many that the Minister of Justice was in some way seeking to shield his son who was an inmate of the Guelph institution from being called upon for active service. It was admitted before us by the Hon. Sir Sam Hughes and by counsel for the Reverend Kennedy H. Palmer that there was no ground whatever for this suspicion or the statements which unfortunately had been widely published by the Reverend Kennedy H. Palmer and others. It was shown that these statements were absolutely unwarranted by the facts. Mr. Marcus Doherty had been examined by the Medical Board at Montreal and was placed in category "E." An endeavour was made in the course of the hearing before us to show that the raiding of this institution had been in express terms authorized by the memorandum of the Minister of Militia and Defence, and by the instructions issued by Captain Burrows. The original memorandum of the Minister was produced in evidence before us, and the copy of the letter of Captain Burrows is a true copy of the letter as written (save for the uncertainty as to whether the expression used was "cleaned up" or "cleaned out".) The suggestion of Major Hirsch and the explicit statement of Captain Macauley that both documents instructed "a raid" are without foundation in fact.

At the hearing before us counsel for the Reverend Kennedy H. Palmer put forward a suggestion that the Jesuit order was an illegal order in the province of Ontario, and that, therefore, although the order was incorporated in the province of Quebec, those who were admitted into the order in the province of Ontario could not by reason of this illegality, become members of the order, and he invited us to express our opinion upon this point. We do not consider that under the terms of the commission we were authorized to enter into any such inquiry. At the same time we think it right to say that we entertain no doubt that the "Society of Jesus" called "The Jesuits" is "a recognized order of an exclusively religious character." There is no question that the order is one of an "exclusively religious character," the only question is whether it can be treated as a "recognized order." In our view the Parliament of Canada must be taken to have intended that all de facto members of any religious order incorporated by any one of the provinces should be included in the wide words of the exception granted.

W. E. MIDDLETON,
J. A. CHISHOLM.

October 6, 1919.

B 42 PETITION FROM MEN OF 1ST CONTINGENT ON
FURLOUGH TO SIR ROBERT BORDEN
[*P.A.C., RG 9, III, v. 90, file 10-12-6X*]

Toronto,
April 10, 1918

We are approaching you on behalf of the married men of the First
Contingent, C.E.F., who have been on constant service in France, and
who are at this time enjoying a short furlough in Canada, with a view of
enlisting your service on their behalf, in order that they may obtain the
same consideration as has been accorded the men of the First Army of
Imperial men and Territorials, who took part in the Battle of the Marne.

As you are no doubt aware, the men of the First British Army, who
survived, were all returned to England, and others sent to the front to
carry on the work, it being considered that these men had done their part.
We do not wish it to be understood that we are unwilling – if need be – to
again take up our task, but since our return we have been astounded to
see the great number of fit men, who have never taken a part in this conflict, and we consider that our families should receive some consideration.

In view of the above, we, therefore, beg to submit the following resolution, which was passed at a meeting held to consider the question, and
further to point out that the number of men affected do not number above
one hundred and fifty.

"Resolved:

Whereas we find that the married men in Canada, have not yet been
conscripted, and that a large number of fit single men are engaged here
in Canada, both in civil and military duties;

We, do therefore, place ourselves on record, as being of the opinion
that it would be only fair on the part of the Government to permit us
to remain in Canada, and take the place of many who could well be
transferred to Britain or France."

Trusting that this, our humble petition may meet with your favourable
consideration, we are, on behalf of the men of the First Division,

Yours most respectfully,

27004 Sgt. Hunter, D., 411 Westmoreland Ave., Toronto,
34565 Sgt. Gwilliam, T.B., 227 River Street, Toronto,
1837 Sgt. Rademacher, H.N., 135 Tyndale Ave., Toronto.

B 43 REPORT ON THE TORONTO RIOTS, SUBMITTED
BY SIR JOHN HENDRIE, LIEUTENANT-GOVERNOR
OF ONTARIO TO MARTIN BURRELL, THE
SECRETARY OF STATE
[*P.A.C., RG 6, A12, v. 10, file 2360*]

Toronto, Ont.
12 August 1918.

I am advised by my Attorney General that this is not a matter respecting which his Department has any official information whatever, nor is it a matter with which they have been called upon to deal, but that he at once communicated with the Toronto police and is informed by them that there have been no anti-Greek riots in any National sense in Toronto; that on Friday night, August 2nd, owing to a rumour that a returned soldier had been seriously assaulted in a café kept by a Greek on College Street, a body of men composed, it is believed, partly of returned soldiers, raided this café destroying property and that, as a result, further raids were made on cafés kept by Greeks and others, some of whom were naturalized British subjects, in Toronto, and some damage done.

The whole affair was over before the police were prepared, but they now state that the matter is completely in hand.

On Saturday night, August 3rd, a collision occurred between the Toronto Police and a small number of soldiers accompanied by a much larger number of citizens. Here a number of injuries resulted both to the Police and to the mob, but the latter was speedily dispersed. A military force of about one hundred was held at the City Hall to assist the civil authorities if such assistance was necessary, but, as the result proved, their presence was not required. Greeks and others are, the Police now state, receiving adequate protection both as to property and person. The Toronto Police also state that they made an explanation of these occurrences to the Greek Consul General for Canada.

B 44 EXTRACTS FROM ANNUAL REPORTS OF LOCAL
MEDICAL OFFICERS OF HEALTH RELATING TO THE
SPANISH INFLUENZA EPIDEMIC
[*Ontario Sessional Papers, 1919, Part V, Number 21,* Report of the
Provincial Board of Health]

LONDON

Early in the autumn, however, we began to hear rumors of cases of influenza occurring in the large eastern cities of the United States, and it was only a few weeks until the disease showed itself in this city. The number of cases rapidly increased, and it was not long until all the doctors and nurses had more work than they could attend to. About this time it was arranged that nurses, trained and practical, could register at the Institute of Public Health for the convenience of physicians needing such help. This arrangement was scarcely under operation when Mrs. J.B. McKillop received a wire from Mr. McPherson, Provincial Secretary, asking her to form a branch of the Women's Volunteer Emergency Auxiliary. This was quickly and ably done by Mrs. McKillop on October 17th, and everything was soon in readiness for the registration of Sisters of Service. This organization had its headquarters at the Institute of Public Health, where Miss J. Fidlar, Statistician, was placed in charge of registration of nurses, and Miss B. Friend, practical nurses, and directed all nurses as to where they should be employed. Nursing aid was sent on advice of physicians or after inspection by the Board of Health. Nursing aid was supplied, in this way, for eleven hundred and fifty nursing days; sheets, bedding, pneumonia jackets, old linen, clothes etc., supplied mostly by the Red Cross, through Mrs. C.R. Somerville, but also by private citizens and firms, were sent out from the office at the Institute of Public Health. In so far as possible, day and night nurses were relieved in the morning and evening, which assured the nurse of certain hours of rest. Nurses were driven from place to place by volunteer automobiles and by those supplied by the Board of Health. Nurses reported to the office by 'phone day and night. Several medical students and other young men volunteered their services, and were a great help in difficult cases.

Two hundred and twenty families, with an average of three patients each, were provided with nurses, of which there were ninety-four who registered. Seventeen women registered who gave assistance in homes as housekeepers where the mother was ill or exhausted.

The work of supplying nourishment for the stricken families and lunches for nurses was undertaken at once by the Women's Volunteer Emergency Auxiliary, and two diet kitchens established, one at the Alexandra School, under Miss Craig, dietician, and one at the Collegiate Institute, under Miss McPherson, dietician.

During the epidemic 187 civilians died. Of these, 67% were persons from twenty to fifty years of age.

The diet kitchen remained in operation for twenty-four hours, during which time twenty-two hundred baskets of food for patients and sixteen hundred lunches for nurses were prepared and sent out.

The distribution of the food was only made possible by the generous way in which the citizens made use of their motors, under the able direction of Mrs. Allan McLean.

An emergency hospital was opened at the Latter Day Saints Church, the use of the building being offered by the pastor, Mr. Gray. No. 4 Division, St. John Ambulance, cared for a number of patients at their quarters.

SUDBURY

During the month of October a serious epidemic of Spanish influenza broke out, and from the 10th to the 15th, we estimated there were some 800 cases. It was deemed advisable at a joint meeting of the Council and Board of Health, held on the 15th, that all public premises, schools, etc., be closed. An emergency committee was formed in charge of Mr. McCarten and Mr. Berlanquet. A volunteer staff of some 150 men, young women and boys got together and gave valuable assistance to the stricken families; the women doing nursing and caring for the houses, boys doing general errands and chores, and the men found endless work in visiting and helping in many ways. We are greatly indebted to these helpers for their valuable work, and to the owners of automobiles for the assistance given. The Daughters of the Empire and Red Cross were untiring in the work of making soups and beef-tea for the hospital and invalid patients at their homes. The ban on public gatherings was raised for churches on the 10th of November, theatres, etc., on the 11th, and schools were opened on the 18th. During the period from October 16th to November 30th some 1,434 cases were reported, making a total, approximately, of 2,230. There were 164 deaths, of which 65 were residents of the town.

OTTAWA

The most outstanding feature of the year was the epidemic of influenza, with its terrible and widespread levy of illness and death, and which but for the splendid way our citizens co-operated to combat this visitation it would have been infinitely worse.

From the commencement, in the latter days of September, the cases developed rapidly, the greater mortality occurring in mid-October, declining rapidly toward the end of that month. During this time 520 deaths were registered from influenza and pneumonia, thus converting an otherwise excellent mortality record into the heaviest for many years.

Drastic steps were taken by the Board to meet the situation, warnings and instructions to the public being issued through the press and circulars distributed by the Boy Scouts. All public gatherings were prohibited, and the hours shortened in mercantile and office work.

The aid of the public was enlisted, and too great praise cannot be given for the wonderful response to the Mayor's appeal to succor the stricken ones. Large relief committees were organized, with headquarters at the City Hall, through whom medical attention, nursing and all requisites were provided for the care of the sick. But for the splendid work done here, in many cases whole families must have gone untended and the suffering and death list have been terribly increased.

The general hospitals, though augmenting their accommodation to the utmost, were inadequate to meet the demands for hospital care.

The May Court Club, Misericordia Hospital and Day Nursery came to the rescue and cared for a large number of patients.

Through the courtesy of the University of Ottawa and the Public School Board we were enabled to open two large emergency hospitals, thus completing a hospital formation adequate to give the requisite care to those in need of it.

Thanks are also due to Queen's University, Kingston, V.A.D., the Militia Department, and other departments of the civil service by whom medical men, nurses and hospital equipment was provided, and to the personnel of the different civic services who were on duty at all hours to assist us.

Charts are appended showing the mortality record, and also the age incidence of those dying, showing the heaviest toll among those at the period of greatest usefulness in life.

The experience gained by many during the epidemic, showing conditions under which our poorer brethren live, must create a greater public interest looking to a betterment of living conditions for everyone. This means sanitary dwellings, but more important still, sanitary dwellers.

RENFREW

The influenza epidemic, which has been universal, visited Renfrew and took a very heavy toll. Accurate figures of the number of cases are not available, as the cases were not required reported, but a fairly conservative estimate would place the number in the neighbourhood of 1,000. There were 67 deaths. The town is almost entirely free of the disease now, although sporadic cases are likely to appear during the next six months. It was early recognized that the disease was of a particularly virulent type and spreading rapidly, so an appeal for outside help (doctors and nurses) was made to the Provincial Health Department. They responded by sending us 13 nurses, and must be credited with doing all in their power to secure outside doctors, but evidently none were available. In addition, 20 nurses were secured privately. These, along with the town and hospital nurses, worked unselfishly and heroically and did an incalculable amount of good. Dr. Maloney, District Health Officer, was also on hand for three days, and gave valuable assistance in organization work. Various women's organizations of the town rendered valuable assistance. To all who assisted in any way in relieving a tense and pathetic situation we are very thankful. It was deemed advisable to close schools, theatres and pool-rooms for a period of three weeks. While expenditure in connection with the epidemic was heavy, it was mostly in supplying nurses for the hospital and charity cases.

C.   LOYALTY IN QUESTION

C 1   THE ALIEN ENEMY REGISTRATION ORDINANCE
[*P.A.C., RG 2, 1, v. 1324   PC 2721 of 28 October 1914*]

The Committee of the Privy Council have had before them a report, dated 28th October, 1914, from the Minister of Justice, stating that it is expedient and necessary to take measures to prevent espionage and also to prevent alien enemies in Canada who are likely to render effective military assistance to the enemy from returning to the enemy's service, and to provide for the proper supervision and control of such aliens as may be so prevented from leaving Canada, and the detention under proper conditions and maintenance where required of such of said aliens as it may be found necessary to intern as prisoners of war, and that it is like-wise desirable considering the lack of opportunity for employment that aliens of enemy nationality who are not likely to add to the strength of the enemy's forces and who desire and have the means to leave the country be permitted to do so.

The Minister observes that it is considered probable that aliens of both classes will be found grouped in particular localities, principally within or in the immediate neighbourhood of the large cities and towns.

The Minister, therefore, recommends that it be enacted by the Governor in Council under the authority of the War Measures Act as follows:–

(1) One or more offices of registration shall be established in such cities, towns and other places as may be from time to time designated by the Minister of Justice, and an officer shall be appointed by the Governor in Council for each of the offices so established who shall be called "Registrars of Alien Enemies".

(2) The Registrars shall be under the immediate direction of the Chief Commissioner of Dominion Police who shall exercise general supervision over them in the performance of their duties and to whom they shall report as may be required. The Minister shall appoint such assistants to such registrars, clerks and other officers as may be necessary for the proper carrying out of the provisions of the present order.

(3) It shall be the duty of a registrar to examine each alien of enemy nationality attending before him, and to register in a book to be provided for the purpose the name, age, nationality, place of residence in Canada and in the country of nationality, occupation, desire or intention to leave Canada and the names of the wife and children (if any) in Canada of every such alien and such other particulars necessary for identification of such alien of enemy nationality or otherwise as may seem advisable.

(4) Every alien of enemy nationality residing or being within any of the cities, towns or places so designated as aforesaid, or within twenty miles thereof, shall as soon as possible after the publication in the Canada Gazette of a proclamation designating such city, town or place as one wherein a registry office is to be established under this ordinance, attend before the registrar or one of the registrars, for the city, town or place within or near which he is or resides and truly answer such questions with regard to his nationality, age, residence, occupation, family, intention or desire to leave Canada, destination, liability and intention as to military service, and otherwise, as may be lawfully put to him by the registrar.

(5) No alien of enemy nationality shall be permitted to leave Canada without an exeat from a registrar; provided that the Chief Commissioner of Dominion Police may in any case, grant or cancel an exeat to an alien of enemy nationality who is registered.

(6) The registrar may issue an exeat to an alien of enemy nationality if satisfied upon the examination and registry that such alien of enemy nationality will not materially assist, by active service, information or otherwise, the forces of the enemy.

(7) If it appears to the registrar that any alien of enemy nationality who is not permitted to leave Canada may consistently with the public safety be suffered to remain at large, such alien of enemy nationality shall be required to declare whether or not he desires and has the means to remain in Canada conformably to the laws and customs of the country, subject to obligation to report monthly to the Chief of Police of the city where or in the neighbourhood of which he is registered. If yea, such alien of enemy nationality may be permitted his liberty, subject to the conditions aforesaid and the provisions of this Ordinance. If nay, he shall be interned as a prisoner of war. The registrar shall report to the Chief of Police the names and addresses of those who elect to remain at liberty. Any alien of enemy nationality who in the judgment of the registrar cannot consistently with the public safety be allowed at large shall be interned as a prisoner of war.

(8) If any alien of enemy nationality who is by the terms of this ordinance required to register, fails to do so within one month after publication of the proclamation referred to in section 4 of this ordinance or within seven days after the date when he shall by reason of his residence come within the description of those required to register, which ever date shall be last, or if he refuse or fail to answer truly any of the questions put by the registrar, or if, being registered he fail to report as hereinbefore required or to observe any of the conditions on which he is permitted to be at liberty, he shall in addition to any other penalty to which he may be therefor by law liable, be subject to internment as a prisoner of war.

(9) Where any alien of enemy nationality interned under the provisions of this order has wife or children living with and dependent on him, such wife and children shall be permitted to accompany him.

(10) Such provision as may be necessary for the maintenance of

aliens of enemy nationality interned as prisoners of war shall be made by the Military authorities who may require such prisoners to do and perform such work as may be by them prescribed.

(11) No alien of enemy nationality who is required to register shall be naturalized unless in addition to other requirements he produces and files with his application a duly certified certificate of a registrar that he is registered pursuant to the provisions of this Ordinance, and that his application for naturalization is approved by the registrar.

C 2 RESOLUTION ADOPTED AT A PUBLIC MEETING IN BERLIN ON 11 FEBRUARY 1916
[Berlin News Record, 11 February 1916, p. 1]

Whereas it would appear that a strong prejudice has been created throughout the British Empire against the name "Berlin" and all that the name implies,

And whereas, the citizens of this City fully appreciate that this prejudice is but natural, it being absolutely impossible for any loyal citizen to consider it complimentary to be longer called after the Capital of Prussia,

Be it therefore and it is hereby resolved that the City Council be petitioned to take the necessary steps to have the name "Berlin" changed to some other name more in keeping with our National sentiment.

C 3 SIR SAM HUGHES'S STATEMENT TO THE HOUSE OF COMMONS, 16 FEBRUARY 1916, REGARDING THE DISTURBANCE AT BERLIN
[Unrevised Hansard, 16 February 1916, pp. 894–895. Copy in P.A.C., RG 24, v. 1256, file HQ 593-1-87]

On the Orders of the Day:

Sir SAM HUGHES (Minister of Militia and Defence): I desire to place the following before the House:

Memorandum regarding disturbance at Berlin, Ont., on Tuesday night, February 15, 1916.

The oral report received from the Officer Commanding is as follows:

1. For some time the feeling of loyal and law-abiding citizens of both British and German extraction in Berlin and Waterloo and adjoining localities, have been more or less exasperated by the language and actions of a Lutheran clergyman – an American citizen named Tappert – and by a German born Canadian subject named Asmussen, who, whether with good or bad intent, have been semi-apologists for German atrocities and Kaiserism. It is asserted that one of these men has recently stated that 'the conduct of the British, in the war, has been about as bad as the conduct of the Germans.' It has not been specifically charged that these utterances have been made with disloyal intent, but merely as seeking not

to justify German brutality as much as to condone it. These utterances, coupled with the general tension of mind throughout the country over the war, gradually wrought up a number of people to a high pitch of feeling.

2. On Sunday last, a young man who had been behind the German lines for some months, as a reporter for an American journal, and who had personally witnessed these horrible atrocities, spoke in Waterloo and Berlin, and in vigorous terms denounced the spirit and recent utterances of the two men above named.

3. The feeling already highly strung on the part of many, found vent on Tuesday evening when ten or fifteen young soldiers, heard that German flags were displayed in a hall in Berlin. They quietly assembled near the place about nine o'clock in the evening, and in the course of a very few minutes had torn the German flags to pieces, while a bust of the former Kaiser William I was carried along the street. There were five policemen within easy call on the street, but the affair seems to have been over so quickly that they did not get time to interfere.

4. Colonel Lochead, on receiving a telephone message at the barracks, immediately repaired to the locality, when order was promptly restored.

I may add further that an inquiry is being held. The civil authorities are also acting in the premises. The authorities have been fully informed that soldiers in uniform lose none of their rights or responsibilities as citizens, and therefore are entitled to all the privileges of the law, but are also subject to its penalties. On the other hand, it will be observed that alien enemies have been treated by the Canadian Government in the most tolerant and lenient manner; but utterances and conduct that even indirectly encourage sedition, treason, or disloyalty, will not be tolerated.

C 4 FINDINGS OF A COURT OF INQUIRY ASSEMBLED AT BERLIN, ONT. ON THE 16TH DAY OF FEBRUARY 1916 BY ORDER OF LIEUT.-COL. W.M.O. LOCHEAD, OC, 118TH OVERSEAS BATTALION, FOR THE PURPOSE OF INQUIRING INTO CERTAIN DISTURBANCES ALLEGED TO HAVE BEEN CREATED BY CERTAIN SOLDIERS OF THE 118TH BATTALION, CEF, ON 15TH FEBRUARY 1916, AND INQUIRING INTO THE NATURE AND EXTENT OF THE DAMAGE (IF ANY) CAUSED BY THEM
[P.A.C., RG 24, v. 1256, file HQ 593-1-87]

The Court of Inquiry having assembled pursuant to order, proceed to read the Order convening the Court and call witnesses to give evidence relevant to the matters subject to investigation.

From the evidence heard by the Court it appears:

1. That about eight o'clock in the evening of February 15th, 1916, the men of the Machine Gun Section of the 118th Battalion, c.e.f., marched in a peaceable manner to Concordia Hall, King Street West, Berlin, and removed therefrom the bust of Kaiser Wilhelm I. Later on in the evening (shortly after nine o'clock) a body of the soldiers, about fifty in number, paraded the main street of Berlin singing patriotic songs. Learning that said Concordia Hall was decorated with German flags, bunting and pictures, about twenty-five of the soldiers entered the hall for the purpose of removing same and found a picture of His Majesty, King George v draped with German flags, upon which the men were enraged to the extent of doing certain damage to the Hall and contents as hereafter appears.

2. That no damage to property was premeditated.

3. That the primary causes of the raid on the Hall are

(a) The spirit of pro-Germanism rampant in certain circles of this city and the general belief that this spirit is founded largely in the Concordia Society which occupies the said Hall.

(b) The general knowledge that the bust of Kaiser Wilhelm I was contained in said Hall.

(c) The desperation of the men at the slowness of recruiting which they attributed to an unchecked anti-British sentiment, well knowing that the membership of said Society includes a great number of young men.

4. That the immediate cause of the damage to property was the finding in the bar-room of the Society of the picture of King George v surrounded with German flags; the general decoration of the walls with German flags and red, white and black bunting; the presence upon the walls of a large number of pictures of the present German Kaiser and other German notables; the entire absence of any British emblems except the King's picture and a Union Jack which is the property of the Berlin School Board; the finding of evidences of habitual occupation of the rooms as a Club in the face of assurances given publicly by the Society officials at the time of the sinking of the *Lusitania* that the Club would be closed until the expiration of the war.

5. That this Court cannot fix individual responsibility for destruction of property.

6. That in the second return to the Hall and in the destruction of property the soldiers were accompanied, aided and abetted by throngs of civilians. No civilian, police officer or municipal or other official interfered or attempted to interfere at any time nor was any notification of the disorder communicated to Battalion Headquarters until nearly the conclusion of the disturbance, and notice was then given only by a non-commissioned officer of the Battalion. Immediately the o.c. with other officers went to the scene and sent all soldiers on the streets back to barracks.

7. That the following damage appears to have been occasioned.

(a) removal of the bust of Kaiser Wilhelm I.

(b) breakage of a number of window panes, glass in partitions, chairs, German pictures.

(c) removal and destruction of two kegs of beer and certain bottles of whisky.

(d) removal and burning of German flags, bunting and books.

(e) removal of the picture of His Majesty King George V.

(f) destruction of a piano by civilians.

Much of the above destruction was done by civilians who were actually selling on the street souvenirs of the occasion, such as piano keys, etc.

C 5 FINDINGS OF A COURT OF INQUIRY ASSEMBLED AT CAMP BORDEN, ONTARIO, ON JULY 25, ADJOURNED TO JULY 26 AND TO AUG. 2 [1916] AT BERLIN, ONT., BY ORDER OF THE OFFICER COMMANDING, 8TH BRIGADE FOR THE PURPOSE OF INQUIRING INTO AND REPORTING UPON ALLEGED DAMAGES TO FURNITURE AND BUILDING KNOWN AS THE CONCORDIA HALL, BERLIN, ONT., ALSO DAMAGES TO LUTHERAN PARSONAGE, ST. MATTHEW'S CHURCH, BERLIN, ONT.
[P.A.C., RG 24, v. 1256, file HQ 593-1-87]

The Court having assembled pursuant to order, finds from the evidence given, also from personal observation of conditions in Berlin and from a thorough inspection of the Concordia Club.

(1st) That conditions were allowed to prevail in Berlin that loyal British citizens found impossible to tolerate.

(2) That the Concordia Club, supposed to be a singing organization, was in reality a strong German club with a large membership of young men and everything we found in connection with the club went to show that it was an organization to foster and maintain a strong German spirit and love for the fatherland.

We found in the club a large pedestal 5 ft. high, built to carry the bust of Kaiser Wilhelm 1st, rescued from the lake in Victoria Park and said to be stored away and covered up. We also found German music, German literature and the scenery for the stage in the hall was German. The only evidence of the English language we saw was a card on the wall back of a counter on which was printed in English, "terms strictly cash."

(3) That this club was closed until the end of the war according to the following which appeared in the News Record, Thursday, May 13th year 1915:

Important Notice
Members of Concordia Society are requested to
attend an important meeting to be held this
Thursday evening in Concordia Hall at 8 o'clock
By Order,
Louis Bardon
President

News item appearing in the *News Record*, Friday May 14th, 1915:

At a special meeting of the Concordia Society held at its club rooms last evening it was voluntarily decided to close the club for pleasure and singing purposes until the end of the war. The meeting was largely attended. Mr. L. Bardon, the president of the club, occupied the chair and Mr. Guetzen acted as secretary. Since the club has leased the present quarters for a certain period of time and is responsible for the rent of the same, the large hall in connection will continue to be leased and used for the purpose of public meetings and assemblies as heretofore. Otherwise the club room will be closed. The decision to close the club was carried unanimously.

The evidence shows the club had not been closed and was still being used as a meeting place.

(4) That the soldiers started the trouble by going after the bust and that soldiers and civilians were equally responsible for the damage. And we place the whole responsibility with the authorities for allowing conditions that were sure to bring trouble ...

C 6   LETTER TO THE EDITOR OF THE BERLIN
News Record FROM W.H. BREITHAUPT,
26 FEBRUARY 1916
[*Berlin* News Record, *26 February 1916, p 6*]

Pennsylvania Germans began settlement of what became Waterloo Township in the year 1800 making this the oldest settlement, of any magnitude, in the interior of Upper Canada. As early as 1803 almost the whole of what is now Waterloo Township was purchased by these people. Benjamin Eby, a liberal minded, far-seeing man, came in 1807. He was made Mennonite Bishop, and at the same time was a very practical man of affairs. He is well entitled to the distinction of being called the founder of Berlin. Whether he gave the place its name is however at best doubtful. Better evidence than that of Ezra Eby's book indicates otherwise.

Germans from Germany, as distinguished from Pennsylvania Germans, began coming here as early as 1819 or 1820. To them and to their later coming compatriots and their descendants, the industrial growth and development of our City is most largely due.

Among the first to come were such men as Gaukel who built the hotel which stood on the corner of King and Queen Streets until replaced by the present Walper House; Kraemer, Hailer, Enslin, and others. Elsewhere in the County there were such men of energy and large undertakings as Hespeler, for whom the village of New Hope changed its name, and Beck, the father of Sir Adam Beck; men like Klotz, a grandson of whom recently gave his life for the honor of Canada, Naftsinger, Schmidt, Ratz, and many others; all Germans until they came to Canada and thereafter patriotic Canadians.

It was fit that the chief place of a settlement of such origin should have a name of German origin and naturally an important name was wanted. Berlin, Canada, was however, not named after the capital of the German Empire for the simple reason that there was at that time no German Empire. Berlin, Germany, was recovering from the ravages of the Napoleonic wars in which her citizens had fought, and finally conquered, side by side with the British.

What is it that gives a name character or nationality? Long association mainly. There are many names of German origin which are now good Canadian or British names. Guelph, for instance, the name of our illustrious Royal family, is a name of German origin. George I was Hannoverian before he was English. Every one who heard him will recall the gracious German address of our Royal Governor-General in front of the City Hall, not two years ago.

What did we think of Botha and Smuts not many years ago, at the time of the Boer war? Now one of these honorable gentlemen is Premier of a unit of the British Empire and the other is a trusted British general.

Berlin, Canada is, by long association, well on to a hundred years, a Canadian name, not German. Long before we were, Berlin Canada was, and will be, long after our bones are dust, even should it try to hide its identity under an assumed name.

We are of German descent, and are not ashamed of it. We are descendants of Germans who came to Canada seeking larger opportunity and larger freedom; of the class of Germans who fought for representative government in the revolution of 1848. Though of German descent we are not Germans nor are we German-Canadians or any variety of Germans or part Germans; not hyphenates as Mr. Weichel has well said. We are Canadians, and yield not an iota, to anyone, in devotion to our country and to the ideals of the British Empire.

...

Is anything to be gained by dropping the venerable name of Berlin, Ontario? Will it make any difference whatever in the cause now most important and most compelling of all, that of British success in the war? Will it not rather demonstrate our lack of dignity and make us a butt of derision from one end of the country to the other?

We are passionately patriotic in making war supplies, at good profit. For the sake of a possible temporary advantage in getting a few more orders we are ready to sacrifice our self respect. And yet, in general, are our factories not well active, and is not our general business condition and outlook steadily improving?

How much nobler to demonstrate the enduring power of British institutions and ideals, which assimilate all that is best in other peoples.

The practical duty is before us – and the privilege of so showing our loyalty – of raising the 118th battalion to full strength as quickly as possible, and this is of infinitely more service to the cause of the British Empire than any futile attempt at change of identity. Berlin, Canada has been an honored name since its existence. Let us now increase its honor by doing our full duty.

On the other hand it is but fair to admit that many citizens – very few of those whose families have been identified with the community's development for more than their own generation – are honestly persuaded that a change of name is desirable. Let them be equally honest in method to bring about the result desired by them.

What are we fighting for if not for the cause of freedom and responsible government, for government by consent of the governed? Or is this a race war, General Sir Sam Hughes to the contrary notwithstanding?

The change of name of our good City is something that affects many of us lightly. To others of us, perhaps more of us, it is a question of vital concern. Under British institutions, on which we pride ourselves, there is a well established method of ascertaining the will of the governed, and that is by ballot. Of all democratic forms of government the British form is most insistent on this. A Parliament will dissolve to get instruction, by ballot, from the people, on a new question of importance arising, and this general method pervades the forms of government of all British Dominions.

Or shall we admit that Prussian ideals of government have already so far impressed us that we are ready to adopt them, ready to impose the will of the few on the many; of the minority on the majority; or in any event to take the risk of so doing?

It is quite possible that a majority of the ratepayers of Berlin Ontario will favor the proposed change. Whether so or not, it is their inherent right to express their will on the question by ballot, and for such ballot there is ample time without interfering with required procedure.

Should such ballot come out about even, although slightly against change, our City legislators can still, with good reason, proceed at their discretion. Should it be strongly adverse there would be an end to the matter.

The News Record has done a public service in printing the names of the signers of the petition presented to the City Council Monday night. Let there be eliminated all names not on the City's voters lists, as such names clearly are on the petition without right. If further there be scratched all names of those to whom the question is wholly indifferent and who signed in complaisance merely, of those who signed under mild coercion such as by a factory proprietor personally making the round of his employees, and lastly such who for any reason would now vote differently from the intent of the petition, let us see what would remain of this sole mandate on which the change of name is to go forward.

There is the further question of adopting a new name, different from either, for the union of the present two municipalities of Berlin and Waterloo. In favor of this there is more to be said than for changing the one name alone. But such consummation does not yet appear to be probable.

C 7   LETTER TO THE EDITOR OF THE BERLIN
News Record FROM W. G. CLEGHORN,
CHAIRMAN OF THE NORTH WATERLOO
RECRUITING COMMITTEE
[*Berlin* News Record, *1 March 1916, p. 4*]

In last Saturday's issue of your paper there appeared a letter over the signature of Mr. W.H. Breithaupt, relative to the proposed changing of the name of Berlin ...

In support of his first contention that the industrial growth of Berlin is largely due to Germans, he mentions many German families who settled here and have become patriotic Canadians. One grows tired of hearing people continually harp upon what the Germans have done for Berlin and Waterloo County. They came from Germany to a veritable garden at an opportune time and prospered. Might one not well ask now whether they did not owe as much to Waterloo County as the County owed to them? However, apart from the fact that the above statement is open to question, in a crisis such as this, when we are engaged in a struggle with the Huns for our very existence, the present is not the time to deal in quibbles as to whether Berlin was built up by Germans, by English, Irish, Canadians or the Breithaupts.

We are surprised too, that a man of Mr. Breithaupt's apparent intelligence should also quibble by saying that Berlin, Ont., was not named after the capital of the German Empire, because there was no German Empire at that time. The fact remains that it was named after the capital of Prussia, and is to-day the capital of the German Empire, whence have emanated the most diabolical crimes and atrocities that have marred the pages of history; an empire that has allied with it the murderous, barbarous unspeakable Turk to help it force its ideas of "Kultur" on the whole world, and gain a "place in the sun." We say "away with a name that has become odious to the civilized world!" If the Germans here had raised one or two battalions who were now fighting in Flanders, Mr. Breithaupt might have some argument for the retention of the name of Berlin. We fail to understand by what line of reasoning he would try to persuade us that the name Berlin should be retained for this city, while

the word Potsdam has been effaced from the Breithaupt Terrace on
Margaret Ave.

Mr. Breithaupt asks what we thought of Botha and Smuts a few years
ago. True, Botha and Smuts fought against Britain, and were conquered.
However, they appreciated so much the British freedom and fair play
which they had received that, when war broke out they shouldered a rifle
like the heroes they were, marched against the Hun, and what is more,
defeated him. That is why these gentlemen are now honored throughout
the British Empire. They did not wait until 18 months had elapsed before they knew how to perform a duty and do it well. They showed that
they, at least, appreciated the privilege of living under the British flag and
fighting for it. We should like to ask Mr. Breithaupt how many of his
name, or of the descendants of the patriotic Germans named by him are
to-day fighting in the cause of liberty as Botha and Smuts did?

Mr. Breithaupt also says "We are Germans and are proud of it." Whom
does he mean by "we?" Does he speak for the community, a certain element in Berlin, or only for hmself? There are thousands of descendants
of Germans in this city to-day who are NOT proud of the fact that they
are German. They approve neither of the purpose for which this terrible
war was forced on the world, nor the ruthless manner in which it has
been carried on. How any one can look back at the countless terrible
outrages – women ravished, children killed, non-combatants drowned at
sea without warning, and still say "we are Germans and proud of it" is
beyond our comprehension. We sincerely hope that Mr. Breithaupt is
the only one who will flaunt such an assertion before the citizens of a
British City at such a crisis. It is bad taste to say the least.

He further says that nothing will be gained by dropping such a venerable name and "we shall be the butt of derision from one end of Canada
to the other." Public opinion as expressed in the papers from coast to
coast has been practically unanimous in requesting the change, and even
suggesting that if we had not the good sense to change it ourselves, that
the Legislature should change it for us. Were it for no other reason we
owe it to the rest of Canada and the Empire to change the name. Berlin
is to-day a name that is "obnoxious" to every loyal British subject
throughout the world. We submit, that if we in addition to changing the
name, do our duty to the Empire by filling the 118th Battalion this city
will be one of the most honored places in Canada, and not the butt of
derision.

Mr. Breithaupt says a far nobler duty lies before us than changing our
name: – that of raising the 118th Battalion to full strength. "Let US" he
continues, "increase the honor of Berlin by doing our full duty." Is Mr.
Breithaupt sincere in this statement?" Since the beginning of the war the
North Waterloo Recruiting Committee has been putting forth every effort
to enlist men for the Empire. Up to the present time, Mr. Breithaupt and
those whom he assumes to represent, have not only [not] taken any part in
recruiting, but have apparently discouraged it in certain quarters; other-

wise why should not their families be represented on the honor roll of their country? Is it fair to say "Let us do our duty to King and Country" while your own kith and kin stand aside, and let other boys go forth to fight their battles?

Mr. Breithaupt says lastly that this question should be submitted to the people. In reply to this statement we beg to say that the Council has decided by a practically unanimous vote to change the name of this city, and we believe that every loyal British subject in Berlin thinks they have taken the proper action. The purpose of the council meeting was well known, and citizens were invited to express their opinions either in favor of or against the proposed change. Why did Mr. Breithaupt not appear before the council and voice his objections?

In conclusion, we would say that even if the question of the change of name of Berlin were submitted to a vote of the people it would afford very little satisfaction to Mr. Breithaupt, as he would have no say in the matter. The Recruiting Committee has evidence that Mr. Breithaupt is not a British subject; is therefore an alien, and would not be entitled to a vote on this question. Such being the case it should have behooved Mr. Breithaupt to keep silent. Has he been voting illegally all these years? Is he to-day qualified for the municipal office which he holds?

C 8 LIEUTENANT-COLONEL W.M.O. LOCHEAD, OFFICER COMMANDING THE 118TH BATTALION, TO COLONEL L.W. SHANNON, OFFICER COMMANDING MILITARY DISTRICT NO. 1
[*P.A.C., RG 24, 1256, file HQ 593-1-87*]

Berlin, Ont.
March 6th, 1916.

I beg to advise that I have, as per the request of the Adjutant-General, forwarded him the following wire:

"Delayed answer pending police court trial of Sergeant who admitted responsibility. stop. Sergeant found guilty and remanded two days for sentence. stop. Have reported fully by telephone and in writing to Colonel Shannon. Stop. Tappert most indiscreet in his language and attitude towards soldiers when asked why he did not leave Canada. Stop. Otherwise he would not have been assaulted. stop. Battalion was officially and sternly warned by myself on different occasions not to approach Tappert or his house. Stop. They disobeyed in my absence and hence to preserve discipline I am lending every assistance to the civil authorities to see that proper punishment is awarded. stop.

You will do well to suggest to the American Consul General that Tappert be advised to leave Canada as soon as possible because he and his family being Prussian at heart are taking advantage of their American citizenship to make themselves most offensive to Canadian soldiers and

Canadian citizens generally. Stop. Get report re Tappert from Colonel Sherwood."

A summary of what took place as per my own investigation and according to the evidence submitted at the police court is as follows:

I returned to my home on Saturday evening from London at about 10:15. I had been in the house but a few minutes when I was advised by the Orderly Officer that a report had reached him that Rev. Mr. Tappert was being badly treated by some soldiers. I told him to lose no time in having Mr. Tappert rescued and escorted home, and the offending soldiers paraded to barracks. This was immediately carried out. On Sunday morning and on Sunday afternoon, I made a full investigation of the circumstances and in this connection, interviewed different officers and men, and Mr. Tappert himself and the police authorities. Before leaving the Chief of Police, I assured him that the arrest and trial of the responsible men would be welcomed by myself and arrangements were accordingly made for the trial of Company Sergeant-Major Blood and of Pte. Schaefer on Monday morning (this morning) at 9 O'Clock these men being the men who conducted Rev. Tappert through the streets. The trial accordingly took place this morning, when Sergt-Major Blood accepted full responsibility for what had taken place. According to his evidence, which same was corroborated by the evidence of others and not in any way refuted by the evidence of Rev. Tappert himself, he and a number of other N.C.O.'s. and men paraded to the residence of the prosecutor to obtain an explanation from him as to why he had not left Berlin, they understanding that he had given his definite promise that he would quit this vicinity by March 1st. On approaching his door they rung the bell but were not permitted to enter. They then held a consultation which resulted in the breaking of the glass between the door. The key, however, had fallen to the floor and hence to gain admission they forced the door. They then entered and demanded an explanation from Mr. Tappert of his continuance in Berlin. Mr. Tappert refused to answer and by his speech and general attitude defied them. They then requested him to put on his coat and hat and accompany them to the barracks, which he refused to do. They, therefore, attempted to lay hands on him when a general scuffle took place and, in his resistance, Mr. Tappert was marked up some little, although he could not make any definite statement as to how or by whom he was actually assaulted. They conducted him from the house and along the street, but gave him up immediately on the arrival of the officers.

The above is a brief but substantial summary of what actually took place. As intimated to you over the telephone, I have at different times appealed to the men to behave themselves and have referred to Mr. Tappert in particular, commanding them to lay no hands on his person or on his property. While, therefore, I am not particularly worrying about Mr. Tappert, as he is not worthy of much consideration, I am nevertheless most anxious to maintain discipline. Hence, I appreciate the necessity of punishing the men responsible for this outrage, and, as intimated above, am acting in full sympathy and active support of the civil authorities. The men must be convinced that they cannot behave in such an un-soldierly and ungentlemanly manner with impunity.

I am particularly disappointed in Sergt-Major Blood, as I have given him different personal talks regarding his duty as an non-commissioned officer. He is an awfully good fellow but suffers his enthusiasm for the British cause to drown his good judgment and sense of proper self-control.

From the above, you will appreciate that I am in no way condoning the action of the soldiers in respect of this or any other outbreak, because I fully realize that any leniency on my part would be fatal to discipline.

I, therefore, request that you make the proper representations to Ottawa; namely, that while Rev. Tappert is not entitled to much consideration, the soldiers yet acted in a disgraceful manner and that I am not endeavoring in the least to shield them.

C 9   REPORT BY C.J. DOHERTY, MINISTER OF JUSTICE, REGARDING THE CLAIM FOR DAMAGES SUBMITTED BY THE ACADIAN CLUB OF WATERLOO, ONTARIO
[P.A.C., RG 24, v. 1158, file HQ 57-4-77]

27 November 1916.

It appears that on the evening of May 5th, 1916, some ten or more soldiers of the 118th Overseas Battalion, C.E.F. ... were allowed admission to the rooms of the Acadian Club in King Street ... for the purpose of obtaining and taking away a bronze bust of the Emperor of Germany; that they carried this bust away but subsequently, about the hour of 11.30 p.m., reinforced by some thirty or forty more soldiers of the same battalion, and organized in the character of a mob, returned ... and practically demolished all the furnishings contained in the said rooms; that the military and civil authorities did not appear to have anticipated these depredations which appear to have been executed without restraint on the part of the military or civil police; that in consequence of these lawless operations on the part of the soldiers, Mr. N.A. Zick, President of the Acadian Club, presented a claim upon the Department of Militia and Defence accompanied by an inventory of the articles alleged to have been destroyed, asking to be indemnified in the sum of $529.75; that a Court of Inquiry was appointed to investigate the affair, and after hearing evidence, reported that the damage ... was done by members of the 118th Battalion, that in view of the racial ill-feeling which appeared to exist in that locality, evidence of which was tendered to, but rejected by the Court, they were not disposed to recommend that the battalion be assessed for the amount of these damages because they feared further ill-feeling might be engendered. They therefore recommended that the damages be paid by the Government ... Mr. Zick represents that ... at the time of the occurrences above described twenty-eight members of the club had enlisted for military service, and that 'the club since the beginning of the war has been patriotic, always welcoming soldiers in their midst, and never giving cause for offence to any one.'

The undersigned, in accordance with the consideration which he has given other claims to compensation arising out of unauthorized wrongful acts on the part of undisciplined soldiers impelled by motives of private malice, has the honour to report that there is no legal responsibility on the part of the Crown in respect of the claim presented by the Acadian Club.

C 10   LIEUTENANT-COLONEL W.M.O. LOCHEAD
       TO MAJOR-GENERAL W.E. HODGINS
       [*P.A.C., RG 24, v. 1256, file HQ 593-1-87*]

Berlin, Ont.
May 20th 1916.

Following my wire sent this morning I have the honor and pleasure to afford you absolute assurance that the conduct of the soldiers throughout yesterday was most commendable in every particular. Those entitled to vote were at intervals given leave during the morning and the battalion carried on in the usual way throughout the day. When the result of the election became known a citizens' parade was formed which was headed by the 108th Regiment band. When this procession passed the home of Mr. Geo. C.H. Lang an incident occurred. Regarding same I beg to give the facts as ascertained from most reliable sources, as follows:

The Langs were bitterly opposed to the changing of the name and took a very active part throughout the day. Naturally the parade stopped at the Lang homestead to give them cheers. Mr. August Lang, who had altercations with different civilians throughout the day, deliberately walked from the house to the street, having in his hand a large walking stick. His manner was most defiant and very apparently was courting trouble. On reaching the street pavement he immediately got in an argument with some civilians which ended in his slashing at one of these civilians with his stick. The blow missed the civilian and fell on a soldier. Mr. Lang then struck out violently with the stick until finally the stick was taken from him and he was escorted back to the house by one of the soldiers. A few soldiers were in the parade, having been invited by different city aldermen to ride on the side of their motorcars. I myself didn't get up town until after the parade was over but I have assurances from the most reliable men in Berlin that Mr. Lang himself was altogether to blame for the little mix-up and that primarily it was an affair which concerned civilians and that any part which the few soldiers did play was most commendable to them. Several of our best citizens assured me that it was deliberately planned by Mr. Lang so that he would be able to report to the authorities bad conduct on the part of the soldiers. Whether this is true or not I cannot say but I can absolutely assure you that no blame can possibly be attached to the soldiers.

The city is tendering us a formal farewell to-day and we expect a good time. We are now busy packing up and making other preparations for our departure for camp on Monday morning.

C 11 STATEMENT IN CONNECTION WITH CHANGE
OF NAME OF BERLIN
[P.A.C., MG 30, B28, John A. Lang Papers]

The Petitioners respectfully submit to the Government for consideration the following facts: –

1. The inaugural meeting of the movement on Feb. 11, was an unadvertised and picked meeting, sprung as a surprise on the general public, who knew of it only when it was past. This was the meeting which was represented to the Private Bills Committee as a "Public Mass Meeting." The attendance, of which a record was kept through the circulation of a petition to the City Council, was approximately 65, including, accidentally, four opponents.

2. The promoters though they acknowledged later (April 15th) that they had considered the movement since the previous fall, appeared with their petition at the last meeting of the City Council (Feb. 21) when that body could act and the requested bill still be advertised the required number of times for passage in the then Session of the Legislature. On this ground the petitioners drove the Council to immediate action that evening before an examination could be made of the petition there presented as signed by 1080 ratepayers and citizens. When the list was published in the following days it was found that approximately only 295 were owners and 115 tenants, ie. only 410 of the 1080 were municipal voters.

3. The effect of the raid on the Concordia Club (Feb. 15) just between Feb. 11 and Feb. 21 was to intimidate the Council on February 21 into passing the request for a change of name without a vote of the citizens. It was the first raid of the kind in Berlin, and there was nothing to provoke it. The Concordia had systematically supported, and given its hall for patriotic purposes, including a smoker by the Officers and soldiers of the 118 Battalion. The result of this and of subsequent raids was that from this time onward, no alderman, newspaper, manufacturer, or citizen was free to oppose the change without risk to himself and his property.

The approximate damage at each of three of these raids was $1,000.00

4. The petition of 1080 was signed largely under coercion; and manufacturers, through dread of raids were forced to sign the special manufacturers' petition. At a meeting of the manufacturers, a motion was introduced to keep records of opponents; and in discussing the motion, a leading promoter proposed to report all such opponents to every business man in Canada, and stated that he and his fellow promoters "would be at some pains to publish the names of those who did not sign and their goods would be boycotted from one end of Canada to another."

5. The attendance of military men at the City Council prevented free discussion and the press was also interfered with by threats of raids.

6. When the Private Bills Committee rejected the Berlin Bill (No. 44) the promoters publicly misrepresented the hearing and grossly attacked the Cabinet (calling it the "rotten Hearst Government") with an unfairness which the petitioners propose yet to expose in print.

At this time also the promoter organ (Berlin Telegraph) threatened to force the Government by disturbances in Berlin; and when the Government passed the special act on the day of the closing of the House, a military officer openly said, "Now we will give you a military election."

7. The wholesale intimidation under which the vote on May 19 was held is shown by the printed slip at the end of this statement, which will form a part of the matter which the petitioners propose to publish. The raids and threats prevented all organized opposition so that there were not even enough opposition scrutineers to man the polls.

8. The majority for the change was insignificant, the matter being as important to this community as local option, where ⅗ are required; and the majority itself was due to a restricted vote and fear of voters to go to the polls. The naturalization test was applied strictly to scores of opponents who had lived here for decades, some 40 and even 50 years. They had voted at every parliamentary and municipal election in all these years, and also done jury duty and fulfilled every other function of complete citizens which they had always held themselves to be. (These same citizens gave sons to the 118 Battalion.)

On the other hand many recent arrivals, unnaturalized citizens of various nationality, including German and Austrian, whom the promoters had induced or coerced to support the change were permitted to vote, no opposition scrutineers being present to prevent them.

9. The promoters controlling the Council broke faith with the citizens in the selection of the new name. The selection of the final list, according to public and signed pledges, was to be left to a representative committee of 99. The Council first left the selection to the 99 under such restrictions that the resulting list of 6 names was the joke of the country.

Then the Council referred the choice to the 99 with less restrictions; and finally, without waiting till the 99 could report or even sit, the Council dismissed that Committee and made the selection itself.

10. The purpose of this arbitrary action was to prevent amalgamation with Waterloo under the name of that corporation.

11. The result of this breach of faith, as well as of all the unfairness of the promoters since the outset of the movement, was the insignificant vote of the citizens on the new name, only 729 in an electorate after deducting repeaters of some 4500. Kitchener, with a vote of 346 has less than 8% of the electors; while the petitioners supporting this statement are numbered by thousands.

12. There is a bitter division at present in the City and many opponents as well as supporters of the change favor amalgamation with Waterloo, under its name, as the best means of allaying the friction. The best opinion of the County also views this solution with favor.

13. The County at large is very anxious that, should there be a change, the new name of the County Seat should correspond with the name of the County.

14. The whole matter is not one of loyalty on the part of the promoters, nor want of patriotism in their opponents. When the result of the vote on May 19th was reported to the King by cable, he practically ignored the message. All that we ask is British fair-play, and a fair review of the question, and especially a consideration of the amalgamation with Waterloo as a possible solution of the present difficulty.

C 12   EDITORIAL REGARDING 'THE OTHER SIDE'
[*Berlin* Daily Telegraph, *24 July 1916. Clipping in P.A.C., MG 30, B28, John A. Lang Papers*]

As a misrepresentation of the attitude and object of a loyal and important class of the population the "scrupulous effort" of the Citizens' League is a huge success ... "The Other Side" is not so remarkable, however, for what it contains as it is for what is missing.

It does not contain a line to show the people who may receive a copy what the Citizens' League or its supporters have done to help the Allies to win the war. There is no information that would lead one to offer congratulations to the League or the "Anti-name-Changers" for the part they had played in recruiting men for the various contingents which have left this city. No reference is made to the fact that after three requests between 700 and 800 aliens of enemy birth in this city, many of whom were on the Voters' Lists, have been registered and are reporting monthly. Above all, it does not offer a single reason why the name "Kitchener" should not be adopted by this industrial centre.

The attempt to belittle the patriotism of the large number of men and women of this city, who have given their husbands and sons to fight for the cause of the Allies will come back sooner or later upon those who are responsible for the composition and circulation of the statement. It must always be kept in mind that Canada is at war as well as Great Britain.

C 13 REPORT BY MAJOR BARON OSBORNE,
ASSISTANT PROVOST MARSHAL, MILITARY DISTRICT
NO. 1, TO THE ASSISTANT ADJUTANT GENERAL,
MILITARY DISTRICT NO. 1
[*P.A.C., RG 24, v. 1256, file HQ 593-1-87*]

London, Ont.
January 4th, 1917.

Acting under instructions, I proceeded to the city of Kitchener on the morning of the 1st instant, leaving London at 6.05 a.m. via Grand Trunk, and reaching Kitchener at 8.20 a.m. I visited the Chief of Police, O'Neil, and handed him list of absentees, men from No. 1 District. I found everything in Kitchener at that time very quiet; no excitement beyond that usually evidenced at election time. At 10.30 a.m. I proceeded by street car to Waterloo. I visited Chief of Police Flynn, of that town, and gave him a description of a man from Special Service Company who was an absentee. We apprehended the soldier the same morning, and returned him to his unit at London.

2. I then returned to Kitchener and booked rooms at the Walper Hotel. Throughout the day everything remained normal as regards the behaviour of the citizens, but great energy seemed to be exercised in getting the voters to the various polls.

3. About 5.30 p.m. people began to gather around the offices of the News-Record, on King Street. This was the organ advocating the platform of the Citizens' League. They were also gathered around the front of The Telegraph, which was the organ supporting the Patriotic League. The crowds gradually increased in numbers, without noise. I was accompanied by three Military Policemen from London, who had also gone to Kitchener to vote. I directed them to mingle with the crowd and listen to the conversations, and without attracting attention endeavour to gain the feeling or possible attitude of the people, as to their future behaviour on this occasion.

4. At about 7 p.m. I was standing outside the office of The Telegraph when I heard a cheer from the direction of the office of the News-Record. I proceeded to the spot quietly, when there, found that the cause of the cheering was that Mayor-elect David Gross junior was heading the poll, also several candidates of the Citizens' League were leading. From that time on the people seemed to become more excited. I proceeded to the office of the Chief of Police at the city hall, with the idea of talking over the situation with him. Whilst in the Chief's office, Mr. W.D. Uttley, editor of the News-Record, came into the office. At that moment the Chief of Police was out of his office, and as old residents of the city Mr. Uttley and I passed the customary New Year's greetings and I asked him to be seated. No mention was made by him or me as to the existing situation. In a few moments the Chief of Police returned. That was about eight p.m. It was then that Mr. Uttley stated to the Chief of Police that

he had been informed that it was the intention of certain people to wreck the office of the News-Record, and he demanded protection as a citizen and ratepayer. I advised the Chief of Police, after he had asked me for advice, to call up the mayor, Dr. Hett; notify him of the situation and request his attendance at the city hall, re the situation. This was done. Also did I advise him to call up the Police Magistrate, J.J.A. Weir. This was done.

5. At about that time two of my police returned and told me that they had heard rumors pass through the crowd that the News-Record office would be "cleaned up," as a certain faction could stand it no longer. At this time also Alderman-elect N. Asmussen, one of the Citizens' League candidates, came to the office and said that he had been struck by a soldier of the 118th Battalion, and that the large plate-glass window of the News-Record had been smashed. He asked me for protection, and what he should do. I advised him to make for some friend's house, and keep off the streets until the feeling more or less subsided. This I believe he did.

6. Immediately after that, the Mayor-elect, David Gross junior, came into the office and stated that a party of soldiers, whom he believed to be members of the 118th Battalion, had visited his residence on Water street North, but not finding him at home had gone away again. He asked me also what I would advise. At this time I knew from reports that a very bitter feeling existed against him. I told him that in my opinion, in the interests of law and order it was absolutely necessary that under the circumstances he go to some friend's house, other than his own, and there keep quiet and let no one know of his whereabouts. He assured me that he would do anything I suggested. He then left the office. It was at this moment that I heard that the window of the News-Record office had been smashed. I immediately proceeded, with two military policemen, to that building and found this to be correct. There was a large crowd at this moment – several hundred people – outside the office. A few soldiers were mingled with this crowd, who seemed to be quiet and acting just as ordinary citizens, interested in the results of the poll. I went into the office, which was crowded with people more or less excited, all civilians. I there learned that Alderman-elect H.M. Bowman had been injured. This I afterwards found to be true, but it was only slight. I believe he struck one of the soldiers.

7. I then recommended the management of the News-Record to request the people to get out of the office, except those connected with the paper. This request was complied with. I then called up the city hall and spoke to Mayor Hett. I explained the situation and asked if he could come down and see for himself. He told me over the 'phone that he had been advised not to come down. I thereupon told him I would go to the police office and speak with him there. I proceeded to carry this purpose into execution.

8. On getting out into the street I heard the singing of the patriotic song, "We'll never let the old Flag fall," and considerable cheering. On looking down King Street in the direction of Waterloo I saw a procession marching

up the street towards me, composed of soldiers and civilians, principally civilians. They were headed by a soldier carrying a Union Jack. I immediately put up my hand and called upon the procession to halt, which was obeyed without hesitation. I then addressed my remarks to the soldiers in the procession, telling them that as soldiers I considered it in the interests of good order and discipline that they should disperse to their homes; and I ordered them, as their superior officer and as Provost Marshal for the District, to immediately obey my orders. Several people in the crowd, whom I did not know, called for three cheers for Major Osborne. After that, they sang, "He's a Jolly Good Fellow" and quietly dispersed. None of the soldiers in the crowd at this time acted otherwise than in harmony with my commands. The procession, to all appearances simply dwindled away.

9. I then went back to the News-Record office for a few moments, and everything seemed to be perfectly quiet. I then went on my mission to the town hall to interview the mayor, whom I found to be there, also Mr. Uttley, editor of the paper previously referred to. The situation was talked over and Mayor Hett seemed very undecided as to the course of action to take. In fact I might state, that none of the civil officials seemed to know what they should do, or what action to take, and constantly referred to me for advice, and seemed to be totally unable to come to any decision as to what they should do under such circumstances. Mr. Uttley was insisting upon protection. Finally the mayor told me that he requested military protection. I told him he would have to make a request in the official manner, when his request would be immediately complied with. He made this request officially, which I here attach.

10. I immediately called up the Officer Commanding the 122nd Battalion, stationed at Galt, and requested that the detachment previously arranged for should be immediately despatched by electric car to Kitchener. I also notified Militia Headquarters, Military District No. 1, London, what I had done, and briefly explained the situation. I called up Galt at 9:35 P.M. This detachment left Galt at 10.01 P.M. I then went down to the city.

11. I met many soldiers, who seemed orderly and well conducted. In fact wherever I appeared, the soldiers were behaving themselves. There were not many soldiers about. Beyond the usual excitement at election times there was nothing out of place.

12. I then proceeded to the car barns on King street to meet the detachment of the 122nd, and conduct them by a quiet route to the market square. A few minutes after 11 P.M. the detachment arrived under command of Captain Carment, 122nd Battalion. On arrival at the market square I went to the police office and informed the mayor and magistrate that the detachment had arrived, and asked them for orders for the disposal of same. They were quite undecided as to what they wanted me to do with these troops, and asked again what I would advise them to do. I told them they would have to give me orders as to what buildings they

required protection for, or what individuals they required protection for, and what steps they required me to take – that I would entirely [act] under their directions, and would carry out all orders given to me by the civil authorities, as was required by law.

13. The mayor then informed me, in the presence of the magistrate and Chief of Police, that he required me to clear King Street from Queen Street to Foundry Street. On the south side of this portion of King Street the Evening Record building is situated. They also told me they required protection for the mayor-elect's residence; and also the button factory on Water Street, owned by the mayor-elect. I then informed them that this would be done immediately, and that I would require a magistrate or justice of the peace to accompany me with each detachment of soldiers in order that if necessary the Riot Act be read, and from whom I would receive orders, which from that time on would have to be in writing.

14. Police Magistrate Weir accompanied the party proceeding to the button factory on Water Street, where he found all quiet, and where a guard was then posted; also a guard on the mayor-elect's residence. After considerable hesitation, Mayor Hett proceeded with me with the detachment to clear King Street. This detachment, with fixed bayonets, formed fours and were marched, under my command down King Street to carry out the above duty. By this time the people had got word of the arrival of the troops from Galt.

15. On the head of my column reaching a point on King Street where Frederick Street crosses, a large crowd of people, creating great noise – shouting, jeering, hooting and hissing, was surging up King Street in the direction of my party. I immediately realized that if I allowed them to surround my party I would become absolutely powerless. I therefore formed line at this point and blocked King Street, and prevented the further passage of the crowd. They came quite close to the soldiers, and appeared to be in a very angry mood. I called upon the people to retire. I waited a few moments and again repeated the order. I saw that determination was required, in order to impress upon them that I was there on serious business and intended to carry it out. My party at this moment was halted. For the third time I called upon the people to disperse, and told them it was my intention to move on down King Street, and that it would be to their interests to quietly give way before the advance of the troops.

16. I again addressed the mayor personally, in a quiet tone, and told him that it was my intention to move at a slow pace down King Street, to carry out these previous orders. I again reminded him that he would, if necessary, have to read the Riot Act, when he remarked that at that time he saw no riot, which in a sense was true. But the people would not obey, and did not seem disposed to move. I brought my men, after cautioning them, to the position of the charge, when the people gradually moved back. At a very slow and steady pace I then moved on down King Street, the people gradually retiring in front of my men.

17. On arriving at Queen Street I threw a cordon across that point, so blocking up that portion of the street. I then moved on and blocked up King Street where Foundry crosses, and then proceeded with the assistance of the civil police to clear the people from the intervening space between Queen and Foundry, quietly passing them through the cordon of soldiers blocking up these points. I found considerable difficulty in getting the people to obey. They did not seem to realize the seriousness of the situation or the observance of authority. Whenever I spoke to soldiers who were in the crowd at this point they immediately moved on, making no remarks or objections.

18. It was here that I found that the whole front of the lower portion of the Record front office had been wrecked. It was about this time − 11.30 − that I received information that some soldiers had entered the back of the building where the Record office is, and had smashed the windows and done other damage. I took a party of twelve men, under a sergeant, to the lane running at the back of the Record building, when I saw that the above statement was correct as regards the smashing of the windows etc., but there was no person other than myself and party at that point when I arrived.

19. After posting the party I returned to King Street. I there saw Mayor Hett again, who asked me if I had any further necessity for his presence. I told him that as first magistrate of the city it was his duty to remain until order had been restored, and moreover I told him I was under the impression that the law called for his presence. However, he seemed to want to get away, and did not want to remain. I thereupon told him, "You are still mayor of the city; do what you think is right," and I proceeded to carry out what I considered to be my duty, absolutely clearing this space as required by the civil authorities so to do. After great trouble I succeeded in carrying this into effect to a reasonable degree, by about one A.M. on the 2nd. I did not see Mayor Hett again until between 2:30 and 2:45 A.M. when I was returning from visiting the detached posts at the button factory and the mayor-elect's private residence on Water Street. When I met him, Mayor Hett was in a cutter driving in the direction of Waterloo, down King Street. He pulled up and asked me what I was going to do, and I told him that I intended to carry out my orders and enforce law and order as he had requested me to do, until such time as he in writing informed me that the services of the Militia were no longer required.

20. He then told me to get all I wanted for the comfort of the men who were there on duty. I then informed him that he as mayor, must understand that the expenses of bringing the troops into the city to meet the existing situation, with which the civil authorities had stated they were unable to cope, would fall entirely upon the city. He thereupon remarked, "Yes, I understand that; that is quite right. Make them as comfortable as ever you can."

21. It would be about two A.M. that I was able to withdraw the cordons of soldiers blocking King Street from Foundry to Queen from those two

posts. The men, after being provided with supper in Geddes' restaurant, were billetted in the old building of W.G. & R., situated on Queen Street South. I left a guard of one sergeant, one corporal and eighteen privates to guard the premises of the News-Record; also a guard on the mayor-elect's residence on Water Street, of one corporal and six privates; also a guard of one sergeant, one corporal and six privates on the button factory on Water Street, which property is owned by the mayor-elect.

22. From that time on things quieted down, and it appeared to me that everything was quietly settling down. After seeing the men fixed up as comfortably as circumstances would permit, in their quarters on Queen Street South, I with the three officers on duty had to take what rest we could at about 3:30 A.M., on the 2nd.

23. At 5:45 A.M. on the 2nd I made another tour of the city, visiting the various guards previously mentioned, and found all quiet. These guards I caused to be relieved at about 9 A.M. on the morning of the second. They remained on duty till about three P.M. on the 2nd, when Mayor Hett again wanted to know what was to be done. I informed him that it was entirely in his hands as to how long he wanted the troops to remain there, and that he having called them out, it was my duty to remain there until he thought fit to instruct me that their presence was no longer required, when, if he gave me an order in writing to the effect that their presence was no longer required, and that I could withdraw them, I would do so.

24. He thereupon gave me an order that I was to withdraw one captain, two subalterns, one company sergeant-major and eighty-two privates, but that I was to leave a guard on the Record office of two sergeants, two corporals, two buglers and eighteen privates. This I did. At four P.M. the portion of the details no longer required returned to Galt by the electric railway.

25. I had that morning ordered the Deputy Assistant Provost Marshal at Galt to report to me at Kitchener by 10 A.M., with one sergeant, one corporal and ten military policemen. I instructed Captain Day, the D.A.P.M., to collect all men of the 118th Battalion, irrespective of the period of their passes, take the passes from them and take measures to ensure their despatch from Kitchener to their unit, stationed at London, by the first available train. About twelve men were sent back from Kitchener at 3 P.M., via Galt, traveling C.P.R. At 3:45 P.M. about thirty men of the 118th Battalion left for London via Grand Trunk.

26. During the day all was quiet, nothing unusual occurring, beyond an incident at the Grand Trunk station, when a party of women, apparently the wives of soldiers at the front, assembled at the station, behaving in a most disorderly manner, jeering and abusing myself and the police and men of the 122nd Battalion. They appeared to be under the impression that we were there solely to protect pro-Germans, or to protect members of the Citizens' League. They did not appear to realize the fact that we were there as required by law, for the protection generally of the community.

27. These same women afterwards caused disturbances on King Street, when Alderman Reid, a member of the Citizens' League, was struck in the face by Mrs. Garner, the wife of a soldier at the front. This woman is well known to the police authorities in Kitchener and seems to be trying to stir up or incite trouble. I believe there is a summons against this woman by the civil authorities for disorderly conduct.

28. At about 1:30 A.M. on the morning of the 3rd, Sergeant Grasser, of the city police, came to my room at the Walper Hotel and informed me that a soldier had rushed across King Street and smashed the window of the News-Record which during the day had been replaced. At this moment I was about to leave the hotel to proceed to the station, to return to London. I therefore immediately went and saw the window had been broken again. I questioned the sentry who was on duty at the News-Record, who told me that the thing was so suddenly done, only one man implicated, and that he was entirely unable to prevent it. I have since been informed it was not a soldier who smashed the window.

29. I then proceeded with Sergeant Grasser in an automobile to the Grand Trunk station. I there found a considerable number of men of various units waiting to return to their stations. I took the passes from all these men in possession of passes and took the names of all others. These men were orderly and seemed well conducted and perfectly sober.

30. At the station I met Lieutenant Bricker, of the 118th Battalion, with whom I returned to London, arriving in London at about five A.M.

31. During my stay in Kitchener, from 8 A.M. on the morning of the 1st, until my departure at about three A.M. on the morning of the 3rd, no officers of the 118th Battalion had reported to me in Kitchener. I did, however, see Captain Routley for a few seconds on the night of the 1st. I was in a great hurry at the time, and could not stop longer than just to pass the remark that I did wish I could get all the soldiers off the streets and to their homes, and would he advise them to that effect if he met any? I think his remark was, "Yes, I will, sir."

32. At about 10:30 A.M. on the morning of the 1st I saw Lieutenant-Colonel Lochead, commanding the 118th Battalion, on King Street, and he asked me if there was any trouble. I told him at that time I could see no trouble. I had not heard of any trouble. He asked me how long was I going to stay. I told him that depended entirely upon circumstances, and asked when he purposed to return. He told me he thought he would return by the 9:20 P.M. train that night, via Grand Trunk railway. I afterwards found out that he had returned to London, but by what train I do not know.

33. There was, when I left Kitchener, a detachment of one lieutenant, two sergeants, two corporals, two buglers and eighteen men guarding the Berlin Record office buildings. Also Captain Day, D.A.P.M., of Galt, one sergeant, one corporal and ten military policemen, making a total of one captain, one lieutenant, three sergeants, three corporals, two buglers and twenty-eight privates. These have since been relieved except a few military police, who remained on duty.

34. Finally I may state positively that during my tour of duty in the City of Kitchener, I had no evidence that the men of the 118th Battalion, or any other men in uniform, had any part in the disturbance, and, as far as I could learn, were in no way responsible for it.

C 14   EXTRACT FROM THE INAUGURAL ADDRESS OF
DAVID GROSS, JUNIOR, MAYOR OF KITCHENER,
8 JANUARY 1917
[P.A.C., MG 30, B28, John A. Lang Papers]

To treat all our citizens with courtesy and consideration having no regard for creed or race and to cultivate genuine good will and unity between all classes of our people.

To do our full share toward every need in the defence of the British Empire. In the past our City has contributed largely to Patriotic, Red Cross and similar funds. We must continue to do so freely and liberally not only out of the civic treasury but also of our own time and money.

During the past year the name of our City has been changed. The agitation for such purpose has raised feelings of bitterness and discord between our citizens. It has led to acts of lawlessness and violence such as were never before known in our City. It has caused the circulation through the public press and otherwise of reports which were in every case distorted and in many cases slanderous and absolutely false. All this has been to the great injury of our City and the reputation of its people.

It will be part of our duty to try to restore peace and harmony in the community – to repress and punish all lawlessness and to hold to strict account any newspapers or persons who may circulate untrue and unfounded reports against our City and its people.

I believe I may say for you as I do for myself that we will not entertain any proposal to rechange the name of the City during our term of office.

D. WOMEN

D 1 'THE WOMEN'S EMERGENCY CORPS,' A STATEMENT PREPARED BY DR. A.H. ABBOTT, SECRETARY OF THE PROVINCIAL ORGANIZATION OF RESOURCES COMMITTEE
[P.A.C., MG 26, H, Borden Papers, RLB file 709(4), pp. 109, 242-109, 242A]

Up to August fifteenth of this year, 358,105 men had enlisted for overseas service with the Canadian Expeditionary Forces. Of this number 152,316 have come from Ontario, that is, 6% of the total population of Ontario (1911 census) are now under arms. These men are almost wholly between 18 and 45 years of age, and, as is natural, are, for the most part, taken from the Canadian and British-born men of the Province. In fact 29% of these two classes have already enlisted. The men of military age constitute also the essential part of the producing forces of the Province. It is, therefore, obvious that the enlistment of 29% of the Canadian and British-born men of military age of the Province, must have a very serious influence in diminishing the producing force, both in the factory and on the farm. This conclusion is confirmed by reports on the labour situation from all over the Province. Considering the industries directly connected with the production of munitions alone, it is found that one of these, which comprises 18 plants, employing approximately 2,000 men and a small number of women, can use at the present time about 500 more workers, and this particular industry is in less need than any other of the many industries concerned in the production of munitions. It is evident, therefore, that many thousands of workers, both men and women, are needed to equip our munition plants so that they can produce up to their capacity.

What is true of munition plants is equally true of most of the other industries of the Province; and the necessity of keeping these producing up to the capacity of the business offering is obvious both for present business and for the maintenance, after the war, of business connections which have been established outside the Province, if returning men are to find employment. There is scarcely a manufacturing establishment of any size in which more workers are not needed. It is not necessary to mention in detail the need for labourers on our farms and for the ordinary unclassified positions in which labour is essential. The effect of enlistment is seen on every hand as soon as the general labour situation is considered. "*The Labour Gazette*" for August, gives statistics on the unemployment on

June 30th, 1916 in organized labour in Ontario. Four-hundred and forty-seven Labour Unions, with a membership of 67,387, report only 625 members out of employment, and of these 525 were in Unions connected with building and construction.

More than that, the industries in which women have been generally employed report difficulty in securing a sufficient number of women workers and it is well-known that many positions for which there is or-dinarily an ample supply of women applicants, such as office-help, general servants, and charwomen, are now filled, either with indifferent help or not at all. While it is therefore true that there is not a sufficient supply of male labour to man our industries, it is also true, though not to the same extent, that there is a shortage of female labour, both for factory and other purposes. This condition has naturally carried with it, under the ordinary law of supply and demand, a general increase in the wages paid, and while this is more strikingly seen in those industries directly connected with the production of war equipment and food, it is generally true that better wages are being obtained to-day by workers than have been re-ceived in the past.

The war is making two great demands on the people of Ontario. The first demand is for men – the strongest and best to be had. The second demand is for increased production, both to meet the need for munitions and to provide money for our necessary patriotic funds and our Canadian War Loans. A moment's reflection will show that these two demands are opposed, and that, therefore, if the first is to be met, as it must be, workers must come from classes which have not been accustomed to labour in factory or on farm, if production is to be maintained, and much more, if production is to be increased.

The Women's Emergency Corps has not been formed to meet an ima-ginary situation. The supply of male labour is exhausted and therefore, women must do the work ordinarily done by men if the productive side of our provincial life is not to suffer. Women who offer themselves for positions ordinarily occupied by men, cannot be looked upon as in any way invading the territory belonging to male labour – they are simply offering their services to fill positions for which no men can be obtained. No man able to work, whether a returned soldier or one unfit for military service, need be out of employment to-day.

The position of the women is, therefore, identical with that taken by every patriotic section of our people, – namely, they are expressing their willingness to serve the Empire in any way in which the need of the hour is greatest. It must not, however, be supposed that changes involving the employment of a great number of women in factories in which ordinarily no women have been employed, can be readily made by our manufac-turers. Nor need it be supposed that manufacturers are anxious to obtain the services of women who have never done the work required, until they are doubly convinced that men cannot be secured. That time has come for some of our manufacturers, and we may be fully convinced that it must come for many more in the near future if they are to do their full duty as patriotic citizens, that is, to give up as many of their male employees as can be used in the army, while they strive to maintain their production.

The example of England is before us. After supplying at least four million men for the Army and millions more for war work, a sufficient number of non-producers have become producers to keep the staple industries running at what must be regarded as a remarkably high state of efficiency under the circumstances. Ontario, which produces more than one half of the annual output of manufactured goods in Canada, must do the same to meet the calls which are made upon it, and women must provide here, as in England, the extra workers to meet the emergency.

Toronto, Sept. 1st, 1916.

D 2   MARK H. IRISH, IMPERIAL MUNITIONS BOARD,
TO LIEUTENANT-COLONEL ERNEST J. CHAMBERS,
CHIEF PRESS CENSOR
[*P.A.C., RG 6, E1, Chief Press Censor, v. 40, file 178-B-5*]

Toronto,
27 October 1916.

Private and Confidential.

I am referred to you by Sir John Willison with whom I have discussed the subject upon which I now advise you.

We are beginning to use female labour in Munition Factories on night shifts as a part of our programme regarding the dilution of labour. It is conceivable, but not probable, that some of these women or girls might be either actually, or in imagination, interfered with on the streets while going to, or coming from, the place of employment. While, of course, no effort should be spared to avoid such occurrence, nor to exact the fullest punishment, yet having regard to the National cause, I submit that Press comments upon such an incident, should it occur, would be most unfortunate, as possibly producing a prejudice against the use of women in projectile production.

I lay the situation before you as I did before Sir John with confidence that you will do what is in the best interests, having regard to all the circumstances.

The matter appealed to Sir John as of sufficient importance to warrant me intruding upon you and he told me that I could feel perfectly confident that it would receive your prompt and sympathetic consideration.

D 3   CIRCULAR LETTER FROM ALBERT H. ABBOTT,
ONTARIO DIRECTOR, DEPARTMENT OF LABOUR OF
THE IMPERIAL MUNITIONS BOARD, TO ALL
TORONTO CONTRACTORS
[P.A.C., RG 24, v. 4376, file 2D. 34-7-61-1]

21 November 1916.

You are doubtless aware that the Department of Labour of the Imperial Munitions Board has been established to assist Contractors, wherever desired, to procure such labour as is necessary to maintain and even increase production.

We believe that Munitions' Contractors will find it to their interest, in view of the probable shortage of male labour next spring, to dilute their labour by the employment of women on all operations which women can successfully perform. The supply of woman labour at the present time is greatly in excess of the demand and the number of women offering their services has become so large that it is quite impossible for this office to handle the matter any longer. We, therefore, have arranged with the Ontario Government to have a Public Employment Bureau opened in Toronto at once under the management of Dr. Riddell, who was recently appointed by the Government as Superintendent of the Trades and Labour Branch. Dr. Riddell is thoroughly trained in the problems affecting labour and understands quite well that no Employment Bureau can be run satisfactorily which is not based solely upon "Efficiency". He, therefore, purposes to employ in this Bureau only those who are competent to decide what kind of work the applicants are fitted to do.

So far as Munitions is concerned Miss Wiseman, Supervisor of Woman Labour for the Imperial Munitions Board, has made a special study of the Plants and operations and has, we believe, conducted the registration which we have done with satisfaction to all our Contractors who have called upon her for assistance. A woman trained by her has been put at the head of the registration in the Government Bureau so that the methods followed by Miss Wiseman will be those adopted in the Government Bureau. We, therefore, suggest that, when you have any need of labour, male or female, you might find it to your advantage to communicate with Dr. Riddell, whose services will be placed at your disposal in the same way as our own. The Government Bureau is to be opened at 164 Bay St., Telephone Adelaide 926, on Wednesday, November 22nd.

Miss Wiseman, being thus relieved of the work of registration, will be able to devote more attention than in the past to the special work she has been appointed by the Board to do, namely, the visiting of Munitions' Plants and the advising of Contractors as to the work which women can do, and the best method of providing accommodation for them. We should be particularly pleased to have you make use of Miss Wiseman's services if you are considering, even remotely, the employment of women.

D 4   EXTRACTS RELATING TO THE EMPLOYMENT OF
WOMEN FROM THE REPORT OF THE TRADES AND
LABOUR BRANCH, ONTARIO DEPARTMENT OF
PUBLIC WORKS, 1917
[*Ontario Sessional Paper No. 16 of 1918*]

ONTARIO GOVERNMENT PUBLIC EMPLOYMENT BUREAUX

The purpose and scope of a provincial system of employment bureaux is set forth in the Report of the Ontario Commission on Unemployment, 1914. There is pointed out the need of intelligent advice for immigrants, the need of quick and reliable information about new openings, both local and in other cities, for men and women out of employment, the need for the Province to take stock of its labour requirements and available supply; in other words, the need of statistics that will interpret existing conditions, supply data for suggestions, enable juveniles to know which occupations are overstocked and which offer a good career, and put the whole question of employment on a scientific basis. All these are the general reasons which make Government employment bureaux a necessary part of the modern industrial world.

But the war has changed and enlarged the immediate purpose of employment bureaux as well as many other departments of Government. As the bureaux have been opened one by one, it has been to meet each time a recognized war need, to act as the machinery to carry out a definite constructive plan. The Toronto, Ottawa and Hamilton Bureaux were opened in November, 1916, December, 1916, and January, 1917, respectively, to meet the need for munition workers. The London Bureau was opened April 9th, 1917, when all bureaux were called upon to handle the placing of farm labour.

When Lloyd George asked for maximum production of munitions, many orders were placed in Canada. Yet everywhere there was a shortage of labour, and men were urgently needed for reinforcements for the army. It was necessary, therefore, to create a new labour supply. The Imperial Munitions Board appointed special officers to study this question and stimulate the training and employment of women in munition factories. There was considerable publicity – badges were given to all those who worked for six months or longer, and wages high enough to attract skilled workers from other trades were offered. As a result thousands of women of all classes offered their services. Two organizations undertook the placing of these women.

In Toronto, in the early stages, the Employment Bureaux of the Women's Emergency Corps sent workers to factories. Later, the Director of Women's Labour of the Imperial Munitions Board endeavoured to interview the hundreds of women who wished to serve in this way. But before long it became evident that the Government must immediately undertake the task of placing munition workers and absorb both these other agencies. On November 24th, 1916, at 164 Bay Street, Toronto, Ontario, there was opened the first office of the Ontario Government Public Employment Bureaux.

The situation confronting the new staff was an exceedingly difficult one. By this time the tales of fortunes made in munition work had caused unparalleled excitement among women workers of every type. During the first week or two over 100 applicants were interviewed daily in the Women's Department. Sewing-machine operators, weavers, stenographers, saleswomen, waitresses, servants, teachers, leisured girls, women of the widest range of strength, skill and intelligence flocked to 164 Bay Street. Many thought that the opening of a Government Bureau meant that the Government was taking over the manufacture of munitions; others came with the plea that a son or husband at the front entitled them to this work.

But it was not so easy to convince the heads of munitions factories that the bureau could send them more satisfactory help than they could get at their doors. At 7 a.m. every morning hundreds of women waited outside the factories. Since there were plenty to choose from, the company's employment agents picked out the promising women, tried them out, and dismissed in a week or two those that seemed unsuitable. As a result there were hundreds hired and an equal number discharged every week, and the latter joined the crowds which went from one factory to another. There had been no central office where they could learn authoritatively just how many workers were needed and where the vacancies were. The result of this was that many other factories were short-handed, while hundreds of workers were idle for weeks, haunting the doors of the munition factories. In the meantime no orders came in to the employment bureaux. Finally one or two of the factories which opened early in the year entrusted their orders to the Government Employment Bureau. The help sent was satisfactory. Before long they made the rule that no applicant would be interviewed without an introduction card from the Bureau. The office staff had time to get a record of each woman's past experience and could, therefore, know how satisfactory she was likely to prove. By degrees, and entirely through the satisfactory way in which the selection of workers was made, many munition factories have come to look to the Bureau for the majority of their help.

In the Men's Department of the Toronto Bureau the demand for munition workers was greater than the supply. In co-operation with the Imperial Munitions Board, machinists and workers of other trades were placed, not only in Toronto, but at outside points such as Paris, Welland, Brantford, etc.

This same need of satisfactory labour for munitions led the authorities interested in the problems created by the war to open an employment bureau for men in Ottawa. In December, 1916, this bureau was taken over by the Trades and Labour Branch. The same demand in Hamilton made it necessary to open there a third office for placing both men and women. In this city too, many of the large firms have made it a rule that all women workers must bring an introduction card from the Bureau. They have learned by experience that the Director has a larger group from which to pick workers, and that her judgment is a valuable asset to the firm. Few men were placed in munitions, owing to a shortage of skilled labour in Hamilton. An unsettled strike of skilled mechanics further complicated the situation.

The placing of munition workers was by no means the only work done by the bureaux, however. In Toronto the Men's Department was steadily working up a connection both in and out of the city. From the Women's Department factories of all kinds were supplied. The Hamilton office handled every type of worker, from social workers, office help, trained nurses to operators, laundresses and houseworkers. In Ottawa a very extensive business was soon established.

The next piece of war work asked of the Trades and Labour Branch was the recruiting and placing of farm workers, needed to increase the production of foodstuffs. The Organization of Resources Committee and the Department of Agriculture had undertaken an educational campaign. Local bodies, such as the Boards of Trade, County Councils, etc., were making surveys, placing men, and encouraging production in every way. It was absolutely necessary, however, to have an organization devoting all its time to this work in order to get workers from the larger cities out on the land. In Toronto a special department was created for the handling of this work, and all departments were moved to 15 King Street East. In London the fourth zone bureau was now opened. It was at the urgent request of the Board of Trade of this city that the bureau was established, and the backing that the bureau received from this body has done much to enable it to meet the needs of this prosperous farming community.

The work of placing labour on farms fell into three divisions: (1) men; (2) women; and (3) students (boys and girls). The campaign to place boys and girls on the land required special plans. Many High School boys had gone out the year before, but for the most part these were farmers' sons returning home. In the spring of 1917 a definite propaganda was carried on to induce city boys to take up this work for the season, and it proved an unqualified success. Men were sent out for the full season for seeding, harvesting and fall ploughing.

One piece of work which shows the part the employment bureaux can play in the life of the Province was the placing of over 1,200 women in the fruit districts. The significance of this piece of work does not lie altogether in the relative importance of saving the fruit crop. More valuable work was done by the men and boys sent out. It lies rather in that fact that such a body as the University students turned to the Department for direction. We were able to get a sceptical body of employers to accept a new type of labour. Moreover, by enlisting the co-operation of other bodies, such as the Young Women's Christian Association, we were able to ensure the safety and well-being of the large number of girls. And this work was done to the satisfaction of the fruitgrowers of each district ...

REPORT OF TORONTO EMPLOYMENT BUREAU

On the 24th of November, 1916, the Women's Department of the Toronto Branch of the Ontario Government Public Employment Bureaux was opened at 164 Bay Street, and ten days later a Men's Department was established at the same address.

At first the offices were swamped with applicants for munition work, and the staff was kept so busy at the work of registration that there was little opportunity to get in touch with employers, and the work of placement was seriously hampered. As soon, however, as it was possible to have personal interviews with employers, and to set before them the advantages of using the Bureau, orders began to come in.

Managers recognized that members of their own staffs were wasting time in fruitless interviews and records, and that the loss the workers sustained in time and energy was still more serious.

The industrial and clerical work of the Bureau was developed gradually. If applicants for munition work were not suitable or could not be placed, employers who were likely to require domestic, other industrial, or clerical help were called up and applicants were frequently placed.

The Farm Department for women was opened in March, 1917, and for men in April.

On the 19th of July, 1917, the Toronto Women's Patriotic League Employment Bureau was taken over by the Government, and the domestic work was then handled as a separate department.

Table 2 – Work of the Women's Department, Toronto Bureau.

Kind of Work	Applications for Work	Help Wanted	Number Placed
Clerical	333	86	69
Day Work	394	1,541	2,211
Domestic	459	1,021	349
Factory	195	655	415
Munitions	6,026	2,824	2,267
Miscellaneous	127	138	97
Total	7,534	6,265	5,408

The large number placed in day work, compared to the number of applicants is accounted for by the successive placement of the same applicants in this line of work.

The apparent discrepancy in the factory figures is due to the diverting of applicants from other lines of work to fill the demand for factory workers.

Table 3 – Percentage of Female Applicants for Munition Work in Age Groups.

City	Under 16	16–20	20–25	25–30	30–35	35–40	40–45	45–50	50–55	55–60
Toronto	1.3	18.1	29.8	21.7	12.7	8.1	6.0	1.5	0.8	
Hamilton	1.5	5.4	17.6	28.3	17.9	12.5	10.4	3.9	1.6	0.9
London		33.8	28.9	15.7	9.6	6.0	2.4	3.6		

Referring to table 3 it will be seen that London had a larger number of applicants for munition work under 20 years of age than Toronto and Hamilton. In each of these cities the greatest percentage of applicants were between 20 and 30 years of age. Hamilton had the largest number of applications of women over 40 years of age.

A few factories preferred young girls, but the greatest call was for women between 20 and 30. Several factories preferred older women, as the managers said they were frequently more conscientious and could do equally efficient work on slow-moving machines.

Table 4 – Conjugal Condition of Female Applicants
for Munition Work.

City	Single	Married	Widowed	Deserted
Toronto	58.7	32.5	7.0	1.8
Hamilton	59.9	33.3	5.8	1.0
London	61.5	31.3	7.2	

It is interesting to notice how closely the percentages of single, married and widowed correspond, in the three cities, as shown in table 4. Many of those offering their services as workers were soldiers' wives; in most cases the woman had a sister, or a mother, who lived with her and took care of her children, but sometimes she paid a neighbour to look after the children. In a number of cases married women asked for night work in order that they might care for their children during the day. One factory refused to employ married women with children unless assured that suitable provision was made for the children during the absence of the mother.

Table 5 – Nationalities of Female Applicants for Munition Work.

City	Canadian	English	Irish	Scotch	American	Other foreign born
Toronto	38.8	34.9	6.9	14.4	1.3	3.7
Hamilton	39.5	39.1	4.4	12.8	2.2	2.0
London	37.3	36.2	9.6	14.5	2.4	

A smaller proportion of foreign women than of foreign men apply at the bureaux, and the foreign women who used the office were found more difficult to place in munitions than the British born.

Table 6 – Previous Occupation of Applicants for Munition Work.

City	Domestic	Factory	Office	Shop	Muni-tions	Lei-sure	Own Busi-ness	Teachers	Nurses	Others
Toronto	14.3	24.9	9.8	9.8	22.2	9.1	2.4	4.1	3.0	0.4
Hamilton	12.5	46.3	6.6	13.4		15.1		2.7	2.2	1.2
London	9.6	54.2	9.7	15.7		1.2	1.2	6.0		2.4

In the three cities compared, in each case the largest number of applications for munition work were received from those who had previously worked in factories, but the proportion of applications from factory workers was much smaller in Toronto than in either Hamilton or London. On the other hand, Toronto had the largest number of applications from domestics, and Hamilton of applications from women of the leisured class.

During the year the percentage of women of the leisured classes applying for work decreased perceptibly. In September and October, when orders for munitions decreased, it was these women who first stopped applying for work. This may be due partly to the fact that newer forms of patriotic work were absorbing their energies.

From the fact that 4.1 per cent of the applicants in Toronto were teachers it cannot be inferred that this number gave up their positions to go into munition work. Most of these applicants came in June when school was about to close and asked for summer work; a few expressed their willingness to give up their work temporarily. Some factories were glad to get teachers for the summer months, when many of the leisured women were leaving.

Table 7 – Percentage of Applicants for
Munition Work Living at Home and Boarding.

City	Living at Home	Boarding
Toronto	39.5	60.5
Hamilton	73.5	26.5
London	77.1	22.9

By reference to table 7 it will be seen that the proportion of applicants for munition work who were boarding was more than twice as great in Toronto as in Hamilton and London.

Wages Asked by Munition Workers

Applicants were requested in filling out forms at the employment bureaux to state the wage they desired and the minimum wage they would take. This information was used as a guide in filling orders.

Table 8 – Percentage of Women Desiring Weekly Wages
Contained in Wage Groups Below.

1.3	$5 to $8
14.6	8 " 10
22.2	10 " 12
37.3	12 " 15
16.3	15 " 18
5.4	18 " 20
2.1	20 " 25
0.8	25 " 30

The majority of applicants did not state wages at all, but of 500 women living in Toronto and 300 in Hamilton, it will be seen that 1.3 per cent asked wages between $5 and $8, and that the wage group $12 to $15 contained the wages asked by the largest number of women in any single wage group.

Table 9 – Percentage of Women Stating as Minimum
Weekly Wages Contained in Wage Groups Below

5.7	$5 to $8
29.2	8 " 10
35.7	10 " 12
20.8	12 " 15
8.0	15 " 18
0.6	18 " 20

Reference to table 9 will show that 5.7 per cent will accept in munitions a wage less than $8 per week, and that the $10 to $12 wage group represents the wages which will be accepted by the largest number of women in any single group.

About 10 per cent of the applicants for munition work had stated that they left their former work on account of low pay ...

REPORT OF THE HAMILTON BUREAU

The Hamilton office of the Ontario Government Public Employment Bureaux was opened in January, 1917. The immediate cause of the opening of the bureau was the need of providing women workers for the local plants engaged in the manufacture of munitions.

In April it was necessary to open a department for placing farm help, and the Men's and Women's Departments were then separated, but the Women's Department continued to place boys under 18 years of age.

Hamilton is situated in the heart of an agricultural and fruit growing belt, but it is essentially an industrial city. It has over 450 manufacturing industries, 50 of which are local branches of American companies that have located in Hamilton during the past three years. About one-half of the industries occupy large premises and employ a large number of hands, considerably over 1,000 in some of the larger iron and steel corporations. Under normal conditions 90 per cent of the raw materials entering into the manufacture of machinery is made in Hamilton, pig and bar iron, steel and grey iron castings, brass castings, structural steel, bar steel screws, tacks, wire, machine tools, hardware, etc. During the past twelve months many of the firms engaged in the foregoing industries have been given over in the main to the manufacture of munitions.

Besides the industries mentioned above employing chiefly men there are large cotton and knitting mills, manufactories of confectionery, clothing, thread, brushes, oils, soap, wire and iron goods, mineral waters, paper and boxes, boots and shoes, which employ some women or in many cases chiefly women. Women are employed also in other processes including packing, press work, bookbinding, canning, upholstering, dyeing, etc.

Women's Department

Munition Work. – The chief work of this department was the placing of munition workers. See Table 18 ... The most suitable were selected, and the rest as far as possible diverted into other employments, for which they were better fitted.

Table 18 – Applications and Number Placed by Women's Department, Hamilton Bureau

Occupations	Applications for work	Help wanted	Number placed
Clerical	123	44	17
Day work	23	88	62
Domestics	304	716	262
Factory	106	288	139
Munitions	1,209	384	381
Miscellaneous	40	31	33
Total	1,805	1,551	894

A study of the table shows that in the case of munitions there were many more applicants than there were placings. In factory work the registrations were fewer in number than the placings. This is due to the fact that some of the applicants for munitions were diverted into this work. The excess of placings over applications for day work is accounted for by the fact that the same applicant is counted on successive occasions ...

REPORT OF LONDON BUREAU

When it was decided to open a Provincial System of Employment Bureaux, London was at once chosen as a place at which a Zone Bureau should be established.

The bureau was opened on April 9th, 1917. Through an arrangement with the Department of Agriculture, temporary offices were shared with the District Representative. In May, the bureau moved to its permanent quarters at 108 Dundas Street, one block from the main business centre and half a block from the Market Square.

Industries of London. – When the bureau opened, the city was prosperous, industrially speaking. There was no serious unemployment, and while the supply was by no means adequate, yet there was no crying need for labour in any particular line. With a population of over 58,000, from 12,000 to 13,000 are employed in its industries. These number 250, and manufacture over 70 distinct lines. There are many metal-working plants, employing nearly 2,700 people, and including the largest stove works in the British Empire, a rolling mill, several foundries and munition and brass working factories. London's annual cigar output from over a score of firms is equalled only by that of Montreal. Two of the largest biscuit and candy works in the Dominion have over 1,100 on their payroll. Garment factories are numerous. Three knitting mills with over 300 employees, several boot and shoe manufactories conclude a list of the more important industries.

If one may judge by the growing registration, the workers have confidence in the bureau's present and future power to help them. School girls eager for berry-picking or truck garden work, were the first women to register. Next came those from every walk of life for munitions, and now the files show records of people experienced in office, store, factory, house and day work. A few professional people have been placed, but this is a department quite undeveloped as yet.

The public mind is not yet entirely disabused of the idea that with the exception of the work of distributing farm help during the war, the bureau is principally a domestic agency.

Women's Department

The work of the Women's Department of the London bureau from its inception April 9th, to October 31st, is shown in the following table:–

Table 19 – Applications for Work and Workers, and Placements in the Women's Department, London

Kind of Work	Registrations	Help Wanted	Placed
Clerical	88	78	29
Day work	30	54	52
Domestic	136	154	76
Factory (other than munitions)	113	98	65
Munitions	104	51	67
Miscellaneous	13		5
Totals	484	435	294

Munitions. – All classes of girls and women applied for munition work. Some of the applicants had High School, Business and University training.

Nearly 34 per cent of the applicants for munition work were under 20 years of age; about 45 per cent between 20 and 30, and 22 per cent over 30. All except two of the registrants were Canadian and British by birth.

The reasons given by the applicants for leaving their previous positions were that they had been laid off; wanted better positions; to go into munitions; wanted change, or higher pay. A small number had left because of sickness or to be married ...

FARM CAMPS FOR WOMEN AND GIRLS

Among the various activities of the Trades and Labour Branch during the summer of 1917 no feature attracted more public attention than the pioneer work accomplished through the medium of the Employment Bureau System, in placing over twelve hundred women and girls on the fruit and truck farms of Ontario. That this work was as satisfactory as it was novel will be seen by the following summary of the means by which a group of patriotic women solved one of the most difficult of the rural labour problems – the gathering and preparing for market of the fruit and vegetable crop. How the scepticism of the growers was overcome, how the problem of housing was solved, how the workers adapted themselves to the different tasks which had to be done, will be briefly described.

Origin of the Movement.

Following an interview which the President of the University had with the Superintendent of the Trades and Labour Branch, it was decided to organize the University women for assisting in the saving of the fruit and vegetable crops.

The Attitude of the Growers.

In other years the growers had been able to cultivate and gather these crops with the aid of Indians and casual labour. But enlistment among the men and the attraction of munition and other well-paid work for the women, produced a great scarcity of workers in the country districts. Farmers were refusing to put in tomatoes, onions and other vegetables which needed continuous cultivation because they had not been able to get them gathered the year before. It was extreme need only that induced the growers to listen to the proposition that city girls should come to fill the gap. Meeting after meeting of the growers was called. The men sat silent and distrustful. "Do you need pickers?" "Yes." "Can you get them?" "No." "Well, do you want to guarantee work to these girls?" Silence. It was only the dire need for workers that finally induced six groups of growers and a farmer in Norfolk County to guarantee work to a definite number of pickers for a stated number of months. The courageous districts were Vittoria, Beamsville, Grimsby, Winona, Oakville and Bronte. The rates of pay were those which had been prevalent in the district for some years.

Assistance Given by the Young Women's Christian Association.

The next problem to be met was the housing of the workers. The National Council of the Y.W.C.A. had been approached on the question and had undertaken to organize the camps. Houses of all sorts were secured in the different districts. They varied from a hired man's house to a small summer hotel, and included a stable which was whitewashed and turned into a dining-room and kitchen, and a big bungalow by the lake shore which boasted running water and a real bath.

A request was sent to the Militia Department, Ottawa, for bell tents, and through the courtesy of the Minister of Militia 150 tents were put at the disposal of the Trades and Labour Branch. Thanks are due to the Senior Ordnance Officer, Military District No. 2, for his kindness in facilitating the distribution of these tents. They were used to supplement the houses provided by the Y.W.C.A.

As well as renting the houses the Y.W.C.A. supplied beds and kitchen and dining-room equipment. In some cases they planted gardens in connection with the camps, from which the season's supply of green vegetables was derived. The girls brought their own bedding and towels and paid $4.00 a week for their board. In addition the girls took turns in assisting with dishwashing and the preparing of luncheons.

Every camp was inspected by a medical health officer.

Other camps were organized by the Fred Victor Mission, by the W.C.T.U., and by the Trades and Labour Branch. There were also camps provided by the growers themselves. The Trades and Labour Branch recognized the work of private groups which undertook to make arrangements for housing the workers. Their only requirement was that the groups should be suitable to have the supervision of camps for girls.

As well as the various camps, there were cases of workers boarding with the growers, or living in a house near work and boarding themselves. Day workers were also sent from Toronto, Hamilton and London.

The size and location of the various groups may be seen from the following tables:

Table 34 – Fruit Pickers Sent Out by the Ontario Government Public Employment Bureau System, 1917.

In Camps –		
1. Y.M.C.A.	584	
2. Fred Victor Mission	89	
3. Trades and Labour Branch Camps	134	
Total		807
On Farms –		
1. Living and boarding in farmer's home	30	
2. Living in military tents and boarding in farmer's home	20	
3. Cooking for themselves in small house on farm	14	
Total		64
Day Workers –		
To points within reach of Toronto by car		17
Unclassified –		
Chiefly grape cutters and day-pickers sent out from Hamilton and London		377
Total		1,265

The following table shows the situation of the camps and the numbers in each.

Table 35

Names of Camps	No. in camps for the season	No. required to keep up the totals
I.–Y.W.C.A. Camps.		
1 Beamsville	70	114
2 Bronte	25	43
3		
4		
5 } Four camps on individual farms at Clarkson	59	72
6		
7 Grimsby	35	95
8 Oakville	25	43
9 Queenston	25	25
10 St. Williams	20	25
11 Vittoria	20	25
12 Winona	55	142
Totals	334	584
II.–Fred Victor Mission Camp	40	89
Totals	40	89
III –Trades and Labour Branch Camps.		
1	50	75
2		
3 } 3 camps on Clarkson farms	22	31
4		
5		
6 } 3 camps in Niagara District	28	28
7		
Totals	100	134

Camps were situated at the Grimsby district (Beamsville, Winona, Grimsby). In the Clarkson district (Lorne Park, Clarkson, Erindale). In Norfolk county (St. Williams, Vittoria, Waterford). In the Queenston district (for peach picking only) (Queenston, St. David's, Niagara-on-the-Lake) ...

A number of private organizations sent out girls; others hired privately with farmers, and many women in the fruit districts, who had previously spent their summers on the verandah, turned out and helped with the crop. It is impossible to estimate the total number of workers added in this way.

Those sent out by the Ontario Government Public Employment Bureau System were drawn from the following groups.

The girls were drawn from 42 different counties in Ontario and 38

Table 36 – Fruit Pickers Sent Out by Department

University students	26.5%
Leisured girls	17.2
High School girls	14.0
Teachers	14.0
Factory and munition workers	8.0
Office workers	5.6
Married women	2.7
Music students and teachers	2.7
Houseworkers	2.0
Others[1]	7.3

[1]These included art students, dressmakers, designers, trained nurses, librarians, salesladies, milliners, civil servants, social workers, bank clerks and furriers.

girls came from Quebec Province. Three private school teachers who could not get home to England came from Nova Scotia; two girls came from New Brunswick, five from the United States, one from each of the prairie provinces, and one from Australia.

Table 37 – Number of Fruit Pickers from each County and District sent out by the Women's Farm Department, Ontario Government Employment Bureaux

(A) Numbers from Ontario

Algoma	3	Muskoka	1
Brant	7	Norfolk	
Bruce	4	Nipissing	8
Carleton	27	Northumberland	8
Dufferin	1	Ontario	1
Dundas	1	Oxford	7
Durham	5	Parry Sound	2
Elgin	2	Peel	17
Frontenac	9	Perth	4
Grey	3	Peterborough	10
Grenville	2	Prescott	1
Haliburton	1	Prince Edward	1
Haldimand	2	Renfrew	3
Halton	9	Russell	2
Hastings	4	Simcoe	9
Huron	4	Victoria	4
Lambton	2	Waterloo	12
Lanark	6	Welland	1
Leeds	1	Wellington	14
Lennox and Addington	3	Wentworth	195
Lincoln	2	York	481
Middlesex	196		

(B) Numbers from Outside of Ontario

Quebec	38	Alberta	1
Nova Scotia	3	Manitoba	1
New Brunswick	2	Saskatchewan	1
United States	5		

The majority of the pickers were young:–
35.7% were in their "teens."
57. "   "   " twenties.
5.2 "   "   " thirties.
1.6 "   "   " forties.
  .5 " over fifty.

Uniform and Badge.

Although no uniform was compulsory, the majority of the pickers wore bloomers and either a middy blouse or smock. In some camps these were made of khaki with red or blue bands on the collar and cuffs. In others they were of grey material smocked with red and belted in at the waist. A few girls wore overalls. When workers went out for a week or two only, old skirts were worn, but from some camps came requests from the matron to urge upon the workers to don bloomers, as skirts were too dangerous when the girls were working in the trees.

A badge was given to every worker by the Trades and Labour Branch and could be retained as her permanent possession if she completed the length of service for which she volunteered. This badge was a blue serge shield. The Farm Service Corps button was given at the end of the season to all who had earned their badges.

Co-Operation of the Press.

The press of Toronto, Hamilton, and other centres gave their hearty co-operation. They were always ready to bring before the public the need for workers and to publish accounts of work in the camps, and incidents of interest. Their unfailing support contributed largely to the success of the work.

The Work of the Camps.

The work done by the girls was of all kinds. The Winona camp was the first to win recognition. The report that the University girls there had hulled strawberries cleaner than any other help, so that less fruit was wasted than in previous years, caused the Toronto office to be swamped with orders.

From one point after another calls came in for camps. Clarkson, Lorne Park and Port Credit, Burlington, Jordan Station and Vineland, Waterford, St. Williams and Fenwick all wanted workers. Orders were filled as far as possible. But it had been so difficult to get the farmers to accept the city workers at all during April and May that the Bureau had been busy telling applicants who wrote in, that the camps arranged for were filled and apparently no further pickers would be accepted. The result was that some three hundred women who might have been available found other work for the summer, and many who had been doubting Thomases lost part of their fruit.

The strawberry-hulling at Winona ended sooner than the manager had led the Bureau to expect, and the cold, wet June delayed the ripening of the fruit. It looked for a time as though the girls were to be at the camps for two or three weeks paying board with no work. Each grower held back, afraid to try these city girls at other work than picking. One man at last was persuaded. He set fifteen girls to clean up an old vineyard which had been neglected for two years. A plough had cleaned between the rows, but there were tall weeds growing along the vines. The soil was heavy clay, now baked hard. It might well have daunted the girls. Hour after hour they hacked and pulled, while the mosquitoes grew thicker as they went farther up the mountain. Some weeks later the grower told them that no man could be got to tackle that vineyard. However, the girls had won recognition. On the second day they were put to varied work on the farm – hoeing, planting, weeding, cultivating, thinning peaches, and after that day in the vineyard no girl in that camp lacked work.

Interest in Work.

The girls took a keen interest in their work and enjoyed it thoroughly, as may be seen from their songs at all the different stages of farm work. Here are some from the Beamsville section:

(Tune: "I love you, Canada.")

I love you raspberries,
  For you mean so much to me,
You mean my board and lodging,
  My dinner and my tea.
You mean my railway ticket
  With which I go back home;
That's why I pick you carefully,
  As up and down the rows I roam.

I hate you raspberries,
  For you've been the death of me;
You broke my back in pieces,
  And you gave me housemaid's knee.
I've had you for my breakfast,
  My dinner and my tea,
That's why I hate the very sight
  Of a red raspberry.

"Raspberries don't pay," was the general comment. Forty to fifty quarts was good picking, and at 2½ c. and 3c. it was hard to make expenses rain or shine. But currants were worse, and gooseberries – well, gooseberries were the limit of endurance.

The songs grew more vigorous.

(Tune: "Pack all your troubles.")

Pick all the currants on the darn old bush,
  And smile if you can.
While you are sitting on the hay-stuffed cush.,
  The stems fall in your pan.
What's the use of hurrying?
  Two cents is not worth while;
So pick all the currants on the darn old bush,
  And smile, smile, smile.

Probably the most famous of the songs was the one to the tune of "We'll never let the old flag fall." Wherever you went, no matter to which camp, wherever the blue shield was seen, you could hear this song:

> We'll never let the old hoe go,
> For we love it so much, you know;
> We don't have to hoe to show our go,
> But when we hoe, we'll hoe, hoe, hoe.
> In rain or shine, we'll never whine,
> But hoe right on to the end of the line.
> When the war is o'er our fame will soar,
> We'll never let the old hoe go.

ON ACTIVE SERVICE AT WINONA, ONTARIO

I am "berry" well.
I have been admitted into the Jam Factory, and am suffering from "smell-shock," "bench-back," and "huller's fingers."
Life here is just one Jam berry after another.
I have had strawberry rash and quite expect to be "berried" soon.
I expect to be sent into the field soon.
This work will soon make us all as cross as "bear-ies."
Signature ....
Date ....
My address is ....

The Active Service Card of the Strawberry Hullers

Hours of Work.

A ten-hour day was the usual thing. At the camps in Oakville, however, the girls decided that they could not work more than nine hours and maintain their efficiency. This was satisfactory to the growers.

Duration of Camps.

The length of time for which the camps were open in the different districts varied according to the need and the supply of workers. The High School girls' camp at Vittoria, which was the first to open, was started in May. Some of the camps were able to keep in full running order until the tree fruits and grapes were picked in the end of October.

Housing Arrangements other than Camps.

Besides the workers in the camps, girls to the number of sixty-four were sent out in numbers varying from two to eight to live and board at the farmers' house. While this plan has met with marked success in two or three places, in the majority of cases it has been unsatisfactory. Growers and girls alike will probably prefer the camp system another year.

Fourteen girls and women were sent to pick fruit and board themselves in a small house provided by the grower. Very few girls like to do this, as it is too strenuous, but the few who do like it will accept no other arrangement. Numbers of women and children also are willing to board themselves. They regard it as a chance to get their children into the country, and the regular camps cannot accommodate them.

Work of Other Bureaux.

Besides the girls sent out from the Toronto office, 349 were sent out by London and Hamilton. London sent 195; Hamilton sent 154. These have not been classified. Most of them, however, went out by the day; a few boarded in farm-houses, and about thirty were sent to camps.

From Hamilton numbers of girls went out each day on the cars, many of them being grape-cutters and peach-pickers. Two High School girls caught the early train each day to Aldershot and worked all summer in a market garden, thus earning exemption from examinations.

From the London Bureau most of the workers went out towards Springbank, by the day.

Although a letter of appreciation was received from the fruit men, saying the labour supply had never been so satisfactory, there was good reason for complaint on the part of the workers. Work was uncertain; rates were low; earnings were not such as to induce any group to continue the work. It was with real difficulty that new groups were obtained. There was one very satisfactory group sent out from this office. Ten girls lived in a cottage on the farm, did their own cooking and housework and were kept busy and contented.

Advantages of This Type of Labour.

The work of the girls proved satisfactory to the farmers. Their inexperience was counterbalanced by the fact that they learned quickly and took a keen interest in their work. Also, they could be depended on to pick the bushes clean and to stay at one farm until the picking was done, and not leave when half the crop was off, as Indians and casual labourers are apt to do. The girls, on their part, gained a knowledge of conditions in the country which they would not otherwise have had.

Appreciation of the Growers.

That the growers appreciated the work of the girls may be seen from the following letter, which was received by the Trades and Labour Branch from the Clarkson Fruit Growers' Association:

I have been instructed by the Fruit-growers' Association to forward to you a copy of a resolution passed at our regular meeting last Saturday evening.

Owing to the very serious situation in which the fruit-growers of this Association were placed with regard to the harvesting of their fruit, and recognizing the self-denial and personal sacrifice made by the many young ladies who volunteered to save the situation, and who so whole-heartedly went at the work, picking and work-ing to the satisfaction of all those by whom they were employed. Be it therefore resolved that the gratitude of this Association be hereby sent to all those who en-listed in the National Service Movement in this district, also to the Employment Bureau of the Ontario Government for the efficient way in which the work was conducted, and to the Militia Department of the Dominion Government for the tents so kindly sent to us for the fruit season.

Signed on behalf of the Clarkson Fruit-growers' Association,

R. H. Lush, President.

W. A. Shook, Secretary.

Wages.

The fruit growers want these workers to come again. The Grimsby farmers sent word to the Trades and Labour Branch that if they were sure of this type of labour permanently, they would break up more ground and put in more varied crops. The Wages paid the girls were not satis-factory, as will be seen from the table below.

Table 38 – Earnings of Girls in Fruit Picking, 1917

1.75%	over $12 a week
1.75%	11
2.25%	10
2.25%	9
4.25%	8
12.0 %	7
24.0 %	6
30.0 %	5
18.0 %	4
3.5 %	under 4

Over half the pickers earned from $5 to $7 per week. Fifty per cent. earned under $6 a week.

Table 39 – Earnings in Different Districts in which Camps
were Established for Two Months and Over

Name of Camp	Percentage earning		
	Over $6	Between $5 & $6	Under $5
Grimsby	93	7	6
Winona	37.15	56.15	6
Oakville[1]	40	10	50
Beamsville	30	58	12
Brant		32	68

1 The girls here worked only a nine-hour day.

Table 40 – Earnings in Camps of Three to Six
Weeks' Duration.

Name of Camp	Percentage	Wages
Clarksons	60	over $6
	22	$5–$6
	18	under $5
Norfolk Co.	15.62	over $6
	40.63	$5–$6
	43.75	under $5
Queenston[1]	2.63	$16
	7.89	15
	7.89	14
	44.73	13
	2.63	12
	7.89	11
	15.82	10
	10.52	9

1 In Queenston the workers went for three or
four weeks for tree fruits only.

Rates of Pay for 1918.

The abnormally poor season is partly accountable for the low earnings. The cold weather kept back the fruit at first, and the intense heat later on dried it up. Also, owing to the farmers' unwillingness to accept this type of labour, it had been impossible to get a working agreement with them which would guarantee steady work. Consequently all loss through weather conditions was borne by the workers themselves. It is hoped that this can be overcome another year. In Grimsby, where the best earnings are recorded, the girls were seldom out of work a single hour, rain or shine. In bad weather they put handles on baskets, potted plants in the green-houses and worked in the canneries.

The experience of the past year seems to make clear that women will take a larger part in agriculture in Ontario. It is planned to establish special training courses for girls in practical agriculture, so that they will be competent to take their place next year on the mixed farms as well as on the fruit and truck farms.

D 5 ADVERTISEMENT FOR THE 118TH BATTALION
[*Berlin* News Record, *15 January 1916, p. 8*]

HAVE YOU MOTHERED A MAN?

There are Women in the noisy cities and in the silent places of Canada to-day who can look the world in the face and truthfully say they have mothered a man. "Somewhere in France" or in the training camps, a Boy of theirs is wearing the Kings Khaki and upholding the most precious right that Britains are heir to, the right of freedom.

It is not without a pang that these noble mothers saw their sons enlist, but it is with a pride which none others know that they cheerfully made the sacrifice.

When the call to arms comes it does not come alone to the physically fit men of military age, it comes also to the women of the land who, by personal sacrifice can give a man to the fighting lines.

Some women have given many sons to the country's cause.

Some women (who can) have not given one.

THIS IS AN APPEAL

to the mothers not to use their influence against the enlistment of sons who are able to take their places with the men who are fighting for Freedom and Liberty and for civilization.

Sisters and Sweethearts

are also urged to place no obstacle in the way of loved ones who are anxious to play the MAN in this great world struggle. In the days to come when history eulogizes the wondrous deeds and splendid heroism of those who saved Democracy for the world, you will have nothing but regret if you know you faltered when the test came.

It is for the sacredness of Home and Womanhood that the Allies are fighting. Women who think these things realize that it is worth while for them to make the sacrifice demanded.

D 6   SELECTIONS FROM 'WIN-THE-WAR
SUGGESTIONS AND RECIPES,' SOLD FOR THE
BENEFIT OF RETURNED SOLDIERS
[P.A.C. Library. Pamphlet number 4435]

This is not a cookery book, only a few recipes and some sketchy hints to help those who want to do more towards economizing our food supply. That economy is one of the most important factors in the successful carrying on of the war, though only one woman in a thousand or so seems to be in the least conscious of the fact.

Food *must* be conserved; the Government *must* have our money; women *must* sacrifice their vanity, their mean self-indulgence and criminal selfishness on the altar of their country's safety. They must do it in order to back up all those who are suffering, and striving, and in such dreadful anxiety at the front; above all, to make good the supreme sacrifice of all the beloved ones who lie forever in the fields of France and Flanders, and those, who, after going through hell, sleep at peace in German prison yards. Every ounce of food saved, *every single solitary ounce*, will do its bit. For every single cent, saved and given or lent to the Government, who can transmute it into munitions while you wait, will tell. "Mony mickles make a muckle," or, as those of us who have the misfortune not to be Scotch can say in a free translation, a mighty lot of nickels will make shells, bullets, guns, tanks, aeroplanes, warships – yes, and the clever magicians of munition can even make warm clothes and bully beef out of them. You save money and the Government does the rest.

Without women's sacrifices there will be but little money, as men can't give if all they earn is squandered or carelessly wasted by their woman-kind. This little book may encourage and decide some women to do *a little* of their bounden duty, and to give their earnest help in getting a proper amount of food over to our own sons, and to that "tight little island" on whose shoulders the greater part of the burden of this terrible war now rests – the nation which has the safety of the world's future welfare in her keeping. She could not feed for a single month all her own hard working, brave, unselfish people, or for a single day, those millions across the channel who are fighting and dying for you, without the precious food you and her other faithful children send over to her. She doesn't even ask you for your comforts, your selfish luxuries (such things are too humiliating to ask for when not given up instinctively, as they should be by every decent-minded man and woman), but only for you to substitute other things for the foods without which no man can fight, or even keep in a working condition; bacon, the lack of which would mean a lowered vitality; without beef, of course, no army *could* fight, and bread is truly what it is called, the staff of life. As an army fights on its stomach, a full adequate supply of those three B's is absolutely necessary for its very existence.

Can't you understand and remember that there are 40,000,000 men fighting, 20,000,000 souls working at high pressure to supply them with munitions? That is, 60,000,000 who produce nothing but use just about five times the amount of food that you use, or that they have used in ordinary times. For there is not only the hideous loss of foodstuffs wantonly destroyed by the submarines – millions of tons – but there is the necessary waste in reducing the bulk and the almost unavoidable loss in perishable stuffs.

All that wastage is inevitable, and it is up to you to make that good, for there isn't actual enough food in the world to send to the army and for you to go on consuming as you have done in the past – and, to their eternal shame, as so many are doing yet. *There is not enough food in all the world* for them, if you refuse to do your *small* individual share, and it is so very little that is asked of you. Only to do without beef and bacon on two days of the week, and to substitute the largest possible percentage of oatmeal, barley, rye, cornmeal or buckwheat for white flour. Cut down sugar to the lowest point. Buy no clothes whatever that are not absolutely needed for protection. Never mind shabby shoes, clothes, hats and furs.

Wool is so scarce, there may be a great difficulty in keeping our defenders warm. Possibly a single unnecessary suit or overcoat may mean frozen limbs for one of your own loved ones; every new dress, woollen garment, those knitted jerseys women have been mad over, may mean for one of our heroes pneumonia, rheumatism, tuberculosis, sending them back to their cruelly selfish and meanly ungrateful country, pitiful, ruined, helpless wrecks of noble manhood.

Every word of this is dreadfully true, not one particle exaggerated. All the stores are crammed with ignoble women spending precious money – and for what? Not merely for "nice clothes." All daughters of Eve crave those, and, though it is inexcusable to gratify that craving in the present hideous state of affairs, it can at least be understood. But no thinking, large-hearted man or woman can understand the wickedness of throwing away money in foolish little frivolities, utterly useless trifles of household articles: in short, cruelly, meanly, utterly selfishly spending for contemptible self-indulgence hundreds of thousands of dollars, refusing even to save and then lend (with wonderful interest and absolute security) to your harassed Government, money to be spent in your own country, and thus increase its and your own prosperity. The wonderful prosperity that has flooded the Dominion through war contracts. Blood money it is to the many greedy corporations, to many more individuals who of their 25 per cent, 50 per cent, and 85 per cent returns, give not even a tithe to help and comfort those who furnished them the cause for making their millions, until a belated law will force the selfish, wantonly ungenerous and unspeakably mean men to give a little of their usury back, often only to gain more contracts.

Look at all the well-managed, hard working war charities – such as the Red Cross, without whose organization the agony, suffering and hideous pain and awful helplessness of millions, yes millions, would be unassuaged, un-relieved, un-helped, and the mortality increased a hundredfold. How many of you have worked for that, as every woman should, or even given to it according to your means? The Y.M.C.A. is blessed by millions of soldiers; yet it must strive, work and beg for the inadequate funds it has to bring some comfort, some joy, some love to our boys at the front. The Soldiers' Comfort Committees are often disheartened, knowing of the suffering men they are unable to relieve or bring some little brightness and pleasure to, for want of the dollar you spent for a new and unneeded necktie, or some other trifle. The funds for the prisoners of war in Germany are pitifully inadequate, though these are the saddest of all our beloved heroes we talk so glibly about at "thé dansants," at afternoon teas, at restaurants, and over the selection of utterly unneeded articles. One would think every expensive dish or selfish tea would, and should, choke you if you could visualize those gaunt, hunger stricken, forsaken forms, waiting like famished animals for the food you waste. One can scarce bear to even mention those millions scattered through every German-invaded district, who are *actually*, *really* starving, dying in the terrible, long-drawn-out anguish of starvation, amid every humiliation, discomfort, and exposure. Still you spend on selfish indulgence, rich and poor (for all but the most unfortunate can save, according to their means), such immense sums that almost every shop has had a record season.

If you refuse to save and give now some terrible calamity may force you to do what a nation of noble and fine souls would do of their own free will – give up all and every extravagance and selfish luxury. Each Canadian can and should begin now, immediately, to take the extra trouble and time to save in little things, ounce by ounce, nickel by nickel, leaving the many millions of precious ounces saved at the disposal of the authorities for your saviours and your starving fellow human beings and your almost equally precious nickels for the helping of the prisoners, the soldiers at the front, the sufferers in hundreds of hospitals, the returned veterans who have stood the heat and burden of the day, and are all more or less handicapped for their future livelihood. Don't, for the love of your womanhood and manhood, go on talking glibly and futilely of "your boys," and "your fine heroes," your "noble defenders of your home and daughters," and – take it out in talking, as many thousands of you do.

Talking with tears in your voices in public is a mighty cheap soft-snap, as our latest and most beloved Allies say, and, as you yourselves say, "soft words butter no parsnips." They certainly don't.

If only every woman that may see the following suggestions, rich and poor, will truly try to follow them patiently for a month or so, to give them a fair trial, and gradually increase the use of them, you will see that the saving for your food controller has been immense. Suppose your family don't like a certain thing, "just hate brown bread," "can't eat porridge," won't even try to get used to cornmeal – then ask them if their fathers, brothers, cousins and friends simply love bully beef 365 times a year, or even the everlasting plum and apple, which they apparently have three times a day the year round. Could your family refuse mutton, kidneys, liver, pigs' feet, tripe, or fish, thoroughly understanding that a shortage of muscle and strength-giving beef would mean a weakened, inefficient army, anaemic, incompetent munition workers?

Not one beefless day, but *one* beef day is what every patriotic man and woman in all this wide Dominion should try for, when beef is not a needed form of food for the work engaged in. Are your families, even the little children, willing to see the dreadful Hun over-run the world because they insist they will eat precious beef, bacon and wheat, because they don't really care much for substitutes? This sounds incredible, but it is just exactly what unthinking Canadians are doing at this moment.

All governments hopefully, though very foolishly, first wait for the patriotic, right-feeling, unselfish and wise inhabitants to answer to the call of their country; but all have found there "ain't no sich person," at least not enough to make the least appreciable difference.

Our loyal neighbours have profited by our hopeful, but sadly mistaken and optimistic rulers, who so flattered us – and, with their usual push, have started right in at a point we have not yet reached after three and a half years. We would be a proud nation if our rulers' ingenuous faith in our innate nobility of soul were justified, and if we Canadians, whose boys have stood so grandly self-forgetful before the hideous German storm of fire, would take the infinitely less difficult stand against our own contemptible foes – against our pitiful indolence, selfishness, indifference, laziness and cruel unhelpfulness – and mow *them* down as our sons mow down the enemy of the world.

There are numbers and numbers of books giving detailed and valuable facts concerning what might be called the science of saving – the saving and economy that will not in the least lessen the nourishment of the food of the new regime, but will answer all bodily requirements of grown-ups and growing children, especially our boys, who must try to fill the place of our many dead and totally disabled.

There are four classes of food required by our body: (1) Fats, which turn into fat and make heat and energy – found in potatoes, bread, sugar, honey, syrup, butter, dripping and meat fat. (2) Those that form muscle – fish, lean meat, eggs, skim-milk, cheese, brown bread, beans, peas, lentils. (3) Those needed for bone, most necessary for all children – milk, fruit, vegetables, brown bread and oat-meal. (4) To keep the body in a proper condition, laxatives are absolutely necessary, and are best supplied by apples, prunes, figs, and other fruits and green vegetables. Any housekeeper with a little study and thought can manage to combine all these properly, and, for less money and no more work, feed her precious family infinitely better and more healthily than she has ever done, to the immense benefit of their future. It is not a question of time, but of patience, to get a start.

White flour bread should, even without consideration for war needs, be used very sparingly, especially for children of any age, as it has comparatively little real value as a food by itself. All other breads can fulfil its use and many other requirements at the same time. Oatmeal is more valuable as a food than almost any other article, excepting milk. The food values are based on the present cost, as a dollar's worth of one of really less food value, being cheaper, will give the same nourishment, or more, for the same money. So, as far as possible, find out the real value. Class 2 are good substitutes for meat, especially beef. Oatmeal, cornmeal mush, hominy, cracked wheat, rye, in one form or other should be used constantly, varied by cornmeal breads and battercakes, rice, buckwheat and whole flour battercakes for breakfast. Frying apples is one of the best ways to prepare them for breakfast, as they lose less bulk and go farther than if prepared in any other way. Milk must be counted as a *necessary*, as well as the use of a little more sugar than is strictly necessary for those who really find it hard to eat cereals without it. Do with less of almost any other foods so as not to cut down the milk and sugar bills. Milk is a sort of fairy godmother in making, adding to, and helping out such an unending variety of valuable dishes. Both skim-milk and buttermilk are as valuable, in some cases actually more valuable than whole milk; especially as a diet for some invalids, buttermilk is in a class to itself. They only lack one thing – the butter-fat – and by some chemical change develop other qualities more valuable. The hardest race in the world, the Scottish Highlanders, have been raised largely on oatmeal and milk and herring, and have plenty of bone, muscle and brain, as most Canadians know.

Next, use brown and whole wheat flour in place of white for *everything* except the very few cakes you are going to make hereafter, and finer kinds of pie crust. For breakfast, dinner and supper, learn to make good palatable scones, shortbread, war breads, oatmeal cakes, and the many suitable cornbreads. Use soups, stews, minces, rissoles, hashes, fish (canned and fresh), pigs' feet, tripe, sausage, fowl, game, macaroni and cheese, baked beans, potato-stew, cheese-potatoes, for both dinner and supper, with only enough of roasts (rarely chops and steaks) and fresh cheaper cuts to keep in a little meat for made dishes for at least one other meal. In very many, even quite well-to-do families, an ordinary supper consisting of a very large bowl of well-made potato-stew, macaroni and cheese, or good soup, made of soup stock thick with bits of meat, vegetables, rice, macaroni, pearl barley – in short, the carefully saved debris of many meals, with brown or corn bread – is all that should be wanted or given, with a little fruit or pudding. Dumplings are filling at the price, even when made of white flour, as with a lot of good gravy they will take the place of half the usual quantity of meat.

All those wise patriotic women who made a serious attempt to put up fruit and vegetables will reap their reward a thousand-fold now and later. Persevere for a while until you have learned some palatable dishes, then have meat only once a day, or for the second time just a little bit in a mostly potato rissole, or some stuffed vegetable, or cottage pie. The cheapest cuts can, by slow simmering, long braising, grinding very finely, be made far tenderer and more palatable than the most expensive cuts, which, as a rule, are very tough.

Try with all your determination to contract the soup habit. Of all ways of helping to conserve food, that is the best, for every tiny scrap of meat, every teaspoonful of left-overs, and every inch of bread, fried as crotons, can be used – even every bacon rind. The very first and most important thing is to keep a pot in which every fragment of meat or bone is put, then boiled, boiled and reboiled each day. If it has jellied when cool it should be poured off and the bits of meat put by. Save the bones till a few more scraps are added, with once a week or so a new 10c. or 15c. soup bone. With jellied stock, you are prepared at an hour's notice, or ten minutes', to serve a delicious, nourishing, economical dish. A tin of corn and one of tomatoes could be kept for several times, or a little kept out when they are used as a vegetable. A soup with the cut-away bits of cabbage, lettuce, cauliflower, onions, boiled absolutely tender, and the leavings of any cooked vegetables, with rice or macaroni or pearl barley, thickened properly and served with fried bread crumbs or toast buttered and brown or stale bread buttered and toasted, is a dish that nine out of ten people like if properly done. All grease being removed while cold.

The plain stock can be served as clear bouillon, with little force-meat balls made of well seasoned bits of meat and boiled egg, rolled in flour and dropped in the rapidly boiling soup for a few minutes. Also, any tinned or powdered soups can be added to the stock to give any flavour desired, which by themselves are devoid of nourishment, and expensive if used for the entire dish. It is easy to keep on hand a few soup vegetables. Vegetable soups are as nourishing and as desirable as any, and not expensive, even counting the milk. With about the same process you can have oyster plant, potato, parsnip, tomato, onion, turnip, in fact almost any vegetable you happen to like. If the family likes corn bread with it and soup an entire meal can be made on a generous quantity, but you must learn to make it good.

SOUPS.

If only each reader would try faithfully for a month or two till she gets the knack of soup making, she will be doing an immense good in the nourishment of her family, in the saving of scraps, and so the saving of money, and incidentally help win this war.

CORNMEAL.

Another habit that is of vital importance to that end is a cornmeal one. The taste can be acquired after a little time, and the dislike quite lost, but, of course, those that don't care for it must go through an apprenticeship. As in the case of all cereals except white flour (for which it is equally as good), soda and sour or butter milk is very much better than milk and baking powder, and far cheaper.

All cornmeals have the same foundation. Use a small tablespoon of lard or dripping to a cup of meal, placed in the centre, enough actually boiling water poured on it till over half is made mush, then a little more to dampen the whole ...

Hoe Cake. – After scalding the meal as above, add enough milk or water and a scant teaspoon of soda, less if water is used, to make the mixture thin enough to drop. Flatten out on griddle till about an inch thick and as large as a battercake. Can be cooked on top of stove like a battercake, or in oven ...

HOMINY.

Hominy, either large or small, is a perfect substitute for potatoes, and the small kind, boiled, not quite done, then fried in cakes, is generally much liked. Both, especially the large hominy, require 2 to 4 hours' cooking. The large is just as good heated over by steaming or in a little milk and water. Both can be added to soups. For all cornmeal dishes, as well as many puddings, a sauce made of dark molasses (not the thick almost black kind that is sold as cooking molasses) and a little butter boiled together, adds immensely to them both in taste and food balance, giving some qualities required that are not found in the other ingredients, and also will help many to acquire that most patriotic cornmeal habit.

CEREALS.

Cereals, including breads, should form at least one-fifth of the bulk of food – as porridge, oatmeal, cornmeal, flaked grains – and to conserve flour, all kinds of meals and other flours can be mixed in whatever proportion you prefer in all kinds of bread, as also can potatoes and rice. They can also be added to any except delicate white flour recipes ...

BROWN OR WHITE YEAST BREAD.

It is better and less wasteful for a woman who can't acquire the knack of bread-making not to persist too long in the attempt, though it saves about one-third the cost of buying bread. Anyone who can make white bread, of course, will succeed in the war varieties. It is best to learn with superior white flour ...

MEAT.

Stews. – Next to soups, there is no war (or any other) economy equal to that of a good stew, for the very cheapest cuts can be made deliciously tender by several hours' careful, slow simmering – and it *must* be both careful and very slow to get the best results. The fuel used is far more than repaid by the saving in the cost and the nourishment obtained. When it is done in the oven, potatoes should be baked in their skins, and other vegetables and pudding also baked when possible, and so save the gas when using a gas stove.

Bake Stew. – That will do for want of a better name. Fry a cup of sliced onions in a little butter, season them (and each other thing as fried) with a little pepper and salt. Then trim skin, not the fat, off the beef, cut in bits two or three inches square, fry in same pan with added butter or dripping, well dredged with brown flour, put into small lard pail, or (much better) a baked-bean pot, with the onions. Cut a cupful each of parsnips, carrots, turnips, about an inch square, fry like the meat, and add to it, covering all with boiling water. Cover tight and cook in slow oven three or four hours till perfectly tender. Some cooked potatoes should be added near the last, so they will not cook too soft. It is generally necessary to add boiling water from time to time, and also a little flour to gravy, if not thick enough. Always skim grease most carefully off all soups and stews. The stew can be closely covered with a plate and slowly stewed on top of stove in frying-pan, but it is not so good. Also, for a change, it can be made without frying the vegetables or meat, and a little milk added to the gravy. Either can be flavoured with celery salt or seed, or curry. Any quantity of any kind of vegetables can be used as desired, also tomato sauce or Worcester sauce.

There is an infinite variety of combinations, after first seeing that the meat is absolutely tender and the stew is perfectly skimmed. Dumplings can be added, but are an unnecessary extravagance if used often. The oftener stews are warmed the better they are (like soups). When there is not enough left to make more than a shadow of a stew, the meat and vegetables, if any, can be kept for soups or hashes or minces, with other left-overs added.

Mutton Stews. – The neck and breast of mutton is only economical and "saving" if plenty of rice and vegetables are used to make the rich gravy of use. As in other stews, the value lies in the extracting of all the nourishment out of the bones, and making palatable several times the bulk of meat with cheaper things, so adding immensely to the value of the amount of meat, which easily goes four or five times as far in filling up your family as meat served alone. Thus one pound cheap beef or mutton, carefully stewed and well made, will easily be far more filling (that phrase is not elegant, but very useful to express the meaning) than four pounds of roast beef or mutton or steaks and chops. Then the bones can be well broken and reboiled in the stock pot ...

Minces. – Minces are useful to disguise the sad fact that not only scraps have been saved, but tiny bits of all *kinds* of scraps, and there is no telling that the mince has not been made from quite extravagant cuts of fresh meat. Either cooked or raw meat is used, as in hash, and there is also no end to their variety, especially as they form the foundation for rissoles, that other stalwart saver.

After mincing in the machine either fine or larger, simmer gently till tender, with seasoning – a little butter, and enough water to keep from burning. After that stage your fancy can have free play. Fry a few onions, add as little curry powder as will flavour it to the meat, and you have Curried Mince. Any possible kind of sauce added, and you have that-kind-of-sauce Mince. It can be quite dry or have a lot of well thickened gravy. Serve with properly cooked rice or mashed (mashed, not lumpy) potatoes, piled in centre. Or a more elaborate style, which of course can be used for any hash, mince or fowl, etc., is to line a mould that has been wet with cold water with boiled rice or mashed or creamed potatoes, carefully pressing the sides and bottom; put in meat, which must not be wet; cover with potatoes or rice, taking care that you join well to sides. Turn out very carefully while still hot. Surround with thickened stewed tomatoes or white sauce. An excellent way to serve an old fowl, after first simmering it tender ...

MILK PUDDINGS.

Of course, milk puddings, rice, tapioca, sago, semolina, custard, etc., are the very best puddings for every person, especially for children, and they are all made in the same way. The milk and one egg needed give their full value, though they don't sound very economical at the present price, but families must be nourished properly. Spend less in every other

way – movies, white gloves, car-fare – and even a family with a very
small income can manage it if they will only get started by giving a little
thought and using a little system in the disposing of what money they
have ...

BAKED APPLES.

Possibly no one article of food is of more value as a regulator. "A
baked apple once a day will make the doctor stay way." Many people, as
Queen Victoria did, have one every day, for some meal. A lot can be
baked whenever the oven is in use and kept for days till needed. Served
with cream, they are good enough for any dinner or supper. Wash, take
out a part of the core, and fill with a tiny bit of butter, a teaspoon of
sugar, a little cinnamon. Place in any baking dish or baking tin, putting
a little water around them, and bake till quite done. Nothing is much
meaner than an apple burnt on one side and raw on the other. Nuts of
any kind add much to the value. The apples can be stuffed with any dried
fruits or nuts ...

BIRDS' NESTS.

This is a most attractive dish, and looks more elaborate and expensive
than it really is. Proceed exactly as above, except peel and core the apples
and drop whole, a few at a time, watching carefully that they cook equally.
Place in a glass dish, pour syrup with a little dissolved isinglass around
them, and with a fork flatten the tops a little, filling in the top of core.
Then place four blanched almonds in the depression thus made, which
makes the dish resemble a bird's nest with eggs. The nuts can be dotted
with some harmless colouring that will make them all the more like tiny
eggs. Serve with whipped cream ...

VEGETABLES.

Vegetables are a very important item of food, as they contain bone-
building, regulating and toning qualities. Potatoes help with the fats. No
article of food is more ruthlessly sacrificed in the cooking, and unless
most of the water is absorbed or kept for boiling soup meat, a large proportion of the useful qualities of the vegetables go down the sink.

Poor potatoes have suffered most. Not only do foolish people throw
away practically the entire nourishment by peeling before boiling, but
generally they are a grey, sodden mass or hard uninviting balls. Don't
on any account peel potatoes before cooking. If you wash them carefully
with a sink brush you will find you can boil them with any other vegetable
and so save fuel, the skins keeping out any other flavour. Boil rapidly
until the fork goes in, take out and press in towel just enough to crack
them. Then stand where they will steam dry quite done. By holding them
in a cloth you can peel them about five times as quickly as when raw.
Try it ...

Potato Stew. – Chop up cooked potatoes about an inch square, season
well with pepper and salt, dredge generously with flour, stirring carefully

enough milk to more than cover them, and simmer very slowly, and be sure not to let them be too done. Small bits of fried bacon add very much to them ...

STUFFED ONIONS, TOMATOES AND GREEN PEPPERS.

Parboil large onions until partly done, in salted water. Take out centre, chopping it with most anything, bread crumbs, bits of meat, ham, green peppers and other vegetables, or even fish, season well, add a little butter and herbs, press down well in onion and pile up. Bake slowly. They can be surrounded with white sauce, good stock, or some of the stuffing ...

CABBAGE.

An exceedingly nice way for supper is to chop cooked cabbage, with or without onion or potatoes, fry in a hot frying pan with a little dripping. When well browned on the under side, fold over like an omelet. Serve hot.

SALADS.

Salads should be considered a necessary adjunct for the helping out of economical meals, and should be far more commonly used by people of small incomes. Olives and olive oil, for their nourishing qualities, are worth the money.

Russian Salad. – Russian salad leads, as all material can be salvaged from the trash heap of many meals. Every kind of cooked meat or fish or vegetable can be used in any possible combination, canned or fresh. Also any kind of dressing is suitable. French dressing is the simplest. Take a spoonful of oil or melted butter to one of vinegar. First season the salad with pepper, salt and onion, or onion salt, then mix them thoroughly. Lettuce, tomatoes, pickled beets, sliced egg, or shredded ends of cabbage leaves, can be used to garnish that or any other salad ...

Apple Salad. – Apple salad looks very elaborate but is not really difficult and is also very cheap. Cut off top, then remove fruit carefully without breaking skin. Chop it with nuts and a very few raisins, season, mix with French Dressing, fill apple skins, replace tops, pick out same size nice looking apples, with the stems on if possible.

BEANS.

Beans are of great importance as a food. All varieties must be soaked at the very least twelve hours and boiled about four till tender. Soy beans must be both soaked and boiled longer.

Butter Beans. – Butter Beans do not require nearly so much time. Boil until tender, season, serve with a little butter and a very little milk. Good for adding to soups and corn.

Haricot Beans. – Haricots are better baked, or used as soup, than served alone. Boil several hours until they are very done, rub through a cullender, season, and a little onion and you have peas porridge ...

OAT, BUCKWHEAT, AND WHOLE WHEAT FLOURS.

All these can be substituted for white flour in any kind of way that is found to be most palatable. Any white flour recipe can be used. An economical way to use flour for afternoon teas, or when appearance and not appetite is considered, is to make a little piecrust (not rich), take bits about as large as a pigeon egg, and roll on a well floured board, until as thin as paper. Bake in quick oven a very light brown. Cut out about two or four inches across. A sheet of iron which just fits the stove is very convenient for baking a lot of small cakes of any kind ...

Graham Gems. – These are not so apt to be successful unless baked in iron gem pans. One teacup sour milk, ½ teaspoon soda, pinch of salt. Stir in enough flour or shorts to make a stiff batter. Have pans very hot, and bake quickly ...

SUGGESTIONS.

By following these suggestions any one can save a great deal, and so have much more to spare for the many funds in such urgent need:

1. People make a big pot of the strongest tea and fill their cups half full of hot water, leaving half of the tea to be thrown away. See just how many of the measures you use are contained in a quarter of a pound of tea. Then see that it lasts just the time it should. After a careful trial you will be surprised to find you have been wasting about one-third.

2. Do the same with coffee. A very economical way to clear coffee is to break an egg, shell and all, into a jelly glass, adding five times its bulk in water. Damp the coffee (heaping spoon of coffee to 2 cups), then stir in a tablespoon of the egg.

3. Often half the suger is left in the bottom of the cup, whereas, by stirring it, much less need have been put in.

4. Scrape out and rinse all saucepans and mixing bowls, so that every particle of the material is saved. This may sound silly, but in the course of the year pounds of nourishment are utilized.

5. In thickening sauces and other things, learn to know the least amount of flour that will do, and don't use a teaspoon more than is required.

6. Never throw away any milk. The sour can be kept in a jug, and any little sweet can be added. It will keep for days in winter, till you are ready to use it.

7. Scrape any kind of fat whatever, collect in a saucepan, boil once or twice in water, carefully scraping off the sediments, and fry out. No taste or odour is then left.

8. Try to get skim milk and buttermilk. They are almost as valuable for food as whole milk.

9. No scrap of meat or vegetable is too small to put by in cold weather. A tablespoon of meat mashed and mixed with boiled egg and bread crumbs, formed into tiny balls, rolled in flour and dropped in boiling soup, make a delicious clear soup.

This saving and scrap-using must be entered into with the right spirit, remembering that we Canadians are about the most wasteful nation in the world. Not so extravagant, as criminally wasteful. Fifty million dollars is thrown away annually in Canadian garbage cans. That is no wild statement, but an ascertained fact. Think if this past year's waste could be restored to us. Fifty million dollars would almost provide for all incapacitated soldiers. And remember, it didn't go out in one or two, or 1,000 cans, but in about 2,000,000 – in yours, and yours, and yours. Each of us should see to it that soon the sight of a slice of bread, a perfectly good bone, or the outside leaves of vegetables, in a garbage can, would give you quite a shock. In England you are fined $50 if the inspector finds any good foodstuff thrown away.

10. Use nut-butter more, or good margarine.

11. All kinds of cold cereal can be saved, and, when not enough to roll in balls to fry, they can be used in batter cakes and corn breads.

12. Keep several cereals on hand, so the family won't get tired of one kind. It's no more expensive in the end.

13. Substitute often rice, macaroni and cheese, dumplings, fried mush and hominy, when potatoes are dear.

14. Cheap tallow rendered down is the cheapest form of dripping. It can be added to what is saved in cooking.

15. Peel adds immensely to all boiled puddings and cakes. Made at home, it costs only the sugar. Grape fruit peel is bitter like some marmalade, so it must not be boiled with the other. And not so much of it should be used.

Cut the fruit in half, take out pulp, taking off a little of the white inside of the peel. Put in a quantity of cold water and boil for hours till tender enough for a straw to pierce very easily. Have ready a hot syrup thick enough to rope when dropped from spoon. Put in enough peel not to be crowded, and simmer very slowly indeed till quite clear. Put on sieve to dry. After the syrup has drained away, roll in sugar and let dry for a day or two. After finishing the lemon and orange, do the grape-fruit.

The syrup left can be used for anything else, or will keep if you want to do just a little of the peel as you have the fruit. Save only the thick skins. If it happens to get too dry or hard, simply soak what you are to use in a little warm water.

16. It is far better to use less butter on the table and have more for cooking. Just try the difference in mince before and after putting in the butter.

17. Careless cooks should take much more pains and cook better. An economical dish should not be blamed for shortcomings when it is the fault of the cooking.

18. Make a sort of game of it. And get your friends to go in for a race with you.

Go to the market, if it is not too far. Walk around and buy at the cheapest places. Many are as dear as the stores.

19. Large families can buy a whole or part of carcass, far cheaper than meat at the butcher's. Or several families who want to do their bit can join. The meat will keep while frozen till used up.

20. Invariably order your bread the day before. About one-fifth is lost by eating the bread fresh. Cut each slice as it is required.

Save every crumb and scrap in a two-pound tin. Grind, grate or roll them when dry, and put in a smaller tin for use.

21. Eat as little cake and pastry as you can.

22. The cheapest tallow, rendered out, can be used for making soft soap. The directions are on the tins of lye. Even bought soft soap is much cheaper to use for rough things, especially dish towels and for floors.

23. Make the following, and save on bought cleansers: 1 pound white sand, 1 pound washing soda, 1 tin soft soap, ½ pound whitening (cheap chalk). Mix well in an open-mouth jar. Keep some in a small jar handy for the sink, also smaller one in bathroom.

24. Instead of one beefless day, why not try for six, to make up for other people less patriotic? Surely in these troubled days all the other kinds of meats and the unwanted parts of beef can fill the other six days perfectly well.

25. By having a plain dinner and good pudding, or vice versa, you can make a good average when your menu is rather sketchy.

It will be a great thing for the country when the vast importance of this "miserly" saving is fully realized. For long after the war is over economy and the greatest care will be needed if the country is to be safe.

There is no doubt that these suggestions are rather bothersome, and carrying them out will take a little more time. Only a little thought and foresight is needed. Arranging for meals the day before, or (better) writing an approximate plan for a week, helps greatly. So does preparing anything you can at the meal before. As you are moving around, it will take no more time to cook rice and anything that is to be used cooked, or get anything done that is to be served cold. With such things done and out of the way, you need not begin the next meal nearly so soon. You will be surprised at the amount of time you do save later.

At a glance, some may think most of these recipes beyond the means of families with very small incomes. But they are not in the least, if well selected, and the whole idea of balanced food values carried out. And the gain is in the greater good received from the money laid out. The little extra trouble of the more elaborate dishes is balanced by the fact that much cheaper things can be used if attractively prepared.

Just 25 per cent of the present amount of beef, bacon and wheat *must* be saved. That means you must do with quarter less of all three. That is very little for each person, but it will amount to millions of pounds.

Do you realize if each of the 7,000,000 Canadians only save a quarter of a pound a week, that means the almost incredible sum of 1,750,000 pounds saved every week?

It is a case of "little drops of water and little grains of sand." So it is more than foolish, it's almost wicked, for anyone to say or think what very little they are able to save won't count.

These recipes are chosen with a view of the *best* economy, nourishing qualities being considered as well as expense.

They are not meant to be recipes de lux.

As this pamphlet has been compiled in less days than it should have taken weeks, faults of omission and commission have been unavoidable.

SAVERS
WILL BE
SAVIOURS

D 7   RECIPE FOR WAR BREAD, FROM A SERIES OF WAR MENUS ISSUED FROM THE OFFICE OF THE FOOD CONTROLLER
[*Kingston* Daily British Whig, *29 October 1917, p. 10*]

2 cups boiling water
½ cup molasses
½ tablespoon salt
1 tablespoon dripping
½ yeast cake dissolved in
½ cup lukewarm water
1 cup rolled oats or oatmeal
4½ cups flour

Add boiling water to oats and let stand one hour. Add molasses, salt, butter, dissolved yeast cake and flour. Let rise, beat thoroughly, turn into buttered bread pans, let rise again and bake.

D 8   RECIPE FOR WAR CAKE
[*Kingston* Daily British Whig, *24 August 1917, p. 10*]

2 cups brown sugar
2 cups hot water
2 tablespoons lard
1 package seedless raisins (or less)
1 teaspoon cloves
1 teaspoon soda
2 cups flour
1 teaspoon cinnamon

Boil all the ingredients except the flour, raisins and soda together for five minutes. When cold add the soda sifted in one-half the flour and the raisins mixed with the rest of the flour.

Bake in loaves 45 minutes in slow oven
Bake in a sheet 30 minutes in a slow oven
Yield: two loaves (8 inches by 2 inches)
Two sheets (9 inches by 1 inch)
Cost of recipe: 32 cents, using one package of raisins

D 9   REPORT OF THE NATIONAL SERVICE
DEPARTMENT OF THE YOUNG WOMEN'S
CHRISTIAN ASSOCIATION, 1916–1917
[*P.A.C., MG 28, I198, YWCA Records, file on war services, 1917–1920*]

1. *Agricultural Work:*

In March the Dominion Council was asked by the Government to co-operate with them by undertaking to provide Hostels and Camps for girls from Colleges and High Schools, and for others who might volunteer to work on the fruit farms of Ontario. The Government Labour Bureau took full charge of the supply of labour, and the Association undertook most, but not all, of the housing. A National Secretary was put in charge of the preparations for opening up the Camps and when the story of the season was told it was found that the Dominion Council had had the oversight of twelve Camps in which about nine hundred pickers and workers had been cared for. These centres were located between Toronto and Niagara, or in the neighbourhood of Lake Erie. As all the preparations had to be made very hurriedly it was not always possible to have the Camps as comfortable and complete as might have been desired, but the spirit of the Campers was so excellent that there was almost a universally cheerful acceptance of the limitations. The health of the workers was on the whole very good, and only two cases of serious illness were reported which is a satisfactory record.

Some of the Camps were not open for more than a few weeks, the crops on certain farms being just strawberries and raspberries, but others were in operation for months. In many of the centres the housing accommodation was increased by the erection of military tents, kindly loaned by the Militia Department, and the girls very much enjoyed being under canvas.

The length of time that the girls remained in the Camps varied, but most of them were anxious to stay as long as possible, and many were in active service for three or four months. Nearly all gained in weight, which indicates that the work was not too strenuous, although besides picking and packing fruit they handled horses, pitched hay, (though this is not work that every girl should be allowed to do) drove motor trucks to market and sold the fruit, sold fruit from stands along the highway, took charge of chicken houses, worked in canning factories, put handles on baskets, hoed for ten hours a day, and put their hands to various other forms of farm work.

The girls are strongly of the opinion that living with the farmers is not the wisest plan, for if they are housed in a central house or camp they can come together in the evenings and enjoy community life. Last year the pickers helped with the dish-washing and preparation of lunches for the next day, but they would very much like to be relieved of this, as it seems quite a burden after coming in weary from the fields.

It was decided that a piano was a necessity, as the workers find real recreation in music, and it also made possible pleasant evenings for the visitors who dropped in from time to time. In some of the Camps a special entertainment was given, the proceeds of which were sent to be applied to the funds of the Dominion Council.

Regarding the labour side of the movement, it may not be out of place in this report to say that the wages which were paid this last year were not satisfactory, as many of the girls, owing partly to the low rate of pay, and partly to the weather conditions, were not able to cover their expenses. The pickers organized and drew up a scale of wages and hours which was submitted to a meeting of the fruit-growers early in December, and it is hoped that this summer more adequate pay may be given. As the rate of wages was low, the Association was only able to charge four dollars a week for board. It can be well understood that with the heavy expense of renting houses, buying equipment, and other necessary outlay, there was a heavy deficit for this first year for the Dominion Council. In the coming year it is hoped that the work may be more nearly financially self-supporting.

The Ontario Government is working out a plan whereby classes may be formed for instruction of girls in general farm work, including milking and the care of horses.

It might be of interest to record that the helpers in the house work in the Camps came from twenty-three different towns, and thus the interest in our work has been increased; many of these helpers have expressed their willingness to come again this year.

The story of the opening up of this new department is not without its chapter of difficulties and discouragements, but the enthusiasm of the whole movement, and the very real value of the service which our Council was able to render, make a record of which we need not be ashamed.

D 10   ARTICLE ON THE KINGSTON STREET
RAILWAY'S CONDUCTORETTES BY NEHNUM MORR
[*Kingston* Daily British Whig, *24 August 1918, p. 9*]

"I understand that you have some vacancies on your line for conductors, Mr. Nickle. I wonder if I could fill the bill?" timidly questioned a female voice.

The manager of the Kingston, Portsmouth and Cataraqui Electric

Railway Company swung round in his easy chair at his desk and, sure enough, there was a tall, handsome young woman looking down at him appealingly. For a moment Hugh C. Nickle was taken aback at the daring request, but a twinkle soon came into his eye as his look of surprise wore off. The young lady was invited to sit down and give her qualifications for a position hitherto always held by a man.

She explained that she had seen the advertisement in the daily papers for conductors, and that she thought she was quite capable to take over the arduous duties. The exigencies of war, she remarked, were taking women into new fields of endeavour, and there was a great need for men in the ranks of the Canadian forces at the front. Women were doing all kinds of work to win the war, and she was quite willing, therefore, to act as conductor while the boys were away doing their bit. The women of England were running trams, and she considered it high time that the Canadians did the same.

The general manager was in a unique position and her argument could not go unheeded. Here was a young lady anxious to do a patriotic service in a time of need, and to release a man for the service of King and country. She was healthy and vigorous and apparently quite able to assume the new duties. Her earnestness did much to convince the perplexed superintendent that she would "make good" and the name of Miss Maude Chart, the first conductorette in Canada, was added to the payroll of the company on October 15th, 1917.

Since that date eleven more girls have entered the ranks of the conductorettes, and the even dozen are just one big, happy family – a unique sight as they come tripping down the main street, laughing and joking, each morning on the way to the street car barns for the day's work. There are no male conductors in the service of the company now, and the ladies have amply justified the hopes and expectations of Mr. Nickle for the success of his novel experiment.

Through the bitter winter and the hot summer they have performed their duties so creditably that they have won the approbation of even the most pessimistic. From the very first, of course, there were some staid, old-fashioned gentlemen who said that Mr. Nickle had been foolish to give the girls an opportunity to show their ability. Men had always been conductors on Kingston street cars, and men should always be conductors according to their views, and not even a great war should make a change. They were dubious about the long hours the girls would have to endure each day and they were not the least reluctant in expressing themselves.

When the girls first came on the cars, and they were somewhat of a novelty, the dear old gentlemen would put their heads together and if the man in the seat behind were to listen he might, too, become the victim of the contagious pessimism.

"You'll see that I'm right," he would hear the first old gentleman remark. "Some of those girls will break down some day when the temperature is about twenty below, and their hands are half frozen to the fare boxes."

And his friend would not be slow in adding, "You know that I think it's criminal to allow them to expose themselves to pneumonia and influenza these cold days. They'll come to an early end, poor dears."

What a dismal picture those pessimists did delight to paint! But they looked at the situation from the wrong angle and they are just now getting the right perspective. The girls did meet with discouraging difficulties, but even in the most trying days when their fingers were blue with cold, they carried on and collected the fares for ten hours at a stretch. Their unfailing politeness and courtesy at all times were commended by visitors as well as citizens, who did not fail to congratulate them on the splendid spirit of service they manifested. As the winter wore on the pessimists became disheartened at their inability to convince themselves and others that the conductorettes were bound to be failures.

A gleam of hope, however, came with the dawn of spring. Summer would soon be here, and the closed winter cars would have to be replaced by the open cars. Ha! ha! Perhaps they were not so wrong after all.

"They may be pretty fair in the winter, but what about the summer?" queried the omniscient pessimist. "They'll never be able to climb along the sides of the car to collect the fares. Mark my words. If Nickle keeps these girls in the summer, there are going to be some dead conductorettes under the sod before the snow comes round again."

And just to make it emphatic the companion in gloom remarked, "I don't see how they'll be able to walk along the sides with their skirts flying around like a couple of flags in a wind storm."

Again the pessimists were to be disappointed. During the summer months the girls have handled tremendous crowds on holidays and on other special occasions, and up to the present only one has been injured – and she was only off duty for half a day with a few bruises. Some of the "Etties" have collected as many as eleven hundred fares during one day, and registered them on an automatic recorder. It has been really wonderful to see them skip along the side steps with remarkable agility and facility. They have been especially gracious in assisting old gentlemen and ladies on and off the cars. They have easily replaced the trolleys on the wires when they slipped off. They have even turned the switches for the motormen. In a word they have performed a score of duties devolving upon them with a grace and cleverness that is exceedingly creditable and gratifying.

Clad in their natty khaki suits, they are an addition to the car service, and their courteous "Fares, please" is a delightful change from the gruff "Fares." Each girl is provided with the material for two uniforms, a peaked, brown straw cap sitting at a jaunty angle on her head under which her hair is neatly tucked, a "slicker" fisherman's hat and rubber boots for rainy days, as well as brown boots and stockings, which complete their attire on sunny days. Their suits are quite plain, consisting of a short skirt and Norfolk coat with shining brass butttons. On very warm days the girls remove their coats, and they look refreshingly cool and comfortable in pongee blouses and khaki middies. They are very business-like in appearance, and in the performance of their duties they will stand no nonsense from any of the male passengers who are of a "flirty" nature, which responds to the attractiveness of the Limestone City's conductorettes.

Their wages are also very generous and many of them make as much as eighteen and nineteen dollars a week. They are paid $2.25 for a ten-hour day, and receive double pay for overtime. At the end of the summer those who have been in the service during the whole of the season are to be granted a substantial bonus by the company as a mark of appreciation for their steady work. Altogether the majority will have averaged about $18.50 a week when their bonus is given.

Some of the girls start as early as six o'clock in the morning on their trips, and Mr. Nickle stated that as a rule they were more regular than the men in arriving for the "dawning" cars. During the day they have few idle moments until the last car enters the barns shortly before eleven o'clock at night.

The girls themselves are delighted with their occupation and are enjoying their novel experience. Most of them have come from some form of indoor work and the change to outdoor duties has benefitted them all physically. One little Yankee girl from Grand Rapids, Mich., found it so exhilarating that she wrote for her sister to join her and they are both now employed as conductorettes. Another girl was married recently and while she collects the fares her husband controls the car as motorman. The names of the girls who have the distinction of being the only conductorettes in the Dominion are Mrs. Gordon Pretty, Mrs. Alfred Kenyon, Miss Margaret Adams, Miss Mabel Brewster, Miss Winnifred Chart, Miss Gladys Fraser, Miss Mamie Fields, Miss Ella Kennedy, Miss Jennie Newman, Miss Elsie Williams, Miss Hilda Williams, and Miss Maude Wilson. Miss Elsie Williams has the record of never being absent or late for duty.

Mr. Nickle is very proud of them and is extremely gratified at the success they have made in the work. "They have acquitted themselves nobly," said he, "and I have absolutely no fault to find with any of them. They are punctual in arriving for work, courteous while performing their duties, and I am convinced that they have been able to collect as many fares as the men. In comparison from every standpoint they are their equal. It was a somewhat radical departure to engage them for the work but they have surpassed our most sanguine expectations and we are proud to be the one company in Canada employing conductorettes. Some of the other cities might gain by our experience in these times when labor is so scarce. The motormen show no antipathy to our employment of them and indeed are co-operating with us in splendid fashion. We are proud to have such patriotic and efficient girls in the employ of the company."

Such a testimony from one who knows should dampen the ardor of those who don't. The world never had any place for the pessimists anyway.

D 11 Sir Joseph Flavelle to Howard Murray, Director of Explosives, Imperial Munitions Board
[*P.A.C., MG 30, B4, Flavelle Papers, v. 11, file 104*]

15 January 1918.

In view of the work which has been done in England by women in explosive plants, I am desirous that early action should be taken to determine what can be done in Canada to make use of women in our explosive plants. Moreover, the increasing necessity for men at the Front, and for men in agriculture, as well as for other activities in the country in which male help only can be used, causes me to see that we have a duty to perform in releasing men wherever possible if women can do the work.

I apprehend that the difficulty at both Trenton, Renfrew and Nobel is the question of suitable housing for the women, and necessary accommodations. These may be prohibitory as regards the entire staff being women. We will not know, however, what will be the difficulties until we fairly face it and make the enquiries. Meantime, are there Departments in Trenton and Renfrew which could be taken over by women operators, – or sections of Departments? If they are so operated, it would be necessary to issue standard clothing for the women. This has been already established in England.

I find that Pirrie confirms what I saw at Gretna where on the Cordite side of the plant it was exclusively operated by women.

If you have an officer available, or if you have not an officer available perhaps you could secure someone who would give sustained attention to this matter so as to give me an intelligent report.

D 12 Howard Murray to Sir Joseph Flavelle
[*P.A.C., MG 30, B4, Flavelle Papers, v. 11, file 104*]

Ottawa,
16 January 1918.

We have not been unmindful of this situation and I brought the matter to the attention of Mr. Mark Irish and Mr. Durkin in October last, as you will note by the attached correspondence. At that time the Conscription Act was facing us. Mr. Irish felt then that any exemptions we required could be obtained. It has been more or less true, but the affects of Conscription have been so far reaching in labour that a broader view must be taken of the entire situation.

You will note that I did take certain definite steps and had Mr. Irish send Mrs. Fenton to Trenton.

You will note by Mr. Durkin's letter of October 11th., that as a result of his review of the situation it was found that we could use at least from one hundred and fifty to two hundred women operators.

It will pay us to put up the accommodation, although Mrs. Fenton's suggestions are more elaborate than we would need to employ. A vital question is as to whether there are sufficient women in the district whom we could obtain or whether it will be possible to draw women from Toronto or other centres of population should accommodation be made for them. I will have a canvass made at once to try to obtain the answers to these questions and will follow the entire matter up with energy.

D 13   SIR JOSEPH FLAVELLE TO MARK H. IRISH
[*P.A.C., MG 30, B4, Flavelle Papers, v. 11, file 104*]

18 January 1918.

I have communicated with Mr. Howard Murray as per attached.

In response he has sent me a file covering letters passing between you and himself in October last.

I will appreciate a careful review of this situation again. The use of women in England in Explosive Plants is a matter of common practice. Do you not think that with present pressure for men for the Front, the pressure for men for agricultural purposes, for the production of coal, and for primary products, that it is the duty of the Board to assist in releasing men wherever possible?

D 14   MARK H. IRISH TO SIR JOSEPH FLAVELLE
[*P.A.C., MG 30, B4, Flavelle Papers, v. 11, file 104*]

Toronto,
21 January 1918.

I have your favour of the 18th inst. in the above connection.

I heartily agree, and always have, with your general proposition that the Board "assist in releasing men wherever possible". I advocated this in the immediate offices of the Board a year ago last September and also in the allied interests of the Board continuously for months past but I must confess that in the first instance, especially in the offices where it was possible without successful contradiction, there was never exhibited any overwhelming enthusiasm. I daresay that this attitude is now changed. I advocated it once and once only in the Inspection Department because the reception there from Major Ogilvie was such as I have seldom received in a business enterprise. So much for the general proposition.

To come to the specific proposition of the employment of women in Explosives Plants: it is my opinion that this branch of employment should constitute our last effort at the Dilution of Labour and not our first. If when we have gone through our offices at Ottawa, Toronto, Montreal and Winnipeg and through, with particular care, the Inspection Department, we still find that the call for men for men's work is pressing, we should then go to our Explosive Plants. To do otherwise is, to my mind, economically unsound and to be deplored from the humane phases of the situation. My reasons are four and as follows:

(1) To introduce women at Trenton and Nobel and have that introduction on lines that will cause us no shame involves a very large expenditure of money. It practically means the establishment of a female colony at each of these points wholly self-contained and reaching to the magnitude of a small town, with health equipment, amusements and all the requisites of a life to be lived within the geographical radius created by the Explosives Department. If the necessity is present and if our list is clean in all other directions then this is a task to which we ought to set our face and I presume that in the last analysis the British taxpayer should fix an example and be prepared to expend the money necessary. Therefore as it is economic it rises only as far as finances play the part.

(2) I am informed that the work for which women are suited in Explosives Plants would not release the number of men in anything like the quantity comparable with the expense involved in equipment and sustained welfare work afterward. The work at Explosives Plants, if my information is correct is to a large measure, necessary of performance by rough labour and while at Trenton, for example, we should have to spend a great many thousands of dollars, we should only facilitate the employment of females to the extent of two hundred.

(3) The inherent danger in an Explosives Plant, no matter how well conducted is such that one must be loath to expose women to it except under dire necessity. If I am correctly informed it was in the Explosives Branch that England last resorted to women.

(4) The fourth reason is humane and relates to health. If you will refer to Memorandum No. 8 of the Health of Munitions Workers Committee, of the Ministry of Munitions, you will see there on pages 4, 5, 6 and 7 a statement of what Explosives work has done toward the permanent disability of women, to say nothing of their irreparable disfigurement, also refer to Dr. Benjamin Moore's article on page 37 of the Pamphlet on the Origin, Symptoms, Etc., in Munitions Workers, published by the Royal Society of Medicine in January 1917 and furnished by the Ministry of Munitions to us.

It may be, of course, that the work at the Plants at Trenton and Nobel would not be of a nature similar to that mentioned by the Health of Munitions Workers Committee but from an interview with Mr. Murray, and devoid of technical knowledge as I am, I formed the impression that women would be exposed to these calamities. If this is correct then it appears to me to afford a strong reason for introducing them into Explosives Plants only as a last resort and I do not think that we have yet approached in Canada this stage and will not until the Federal Government differentiates between essential and non-essential production and we have used the Labour after this differentiation to the full.

D 15 'SOCIAL REACTIONS OF THE WAR'
[*Editorial in the* Globe, *4 February 1918, p. 4*]

The war has brought Canadian women together as never before by a common bond of sympathy and sacrifice, and co-operation in the many activities in which their patriotism has found such useful expression. In every community war work has done much to break down the class distinctions and the snobbery which flourished in this young country as in older lands ...

The class barriers which have been burned away in the fires of the war ought not to be rebuilt. Perhaps the new and wider opportunities of public service opening to women, and the interest in politics and problems of government which will be stimulated by woman's franchise, will turn into rational channels much of the energy hitherto wasted in a rapid round of pleasures. It would be a great gain if the serious outlook and ideal of service which many fashionable women have acquired during the war become the habit and custom. Certainly during this period of testing the Canadian women have developed a capacity for leadership and for organization which has set the pace for the men.

E. SCHOOLS

E 1 FIRST PRIZE ESSAY WRITTEN BY
RUTH MCKINNON OF CHATSWORTH HIGH SCHOOL
[Public Service Bulletin, *November 1917, pp. 82–3*]

HOW CAN THE ONTARIO HIGH SCHOOL BOY BY WORKING ON A FARM THIS
SUMMER HELP HIMSELF, THE FARMER, AND THE EMPIRE.

The production of food in Canada has hitherto been regulated by the
law of supply and demand. Farmers devoted themselves to raising the
products which they thought would be profitable and marketable. But,
for the present at least, all this is changed. Food production has been
lifted to the plane of a religious and patriotic duty. The withdrawal of so
many millions of men from industrial pursuits into the armies of the
various warring nations has resulted in a scarcity of food all over the
world and this situation can be relieved only by the most strenuous efforts
of all who remain at home, men and women, boys and girls. We must
squarely face this serious situation and face it in the spirit which has
taken our boys to the front, the spirit of service to our country and to
humanity.

So the Ontario High School boy, not old enough, or not strong enough
perhaps to don the khaki, can in this great food crisis play a man's part
and do a work hardly less important than that of our gallant boys in
France. And in doing this many benefits will be reaped by the boy himself. In the first place he will have the feeling that he is performing a
patriotic service, and that thought alone ought to make a boy more manly
and give him a self-respect and a strength of character that will help fit
him for the battle of life. Physically it will be an ideal service. In it he will
get a change from the life of a student, which change will not only benefit
him physically but will also help him mentally. When he returns to his
studies in the autumn he will find that many a cobweb has been cleared
from his brain and that he will have a mental alertness surpassing anything he has hitherto known. The exercise in the fresh air and sunshine,
the sound refreshing sleep, the "early to bed" and the "early to rise"
which the old proverb says "makes a man healthy, wealthy and wise,"
will tend to develop in him a strong physique. The thought that he is
unselfishly trying to "do his bit" will give him a feeling of happiness and
contentment, which will be worth far more to him than the money he
will earn; but from the financial standpoint also it is an opportunity not
to be despised, for many a student finds the money problem a serious
one. Then, too, his opportunity of studying nature at close range, the
birds and trees and wild flowers – especially the city student to whom

many of these things will be quite new – ought to be a means of culture to him, that will make life richer for him all his days. He will also learn something of the land, the processes of crop production, and the farmer's point of view – advantages of great value in his education and his equipment for his life work.

And how can our High School boy help the farmer? Farmers stand in dire need of labour now. There is today in Ontario an average of one man for a hundred acres, not nearly enough and unless help is forthcoming in large measure, the farmer cannot sow even a normal crop much less the twenty per cent increase, which the Motherland has called upon Ontario to produce. The three vital needs for victory are men, food and money. The farmer stands out pre-eminently as the man responsible for feeding the Empire. And the High School boy can help the farmer to "do his bit" and to reap the benefits financially by meeting the great demand for food and getting the high price.

And then the Empire – the world's available surplus of food is gone. There is a pressing need for food on the part of Great Britain and our Allies, who look to Canada, the world's granary for supplying that need. All eyes turn now to the Canadian farmer for he can render the Empire special service in this, the sternest year of the great war. The Motherland is far from feeding herself under normal conditions. Her difficulties have been greatly increased by the submarine menace and Canada is in the best position to help because she is the nearest great source of supply. Statesmen and economists agree that the universal food shortage is today the most dangerous menace of all. Lloyd George declares that one year's unselfishness will save the British Empire – will save humanity. Words like these make us realize how grave the situation is and how loudly the call of Empire comes to all – High School boys included – who are able to help solve this serious problem.

Thus the Ontario High School boy, laying aside the idea that he is going on a picnic for the summer, and bracing himself for real hard work, can very effectively help himself, the farmer and the Empire.

E 2   REPORT ON STUDENT FARM WORKERS DURING
THE SUMMER OF 1917
[Ontario Sessional Paper number 16 of 1918. Annual Report of the Department of Public Works, Trades and Labour Branch]

The campaign for securing boys from the secondary schools was launched early in March. The Department of Education had made regulations in 1916 permitting High School boys who passed a preliminary examination to leave school any time between April 20th and May 20th for the purpose of working on a farm. Their standing was granted to them when they had furnished proof of three months' satisfactory work. These regulations applied to all High School boys with the exception of those taking their final examination for teachers' certificates. Two thousand seven hundred and seventeen boys fulfilled the requirements of the Department and obtained their standing by means of farm work.

In 1917 the Department of Education passed a further regulation which permitted girls to do farm work under the same conditions, with the proviso that the girls should find their own employment through parents or teachers. In order to maintain the standard of the schools, a further regulation provided that boys who had obtained their departmental standing by farm work during the summer of 1916 could not again secure their standing by the same means.

The campaign was carried on partially by newspaper and magazine publicity, and partially by personal appeal. A series of advertisements was prepared, urging the boys of the Province to heed the urgent call of the Empire for greater production and pointing out the opportunity which was before them to render practical aid to their older brothers who were fighting across the seas. Three University professors visited the principal High Schools and Collegiate Institutes and addressed the students on the importance of securing every student who could possibly assist in farm work. The Young Men's Christian Association also loaned a number of their boy secretaries, and in this way all the principal schools of the Province were visited.

Copies of a pamphlet entitled "The High School Campaign for Farm Labour" were distributed in the schools for the students to take home, in order that the plan might be understood by the parents. An essay contest was arranged by the Organization of Resources Committee on the subject, "How best can the High School boy working on a farm benefit himself, the farmer and the country?" Prizes of five, three and two dollars were offered in each of the secondary schools, and grand prizes of twenty-five, ten and seven dollars for the three best essays from any of the schools in the Province. Students in more than 200 schools entered the Essay Contest. Thousands of boys and girls put their best efforts and thought into the subject, with the result that hundreds of intelligent boys and girls engaged in food production last summer when they might otherwise have spent their time less productively.

During the annual Teachers' Convention in April a luncheon was given for all school principals. At this luncheon an urgent plea for greater production was made and the principals were asked to co-operate in every possible way in the recruiting of the army of High School students.

Getting in Touch with the Farmers.

At the same time a campaign was carried on to induce the farmers to avail themselves of the services of this comparatively unknown labour supply. A series of advertisements, which included an application form, was run in the rural papers, and the farmers were asked to send the application blank to the nearest branch of the Ontario Government System of Public Employment Bureaux. In some counties the farmers welcomed the opportunity of securing the boys; in others, it was not until a few boys had gone out and given satisfaction that the men had sufficient faith even to send in applications. All applications from farmers for High School boys were sent either to the District Representative of the Department of Agriculture, to the nearest employment bureau, or to the office of the Superintendent of Trades and Labour. Eventually, however, all the boys in the rural counties were placed by the District Representatives. A large reserve of boys was obtained from the cities and towns, and these boys were sent out either directly from the Zone Bureaux, or through the Agricultural Representatives.

Response on the Part of High School Students.

Over five thousand boys filled in the Government's Student's Registration Form for Farm Work. This number does not, of course, include the hundreds who found their own employment and did not report to the Trades and Labour Branch. Over eight thousand High School boys and girls participated in food production during the summer of 1917.

Many of the boys and girls worked on farms at considerable sacrifice of their own interests. There were many cases brought to the attention of the Department where enjoyable vacation trips were refused by students who preferred to do their bit by assisting in food production.

A small percentage of the boys and girls sent out were too young to do efficient work. The greater number, however, were from fourteen to sixteen years of age and proved satisfactory workers.

An attempt was made to keep the boys in touch with representatives of their own religious denominations, and for this purpose a record was kept of the religious faith of each applicant ... About half the boys had worked on farms before. Of the remainder some had worked as delivery boys and were, therefore, able to handle horses ...

A letter was sent to the principals of all the Secondary Schools in the Province asking for a report on the farm work during 1917, of all the students who had been engaged in food production. The tabulated results of the questionnaires sent out with the letter follow.

Summary of Returns re Farm Work, 1917.

Pupils in Secondary Schools who Engaged in Farm Work during 1917

Total number of Students in Schools		Total number who were engaged in farm work for any period		Total number who worked for at least three months		Number who were parents of children residing on farms	
Boys	Girls	Boys	Girls	Boys	Girls	Boys	Girls
14,318	19,597	4,867	4,036	4,235	3,351	2,381	2,893

Percentage of Pupils of Secondary Schools who Engaged in Farm Work during 1917

School	Boys	Girls
High	39.68	25.67
Continuation	49.96	26.81
Collegiates	26.01	14.36

In all, 33.99 per cent of the total number of boys and 20.59 per cent of the girls in the secondary schools of the Province received badges from the principal of the school for their farm work during 1917. This does not include the very large number who received their badges in other ways.

Of the boys who worked on the farms 87 per cent worked for three months or more, and of the girls 83.02 per cent.

Percentage of Farm Workers who were Children of
Parents Residing on Farms

School	Boys	Girls
High Schools	61.97	74.17
Collegiates	40.68	65.39
Continuation	39.33	79.56
All Secondary Schools	48.92	71.68

The great difference between the percentage of girls residing on farms and that of boys is due to the fact that no special effort was made in 1917 to induce girls from the secondary schools to do farm work, whereas the s.o.s.[1] movement recruited a large percentage of boys from cities and towns.

Farm Service Corps Badges.

In order that the boys and girls might realize that they were members of a great organization to aid production, farm service corps badges were designed and awarded to every applicant upon presentation of evidence of a satisfactory length of service ...

During the summer large numbers were also given out by the s.o.s. Supervisors working under the direction of the Young Men's Christian Association. The meetings which the supervisors arranged largely included other items on their programme, as well as the badge distribution, but this aspect of each meeting was featured in the advertising, and was undoubtedly the means of attracting large numbers, who otherwise might not have attended.

At a typical badge distribution meeting arranged by Zone Supervisor R.C. Sidenius in Dundas, the programme consisted of short addresses to the boys delivered by the mayor of the town, local representatives of the clergy, and by a representative of the Trades and Labour Branch. Sports were engaged in during the afternoon of the meeting and the programme included an explanation and an exposition of the Canadian Standard Efficiency Tests.

The actual presentation of badges to the boys took place around a camp fire, and a great deal of interest was manifested by those present in the pinning on the boy's coat of the Government's recognition of his efforts as a farm worker.

[1]Soldiers of the Soil.

The meeting described above is fairly representative of the button distribution meetings held under the direction of the Zone Supervisors. These gatherings included not only the boys, but also in many cases their parents and their farm employers, and there was a marked spirit of co-operation between town and country manifested on every occasion.

Co-Operation of Young Men's Christian Association.

The Young Men's Christian Association played an important part in the High School campaign for farm labour both during the drive for volunteers and after the boys had actually started work. A Zone Supervisor was appointed for each of the four districts into which the Province was divided. These men, all of whom had previous training in boys' work, visited many farms where boys were working, and took a friendly interest in the boys' general welfare. The Young Men's Christian Association is to be congratulated upon the efficient way in which it organized and conducted the follow-up work in connection with the employment of boys on the land.

Attitude of the Boys.

From the replies to the questions asked on the Farm Service Badge receipt form, it has been possible to obtain much valuable information as to the general conditions of employment, the wages paid, and the hours of labour. The majority of the boys have expressed themselves as satisfied with the treatment which they received, and many have already made arrangements to spend the summer of 1918 with their farm employer of last year. Eight out of every ten boys who engaged in farm work during the summer stayed for at least three months, and gave satisfactory service to the farmers. The average length of service was three months.

A few quotations from letters received from boys who had spent the summer on farms will serve to indicate the splendid spirit of the boys:

I am in the best of health and am sure enjoying myself, even though the work is hard. I get the best of meals, and a good bed with plenty of covers to keep me warm. I get up at half-past five, and go to bed at eight o'clock, and am treated just as I was at home, so you can just bet I'm glad I came out to the farm.

Just a line to let you know I am getting along fine here. We have started harvesting, and the two of us are bringing all of it in ourselves from 80 acres.

I like the farmer and the farm all right and am getting on fine. I drive a team harrowing and cultivating. At the present time we get up at half-past six, have an hour for each meal, and we get finished supper and all the chores by seven o'clock. My wages will be $20 a month, and the farmer wants me to stay till the end of September.

I am getting along fine and like the place very well. Mr. W. is a nice man, and so is his wife. (!)

Living Conditions.

In practically all cases the boy or boys lived and boarded at the farmer's house. A very few boys, however, cooked for themselves ... Four Toronto High School boys lived [in a shack] near Niagara-on-the-Lake.

They slept on canvas cots and did all their cooking on an oil stove. Vegetables and fruits were supplied by the farmer, but they had to purchase butter and eggs. The price of the milk the boys used was deducted from their wages at the close of their term of engagement. While the boys enjoyed the advantages incidental to camp life, it cannot be said that the plan was a financial success.

Attitude of the Farmers.

The farmers have also written many letters which indicate their satisfaction with the High School student as a "hired man." The following are typical:

"Nobody but the farmer himself knows the vast difficulties that can be overcome with a pair of extra hands. The boy that you sent me was totally ignorant of farm work; in fact, I never saw a chap who knew so little about agricultural things, but he is willing to learn and so far is doing splendidly. The very first day I put four horses on the cultivator and gave him the lines. He had never had hold of lines before, but with a round or two of the field he has driven ever since. Again I thank you."

Another farmer said: "The boy you sent me only knew the country from the summer resort viewpoint, yet he has adapted himself wonderfully well. He could scarcely be more interested if the farm belonged to him. He is going to try to persuade his people to allow him to be a farmer."

At the outset of the season it was decided that no High School boy should be sent out to do farm work at a wage less than twelve dollars a month. There was a slight difference in the rates of wages asked for and received in the different sections of the Province.

At the Toronto Bureau the wages offered ran from eight to twenty-five dollars a month. Those in the centres west of Toronto and in the Niagara district averaged higher than those in Durham, Peterborough, Northumberland and Victoria Counties. The wages, as shown by the Badge Receipt cards, were in advance of the amounts originally offered by the farmers at the beginning of the season. This is in itself sufficient evidence of the satisfactory service rendered by the boys. Many boys who began work at fifteen and twenty dollars a month were increased to twenty and twenty-five dollars a month before the season ended. There were no offers from farmers applying to the Toronto Bureau to pay boys above thirty dollars a month, yet thirty, thirty-five and even forty dollars a month with board is stated as the amount actually paid in some instances.

At the Hamilton Bureau there were comparatively few calls for student farm labour, but the wages offered averaged eighteen dollars per month, ranging from ten to twenty-five dollars. More boys applied for work at Hamilton than could be placed in that zone. In the Ottawa Bureau, the wages offered for boys in the early part of the season were around nine dollars a month. Later the wage offered rose to twenty dollars a month, and the demand for boys steadily increased.

The wages offered at the London Bureau were as high as twenty-eight to thirty dollars a month, and the demand greatly exceeded the supply. The average wage was slightly over twenty dollars.

The Trades and Labour Branch did not undertake the placing of High School girls individually on farms as in the case of the boys, it being deemed more advisable to have the girls procure their own farm employment through friends and relations. For the girls who were unable to obtain employment in this way, ample opportunity was afforded for farm service through the girls' camps, which were organized by the Trades and Labour Branch in various fruit and truck farming sections of the Province.

E 3   LETTER TO THE *Globe* FROM PROFESSOR C.B. SISSONS
[Globe, *12 February 1918, p. 4*]

The case of Miss Freda Held cannot be allowed to drop if the good name of Toronto is to be maintained and a grave injury to the teaching profession and the children of the city is to be avoided. Miss Held's statement presented in the board meeting of last Thursday evening forms a serious indictment of the administration of the public schools of the city. It puts the board and the public, whose servant the board is, on the defence.

Miss Held is a British subject by birth.[2] The mere fact that she is of German extraction should not be counted against her. To say nothing of royalty, Viscount Milner, who is a member of the War Cabinet, has German blood in his veins and was actually born in Germany where he received his early education. Britain's greatness has been due largely to the fact that she has kept open house and has been willing to defend the rights of those who have been willing to become her subjects. Miss Held says: "I do not speak German and never was in Germany. My education has been entirely English, and my whole habit of thought and all that I have and am are British and Canadian."

The following evidence has been brought against her:

(1) The fact that she taught one of Tom Moore's poems too effectively to satisfy one of the inspectors. He complimented her on her lesson at the time (last March), but afterwards concluded that the spirit and feeling with which she presented the lesson indicated sympathy with Sinn Fein. But he said nothing of the sort to herself or the principal.

(2) The fact that two teachers of the school bore witness against her before an unofficial committee consisting of the inspector in question, his chief, the Chairman of the Board and two other members. The evidence was unsubstantial and was weakened by the fact that a charge laid

[2] Miss Held was a native of London, England, and received her teacher training there.

by one of the teachers at the first session of the committee was with-
drawn at the second session. The whole investigation, which was held in
camera, appears to have been of the nature of an inquisition rather than
an inquiry.

(3) The fact that Miss Held objected to singing the second verse of the
National Anthem.[3] She admits this charge, and says she thinks the verse
inconsistent with the golden rule. In this she is in good company. It will
be remembered that an influential section of the Anglican Synod was
opposed to its use even in war-time.

(4) A letter from a Mrs. Anning, now resident in Michigan, which attributes disloyalty to the family of Miss Held. This woman's acquain-
tance with the family is confined to the few hours during which she was
the guest of that family for supper. Apparently both her daughter, who
has lived with the Helds for three years, and her son, who spent his last
leave there before going overseas and has been the recipient of good
things from the Held kitchen ever since, do not agree with the mother.

Over against these charges must be set the opinion of the teachers in
the school, except the two mentioned, and the unanimous opinion of the
parents of the children in her room. They all speak in her favour and see
no reason to doubt her loyalty. Indeed, her statement shows her to be a
young woman with just those qualities which are needed in the difficult
and important public service to which she has devoted herself. Not even
in respect to her one strategical mistake, that of handing in her resignation at the chief inspector's suggestion, should she be criticized. Few
men and fewer women in the circumstances would have chosen the publicity and strife unavoidable in case she refused to accept his recommendation.

The public, however, has a right to object to the whole procedure. It
has a right to object to the attitude of an inspector who regards his relation to the teachers in the light of a detective, rather than a friend: to the
private session of a self-appointed committee of the board making a
private recommendation to this teacher that she resign, lest a worse evil
befall her; and, finally, to any closing of the question before Miss Held
has every opportunity, without recourse to the law, of disproving the
charges privately and publicly made against her.

The tablet erected in memory of Harry Lee in the Annette Street
School should stand as a warning to those who mistake loyalty to convention for loyalty to country. Above all things, our teachers must feel
free to think for themselves, and if at times they are in error, should ex-

[3]The second verse of the national anthem (*God Save the King*):
>Oh, Lord, our God arise,
>Scatter his enemies,
>And make them fall;
>Confound their politics,
>Frustrate their knavish tricks,
>On thee our hopes we fix,
>God save us all.

pect warning and guidance, rather than the methods of the Star Chamber. British justice to a British subject demands the reconsideration of the case of Miss Freda Held.

E 4 MISS FREDA HELD'S LETTER OF RESIGNATION
[Globe, *3 May 1918, p. 8*]

In view of the fact that I have been refused the opportunity in a public investigation of clearing myself of all suspicion of disloyalty, I ask to be relieved of any further duties as a teacher on the staff.

I trust the board will appreciate how keenly I have felt the accusations which have been made against me. I was born and have lived all my life under the British flag. I am a British citizen, and love the free democratic institutions of my country.

I abhor the autocracy and militarism of Germany, and believe with all my heart that the world will only be safe for future generations when they are crushed.

It is a cause of great satisfaction to me to feel that all who really know me have never doubted me. Twenty-two teachers on the staff of Carlton Street School have testified for me. The parents of the children whom I have taught do not doubt me. Many citizens of the school community have endorsed me. A majority of the board have voted for my reappointment.

All this, in these abnormal times, when prejudice might naturally be expected, is evidence of the great and dominating force of British fair play and British justice.

Under these circumstances a further justification seems unnecessary. The publicity to which I have been subjected is most distasteful. I would therefore request that the incident be closed by the acceptance of my resignation.

E 5 'ONTARIO'S PART IN THE GREAT WAR' IN THE ONTARIO EDITION OF THE
Canada War Thrift Book

In the *Canada War Thrift Book* the boys and girls of the schools of Ontario will read what our great Dominion has done to aid the Mother Country in the war for the freedom of the world. And they may ask themselves, or their parents, or their teachers, "What has Ontario done?" Now, there is not, and there should not be, any feeling of rivalry among the Provinces of Canada. We are all Canadians. But there is a healthful spirit in each Province – a spirit which makes the nine Provinces of the Dominion act like nine sisters in a family, each of whom says to herself, "I must do as much as I can to help our mother – I must excel all of my sisters in this great labour of love." And, being one of the older sisters in the great family, this is how Ontario feels and acts.

It is but natural, and it is but right, that those who live in Ontario should think that they are citizens of the "Banner Province" of the Dominion. To this distinctive name Ontario had many good claims before the war. She has more right to that high honour now. The story of what Ontario has done should produce in every pupil, not a spirit of boastfulness, but a just pride that this Province has so nobly done what she could for the cause of civilization.

Most young people care little for statistics — they like to think in general terms; and so this story must be as free as possible from figures, which are usually so meaningless. But everyone knows that Ontario has sent thousands of the fairest and the finest of her sons to join the Empire's fighting forces in all parts of the world. Up to June 17th, 1918, Canada had raised for her army 538,283 men; of these 231,191 came from Ontario. In what way could the patriotism of this Province be more clearly shown than in this magnificent contribution? But this is not all. Thousands of brave young fellows joined the Royal Air Force and the Canadian Naval Service; thousands more were trained in the University of Toronto Officers' Training Corps and entered the Imperial Army, leading their men in France, in Flanders, in Mesopotamia, in Palestine, in the Balkans, and wherever else Great Britain's battles were fought.

What of Ontario's daughters? Hundreds of them went to the front as nurses; others served as workers in munition factories; some performed clerical or mechanical duties in various departments of war work. In every city, town, village, hamlet, and rural section of the Province, women worked as women never worked before, sewing, knitting, preparing hospital supplies, packing overseas boxes, sending comforts, raising money, doing anything and everything that would assist in the prosecution of the war and in the relief of suffering.

Young people are interested in their teachers and their schools. What have the teachers done? There are relatively few men engaged in teaching in this Province, yet 519 of them enlisted and 34 of them have given their lives for the cause of freedom. The teachers of Ontario have enthusiastically taught the war and its lessons to their pupils; they have instilled patriotism; with zeal and with fidelity they have exerted themselves in all forms of patriotic work. They have organized their pupils to collect for Red Cross Funds, for the Patriotic Fund, for the Navy League, for work in knitting socks and in forwarding comforts to soldiers. No class of people has been more earnest and more energetic in war work than the teachers in the schools. And does anyone imagine that the soldiers could have fought with such gallantry, that they could have endured hardships with such fortitude, that they could have shown such courage, such faith, such loyalty, such true and clean uprightness, if the teachers of the present time and those of earlier years had not taught them well and had not set before them noble examples of all that is best in life. This country will not soon forget the work done in the schools in preparing the youth in mind and in character to meet and sustain the severe test imposed by the war.

What of the youth of Ontario? Have they done their share? Everywhere students who were of sufficient age enlisted. In the secondary schools, in the two years, 1916 and 1917, 549 of them obtained certificates without writing on examinations – they enlisted instead. In the same two years 9,776 boys and girls of the secondary and elementary schools secured their class standing or their certificates under the regulation which allows farm employment to be substituted, during certain months, for school attendance and study.

For winning a war there must be soldiers, nurses, and workers of all kinds, but there must also be money. And Ontario has not been behind with her gifts. To estimate what the people have given, in cash and in supplies, would be an impossible task. Every appeal has met with a splendid response. Ontario has earned a reputation for magnificent generosity. However, people give not only as individuals, but they also give through their Government. In this Province a tax of one mill has been levied on all property, and the receipts from that source amount to about two million dollars a year – all this is used for war purposes only.

Immediately on the outbreak of the war Ontario presented the Motherland with 250,000 bags of flour to help feed her soldiers and also sent provisions and supplies for the unfortunate Belgians. These gifts cost nearly one million dollars.

Have all the boys and girls heard of the Ontario Military Hospital at Orpington, England? This is, perhaps, Ontario's greatest single gift to the cause in which all are interested. In 1915 there were in England only two Canadian hospitals, with accommodation for only 165 patients, and wounded Canadian soldiers were being placed in hospitals in various cities in the British Isles. Of course, they were well cared for, but they preferred to be together – among comrades with whom they had a good deal in common. And so the Ontario Government sent its Minister of Education to England to arrange for a really large hospital for Canadian soldiers. It was established at Orpington, and it contains 2,000 beds. The cost to the Province has been more than one and a quarter million dollars.

It is necessary that wounded soldiers receive every attention and it is also necessary that soldiers who are sent back to England "on leave" – to spend a brief vacation – should have a place to rest and to enjoy wholesome recreation. In response to this latter need Ontario established in London, England, four Maple Leaf Club Houses. These provide meals and sleeping accommodation and a homelike atmosphere for which Canadian soldiers are very grateful.

Would a long list tire the young people in the schools of Ontario? Not when it has to do with the war. In addition to the gifts mentioned, grants have been made to the Patriotic Fund (over one and a quarter millions of dollars in 1918), to Belgian Relief, to the Navy League, to the British

Sailors' Relief Fund, to King George's Fund for Sailors, to the Great War Veterans' Association, to a Khaki Club, to the overseas work of the Y.M.C.A., to the Boy Scouts' Association, for soldiers' comforts, for athletic supplies for overseas troops, to the Palestine War Relief Commission, to the Italian Red Cross, to the Secours National, for Polish Relief and Serbian Relief, to the Seamen's Hospital, to the Canadian Chaplains' Association, for horse and motor ambulances, for machine guns, for evaporated apples, to Tuberculosis Sanitaria, to the Canadian Aviation Fund, for the relief of Halifax sufferers, for recruiting, for organization of resources, for increased production, for soldiers' hospitals and libraries, and to the Soldiers' Aid Commission. To all these the Government of Ontario has given $8,281,624.96 – a huge total, indeed!

It may not be generally known that the Ontario Board of Health has, since the beginning of the war, supplied, free of cost, all the typhoid vaccine and paratyphoid vaccine used by Canadian troops. The value of this, at commercial rates, is over $170,000.

Ontario, it will be agreed, has done well in giving. She has also done well in lending. Of the total of $417,000,000 subscribed to the Victory Loan of 1917, $203,000,000 was supplied by the people of this Province. Details of the Victory Loan of 1918 are not, at this writing, available, but there is no doubt – there never is a doubt about Ontario – that this Province will again be the source of nearly half of all the money obtained.

Every boy and girl knows the importance of food in winning the war. The Government of Ontario has taken every means to encourage increased production – the Department of Education has made it easy for the pupils of the schools to spend a good deal of time at farm work without losing credit for their work in school. This year there have been under cultivation 300,000 acres of land more than before the war – an addition of the equivalent of 3,000 ordinary farms! Just two more figures – in 1914 the value of Ontario's field crops was $199,152,945; in 1917 it was $333,691,563. These statistics tell their own story of what the farmers of this Province have been doing.

In the country increased production has been and is the order of the day; in the cities the emphasis was on the making of munitions. The factories of Ontario manufactured shells, aeroplanes, engines, and other necessaries at a wonderful rate. With the close of the war munition-making ceases, but increased production of food will be almost as necessary as ever.

So much for Ontario's part in winning the war. Now the great conflict is over. Is there, then, anything more to do? There is. The soldiers, who have fought for their country and for its people, must be cared for, must be given a new start in life. The Government of Ontario has given the most hearty support to every good scheme having for its object the resettlement in life of the returned soldier. For this purpose a plan of settlement is actually in operation, and a community of soldiers is already established in Kapuskasing, in Northern Ontario. Every provision is made for training the soldier in farm work and for supporting him and his family until he is able to use the farm which the Government presents to him. And this offer is open not only to Ontario's soldiers, not only to Canadian soldiers, but to British soldiers as well.

Not all returned soldiers can or will take up farm work. To provide for those who need other employment the Soldiers' Aid Commission of Ontario was appointed in 1915. By means of this organization every returned man is carefully looked after and is suitably located. The Government of Ontario, in conjunction with the Dominion Government, is providing for vocational training and the re-education of returned soldiers through the development of a complete system of agricultural, commercial, and technical colleges and schools.

And what is expected of the youth of Ontario? That they will not waste time in school, but will be ready as soon as possible to do the most effective work as men and women – they will be needed; that they will be loyal citizens who will take advantage of every opportunity to serve Canada; that they will give as freely as they may be able to every worthy cause; that they will save their money and lend it to the Government of Canada by investing it in War Savings Stamps.

F. UNIVERSITIES

F 1 'REPORT REGARDING NATIVE-BORN GERMANS
WHO ARE SERVING ON THE STAFF OF THE UNIVERSITY
OF TORONTO,' READ BY PRESIDENT FALCONER TO
THE BOARD OF GOVERNORS ON 3 DECEMBER 1914
[*University of Toronto Archives. Falconer Papers. "Germans" File*]

Owing to the strong feeling that has been aroused in the minds of
many people by the fact that several native-born Germans are serving
on the staff of the University of Toronto, I desire to make the following
statement in justification of their being continued in their positions.

1. Their Appointments.

(a) Dr. Immanuel Benzinger is Professor of Oriental Languages in
University College. When Dr. Richard Davidson was appointed to a
chair in Knox College in 1910, the place was not filled immediately
owing to the difficulty of finding at that time a suitable successor. In 1912
Dr. McCurdy, who had been holding the position of Director of the
School of Archaeology at Jerusalem, advised me to consider the name of
Dr. Benzinger, who for family reasons would be willing to leave Palestine
after ten years' residence; leading Semitic scholars of Britain also spoke
to me very highly of Dr. Benzinger's attainments. He was made associate-
professor of Oriental Languages in the autumn of 1912. After two sessions' experience there was no hesitation in appointing Dr. Benzinger
full professor last spring when Dr. McCurdy resigned, and we deemed
ourselves fortunate in having secured a teacher and scholar of international reputation to follow a man who has conferred so much distinction on this University.

(b) Mr. P.W. Mueller is associate-professor of German in University
College. Mr. Mueller who is a graduate of this university was recommended some years ago by Professor vander Smissen as a lecturer in the
German language. His ability as a teacher was soon recognized, he has
received rapid promotion and now fills a position that we should otherwise find great difficulty in providing for.

(c) Mr. B. Tapper came to the University in October 1913 as a temporary lecturer in German. On account of the illness of Dr. Toews it was
necessary to secure temporary help, and after some delay and no little
trouble Mr. Tapper was found and induced to abandon his postgraduate
work in the University of Chicago. He gave such satisfaction that we were
glad to appoint him again for this session, and all the reports of his work
that I have received are most favourable. That we have been unable to

fill another position in German this winter and are thus one man short, is evidence of the difficulty we experience in securing suitable teachers for such positions in this subject.

2. Their Attitude and Conduct in the Present Crisis.

For native-born Germans holding positions in a provincial university the present as a most trying situation. Of the two who have permanent appointments one has been absent from Germany for twenty-one years and has made his home in Toronto since 1893; the other who has not resided in Germany for thirteen years came to Toronto with the full intention of making his permanent home in Canada and of becoming a Canadian citizen. They therefore regard this as their home. They have also made Statutory declarations to the effect that they are not reservists in the German army, have never at any time given information which could be used in any way to the disadvantage of the Allied Forces in the present war, have made no reference whatever to the present war in their classes or in their intercourse with students of the University, have adhered both in letter and spirit to the promise that they made to the President at the beginning of the session to maintain silence with regard to their opinion as to the rights of the present war and agree to abide by that promise in the future.

When I heard from the Editor of one of the daily papers that Dr. Benzinger on the day of his arrival had given an interview on matters concerned with the situation in Europe I asked that it should not be printed, because I thought that the maintenance of silence was the only wise procedure. What was in that interview I do not know. At once I enjoined silence on Dr. Benzinger for the future and he heartily agreed to observe my desire.

3. Recommendation that their services be retained.

Taking account of their previous service to this University, the satisfactory performance of their present duties which constitutes a real benefit to the university, their conduct in a difficult situation, the fact that there are no grounds for suspicion that they are in any way misusing their position, and their promises for the future I believe that it is only just and right that these gentlemen should be kept in their present positions. For the university to take this attitude is to act according to the spirit of the Proclamation of the Governor-General made on August 15th, 1914. "Whereas there are many persons of German and Austro-Hungarian nationality quietly pursuing their usual avocations in various parts of Canada, and it is desirable that such persons should be allowed to continue in such avocations without interruption: Therefore His Royal Highness the Governor-General in Council is pleased to order and it is hereby ordered as follows: – that all persons in Canada of German or Austro-Hungarian nationality so long as they quietly pursue their ordinary avocations, be allowed to continue to enjoy the protection of the law, and be accorded the respect and consideration due to peaceful and law-abiding citizens; and that they be not arrested, detained or interfered with unless there is reasonable ground to believe that they are engaged in espionage, or engaging or attempting to engage in acts of a hostile nature, or are giving or attempting to give information to the enemy, or unless they otherwise contravene any law, Order-in-Council or proclamation."

There being no reasonable grounds to believe that they "are engaged in espionage or engaging or attempting to engage in acts of a hostile nature, or are giving or attempting to give information to the enemy, or are otherwise contravening any law, Order-in-Council or proclamation", I am unable to make any recommendation which would disregard the proclamation that these persons "so long as they quietly pursue their ordinary avocations be allowed to continue to enjoy the protection of the law, and be accorded the respect and consideration due to peaceful and law-abiding citizens", or to recommend any course which, it has been suggested to me, might interfere with their contracts of service with the University.

F 2 CONCLUSION OF THE UNIVERSITY SERMON, DELIVERED BY PRESIDENT R.A. FALCONER OF THE UNIVERSITY OF TORONTO ON 29 SEPTEMBER 1914 [*Quoted in G. Oswald Smith,* The University of Toronto Roll of Service, *1914–1918, Toronto, 1921, p. xi*]

This is the greatest of moral struggles. Are there to be free democracies who only need to police themselves against the force-attacks of the barbarous? Or will force tower arrogantly above freedom and enslave intellect? The struggle had to come. It is well to have it decided one way or other finally, for our own sakes and for our children's. This struggle I want you to think about. Many of our members have already heard the call and have left to take their share in the war. Some of them will lay down their lives for our sakes. Others of you will doubtless go later. Most of us will, I suppose, remain at home. But do not shirk whatever sacrifice is necessary. Be ready to defend your life which, with its freedom, has been won for you by others. Live a life of sacrifice this winter and thereby contribute something to help the nation in relieving its suffering. Do not be light-hearted. You cannot be as merry as yesterday, nor as blithe as we hope you will be in the world's tomorrow. The world is in agony, let this agony reach the depths of our nature also, so that it may purge our selfishness. If we shall not be called upon to die or be wounded in the flesh, I hope that we may carry into the revived life of our nation, when it issues from the struggle, the healed wounds of the spirit that will be the sign of the battle in which we have won over again the right to call ourselves freemen in a real democracy.

F 3   Extract from the Annual Report, 1914–
1915, of Principal D.M. Gordon of Queen's
University
[Copy in P.A.C. Library, pp. 6, 41]

As the Officers' Training Corps was formed early in the Session the Senate agreed that each member of the Corps who secured certificate in drill and musketry instruction might have the training count as substitute for one pass class in his course, the selection of such class to be subject to the approval of the Faculty. This arrangement affected the attendance at a number of the Arts Classes, as there were about 250 Arts students members of the OTC.

. . .

Much should be said of the enthusiasm shown by all members of the Corps, in view of the exceptional difficulties encountered throughout the Session; no uniforms could be procured; there was a great shortage of drill books, some, indeed, could not be procured at all, although the examination is based on them: rifles were not obtained until the end of January; and the Government was unable to provide any ammunition for rifle practice, so that it had to be bought privately.

F 4   Principal D.M. Gordon of Queen's
University to William Lawson Grant
[P.A.C., MG 30, D20, Grant Papers]

18 July 1917.

The sick & wounded soldiers are coming to us pretty steadily now, although we are not yet up to full capacity. you wd. be amazed & delighted to see what a splendid up-to-date hospital Grant Hall and the Arts B'ld'g form. The soldiers are more than delighted with their quarters & the campus forms a charming lounging ground for them. It is a pleasure to give them our best. When it was first proposed to surrender the buildings for hospital purposes, it seemed impossible: but a little more thought & a little more spirit of Queen's succeeded in accomplishing the impossible.

G. ONTARIO'S BLACK VOLUNTEERS

G 1 GEORGE MORTON TO SIR SAM HUGHES
[*P.A.C., RG 24, v. 1206, file HQ 297-1-21*]

52 Augusta St.,
Hamilton, Ont.
Sept. 7, 1915.

A matter of vital importance to my People (the colored), in reference to their enlistment as soldiers, provokes this correspondence with you.

In behalf of my people I respectively desire to be informed as to whether your Department has any absolute rule, regulations or restrictions which prohibits, disallows or discriminates against the enlistment and enrolment of colored men of good character and physical fitness as soldiers?

And whether you as the well-qualified, popular and Honorable Head of said Department, have issued instructions to this effect, to your subordinates?

The reason for drawing your attention to this matter, and directly leading to the request for this information, is the fact that a number of colored men in this city (Hamilton), who have offered for enlistment and service, have been turned down and refused, solely on the ground of color or complexioned distinction; this being the reason given on the rejection or refusal card issued by the recruiting officer.

Now among the recruiting officers here, in respect to this matter, there seems to be a difference and conflict of opinion. Some officers aver that there are no regulation orders or rules making such invidious discrimination and distinction.

A number of leading white citizens here, whose attention I have drawn to this matter, most emphatically repudiate the idea as being beneath the dignity of the Government to make racial or color distinction in an issue of this kind. They are firm in their opinion that no such prohibitive restrictions exist and have assured me they would very deeply deplore and depreciate the fact if it should turn out that such was in force and they have urged me to communicate with you as to the real existing facts.

Notwithstanding this kindly expressed opinion, there still remains this cold and unexplained fact that the proffered service of our people have been refused. Now our people feel most keenly this unenviable position in which they seem placed and they are very much perturbed and exercised over the matter as it now stands. The feeling prevails that in this so-called Land of the Free and the Home of the Brave that there should be no color lines drawn or discrimination made. As humble, but as loyal subjects of the King, trying to work out their own destiny, they think they should be permitted in common with other peoples to perform their part and do their share in this great conflict. Especially so when gratitude leads them to remember that this country was their only asylum and place of refuge in the dark days of American slavery and that here, on this consecrated soil, dedicated to equality, justice and freedom, that under the all-embracing and protecting folds of the Union Jack, that none dared to molest or to make them afraid.

So our people, gratefully remembering their obligations in this respect, and for other potential reasons, are most anxious to serve their King and Country in this critical crisis in its history and they do not think they should be prevented from so doing on the ground of the hue of their skin.

If there are restrictive regulations as regards our peoples' enlistment (which I trust there are not), a knowledge of this fact, unpleasant as it may be, will prevent them from further offering their services in the hour of their country's great need, only to suffer the humiliation of being refused solely on color lines.

It at your earliest opportunity you will honor me with a reply to the information herein asked for, I will deeply appreciate it.

In closing, permit me, Hon. Sir, in behalf of our people, to offer our humble congratulations to you on the recent signal honor so worthily conferred upon you by His Most Royal Majesty The King, for your distinguished services to the country.

G 2   ARTICLE IN THE *Canadian Observer*,
8 JANUARY 1916
[*Copy in P.A.C., RG 24, v. 1206, File H.Q. 297-1-21*]

General Hughes has approved of our plan for a Colored Platoon. For the government to take official action we must be ready to present sixty available men.

We do not believe that there will be the slightest difficulty in raising immediately the sixty men required as a nucleus. And may we soon have sufficient number for a company, and we hope at least a full battalion.

We appeal to our people all over Canada to take this matter up and show by a quick response the depth of their loyalty and patriotism. Prominent men of our race in Toronto think that this is a splendid movement and should receive unqualified support from all sections of Canada. The Toronto Star on Jan. 3rd published the following:

"Preparations for an extensive recruiting campaign are now under way. New regiments will shortly be authorized for the various cities, towns and rural districts thruout Canada. In addition to these the minister of militia declares that he has decided to raise several special regiments including two or more Indian regiments, a Metis regiment, a naturalized Japanese-Canadian regiment, and a colored regiment."

G 3   EDITORIAL IN THE *Canadian Observer*,
8 JANUARY 1916
[*Copy in P.A.C., RG 24, v. 1206, File H.Q. 297-1-21*]

Justice has not been dealt us in every pursuit in life in Canada. Others enjoy it in its fullest sense, yet we have come in contact with a few of the narrow-minded individuals, who in many cases have made the road very hard for us. However, we will take the stand for justice, and purpose dealing squarely with our country and its cause. The Prime Minister is calling for 500,000 men to assist the Empire in fighting for justice and liberty. Are we going to stand back and say let them fight and establish justice without taking a part? No! Most emphatically, No! We are going to do our bit in this great struggle for justice. Our men have been falling in the ranks one by one here and there, but now a more urgent appeal is made to form a company, or a platoon, and in unity let us prove our worth to the country and the Empire. Let us show we stand for justice, and we really know what it means.

If we work together our united efforts will count for something, and whatever position we gain will prove a lasting credit to the progress of our race.

H. INDIANS

H 1   ANNUAL REPORT OF THE DEPUTY
SUPERINTENDENT GENERAL OF INDIAN AFFAIRS
[*Canada Sessional Paper No. 27 of 1920, pp. 14–17, 25–6*]

ONTARIO

Ojibwa Bands. The majority of the Indian bands in Ontario belong to the Ojibwa or Chippewa tribe, which is the largest subdivision of the great Algonkin linguistic stock ... The enlistment average during the late war was exceptionally high and many of their bands sent practically all their eligible members to the front.

Special mention must be made of the Ojibwa bands located in the vicinity of Fort William, which sent more than one hundred men overseas from a total adult male population of two hundred and eighty-two. Upon the introduction of the Military Service Act is was found that there were but two Indians of the first class left at home on the Nipigon reserve, and but one on the Fort William reserve ... The Indian recruits from this district for the most part enlisted with the 52nd, popularly known as the Bull Moose Battalion. Their commanding officer, the late Colonel Hay, who was killed, stated upon frequent occasions that the Indians were among his very best soldiers. Their gallantry is testified by the fact that the name of every Indian in this unit appeared in the casualty list. The fine appearance of these Indian soldiers was specially commented upon by the press in the various cities through which the battalion passed on its way to the front ...

The Chippewas of Rama sent thirty-eight men to the front from a total adult male population of 110 ...

Among the Mississaugas of Rice Lake, forty-three enlisted from a total male population of eighty-two ... Upon the introduction of the Military Service Act it was found that not a single man of the class called remained at home among the Chippewas of Nawash, located at Cape Croker. Thirty-one Mississaugas of Alnwick enlisted from a total male population of sixty-four ...

The Indian bands located on Manitoulin Island ... sent about fifty men to the front ...

About twenty Indians enlisted from the Parry Sound district. One of their number, Corporal Francis Pegahmagabow, won the Military Medal and two Bars. He enlisted in 1914 with the original 1st Battalion. He distinguished himself signally as a sniper and bears the extraordinary record of having killed 378 of the enemy. His Military Medal and two

Bars were awarded for his distinguished conduct at Mount Sorrell, Amiens and Passchendaele. At Passchendaele, Corporal Pegahmagabow led his company through an engagement with a single casualty, and subsequently captured 300 Germans at Mount Sorrell ...

Forty-two Moravians of the Thames went to the front from a total adult male population of seventy-nine ...

Among the other Ojibwa bands in Ontario that have notable enlistment records are the Chippewas of Saugeen, who sent forty-eight from a total adult male population of one hundred and ten; the Chippewas of Georgina and Snake Islands, who sent eleven from a total adult male population of twenty-three; the Chippewas of the Thames, who sent twenty-five from a total adult male population of one hundred and ten; the Chippewas and Pottawatomies of Walpole Island, who sent seventy-one to the front from a total adult male population of two hundred and ten; the band located at Sturgeon Falls, which sent thirty-five from a total adult male population of one hundred and three; the bands in the Chapleau district, which sent forty from a total adult male population of one hundred and one; the Mississaugas of the Credit, located near Hagersville, who sent thirty-two from a total adult male population of eighty-six, and the Munsees of the Thames, who sent eleven from a total adult male population of thirty-eight.

Special mention must be made of the remarkable response to the call to arms among the Mississaugas of Scugog. This little band has only thirty of a population, and when the war broke out but eight of these were adult males. These eight men all enlisted without exception, thereby establishing what is probably an enlistment record unequalled in the annals of the great war. Another outstanding case is that of the Algonkins of Golden Lake, who sent twenty-nine soldiers to the front, leaving only three men on the reserve.

IROQUOIS BANDS

There are a number of populous Iroquois bands in Ontario, and these also like those of the Ojibwa race have a proud record in the great war ... The largest band of Iroquois is the Six Nations of Brantford. This band sent two hundred and ninety-two warriors to the front, of whom twenty-nine were killed in action, five died from sickness, one is missing, fifty-five were wounded, and one was taken prisoner of war ...

The great majority of these Six Nations soldiers enlisted with the 114th Battalion, which was organized in the fall of 1915, under the command of Colonel E.S. Baxter of Cayuga, then commanding officer of the Haldimand Rifles, a well known militia battalion. Colonel Baxter died in 1916 and was succeeded by Lieut.-Colonel Andrew T. Thompson of Ottawa. Colonel Thompson had also for some years commanded the Haldimand Rifles, the left half of which was made up of Six Nations Indians. Colonel Thompson is an honorary chief of the Six Nations Indians and his position at the head of the battalion did much to stimulate recruiting among the Indians. Many Indians from other bands also joined this unit, among whom were a large number from the Caughnawaga and St. Regis bands, in the province of Quebec, which also belong to the Iroquois race. Two entire Indian companies were formed in the 114th Battalion, and the majority of the officers of these companies were also Indians. In recognition of the fact that among its Indian members were many who were descendants of warriors who fought at the battle of Queenston Heights under General Brock, the battalion received the name of Brock's Rangers, and the device of two tomahawks became part of the regimental crest. A singularly beautiful regimental flag was worked for the Rangers by the Six Nations Women's Patriotic League. This is adorned with figures symbolic of various tribal legends and has been the subject of much comment and admiration. The 114th regimental band, composed almost entirely of Indians, toured the British Isles for recruiting and patriotic purposes ...

The other Iroquois bands in Ontario are the Mohawks of the Bay of Quinte, and the Oneidas of the Thames; both these bands have an exceptionally high enlistment record. Eighty-two Mohawks of the Bay of Quinte enlisted from a total adult male population of three hundred and fifty-three, and forty-eight Oneidas of the Thames enlisted from a total adult male population of two hundred and twenty ...

The Indian women on many of the reserves formed Red Cross societies and Patriotic leagues. These organizations corresponded to similar societies in white communities. They carried on their work with energy and efficiency and were successful in the accomplishment of excellent results. They made bandages and provided various comforts for the soldiers, knitted socks, sweaters and mufflers, and also raised money for patriotic purposes by holding card parties, bazaars, and other social entertainments. The making of baskets and beadwork is a native industry among the Indians, and the Indian women found a novel and very successful means of securing funds for war needs by the sale of these wares.

The first of these organizations ... to be formed on a reserve was the Six Nations Patriotic League, which was organized in October 1914, and continued in operation with great success until the conclusion of the war. Upon the mobilization of Brock's Rangers ... another women's patriotic society was formed on the Six Nations reserve under the name of the Brock's Rangers' Benefit Society. The purpose of this society was to provide for the needs of the Indian companies of this battalion. The society was very painstaking in its work and no Indian member of the battalion failed to benefit as a result of its efforts.

The Indian women of the Oneidas of the Thames, another Iroquois band, which sent a large number of its members to the front, also formed a patriotic league in 1916 in order to provide comforts for their soldiers. In the first year of its existence this society sent twenty-five boxes overseas; in 1917, one hundred and four; and in 1918, seventy-four up to the signing of the armistice. Each of these boxes contained thirty pairs of socks and twenty-four khaki sweaters.

A Red Cross society was formed by the Chippewas of Saugeen to provide comforts for the members of the band who were at the front. This organization raised more than $400 for the benefit of their soldiers by holding a series of box socials.

H 2   WILLIAM HAMILTON MERRITT TO LIEUT.-COL. E.A. STANTON
[P.A.C., RG 7, G21, v. 549, file 14071F]

> Territet (Montreux)
> Switzerland
> 2/1/15

With reference to my letter of 31st ult. relative to cutting out the name of the Six Nations, I have the honour to say that I should like to slightly modify the suggestion made in my letter above mentioned.

If it cannot be conceded that the past services to the Crown of the Six Nations Indians warrant the exception being made of a unit bearing their name, it would seem that possibly our Indians as a whole have proved themselves worthy of some consideration, and therefore, if it is desired that the offer of a contribution made 21st Sept. should be modified please allow it to stand as follows, namely, that £5000 will be placed at the disposal of H.R.H. for two companies to be composed of members of the Six Nations Indians, as a Centenary tribute to them for their vital aid in helping to save Canada to the Crown in 1812–14, provided the other two companies of the Battalion to which they are posted are also composed of Canadian Indians. I do not make any suggestion with reference to officers. In other words one Battalion of the Canadian forces to be composed of Indians with two companies of the Six Nations Indians and the officers to be Indian or white as may be deemed advisable.

H 3   WILLIAM HAMILTON MERRITT TO LIEUT.-COL. E.A. STANTON
[P.A.C., RG 7, v. 549, file 14071F]

> Territet, Switzerland
> 6th Feb. 1915.

I have received your letter of 19th of January in which you are good enough to explain the very good reason why H.M. the King could not ask for the services of all the Indian bands in Canada. It is very obvious that such an appeal to all of the scattered remnants of tribes throughout the immense domain, and in their varying degrees of civilization, would be practically impossible.

I indicated in my letter of 2nd January that as an alternative to a detachment of 2 companies bearing the Six Nations' name, which I should prefer, the contribution offered would be available towards a Battalion composed of our Indians, two companies to be Six Nations Indians.

I have written to the Brantford, Bay of Quinte, and Caughnawaga Reserves asking them to let H.R.H. know if they should decide to offer their services instead of waiting to be asked. From Brantford one company, and a half company from each of the others.

If they should not make definite offer, that circumstance would, I take it, end the possibility of a separate detachment bearing their name as a centenary tribute to their splendid aid in 1812–14 in helping to save Canada to the Crown; but I do not suppose that it would prevent the Militia Council from authorizing and recruiting, in the usual manner, a Battalion from among the civilized & educated Indian communities of Eastern Canada.

It has always been our boast that the just treatment of our Indians by the British Government has led to happy results & relations, and if, as a reward, they were now to be given recognition as a race, in a unit of their own, along-side their white fellow-subjects it would undoubtedly be welcomed with a thrill of gratitude and appreciation by all of the scattered bands, whose number and isolation render it impossible to give them individual consideration.

There is no question whatever in my mind about the response, and that the Battalion could easily be raised, and it might well call general attention to the fealty of our Indian Allies in North America and furnish another instance of the justice of Britain's rule.

H 4 LIEUTENANT-COLONEL G.H. JONES, OFFICER COMMANDING 227TH BATTALION, TO THE ASSISTANT ADJUTANT GENERAL, MILITARY DISTRICT NO. 2
[P.A.C., RG 24, v. 4383, file 2D. 34-7-109]

Sault Ste. Marie,
4 May 1916.

I have the honor to refer to our former correspondence about recruiting Indians on the Manitoulin and still await an answer to my letter of April 12th. I beg particularly now to ask for authority to recruit Indians, and wish to point out that I can recruit these men better than Brock's Rangers can.

I wish to point out this, that may perhaps have been overlooked, that in taking these Indians and putting them in a battalion in the eastern part of the Province quite a traditional point is overlooked, namely, that these Manitoulin Indians are asked to band themselves with Mohawk

Indians. It has been openly said that they do not like to do this but would rather come with their white friends from the Manitoulin.

If I am restricted from recruiting Indians it simply means that another important factor that I counted on in connection with the recruiting of this battalion is lost to me and that the task of recruiting, which is hard enough under any circumstances in this sparsely populated area, becomes almost impossible in the time it will be expected to recruit it. I beg to ask therefore that I be allowed to recruit Indians.

H 5   MINUTE OF THE SIX NATIONS' COUNCIL
[*Quoted in the* Brantford Expositor, *3 January 1919*]

Ohsweken Council House
September 15, 1914

The chiefs of the Six Nations' Council decided to contribute $1500 from the capital funds of the Six Nations to the patriotic funds, this amount to be restored from the interest account semi-yearly for 15 years to restore the impaired capital and would ask the Department of Indian Affairs to pay this amount to their brother, Chief Ka-rah-kon-tye, the Duke of Connaught, Governor General of Canada, who will forward the same to the Imperial authorities to be used at their discretion either for the Patriotic or War funds in England as a token of the alliance existing between the Six Nations and the British Crown. They also expressed their willingness to offer their warriors to help in accordance with their ancient custom if their services should be required.

H 6   F.W. JACOBS, PRESIDENT, GRAND INDIAN COUNCIL, TO THE CHIEFS OF THE DIFFERENT BANDS IN ONTARIO
[*P.A.C., RG 10, v. 2640, Red Series file 129690-3*]

Sarnia, August 17th, 1917.

At the urgent request of several of the Chiefs of the different Reserves:

I feel it to be my duty to call the Grand Indian Council to meet at Chemong Reserve on 2nd of October, 1917. I hope that all the Reserves within the Province will be represented by at least one or two of the most progressive and up-to-date men as delegates from each Reserve. We as Indians are at a crucial stage of our lives, whilst our young men are at the Front fighting the battles of our Noble King, and our Country, we cannot say that they are fighting for our liberty, freedom and other privileges so dear to all nations, for we have none; it is our duty to bring forth our requests at this time to the Government. It is then most important that we should get together to discuss matters that are of most vital importance to the well-being of our race. In looking ahead under our present condition the scene is not very bright and it is plain that something must be done by ourselves and that soon. We Indians, like all humanity are endowed with the same instincts, same capabilities, and it only remains for the Government to give us a chance to develop those qualities. The Government may be bound by Treaties to certain lines of protection to the Indian people, and it is apparent that we must co-operate with the Government to abrogate those Treaties, which will liberate our people, and we will then become identified with the peoples of this country and become factors side by side with them in shaping the destinies of our country. Our task is difficult, it requires our most careful consideration. Our people are difficult to handle owing to the transformation that is taking place amongst them, from the old life into the new and it is therefore very necessary that each Reserve should appoint the most progressive men, who will represent them in the coming Grand Council. Every reserve must be represented if possible, as united action is more effective, and above all we must depend upon the Giver of all wisdom for guidance.

H 7   DUNCAN CAMPBELL SCOTT TO G.A. MORROW,
ASSISTANT TO DIRECTOR OF AVIATION,
IMPERIAL MUNITIONS BOARD
[P.A.C., RG 10, v. 7615, file 13034-375]

April 18th, 1917.
    The Council of the Mohawks of the Bay of Quinte having passed a resolution in favor of granting the use of the "Plains" on the Tyendenaga reserve for an aviation school, during the continuance of the war, I have pleasure in expressing my approval of their action and in granting you authority to occupy the said "Plains" for the above mentioned purpose.
    The Indians have made this concession purely from patriotic motives and ask no remuneration, except that the Imperial Munitions Board pay the sum of $500, annually, in advance to cover the expense of engaging a herder for the cattle grazing on the "Plains" during the summer months. It is also stipulated that the Board is to be responsible for any damage done to fences or buildings or other possessions of the Indians.

I. ONTARIO'S FIRST WAR ARTIST

I 1 SIR SAM HUGHES TO SIR ROBERT BORDEN
[*P.A.C., MG 27, II D9, Kemp Papers, v. 112, file 95*]

Ottawa, February 25, 1916

At the time the Camp was on at Valcartier, I met Mr. Homer Watson of Doon, Ont., a bosom friend of the late Honourable George Clare.

He expressed his desire to paint a couple of pictures of the Force for our Canadian Archives. I remember encouraging him to go ahead, and I always intended bringing it up before the Council, but everything was in a hurry and I completely forgot it.

He has three pictures done; two of them are regarded as very fine. They are, I believe, in Rae's Store in Ottawa here.

I would be very pleased if you could take a look at them.

Meantime, Mr. Watson has, through our mutual friend F.S. Scott, M.P. of Galt asked me for two or three thousand dollars.

How would it do for you, White and others of Council to go over and look at them? I understand from those who have seen them here, that the light on them is very bad, but nevertheless they show up well.

I 2 SIR SAM HUGHES TO THE DEPUTY MINISTER OF
MILITIA AND DEFENCE
[*P.A.C., MG 26, H1(c), Borden Papers, v. 214, file RLB 1175,
p. 121221*]

May 30, 1916.

When the troops had assembled at Valcartier in 1914, it was suggested by many notable persons in Canada, that a painting should be had of the historic Camp.

Accordingly, Mr. Homer Watson, who spent several days there, painted three scenes; – one – a general one of the Camp; – another – showing one of the historic reviews, and a third, – showing the soldiers at target practice on the long range. These three paintings are now in the halls of the temporary Parliament Buildings – the Museum – at Ottawa.

No price has been fixed by Mr. Watson, but it is strongly recommended that the pictures be purchased by the Canadian Government – that Mr. Watson be advanced three or four thousand dollars upon them, for he is in need of some money, and that the balance be paid him as soon as a satisfactory price can be agreed upon for the three paintings.

To arrive at the latter, it is suggested that a committee take the matter into consideration.

I 3   SIR SAM HUGHES TO THE GOVERNOR GENERAL
IN COUNCIL
[P.A.C., Borden Papers, v. 214, file RLB 1175, p. 121219]

Ottawa,
May 30, 1916.

The undersigned has the honour to report that, acting under his instructions, Mr. Homer Watson has painted three large pictures of Valcartier Camp, as the Camp appeared in September, 1914, when the First Canadian Contingent was mobilized there. These pictures have been placed in the Royal Victoria Museum.

Mr. Watson asks as remuneration for his services in painting these pictures, the sum of $20,000.00.

The undersigned considers the price asked by Mr. Watson as fair and reasonable, and recommends payment of the same for the favourable consideration of Your Royal Highness, and that the payment be made a charge against the War Appropriation.

I 4   SIR ROBERT BORDEN TO HOMER WATSON
[P.A.C., Borden Papers, v. 214, file RLB 1175, p. 121231]

Ottawa,
13th July, 1916.

The difficulty about the paintings is that you were engaged by General Hughes without any communication to or authority from Council. Moreover, no appropriation was made available except that which is placed annually at the disposal of the Government to be expended under the direction of the Advisory Arts Council. For this reason the matter has been referred to that Council but up to the present no report has been received. If the Minister had brought the subject to my attention in the first instance the difficulty would not have occurred.

I 5   SIR THOMAS WHITE TO SIR ROBERT BORDEN
[P.A.C., Borden Papers, v. 214, file RLB 1175, p. 121234]

Ottawa, July 26th, 1916.

Referring to your letter to Mr. Homer Watson respecting the paintings executed by him for the Government I would suggest that the price which he places upon them should be taken under review by the Committee which purchases for the Art Gallery. The figure which he is asking appears to me to be extortionate and if he is not willing to agree to an arbitration which would fix a fair price my view would be that he should be allowed to sue the Government when the whole question as to value of these paintings could be gone into. Personally I am strongly opposed to paying him anything like the amount which he asked. It seems to me to be a clear case of hold-up.

I 6   SIR EDMUND WALKER TO SIR ROBERT BORDEN
    [*P.A.C., Borden Papers, v. 214, file RLB 1175, p. 121235*]

August 1st, 1916.

In reply to your letter of June 9th 1916 regarding the three pictures of Valcartier Camp painted by Mr. Homer Watson R.C.A., I am authorized to report, that in view of the pictures having been executed by instructions from the Minister of Militia: of the scale of the work: and the circumstances surrounding the painting thereof: of the historical interest attached to the pictures, and of the high expectations as to price entertained by the artist: the Advisory Arts Council suggest that Ten Thousand Dollars ($10,000.00) would be a suitable remuneration for the pictures.

I 7   HOMER WATSON TO SIR ROBERT BORDEN
    [*P.A.C., Borden Papers, v. 214, file RLB 1175, pp. 121243–121243A*]

Doon,
November 21st.

On coming home I have made a decision to accept your offer. Needless to say I was disappointed at the report of the Advisory Arts Board; for I thought in view of the trouble and expense I had been put to they would have dealt with the matter in a spirit of reporting for me a price in keeping with prices I had been getting for the past fifteen years. If the chairman of the board had based his report on what he himself gave me for a National Gallery picture the amount would have come to three thousand dollars more than my account asked; for I have always sold my pictures according to size. This National Gallery price was not the highest either I had received for the same sized picture. I thought I might as well go into this so as to make it clear my account was not excessive.

I know that some of the best work of my life has gone into those camp pictures.[1] My friends here when they saw the Minister of Militia early last

[1]Writing about Homer Watson in *Sons of Canada* (Toronto, 1916), Augustus Bridle commented: 'One passes over the epic sonata of canvases which he did on commission in 1915 for the Canadian Government impersonated by Sir Sam Hughes. They may have been good pictures of Valcartier, but they were neither good typical Watsons, nor first-rate pictures of a war camp.' Two of the paintings, *Camp at Sunrise* and *The Birth of an Army*, are now in the Canadian War Museum. The third, *The Review*, was destroyed in a Canadian Legion Hall fire in Edmonton.

winter based their claim for me on a feeling I was entitled to the amount asked. They knew what I had been put to in producing them and the success of their reception by the public.

In accepting the offer do you not think it would be fairer to me considering the low value put on this work that I should be allowed something for my expenses in addition to what is recommended in the report of the Advisory Arts Council? However I will leave this to you knowing that it is a delicate situation and you will do the best you can.

I 8   MEMORANDUM PREPARED BY T.C. BOVILLE,
DEPUTY MINISTER OF FINANCE
[P.A.C., Borden Papers, v. 214, file RLB 1175, pp. 121245–6]

December 18th, 1916.

The sum of $10,000 has been arrived at as the cost of these pictures. The Minister of Finance has given instructions to have this sum placed in the Estimates.

The pictures are in the possession of the Government in the Victoria Museum. It is not known whether they are under the control of the National Gallery or the House of Commons.

If it is desired to avoid a discussion in the House, which an item of this kind will no doubt cause, it is suggested that the paintings be handed over to the National Gallery and paid for by the trustees out of the vote in Miscellaneous Public Works of $25,000 – "The National Gallery of Canada, including the purchase of paintings by the Board of Trustees".

An examination of the ledger shows that there is about $10,000 of this vote not yet expended. A part payment could be made to Mr. Watson and next year's Estimates could be increased by $10,000 to cover the matter. In this way it could be disposed of without charging the expenditure to War Appropriation. Probably this could be arranged through Sir Edmund Walker, one of the trustees.

I 9   SIR EDMUND WALKER TO SIR THOMAS WHITE
[P.A.C., RG 2, 1, v. 1432]

Toronto, 26 December 1916.

At the request of the Premier I made a report as Chairman of the Advisory Arts Council suggesting the price to be paid to Mr. Homer Watson, not because of the artistic value of the pictures but because of the various circumstances surrounding the order given by the late Minister of Militia. My action as Chairman of the Advisory Arts Council has of course nothing to do with the National Gallery. It would be quite impossible to take the sum out of the reduced appropriation now made for the National Gallery, every penny of which is earmarked for the present year, nor could we think of hanging the pictures in the Gallery. If they are thought worthy they should, I suppose, in the end find a place in the gallery of historical pictures which will undoubtedly grow out of the work of the Archives Department.

While the pictures are hanging in the Victoria Museum they are not in the custody of the National Gallery.

J. ARMISTICE

J 1 FIRST NEWS OF THE ARMISTICE IN TORONTO
[Globe, *11 November 1918, p. 1*]

Toronto was awakened from its slumbers at 2.55 o'clock this morning. The first flash bulletin that armistice had been signed came through over the Associated Press wires to the newspapers at that hour. Within a few minutes many whistles in all parts of the city were blowing full blast. Eaton's big "wildcat" siren awakened the whole city. Toronto citizens rubbed their eyes and could not believe their senses. The newspaper offices were swamped with telephone calls.

At a little after 3 o'clock a procession, mostly of women munition workers, paraded Yonge Street, cheering, wildly beating tin pans and blowing whistles. By this time a crowd began to gather all along Yonge Street, motor cars came tearing down street, reckless of all speed laws, tooting their horns and awakening the entire city. Long distance calls from all parts of the country assisted in fairly swamping the telephone exchanges with work. The girls worked heroically without any let up to help give the wonderful tidings to all parts of the waiting, anxious but sleeping Province.

J 2 ARMISTICE CELEBRATIONS IN ALBANY *
[*Anglican Church Archives, Moosonee Collection,*
Box 2 (Albany). Journal of Albany Mission]

Feb. 5th, 1919. Peter Iserhoff, John Bluff & Alick Lazarus arrived this morning from Ghost River and brought the good news that the War was stopped. An Armistice had been signed about the middle of Nov. The news had been passed along by the different Indians hunting along the Albany River.
Feb. 7th. We received letters & Papers on the arrival of the Packet today from Moose giving us full information of the Glorious Victory for the Allies.
"Praise God from whom all blessings flow."
GOD SAVE THE KING
Feb. 16th. Thanksgiving Services for Peace were held today, we had the Church decorated with all the Flags available & it looked quite National, nearly everyone was present.

*My thanks to Jennifer Brown for drawing this document to my attention.

J 3   ARMISTICE CELEBRATIONS IN ONTARIO
[Globe, *12 November 1918, p. 16*]

Inspired by a common impulse, ten thousand citizens of Windsor gathered on Ouellette Square in the morning and joined in a spontaneous outburst of thanksgiving to Almighty God because of the termination of hostilities. It was one of the most impressive religious services ever held on this Canadian border, and the entire lack of formality lent added power to the words of the clergy who addressed the huge open-air congregation.

The celebration started promptly on time this morning, the fire bells carrying to citizens the news of victory a few minutes after 3 a.m. Soon the ferries and car boats added their deep tones to the babel of sound and everywhere sleep was impossible.

At 7 o'clock the streetcar men quit work, leaving people on the outskirts dependent upon the good nature of autoists to get them into the city. All day long the din and cheering kept up, while employees of factories, shops and manufacturing plants joined in the impromptu parades that filled the streets ...

Kingston was still celebrating the armistice late last night. The whole city was on the streets from early morning, and there was continual clamour. The mayor's holiday proclamation was never so well obeyed. Even the street car conductorettes quit work, and the cars had to stay in the barns while they joined the parades. Milkmen feared to make their deliveries, lest the crowds confiscate their 14 cents a quart milk, but there was no outcry. All local industries were shut down, and Labor turned out for an immense parade at 1.30, and returned soldiers and citizens joined them in hundreds. At night a huge bonfire burned on the Market Square, and 25,000 people cheered themselves hoarse. Addresses were given on the Square and at 9 o'clock there was a parade two miles long, that would have done credit to a metropolis. Soldiers, students, workmen, women, children, clergymen were in it, and with six bands and fireworks it was an imposing sight ...

Mayor Mitchell of Bowmanville proclaimed a half-holiday. At 7.30 p.m. the people renewed the celebration in real earnest, whistles, bells, bands, horns and shouting combined to create a pandemonium. Industries turned out a half dozen beautiful floats, girls, patriotic societies, the Citizens' Band and scores of automobiles joined in the parade. Halting at the post office, Mayor Mitchell called the crowd to order. Revs. S. Sellery and C.P. Muirhead offered prayer, and Rev. D.W. Best delivered a ten-minute address, reviewing the wonderful achievements of the allies. Cheers for the King, the Empire, Marshal Foch and all his officers, and the brave Canadians were given. A huge bonfire on the main four corners brought an end to the biggest celebration ever seen in Bowmanville ...

The thousands wending their way to work at Kitchener at 6 a.m. found the factories closed, and parades were immediately started. The Great

War Veterans' Association took charge of the celebration, organizing a general parade for 2 o'clock in the afternoon. There were no disturbances of any kind. The exceptional feature of the morning's program was the escorting of Ald. A.L. Bitzer of the City Council from his office to the City Hall, where he was compelled to kiss the Union Jack, amid the tremendous cheers of the crowd. Other Aldermen were sought, but could not be found.

In the afternoon a parade over two miles in length attracted the largest crowd ever witnessed in this city. More than a dozen effigies of the Kaiser, floats and other features aroused the enthusiasm of the spectators. The 108th Regiment Band led the parade, followed by the Great War Veterans, Daughters of the Empire, Red Cross workers, Victory Bond canvassers, city officials, scores of floats and hundreds of gaily decorated automobiles. When the procession returned to the City Hall two monster meetings were held in front of the band stand and the City Hall ...

Continuous services were held in all the city churches and at night mass meetings were held in all the Evangelical churches ...

Receipt in London of the news of the capitulation of Germany at 3 o'clock yesterday morning was the signal for the commencement of a jubilation the like of which had never been experienced here before. It continued unabated through the day, which was proclaimed a public holiday by Mayor C.R. Somerville. Even the Victory Loan bond salesmen were compelled to call off their canvass for the day. London did not want to talk any kind of business. Unable to wait for the official celebration of the afternoon, thousands crowded into the business district, and before daybreak burned Kaiser Wilhelm in effigy on a bonfire built at the corner of Dundas and Richmond streets. In the afternoon a procession which took more than two hours to pass a point was organized and was participated in by the troops of London Camp, Red Cross workers, headed by Lady Beck, and hundreds of women munitions makers and members of auxiliary army units.

At night a carnival was held in the streets. Lest any excesses should be attempted the police maintained a strong guard at E.B. Smith's liquor store, the Government dispensary for western Ontario, and as an added precaution steel bars were erected before doors and windows ...

Mayor Stewart of Seaforth proclaimed a holiday. At 2 o'clock a monster procession was formed at the GTR depot and proceeded to Victoria Park, where an outdoor religious service was held by the clergy and participated in by an immense crowd. Special music was rendered by the united choirs of the town. The Anglican Church held a service shortly after the news of peace was received, and tonight a union service filled the Methodist Church to overflowing. Large crowds again gathered on the streets at night where towering bonfires lit up the town. Although the rejoicing was general, it was mixed with sadness, owing to the large casualty list in the 161st Huron Battalion ...

At Thamesville a public holiday was proclaimed by Reeve MacKenzie and in a few hours the town was gaily decorated and a splendid parade formed, which was over half a mile long, headed by the Victory Loan honor flag with its nine crowns and the local canvassers, decorated with Victory Loan posters. Decorated autos carrying relatives of all Thamesville soldiers who have fallen in France were followed by platoons representing various allied nations, the Council, school children; the Soldiers' Service Society, dressed as Red Cross nurses; the Red Cross ladies carrying peace banners and various floats, including one with an effigy of the Kaiser suspended from a scaffold. On the Town Square national airs were sung and short addresses given ... In the evening a short service of thanksgiving was held, followed by a torchlight procession and the burning of the Kaiser's effigy. The announcement was received with cheers at the celebration that this village would reach $100,000 in the Victory Loan campaign.

SELECTED
BIBLIOGRAPHY
AND
INDEX

SELECTED
BIBLIOGRAPHY

MANUSCRIPTS

CANADA

Public Archives of Canada (P.A.C.)

(1) Private papers and records of organizations
   Sir Robert L. Borden (Manuscript Group 26, H)
   George T. Denison (MG 29, F 13)
   George Desbarats (MG 30, E 7)
   Sir Joseph Flavelle (MG 30, B 4)
   John M. Godfrey (MG 30, E 19)
   W.C. Good (MG 27, III C 1)
   William L. Grant (MG 30, D 20)
   George Keen (MG 30, B 11)
   Sir A.E. Kemp (MG 27, II D9)
   W.L. Mackenzie King (MG 26, J)
   John A. Lang (MG 30, B 28)
   National Council of Women (MG 28, I 25)
   Ottawa Women's Canadian Club (MG 28, I 35)
   W.N. Ponton (MG 30, E 5)
   N.W. Rowell (MG 27, II D 13)
   C.B. Sissons (MG 27, III F 3)
   Toronto District Labour Council (MG 28, I 44)
   Sir John Willison (MG 30, D 14)
   Young Women's Christian Association (MG 28, I 198)

(2) Records of federal government departments and offices
   Chief Press Censor (Record Group 6, E 1)
   External Affairs (RG 25)
   Governor General's Office (RG 7)
   Indian Affairs (RG 10)
   Militia and Defence (RG 9)
   National Defence (RG 24)
   Parliament (unpublished Sessional Papers) (RG 14, D 2)
   Privy Council (RG 2)
   Secretary of State (RG 6)

Ontario

Department of Public Records and Archives (P.A.O.)
    Office of the Premier. Sir William Hearst (RG 3)
    Department of Provincial Secretary and Citizenship (RG 8)
    Hearst Papers

University of Toronto Archives
    Sir Robert Falconer Papers
    Minute Books, Board of Governors

Toronto City Archives
    Records of Board of Control

Anglican Church. General Synod Archives
    St Paul's Church Mission, Albany

GOVERNMENT PUBLICATIONS

Statutes of Canada
Statutes of Ontario
Canada Sessional Papers
Ontario Sessional Papers
Journals of the Legislative Assembly of Ontario
Report of the Director of the Military Service Branch to the Honourable the Minister of Justice on the Operation of the Military Service Act, 1917 (Ottawa, 1919).
Returned Soldiers. Proceedings and Report of a Special Committee of the House of Commons Appointed to Inquire into and Report upon the Reception, Treatment and Future Disposition of Returned Soldiers of the Canadian Expeditionary Forces (Ottawa, 1917).
Internment Operations, 1914–1920. Final Report of Major-General Sir William Otter (Ottawa, 1921).

NEWSPAPERS AND PERIODICALS

[Only those newspapers and periodicals which were used frequently in the course of research are listed below.]
Toronto *Globe*
Kingston *Daily British Whig*
London *Free Press*
Berlin *Daily Record*
Ottawa *Citizen*
Toronto *Daily Star*

The Veteran
Public Service Bulletin
The Canadian Magazine

PAMPHLETS

ABBOTT, ALBERT H., *The Women's Emergency Corps* (Toronto, 1916).

HENDRIE, JOHN S. and C. A. MASTEN, *Report of the Executive Committee of the Speakers' Patriotic League, Central Ontario Branch, Covering Operations from the Date of Organization to May 31st, 1916* (Toronto, 1916).

HERRIDGE, W.T., *'The Call of War', A Recruiting Sermon Preached in St. Andrew's Church, Ottawa on June 27, 1915* (Ottawa, 1915).

ANONYMOUS, *Circulars* of the Organization of Resources Committee.

———— *Report of the Women's Convention on Food Conservation, Held in Convocation Hall, University of Toronto* (Toronto 1917).

———— *A Double Collapse of Bigotry* (London, 1919).

———— *Win-the-War Suggestions and Recipes* (n.p., n.d.).

———— *The Other Side, An Appeal for British Fair Play* (Kitchener, 1916).

———— *Soldiers' Aid Commission 'Appreciatory'* (Toronto, 1919).

———— Brochure of the Speakers' Patriotic League (Central Ontario Branch) (Toronto, 1915).

BOOKS

ALLEN, RALPH, *Ordeal by Fire* (Toronto, 1961).

ALLEN, RICHARD, *The Social Passion. Religion and Social Reform in Canada, 1914–1928* (Toronto, 1971).

ANONYMOUS, *The Canada War Thrift Book* (Ottawa, 1919).

BANK OF COMMERCE, *Letters from the Front,* (2 vols.), n.p. [1920].

BORDEN, HENRY, ed., *Sir Robert Laird Borden: His Memoirs*, (2 vols, Toronto, 1938).

BOWRING, CLIFFORD HENRY, *Service; the Story of the Canadian Legion, 1925–1960* (Ottawa, 1960).

BROWN, ROBERT CRAIG and RAMSAY COOK, *Canada 1896–1921. A Nation Transformed* (Toronto, 1974).

CALVIN, D.D., *Queen's University at Kingston* (Kingston, 1941).

CARNEGIE, DAVID, *The History of Munitions Supply in Canada, 1914–1918* (London, Toronto, 1925).

CLEVERDON, CATHERINE LYLE, *The Woman Suffrage Movement in Canada* (Toronto, 1950).

COLLINSON, J.H. and Mrs BERTIE SMITH, *The Recruiting League of Hamilton* (Hamilton, 1918).

DRURY, E.C., *Farmer Premier* (Toronto, 1966).

FIRTH, EDITH, ed., *Profiles of a Province* (Toronto, 1967).

FROST, LESLIE M., *Fighting Men* (Toronto, 1967).

GLAZEBROOK, G.P. DET., *Life in Ontario. A Social History* (Toronto, 1968).

GOOD, W.C., *Farmer Citizen* (Toronto, 1958).

GRANATSTEIN, J.L. and R.D. CUFF, eds., *War and Society in North America* (Toronto, 1971).

HALLOWELL, GERALD A., *Prohibition in Ontario, 1919–1923* (Ottawa, 1972).

HARSHAW, JOSEPHINE PERFECT, *When Women Work Together. A History of the Young Women's Christian Association in Canada, 1870–1966* (Toronto, 1966).

HERRINGTON, W.S. and A.J. WILSON, *The War Work of the County of Lennox and Addington* (Napanee, 1922).

HOPKINS, J. CASTELL, *The Canadian Annual Review, 1914–1918* (Toronto, 1915–1919).

——— *The Province of Ontario in the War* (Toronto, 1919).

INNIS, MARY QUAYLE, *Unfold the Years. A History of the Young Women's Christian Association in Canada* (Toronto, 1949).

IRVINE, WILLIAM, *Farmers in Politics* (Toronto, 1920).

MORRIS, PHILIP H., *The Canadian Patriotic Fund. A Record of its Activities, 1914–1919* (n.p., n.d.).

MORTON, DESMOND, *The Canadian General. Sir William Otter* (Toronto, 1974).

NELLES, H.V., *The Politics of Development. Forests, Mines and Hydro-Electric Power in Ontario, 1849–1941* (Toronto, 1974).

NICHOLSON, G.W.L., *Canadian Expeditionary Force 1914–1919* (Ottawa, 1962).

Number 4 Canadian Hospital. The Letters of Professor J.J. Mackenzie from the Salonika Front, with a Memoir by his wife, Kathleen Cuffe Mackenzie (Toronto, 1933).

PLEWMAN, W.R., *Adam Beck and Ontario Hydro* (Toronto, 1947).

PRANG, MARGARET, *N.W. Rowell: Ontario Nationalist* (Toronto, 1975).

QUEEN'S UNIVERSITY, *Annual Reports* (1914–1917).

REVILLE, F. DOUGLAS, *History of the County of Brant*, Vol. 2 (Brantford, 1920).

SISSONS, C.B., *Nil Alienum: The Memoirs of C.B. Sissons* (Toronto, 1964).

SMITH, G. OSWALD, *University of Toronto Roll of Service 1914–1918* (Toronto, 1921).

SPENCE, RUTH ELIZABETH, *Prohibition in Canada. A Memorial to Francis Stephens Spence* (Toronto, 1919).

STACEY, C.P., ed., *Historical Documents of Canada, Volume 5: The Arts of War and Peace, 1914–1945* (Toronto, 1972).

STAPLES, M.H., *The Challenge of Agriculture* (Toronto, 1921).

TALMAN, J.J. and RUTH DAVIS, *'Western,' 1878–1953* (London, Ont., 1953).

WINKS, ROBIN W., *The Blacks in Canada. A History* (Montreal, New Haven, and London, 1971).

ARTICLES

ABBOTT, ALBERT H., 'University Extension and the War,' *The Varsity War Supplement* (1915) p. 47.

'A Graduate,' 'Fifth F.C.C. Engineers at Valcartier,' *Queen's Quarterly*, 22 (1914–1915) pp. 294–8.

BARBER, MARILYN, 'The Ontario Bilingual Schools Issue: Sources of Conflict,' *Canadian Historical Review*, 47 (1966), pp. 227–48.

BLISS, J.M., 'The Methodist Church and World War I,' *Canadian Historical Review*, 49 (1968) pp. 213–33.

BRAITHWAITE, J.V.M., 'Year of the Killer Flu,' *Maclean's Magazine*, 66 (1 Feb. 1953) pp. 10–11, 43–4.

D.M.G., 'Queen's and the War,' *Queen's Quarterly*, 22 (1914–1915) pp. 384–8.

ENNS, GERHARD, 'Waterloo North and Conscription 1917,' Waterloo Historical Report, (1963) pp. 60–9.

EVANS, A. MARGARET and R.W. IRWIN, 'Government Tractors in Ontario, 1917 and 1918,' *Ontario History*, 61 (1969) pp. 99–109.

GREEN, ERNEST, 'Upper Canada's Black Defenders,' Ontario Historical Society *Papers and Records*, 27 (1931) pp. 365–91.

HEICK, WELF H., 'Becoming an Indigenous Church: The Lutheran Church in Waterloo County,' *Ontario History*, 56 (1964), pp. 249–60.

KERR, ESTELLE M., 'Those War-Time Jig-Saw Toys,' *Canadian Magazine*, (Dec. 1915) pp. 93–9.

McNAB, DAVID, 'Peter McArthur and Canadian Nationalism,' *Ontario History*, 64 (1972) pp. 1–10.

MOORE, MARY MACLEOD, 'Canadian Women War Workers Overseas,' *Canadian Magazine*, (Jan. 1919) pp. 737–51.

MORTON, DESMOND, 'Sir William Otter and Internment Operations in Canada During the First World War,' *Canadian Historical Review*, 55 (1974) pp. 32–58.

OLIVER, PETER, 'Tory Hatchet Man: Howard Ferguson on the Whitney Backbenches,' *Ontario History*, 61 (1969) pp. 121–35.

PRANG, MARGARET, 'Clerics, Politicians and the Bilingual Schools Issue in Ontario, 1910–1917,' *Canadian Historical Review* 41 (1960) pp. 281–307.

ROBIN, MARTIN, 'Registration, Conscription and Independent Labour Politics, 1916–1917,' *Canadian Historical Review*, 47 (1966) pp. 101–18.

TENNYSON, BRIAN D., 'Sir Adam Beck and the Ontario General Election of 1919,' *Ontario History*, 58 (1966) pp. 157–62.

————— 'Premier Hearst, The War, and Votes for Women,' *Ontario History*, 57 (1965) pp. 115–21.

————— 'The Succession of William H. Hearst to the Ontario Premiership, September 1914,' *Ontario History*, 56 (1964) pp. 185–9.

————— 'Sir William Hearst and the Ontario Temperance Act,' *Ontario History*, 55 (1963) pp. 233–45.

WILLMS, A.M., 'Conscription, 1917: A Brief for the Defence,' *Canadian Historical Review*, 37 (1956) pp. 338–51.

YOUNG, W.R., 'Conscription, Rural Depopulation and the Farmers of Ontario, 1917–1919,' *Canadian Historical Review*, 53 (1972) pp. 289–320.

INDEX